ULTIMATE
BEEF
CHICKEN & PORK
COOKBOOK

TASTE OF HOME BOOKS ● RDA ENTHUSIAST BRANDS, LLC
MILWAUKEE, WI

Taste of Home

EDITORIAL

Editor-in-Chief: Catherine Cassidy
Vice President, Content Operations: Kerri Balliet
Creative Director: Howard Greenberg

Managing Editor, Print & Digital Books: Mark Hagen
Associate Creative Director: Edwin Robles Jr.

Editors: Amy Glander, Hazel Wheaton
Art Director: Maggie Conners
Graphic Designer: Courtney Lovetere
Editorial Services Manager: Dena Ahlers
Editorial Production Coordinator: Jill Banks
Copy Chief: Deb Warlaumont Mulvey
Copy Editors: Dulcie Shoener (senior), Ronald Kovach,
Chris McLaughlin, Ellie Piper
Editorial Services Administrator: Marie Brannon

Content Director: Julie Blume Benedict
Food Editors: Gina Nistico; James Schend; Peggy Woodward, RDN
Recipe Editors: Sue Ryon (lead), Irene Yeh

Culinary Director: Sarah Thompson
Test Cooks: Nicholas Iverson (lead), Matthew Hass
Food Stylists: Kathryn Conrad (lead), Lauren Knoelke, Shannon Roum
Prep Cooks: Bethany Van Jacobson (lead), Melissa Hansen, Aria C. Thornton
Culinary Team Assistant: Maria Petrella

Photography Director: Stephanie Marchese
Photographers: Dan Roberts, Jim Wieland
Photographer/Set Stylist: Grace Natoli Sheldon
Set Stylists: Melissa Franco (lead), Stacey Genaw, Dee Dee Schaefer
Set Stylist Assistant: Stephanie Chojnacki

Business Architect, Publishing Technologies: Amanda Harmatys
Business Analyst, Publishing Technologies: Kate Unger
Junior Business Analyst, Publishing Technologies: Shannon Stroud
Editorial Business Manager: Kristy Martin
Rights & Permissions Associate: Samantha Lea Stoeger
Editorial Business Associate: Andrea Meiers

BUSINESS

Vice President, Group Publisher: Kirsten Marchioli
Publisher: Donna Lindskog
Business Development Director, Taste of Home Live: Laurel Osman
Strategic Partnerships Manager, Taste of Home Live:
Jamie Piette Andrzejewski

TRUSTED MEDIA BRANDS, INC.

President & Chief Executive Officer: Bonnie Kintzer
Chief Financial Officer: Dean Durbin
Chief Marketing Officer: C. Alec Casey
Chief Revenue Officer: Richard Sutton
Chief Digital Officer: Vince Errico
Senior Vice President, Global HR & Communications:
Phyllis E. Gebhardt, SPHR; SHRM-SCP
General Counsel: Mark Sirota
Vice President, Magazine Marketing: Christopher Gaydos
Vice President, Product Marketing: Brian Kennedy
Vice President, Operations: Michael Garzone
Vice President, Consumer Marketing Planning: Jim Woods
Vice President, Digital Product & Technology: Nick Contardo
Vice President, Financial Planning & Analysis: William Houston

For other *Taste of Home* books and products, visit us at **tasteofhome.com**.

International Standard Book Number: 978-1-61765-648-4

Library of Congress Control Number: 2016961392

Pictured on front cover (left to right): Fajita in a Bowl, page 37;
Feta Chicken Burgers, page 205; Grilled Dijon Pork Roast, page 239
Pictured on title page (left to right): Oven-Baked Brisket, page
60; Apple-Butter Barbecued Chicken, page 134; Apple-Pecan Pork
Tenderloin, page 266
Pictured on back cover (left to right): Steaks with Cherry-Chipotle
Glaze, page 33; Family-Favorite Fried Chicken, page 149; Holiday Crown
Pork Roast, page 271
Illustrations: Metal plate: donatas1205/Shutterstock; Small animals:
ps-42/Shutterstock; Back cover animals: CHEMADAN/Shutterstock

Printed in China.
1 3 5 7 9 10 8 6 4 2

GET SOCIAL WITH US

To find a recipe tasteofhome.com
To submit a recipe tasteofhome.com/submit
To find out about other *Taste of Home* products shoptasteofhome.com

LIKE US
facebook.com/tasteofhome

PIN US
pinterest.com/taste_of_home

FOLLOW US
@tasteofhome

TWEET US
twitter.com/tasteofhome

[CONTENTS]

BACON CHEESEBURGER SLIDER BAKE, PAGE 17

BEEF

CHICKEN

SAUCY BARBECUE DRUMSTICKS, PAGE 137

PORK

PORK TENDERLOIN WITH CRANBERRY-ORANGE RELISH, PAGE 235

LET'S EAT!

FETA STEAK TACOS, PAGE 53

A HEARTY MEAL IS ALWAYS ON HAND WITH THIS THREE-IN-ONE COOKBOOK.

Sink your teeth into 375 sensational dishes with this collection of all-time family favorites! Whether you're looking for a succulent steak cooked to perfection on the grill, fried chicken that's sure to satisfy or pulled pork sandwiches loaded with crowd-pleasing appeal, you'll find just the right dish with *Taste of Home Ultimate Beef, Chicken & Pork Cookbook*.

Best of all, this fantastic collection is really three cookbooks in one! Take a look inside and you'll find lip-smacking recipes organized into three easy-to-navigate sections.

RESTAURANT-STYLE PRIME RIB, PAGE 69

CHICKEN BURRITO SKILLET, PAGE 149

PULLED PORK NACHOS, PAGE 287

BEEF: Satisfy the meat-and-potato lovers in your family with the **129 recipes** in this meaty section. From flame-broiled burgers and juicy steaks to savory tacos and spaghetti dinners made easy on the stovetop, this section has it all! You'll even find 23 specialties for the slow cooker, plus man-sized sandwiches and comforting stews.

CHICKEN: When it comes to dinnertime lifesavers, chicken is a no-brainer. Turn to this section for **125 meals** that'll have the gang asking for seconds every time. Enjoy classics like Chicken Parmigiana (page 173) and Super Quick Chicken Fried Rice (page 153) as well as modern comforts such as Barbecued Strawberry Chicken (page 175) and One-Dish Moroccan Chicken (page 187).

PORK: You just can't beat the flavor and versatility of pork, ham, bacon and sausage. Check out any of these **121 dishes** and see for yourself! Find shredded pork sandwiches, subs piled high with deli meats, pork tenderloins and juicy baked ham. In the chapter On the Stovetop (page 244), discover an assortment of pork chops you can make fast in a skillet; Slow-Cooked Staples (page 278) will show you simmering specialties that are ready when you are!

Each section includes appetizers and snacks that are substantial enough to satisfy everyone on your guest list, as well as wraps, soups, main-dish salads and more. Handy tips and tricks to help cut kitchen time are scattered throughout the book, and you'll also find **332 appetizing color photos.**

So get cooking tonight with any of the extraordinary selections in this three-in-one collection. With ***Ultimate Beef, Chicken & Pork Cookbook,*** you'll have mouths watering in no time!

FINDING THE RIGHT DISH JUST GOT EASIER!

WATCH FOR THESE HANDY ICONS

FAST FIX Beat the clock with recipes that are on the table in 30 minutes or less!

5 INGREDIENTS These dishes call for just five staples—not including water, oils, salt, pepper and optional ingredients.

EAT SMART Lighten up meals by trimming back on calories, fat, carbs and/or sodium.

Sink your teeth into any of the meaty staples found in this section. From grilled greats to sandwiches piled high with deli favorites, you can't go wrong with these beefy classics.

BEEF

BEEF [101]

Bone up on the facts behind one of our favorite main-course meats.

Beef is a staple in kitchens from coast to coast.
From succulent steaks and juicy burgers to savory meatballs and sizzling fajitas, it's the cornerstone of hearty dinners loaded with comforting appeal.

Review these pointers and then dig into the beefy recipes that follow. Whether grilled, slow-cooked or simmered on the stovetop, the meals in this section come together quickly and easily for lip-smacking dinnertime success!

BECOME A BEEF BARON...

- Look for a bright cherry red color in ground beef, steaks and roasts. Avoid meat with gray or brown patches.

- Watch for excessive liquid in the package, which can indicate improper storage.

- Select items with sell-by dates that are later than the day of your purchase. If it's the same date, use the beef that day or freeze it for later.

- Can't find what you need? Ask the butcher! The team behind the counter might have some cuts in back or be able to suggest substitutes.

WHERE'S THE BEEF?

- Tender cuts of beef are the rib (both rib roasts and rib steaks), short loin (including T-bone, porterhouse, strip and tenderloin steaks) and top sirloin.

- Ground beef, beef stew meat and cubed steak are generally considered tender cuts.

- Less tender cuts include chuck, bottom sirloin (tri-tip roast), plate (skirt steak), flank steak, top round steak, shank and brisket.

LOVE 'EM TENDER

- Moist-heat techniques (slow-cooking, braising and simmering) work well for less tender cuts of beef.

- Marinating tenderizes tough cuts while adding flavor.

- Consider dry-heat methods such as grilling, roasting, pan-frying and broiling when preparing tender cuts.

TENDERLOIN STEAK DIANE, PAGE 54

GRILLING GUIDELINES

Everyone loves a flame-broiled specialty sizzling hot from the grill. When heating up a charcoal grill, leave the vents open. This allows air to escape through the top, ultimately pulling air in through the bottom vent and heating up the coals.

Check for doneness with an instant-read thermometer. First, remove the beef from the grill. Carefully insert the thermometer horizontally from the side, and try to get the reading from the center of the beef.

HAVE IT YOUR WAY! A MEAT THERMOMETER SHOULD READ

145° for medium-rare
160° for medium
170° for well-done

SOUTHWEST FLANK STEAK, PAGE 35

Neck · Chuck · Fore Rib · Thick Rib · Thin Rib · Brisket · Shin · Sirloin · Flank · Rump · Silverside · Topside · Thick flank · Leg

[BEEF UP YOUR MENUS]

What are you waiting for? It's easy to beef up dinners, lunches and munchies for the man cave. Just turn the page to check out all of the hearty beef dishes waiting to tempt your taste buds—and give hunger the cold shoulder.

SICILIAN
NACHOS,
PAGE 20

ROAST BEEF FINGER SANDWICHES, PAGE 17

QUICK BITES

Beef up your appetizer lineup with these **hearty snacks** that are sure to satisfy a crowd. Roast beef, flank steak, ground beef and thinly sliced sirloin lend familiar appeal to these **substantial party starers.** Try any of these beefy bites the next time you're hosting the gang. You'll find **16 new favorites** among the following pages.

MINI ROSEMARY-ROAST BEEF SANDWICHES, PAGE 21

STEAK & PEPPER QUESADILLAS, PAGE 20

REUBEN WAFFLE POTATO APPETIZERS

REUBEN WAFFLE POTATO APPETIZERS

I turned the classic Reuben sammie into a fun appetizer by stacking corned beef and sauerkraut on waffle fries.
—GLORIA BRADLEY NAPERVILLE, IL

PREP: 30 MIN. • **BAKE:** 10 MIN./BATCH
MAKES: ABOUT 4 DOZEN

- 1 package (22 ounces) frozen waffle-cut fries
- 4 ounces cream cheese, softened
- 2 cups shredded fontina cheese, divided
- ⅓ cup Thousand Island salad dressing
- 3 tablespoons chopped sweet onion
- 1½ teaspoons prepared horseradish
- 12 ounces sliced deli corned beef, coarsely chopped
- 1 cup sauerkraut, rinsed, well drained and chopped
- 2 tablespoons minced fresh chives

1. Prepare waffle fries according to package directions for baking. Meanwhile, in a small bowl, beat cream cheese, 1 cup fontina cheese, salad dressing, onion and horseradish until blended.
2. Remove fries from oven; reduce oven setting to 400°. Top each waffle fry with about ¼ ounce corned beef and 1 teaspoon each cream cheese mixture, sauerkraut and fontina cheese. Bake 8-10 minutes or until cheese is melted. Sprinkle with chives.
PER SERVING 1 appetizer: 62 cal., 4g fat (2g sat. fat), 12mg chol., 168mg sodium, 4g carb. (0 sugars, 0 fiber), 3g pro.

TOP TIP

EASY DINNER
These substantial appetizers can also make for a fast, comforting meal. Simply serve them alongside piping hot bowls of soup and a fresh green salad for a no-fuss dinner any night of the week.

TERIYAKI BEEF JERKY

Jerky is a portable, chewy snack—and you can make your own with our recipe. The meat has a savory flavor and a bit of heat.
—*TASTE OF HOME* TEST KITCHEN

PREP: 40 MIN. + MARINATING • **BAKE:** 4 HOURS
MAKES: 8 SERVINGS

- 1 beef flank steak (1½ to 2 pounds)
- ⅔ cup reduced-sodium soy sauce
- ⅔ cup Worcestershire sauce
- ¼ cup honey
- 3 teaspoons coarsely ground pepper
- 2 teaspoons onion powder
- 2 teaspoons garlic powder
- 1½ teaspoons crushed red pepper flakes
- 1 teaspoon liquid smoke

1. Trim all visible fat from steak. Freeze, covered, 30 minutes or until firm. Slice steak along the grain into long ⅛-in.-thick strips.

2. Transfer to a large resealable plastic bag. In a small bowl, whisk remaining ingredients; add to beef. Seal bag and turn to coat. Refrigerate 2 hours or overnight, turning occasionally.

3. Preheat oven to 170°. Transfer beef and marinade to a large saucepan; bring to a boil. Reduce heat; simmer 5 minutes. Using tongs, remove beef from marinade; drain on paper towels. Discard marinade.

4. Arrange beef strips in single layer on wire racks placed on 15x10x1-in. baking pans. Dry in oven 4-5 hours or until beef becomes dry and leathery, rotating pans occasionally. (Or use a commercial dehydrator, following manufacturer's directions.)

5. Remove from oven; cool completely. Using paper towels, blot any beads of oil from jerky. For best quality and longer storage, store jerky, covered, in refrigerator or freezer.

PER SERVING *1 ounce: 132 cal., 6g fat (3g sat. fat), 40mg chol., 139mg sodium, 2g carb. (1g sugars, 0 fiber), 17g pro.*

SMOKED GOUDA & ROAST BEEF PINWHEELS

SMOKED GOUDA & ROAST BEEF PINWHEELS

Our local deli makes terrific roast beef sandwiches; I made this pinwheel appetizer to re-create that taste. So much flavor in such little treats!
—**PAMELA SHANK** PARKERSBURG, WV

PREP: 20 MIN. • **BAKE:** 15 MIN./BATCH
MAKES: 4 DOZEN

- ¾ pound sliced deli roast beef, finely chopped
- 1 package (10 ounces) frozen chopped spinach, thawed and squeezed dry
- 1 package (6½ ounces) garlic-herb spreadable cheese
- 1 cup shredded smoked Gouda cheese
- ¼ cup finely chopped red onion
- 2 tubes (8 ounces each) refrigerated crescent rolls

1. Preheat oven to 375°. In a small bowl, mix the first five ingredients until blended. On a lightly floured surface, unroll one tube of crescent dough into one long rectangle; press perforations to seal.

2. Spread half of the roast beef mixture over dough. Roll up jelly-roll style, starting with a long side; pinch seam to seal. Using a serrated knife, cut roll crosswise into twenty-four ½-inch slices. Place on parchment paper-lined baking sheets, cut side down. Repeat with remaining crescent dough and roast beef mixture.

3. Bake 12-14 minutes or until golden brown. Refrigerate leftovers.

PER SERVING *1 appetizer: 71 cal., 5g fat (2g sat. fat), 11mg chol., 160mg sodium, 4g carb. (1g sugars, 0 fiber), 3g pro.*

GROUND BEEF
TACO DIP

GROUND BEEF TACO DIP

It's not a football party without taco dip! This version, made with spicy ground beef and fresh toppings, does not disappoint the diehards. It's full of classic flavors and is a little extra filling for game day appetites.

—PACKERS WOMEN'S ASSOCIATION
GREEN BAY, WI

START TO FINISH: 25 MIN.
MAKES: 24 SERVINGS

- 1 **pound lean ground beef (90% lean)**
- ¾ **cup water**
- 2 **envelopes taco seasoning, divided**
- 1 **container (16 ounces) fat-free sour cream**
- 1 **package (8 ounces) cream cheese, softened**
- 2 **cups shredded iceberg lettuce**
- 1 **cup shredded cheddar cheese**
- 3 **medium tomatoes, finely chopped**
- 1 **medium green pepper, finely chopped**
- 1 **can (2¼ ounces) sliced ripe olives, drained**

1. In a large skillet, cook and crumble beef over medium heat until no longer pink, 4-6 minutes; drain. Add water and one envelope taco seasoning; cook until thickened. Cool slightly.
2. Beat sour cream, cream cheese and remaining taco seasoning until blended. Spread in a 3-qt. dish; add ground beef. Top with lettuce, cheddar, tomatoes, pepper and olives.
PER SERVING *½ cup: 116 cal., 7g fat (3g sat. fat), 30mg chol., 378mg sodium, 7g carb. (2g sugars, 0 fiber), 7g pro.*

GRILLED STEAK APPETIZERS WITH STILTON SAUCE

Here's a hearty appetizer that will get any gathering off to a delicious start. The rich, elegant Stilton cheese sauce complements the grilled steak to perfection.

—RADELLE KNAPPENBERGER OVIEDO, FL

PREP: 25 MIN. • **GRILL:** 10 MIN.
MAKES: 20 APPETIZERS (¾ CUP SAUCE)

- 2 **boneless beef top loin steaks (8 ounces each)**
- ¼ **teaspoon salt**
- ¼ **teaspoon pepper**
- ½ **cup white wine or chicken broth**
- ⅓ **cup heavy whipping cream**
- 3 **tablespoons sour cream**
- 2 **ounces Stilton cheese, cubed**

1. Sprinkle steaks with salt and pepper. Grill steaks, covered, over medium heat for 4-6 minutes on each side or until meat reaches desired doneness (for medium-rare, a meat thermometer should read 145°; medium, 160°; well-done, 170°). Remove meat to a cutting board and keep warm.
2. In a small saucepan, bring wine to a boil; cook until reduced by half. Add cream. Bring to a gentle boil. Reduce heat; simmer, uncovered, until thickened, stirring occasionally. Remove from the heat. Add sour cream and cheese; stir until cheese is melted.
3. Cut steaks into 1-in. cubes; skewer with toothpicks. Serve with sauce.
NOTES *Top loin steak may be labeled as strip steak, Kansas City steak, New York strip steak, ambassador steak or boneless club steak depending on your region. You may substitute ⅓ cup crumbled blue cheese for the Stilton cheese.*
PER SERVING *1 appetizer: 60 cal., 4g fat (2g sat. fat), 19mg chol., 64mg sodium, 0 carb. (0 sugars, 0 fiber), 6g pro.*
Diabetic Exchanges: 1 lean meat, ½ fat.

SPICY BEEF SKEWERS

The fragrant spices and full flavors of North African cuisine make these kabobs tasty and distinctive party fare.

—ROXANNE CHAN ALBANY, CA

PREP: 35 MIN. • **BROIL:** 5 MIN.
MAKES: 2 DOZEN (½ CUP SAUCE)

- 1 **cup white wine vinegar**
- ¾ **cup sugar**
- ½ **cup water**
- 1 **tablespoon orange marmalade**
- ¼ **teaspoon grated orange peel**
- ¼ **teaspoon crushed red pepper flakes**
- ½ **cup finely chopped salted roasted almonds**
- 2 **tablespoons minced fresh mint**
- 1 **green onion, finely chopped**
- 1 **tablespoon lemon juice**
- 1 **garlic clove, minced**
- ¼ **teaspoon each ground cinnamon, cumin and coriander**
- 1 **pound lean ground beef (90% lean)**
  Minced fresh parsley

1. In a small saucepan, combine the first six ingredients. Bring to a boil. Reduce heat; simmer, uncovered, about 25 minutes or until reduced to ½ cup.
2. Meanwhile, in a large bowl, combine almonds, mint, onion, lemon juice, garlic and spices. Crumble beef over mixture and mix well. Divide into 24 pieces. Shape each piece into a 3x1-in. rectangle; insert a soaked wooden appetizer skewer into each.
3. Broil 6 in. from the heat 2-4 minutes on each side or until a thermometer reads 160°. Arrange on a serving platter. Drizzle with sauce mixture and sprinkle with parsley.
PER SERVING *1 appetizer with 1 teaspoon sauce: 77 cal., 3g fat (1g sat. fat), 12mg chol., 20mg sodium, 8g carb. (7g sugars, 0 fiber), 4g pro.*

MINI BEEF CHIMICHANGAS

The first time I made these, I was looking for a way to jazz up some leftover roast meat. Now we make them for parties all the time. The crisp, golden chimis are excellent served with guacamole or all on their own.
—DANIELLE LUADERS CLEVER, MO

PREP: 30 MIN. • **COOK:** 5 MIN./BATCH
MAKES: 20 MINI CHIMICHANGAS

- 2 **cups shredded pepper Jack cheese**
- 1 **can (15 ounces) black beans, rinsed and drained**
- 1 **cup (8 ounces) sour cream**
- 1 **cup shredded Colby-Monterey Jack cheese**
- 1 **can (4 ounces) chopped green chilies**
- 2 **teaspoons ground cumin**
- 1 **teaspoon salt**
- ½ **teaspoon garlic powder**
- ½ **teaspoon crushed red pepper flakes**
- 2 **cups shredded cooked roast beef**
- 1 **package (16 ounces) egg roll wrappers**
  Oil for deep-fat frying
  Guacamole, optional

1. In a large bowl, combine the first nine ingredients. Stir in cooked beef.
2. Place ¼ cup filling in the center of one egg roll wrapper. (Keep remaining wrappers covered with a damp paper towel until ready to use.) Fold bottom corner over filling. Fold sides toward center over filling. Moisten remaining corner with water; roll up tightly to seal. Repeat with remaining wrappers and filling.
3. In an electric skillet or deep fryer, heat oil to 375°. Fry chimichangas in batches for 1-2 minutes on each side or until golden brown. Drain on paper towels. Serve warm with guacamole if desired.
PER SERVING *1 chimichanga: 284 cal., 18g fat (6g sat. fat), 35mg chol., 423mg sodium, 18g carb. (1g sugars, 1g fiber), 13g pro.*

BARBECUE GLAZED MEATBALLS

BARBECUE GLAZED MEATBALLS

Stock the freezer with these meatballs and you'll always have a tasty snack available for unexpected guests. We like to eat them as a main dish with rice or noodles on busy weeknights.
—ANNA FINLEY COLUMBIA, MO

PREP: 30 MIN. • **BAKE:** 15 MIN./BATCH
MAKES: 8 DOZEN

- 2 **cups quick-cooking oats**
- 1 **can (12 ounces) fat-free evaporated milk**
- 1 **small onion, finely chopped**
- 2 **teaspoons garlic powder**
- 2 **teaspoons chili powder**
- 3 **pounds lean ground beef (90% lean)**

SAUCE

- 2½ **cups ketchup**
- 1 **small onion, finely chopped**
- ⅓ **cup packed brown sugar**
- 2 **teaspoons liquid smoke, optional**
- 1¼ **teaspoons chili powder**
- ¾ **teaspoon garlic powder**

1. Preheat oven to 400°. In a large bowl, combine the first five ingredients. Add beef; mix lightly but thoroughly. Shape into 1-in. balls.
2. Place meatballs on greased racks in shallow baking pans. Bake 15-20 minutes or until cooked through. Drain on paper towels.
3. In a Dutch oven, combine sauce ingredients. Bring to a boil over medium heat, stirring constantly. Reduce heat; simmer, uncovered, 2-3 minutes or until slightly thickened. Add meatballs; heat through, stirring gently.
FREEZE OPTION *Freeze cooled meatball mixture in freezer containers. To use, partially thaw in refrigerator overnight. Microwave, covered, on high until heated through, gently stirring and adding a little water if necessary.*
PER SERVING *1 meatball: 42 cal., 1g fat (0 sat. fat), 9mg chol., 93mg sodium, 4g carb. (3g sugars, 0 fiber), 3g pro.*

BACON CHEESEBURGER SLIDER BAKE

Take these to a potluck or serve them up at a big house party. The hearty sliders are just terrific! You can even assemble them ahead of time and freeze.
—*TASTE OF HOME* **TEST KITCHEN**

PREP: 20 MIN. • **BAKE:** 25 MIN.
MAKES: 2 DOZEN

- 2 **packages (18 ounces each) Hawaiian sweet rolls**
- 4 **cups shredded cheddar cheese, divided**
- 2 **pounds ground beef**
- 1 **cup chopped onion**
- 1 **can (14½ ounces) diced tomatoes with garlic and onion, drained**
- 1 **tablespoon Dijon mustard**
- 1 **tablespoon Worcestershire sauce**
- ¾ **teaspoon salt**
- ¾ **teaspoon pepper**
- 24 **bacon strips, cooked and crumbled**

GLAZE
- 1 **cup butter, cubed**
- ¼ **cup packed brown sugar**
- 4 **teaspoons Worcestershire sauce**
- 2 **tablespoons Dijon mustard**
- 2 **tablespoons sesame seeds**

1. Preheat oven to 350°. Without separating rolls, cut each package of rolls horizontally in half; arrange bottom halves in two greased 13x9-in. baking pans. Sprinkle each pan of rolls with 1 cup cheese. Bake 3-5 minutes or until cheese is melted.

2. In a large skillet, cook beef and onion over medium heat 6-8 minutes or until beef is no longer pink and onion is tender, breaking up beef into crumbles; drain. Stir in tomatoes, mustard, Worcestershire sauce, salt and pepper. Cook and stir 1-2 minutes or until combined.

3. Spoon beef mixture evenly over rolls; sprinkle with remaining cheese. Top with bacon. Replace tops. For glaze, in a microwave-safe bowl, combine butter, brown sugar, Worcestershire sauce and mustard. Microwave, covered, on high until butter is melted, stirring occasionally. Pour over rolls; sprinkle with sesame seeds. Bake, uncovered, 20-25 minutes or until golden brown and heated through.

FREEZE OPTION *Cover and freeze unbaked sandwiches; prepare and freeze glaze. To use, partially thaw in refrigerator overnight. Remove from refrigerator 30 minutes before baking. Preheat oven to 350°. Pour glaze over buns and sprinkle with sesame seeds. Bake sandwiches as directed, increasing time by 10-15 minutes or until cheese is melted and a thermometer inserted in center reads 165°.*

PER SERVING *1 slider: 430 cal., 26g fat (13g sat. fat), 93mg chol., 668mg sodium, 29g carb. (13g sugars, 2g fiber), 20g pro.*

FAST FIX

ROAST BEEF FINGER SANDWICHES (PICTURED ON PAGE 11)

These simple sandwiches are ideal for a brunch or quiet get-together, when the menu is a bit more substantial. The mustard adds a nice kick without being overly spicy.
—**ANNDREA BAILEY** HUNTINGTON BEACH, CA

START TO FINISH: 15 MIN.
MAKES: 1½ DOZEN

- ½ **cup butter, softened**
- ½ **cup chopped pitted Greek olives**
- ¼ **cup spicy brown mustard**
- ¼ **teaspoon pepper**
- 6 **slices whole wheat bread, crusts removed**
- 6 **ounces thinly sliced deli roast beef**
- 6 **slices white bread, crusts removed**

Place butter, olives, mustard and pepper in a food processor; pulse until chopped. Spread butter mixture over wheat bread; top with roast beef and white bread. Cut each sandwich crosswise into thirds.

PER SERVING *1 finger sandwich: 98 cal., 7g fat (4g sat. fat), 19mg chol., 240mg sodium, 5g carb. (1g sugars, 1g fiber), 3g pro.*

BACON CHEESEBURGER SLIDER BAKE

(5) INGREDIENTS FAST FIX
MINI PARTY BURGERS

In the South, we love our finger foods. For a party, I make these mini burgers in advance, then wrap, bake and serve them with an assortment of sauces.
—**MONICA FLATFORD** KNOXVILLE, TN

START TO FINISH: 30 MIN.
MAKES: 8 SERVINGS

- ½ **pound ground beef**
- 1 **envelope ranch salad dressing mix**
- 1 **large egg**
- 1 **teaspoon water**
- 1 **sheet frozen puff pastry, thawed**
- 4 **slices Havarti cheese (about 4 ounces), quartered**

1. Preheat oven to 400°. Place beef in a small bowl; sprinkle with dressing mix and mix lightly but thoroughly. Shape into eight ½-in.-thick patties.

2. In a large nonstick skillet, cook burgers over medium heat 3-4 minutes on each side or until a thermometer reads 160°. Remove from heat.

3. Meanwhile, in a small bowl, whisk egg with water. On a lightly floured surface, unfold puff pastry; roll into a 12-in. square. Cut pastry into four 6-in. squares; cut squares in half to make eight rectangles. Place a burger on one end of each rectangle; top with cheese. Brush edges of pastry with egg mixture. Fold pastry over burger to enclose; press edges with a fork to seal.

4. Transfer to a parchment paper-lined baking sheet. Brush tops with egg mixture. Bake 15-20 minutes or until golden brown.

PER SERVING *1 appetizer: 271 cal., 16g fat (6g sat. fat), 54mg chol., 488mg sodium, 20g carb. (0 sugars, 2g fiber), 11g pro.*

PHILLY CHEESESTEAK BITES

Here's a deliciously downsized version of the ever-popular Philly cheesesteak. For perfect bite-size snacks, the sandwich ingredients are layered on waffle-cut fries instead of buns.

—TASTE OF HOME TEST KITCHEN

PREP: 30 MIN. • **COOK:** 5 MIN.
MAKES: 1½ DOZEN

- 1 package (22 ounces) frozen waffle-cut fries
- 1 medium onion, halved and sliced
- ½ small green pepper, halved and sliced
- ½ small sweet red pepper, halved and sliced
- 3 tablespoons canola oil, divided
- ½ teaspoon salt, divided
- ¾ pound beef ribeye steak, cut into thin strips
- ¼ teaspoon pepper
- 3 tablespoons ketchup
- 6 tablespoons process cheese sauce

1. Bake 18 large waffle fries according to package directions (save remaining fries for another use). Meanwhile, in a large skillet, saute onion and peppers in 1 tablespoon oil until tender. Sprinkle with ⅛ teaspoon salt. Remove and keep warm.
2. In the same pan, saute steak in remaining oil in batches for 45-60 seconds or until desired doneness. Sprinkle with pepper and remaining salt. On each waffle fry, layer the beef, onion mixture, ketchup and cheese sauce. Serve warm.

PER SERVING *1 appetizer: 106 cal., 7g fat (3g sat. fat), 15mg chol., 201mg sodium, 6g carb. (1g sugars, 1g fiber), 4g pro.*

BEEF SPIEDINI

An Italian favorite, *spiedini* are great for holidays and other special occasions. The hearty skewers hold marinated steak pinwheels that are stuffed with a marinara-and-crumb filling.

—DESTY LORINO SHOREWOOD, WI

PREP: 45 MIN. • **BROIL:** 5 MIN./BATCH
MAKES: 40 APPETIZERS

- 1 beef top sirloin steak (1 inch thick and 1½ pounds)

MARINADE
- ½ cup olive oil
- 1 tablespoon lemon juice
- ½ teaspoon salt
- ½ teaspoon pepper

BREADING
- 1¼ cups seasoned bread crumbs
- ⅓ cup grated Parmesan cheese
- 2 tablespoons minced fresh parsley
- ⅛ teaspoon salt
- ⅛ teaspoon garlic powder
  Dash pepper
- ¾ cup marinara sauce

ASSEMBLY
- 1 medium red onion
- 40 fresh sage leaves
- ¼ cup olive oil

1. Thinly slice steak widthwise into 5-in. strips. In a large resealable plastic bag, combine the marinade ingredients. Add beef; seal bag and turn to coat. Refrigerate for 4 hours or overnight, turning occasionally.
2. Combine the bread crumbs, cheese, parsley, salt, garlic powder and pepper. Transfer half of the mixture to a shallow bowl; set aside. For filling, add marinara

BEEF SPIEDINI

sauce to the remaining crumb mixture and mix well. Spread 1 teaspoon filling over each beef strip and roll up into pinwheels. Coat with reserved crumb mixture.
3. Cut onion into 1-in. pieces and separate into layers. Thread a piece of onion, a sage leaf and a beef pinwheel onto a soaked wooden appetizer skewer; repeat. Drizzle lightly with oil and place on a greased 15x10x1-in. baking pan.
4. Broil 3-4 in. from heat for 5-7 minutes or until beef reaches desired doneness, turning once.

TO MAKE AHEAD *Skewer spiedini as directed but do not add sage and onion. Freeze unbaked spiedini in a single layer on a waxed paper-lined baking sheet. Once frozen, transfer to a freezer container and freeze for up to 1 month. To use frozen spiedini, thread sage and onion as directed. Bake at 375° for 13-15 minutes or until beef reaches desired doneness, turning once.*

PER SERVING *1 appetizer: 59 cal., 3g fat (1g sat. fat), 7mg chol., 101mg sodium, 3g carb. (1g sugars, 0 fiber), 4g pro.*

TOP TIP

MAKE SAFETY AN ISSUE

Party foods left out for too long offer the perfect environment for bacteria to grow, so it's important to keep an eye on them. The USDA says foods shouldn't sit at room temperature longer than 2 hours. That said, it's better to place small portions on the buffet table and replenish dishes often. Store hot backup dishes in a 200-250 degree oven or in a slow cooker.

SICILIAN NACHOS

STEAK & PEPPER QUESADILLAS (PICTURED ON PAGE 11)

Great Southwestern flavors combine in this finger-food favorite. The recipe makes a fabulous appetizer or party food, as well as a quick and easy lunch.

—**SHARON SKILDUM** MAPLE GROVE, MN

START TO FINISH: 30 MIN.
MAKES: 4 SERVINGS

- ½ **pound beef top sirloin steak**
- ½ **each medium green, sweet red and yellow pepper, julienned**
- 1 **tablespoon chopped red onion**
- 1 **garlic clove, minced**
- 1 **tablespoon minced fresh cilantro**
- ¼ **teaspoon dried rosemary, crushed**
- 4 **flour tortillas (6 inches)**
- 12 **cherry tomatoes, halved**
- 1½ **cups shredded cheddar cheese**

1. On a greased grill rack, grill steak, covered, over medium heat or broil 4 in. from the heat for 4 minutes on each side or until meat reaches desired doneness (for medium-rare, a meat thermometer should read 145°; medium, 160°; well-done, 170°). Let stand for 10 minutes.
2. Meanwhile, in a large skillet coated with cooking spray, saute peppers and onion for 5-6 minutes or until tender. Add garlic; cook 1 minute longer. Sprinkle with cilantro and rosemary.
3. Place two tortillas on a baking sheet coated with cooking spray. Cut steak into thin strips; place on tortillas. Using a slotted spoon, place pepper mixture over steak. Top with tomatoes, cheese and remaining tortillas; lightly spray top of tortillas with cooking spray.
4. Bake at 425° for 5-10 minutes or until golden brown and cheese is melted. Cut each quesadilla into four wedges.
PER SERVING *2 wedges: 336 cal., 18g fat (10g sat. fat), 68mg chol., 511mg sodium, 20g carb., 1g fiber, 25g pro.*

SICILIAN NACHOS

Crispy slices of French bread replace classic tortilla chips in this version of nachos, and a savory meat sauce tops things off. My hearty appetizer easily doubles as a main dish—add a salad and you have a comforting dinner!

—**SONYA LABBE** WEST HOLLYWOOD, CA

PREP: 20 MIN. • **COOK:** 35 MIN.
MAKES: 12 SERVINGS

- 1 **pound ground beef**
- 1 **small red onion, finely chopped**
- 1 **small carrot, finely chopped**
- 4 **garlic cloves, minced**
- ¾ **teaspoon crushed red pepper flakes**
- ½ **cup dry red wine or beef broth**
- 1 **can (15 ounces) crushed tomatoes, undrained**
- 1 **can (8 ounces) tomato sauce**
- ½ **cup vegetable broth**
- 1 **bay leaf**
- ¼ **teaspoon salt**
- ¼ **teaspoon pepper**
- 2 **tablespoons minced fresh basil or 2 teaspoons dried basil**
- 48 **slices French bread baguette (¼ inch thick)**
- 2 **garlic cloves, halved**
- ⅓ **cup olive oil**
- 1 **cup shaved Parmesan cheese**

1. In a large skillet, cook the first five ingredients over medium heat until beef is no longer pink; drain. Add wine, stirring to loosen browned bits from pan.
2. Stir in the tomatoes, tomato sauce, broth, bay leaf, salt and pepper. Bring to a boil. Reduce heat; simmer, uncovered, for 20-25 minutes or until thickened. Discard bay leaf. Stir in basil.
3. Rub baguette slices with garlic halves; place on ungreased baking sheets. Brush lightly with oil. Bake at 400° for 3-5 minutes or until lightly browned.
4. Arrange toast on serving platters; top with beef mixture and cheese. Serve immediately.
PER SERVING *212 cal., 12g fat (4g sat. fat), 28mg chol., 455mg sodium, 14g carb. (1g sugars, 1g fiber), 10g pro.*

MINI ROSEMARY-ROAST BEEF SANDWICHES

Roast beef sandwiches never last long at a party, especially if you dollop on the mayo, mustard, horseradish and pickled giardiniera relish. Give them a try!

—SUSAN HEIN BURLINGTON, WI

PREP: 25 MIN. + CHILLING
BAKE: 50 MIN. + CHILLING
MAKES: 2 DOZEN

- 1 **beef top round roast (3 pounds)**
- 3 teaspoons kosher salt
- 2 teaspoons crushed dried rosemary
- 2 tablespoons olive oil, divided
- 2 teaspoons pepper
- 2 cups mild giardiniera, drained
- 1 cup reduced-fat mayonnaise
- 2 tablespoons stone-ground mustard
- 1 to 2 tablespoons prepared horseradish
- 24 Hawaiian sweet rolls, split

1. Sprinkle roast with salt and rosemary; wrap tightly in plastic. Refrigerate at least 8 hours or up to 24 hours.

2. Preheat oven to 325°. Unwrap roast and pat dry. Rub roast with 1 tablespoon oil; sprinkle with pepper. In a large ovenproof skillet, heat remaining oil over medium-high heat. Brown roast on both sides.

3. Transfer to oven; roast 50-60 minutes or until a thermometer reads 135° for medium-rare. (Temperature of roast will continue to rise about 10° upon standing.) Remove roast from skillet; let stand for 1 hour. Refrigerate, covered, at least 2 hours or until cold.

4. Place giardiniera in a food processor; pulse until finely chopped. In a small bowl, mix mayonnaise, mustard and horseradish.

5. To serve, thinly slice cold beef. Serve on rolls with mayonnaise mixture and giardiniera.

PER SERVING *1 mini sandwich: 220 cal., 9g fat (2g sat. fat), 50mg chol., 166mg sodium, 18g carb. (7g sugars, 1g fiber), 17g pro.*

MINI ROSEMARY-ROAST BEEF SANDWICHES

GRILLED STEAKS WITH CILANTRO SAUCE , PAGE 35

GRILLED SIRLOIN KABOBS WITH PEACH SALSA, PAGE 32

FLAME-BROILED FAVES

Firing up the grill? Turn here for all the **stick-to-your-ribs** entrees you could ask for! From steaks to burgers and from kabobs to fajitas, this beefy selection of **fiery greats** guarantees success every time you light the coals. Try some **new favorites,** too, such as meat loaf, tacos and meatballs made over an open flame.

SIZZLING ANCHO RIBEYES, PAGE 31

SESAME BEEF SKEWERS, PAGE 37

GRILLED FLANK STEAK WITH SUMMER RELISH

GRILLED FLANK STEAK WITH SUMMER RELISH

My garden produces a full harvest of produce, and I use all of it to make the flavor-packed relish for this tasty steak.

—BRENDA WASHNOCK NEGAUNEE, MI

PREP: 25 MIN. + STANDING • **GRILL:** 20 MIN.
MAKES: 4 SERVINGS

- 3 garlic cloves, minced
- 1 teaspoon sea salt
- 1 teaspoon dried rosemary, crushed
- 1 tablespoon olive oil
- 1 beef flank steak (1½ pounds)

RELISH

- 4 large ears sweet corn, husks removed
- 4 green onions
- 2 medium tomatoes
- 1 poblano pepper
- 2 tablespoons olive oil, divided
- 1 medium ripe avocado, peeled and cubed
- 1 teaspoon balsamic vinegar
- ½ teaspoon salt

1. Mix garlic, salt, rosemary and oil; rub over both sides of steak. Let stand at least 30 minutes. Meanwhile, brush corn, onions, tomatoes and poblano with 1 tablespoon oil. Grill, covered, over medium-high heat 5-10 minutes or until vegetables are charred and tender, turning occasionally.

2. Grill steak, covered, over medium heat 5-8 minutes on each side or until meat reaches desired doneness (for medium-rare, a thermometer should read 145°; medium, 160°; well-done, 170°). Let stand 5 minutes.

3. When corn is cool enough to handle, cut kernels from cobs; place in a large bowl. Remove skin and seeds from tomatoes and poblano. Chop onions, tomatoes and poblano; add to bowl. Gently stir in avocado, vinegar, salt and remaining oil. Thinly slice steak across the grain. Serve with relish.

PER SERVING *5 ounces cooked beef and 1 cup relish: 547 cal., 30g fat (8g sat. fat), 81mg chol., 907mg sod., 36g carb. (12g sugars, 7g fiber), 39g pro.*

GRILLED STUFFED MEAT LOAF

Meat loaf on the grill? Absolutely! A twist on the traditional, this meat loaf recipe lets you get out of the kitchen. My husband enjoys it served with grilled corn on the cob.

—MELISSA MASEDA DIXON, CA

PREP: 25 MIN. • **GRILL:** 50 MIN. + STANDING
MAKES: 8 SERVINGS

- 2 cups sliced fresh mushrooms
- 1 medium onion, thinly sliced
- 1 tablespoon butter
- 1 large egg, lightly beaten
- ⅓ cup whole milk
- ½ cup old-fashioned oats
- ½ teaspoon salt
- ¼ teaspoon pepper
- 1½ pounds ground beef

SAUCE

- ½ cup ketchup
- 2 tablespoons brown sugar
- 2 teaspoons prepared mustard

1. In a large skillet, saute mushrooms and onion in butter until tender; set aside.

2. In a large bowl, combine the egg, milk, oats, salt and pepper. Crumble beef over mixture and mix well. On a large piece of heavy-duty foil, pat beef mixture into a 12x8-in. rectangle; spoon mushroom mixture to within 1 in. of edges. Roll up jelly-roll style, starting with a short side and peeling foil away while rolling. Seal seam and ends. Discard foil.

3. Prepare grill for indirect heat, using a drip pan. Form a double thickness of heavy-duty foil (about 14 in. square); cut three slits in foil. Place meat loaf on foil; place on the grill rack over drip pan.

4. Grill, covered, over indirect medium heat for 35 minutes. Combine sauce ingredients; brush over loaf. Grill, covered, 15-20 minutes longer or until meat is no longer pink and a thermometer reads 160°. Let stand for 15 minutes before slicing.

PER SERVING *1 slice: 266 cal., 14g fat (6g sat. fat), 96mg chol., 434mg sod., 14g carb. (9g sugars, 1g fiber), 21g pro.*

BALSAMIC-GLAZED BEEF SKEWERS

EAT SMART · **⑤ INGREDIENTS** · FAST FIX

BALSAMIC-GLAZED BEEF SKEWERS

With just five simple ingredients, these mouthwatering kabobs are a summertime favorite in our family.

—CAROLE FRASER TORONTO, ON

START TO FINISH: 25 MIN.
MAKES: 4 SERVINGS

- ¼ cup balsamic vinaigrette
- ¼ cup barbecue sauce
- 1 teaspoon Dijon mustard
- 1 pound beef top sirloin steak, cut into 1-inch cubes
- 2 cups cherry tomatoes

1. In a large bowl, whisk vinaigrette, barbecue sauce and mustard until blended. Reserve ¼ cup mixture for basting. Add beef to remaining mixture; toss to coat.

2. Alternately thread beef and tomatoes on four metal or soaked wooden skewers. Lightly grease grill rack.

3. Grill skewers, covered, over medium heat or broil 4 in. from heat 6-9 minutes or until beef reaches desired doneness, turning occasionally and basting frequently with reserved vinaigrette mixture during the last 3 minutes.

PER SERVING *194 cal., 7g fat (2g sat. fat), 46mg chol., 288mg sod., 7g carb. (5g sugars, 1g fiber), 25g pro.* **Diabetic Exchanges:** *3 lean meat, 1½ fat, ½ starch.*

GRILLED BEEF CHIMICHANGAS

GRILLED BEEF CHIMICHANGAS

I created this recipe when I didn't have the ingredients for my go-to dish. After making these chimis, they became my new go-to dish!

—JACKIE BURNS KETTLE FALLS, WA

PREP: 25 MIN. • **GRILL:** 10 MIN.
MAKES: 6 SERVINGS

- 1 pound lean ground beef (90% lean)
- 1 small onion, chopped
- 2 garlic cloves, minced
- 1 can (4 ounces) chopped green chilies
- ¼ cup salsa
- ¼ teaspoon ground cumin
- 6 whole wheat tortillas (8 inches)
- ¾ cup shredded Monterey Jack cheese
  Reduced-fat sour cream and
    guacamole, optional

1. In a large skillet, cook beef, onion and garlic over medium heat 6-8 minutes or until beef is no longer pink and onion is tender, breaking up beef into crumbles; drain. Stir in chilies, salsa and cumin.
2. Spoon ½ cup beef mixture across center of each tortilla; top with 2 tablespoons cheese. Fold bottom and sides of tortilla over filling and roll up.
3. Place chimichangas on grill rack, seam side down. Grill, covered, over medium-low heat 10-12 minutes or until crisp and browned, turning once. If desired, serve with sour cream and guacamole.
PER SERVING *1 chimichanga (calculated without sour cream and guacamole): 295 cal., 12g fat (5g sat. fat), 60mg chol., 370mg sod., 25g carb. (1g sugars, 4g fiber), 22g pro.* **Diabetic Exchanges:** *2 lean meat, 1½ starch, 1 fat.*

FAST FIX

SUPREME PIZZA BURGERS

One night I couldn't decide what I wanted more: pizza or hamburgers. So I combined the two to make pizza burgers. My daughter cheers every time these are on the menu.

—ANNA RHYNE KERSHAW, SC

START TO FINISH: 30 MIN.
MAKES: 4 SERVINGS

- ⅓ cup each chopped fresh mushrooms, onion and green pepper
- ⅓ cup chopped ripe olives
- 10 slices turkey pepperoni
- 2 tablespoons tomato paste
- 2 teaspoons Italian seasoning
- ¼ teaspoon garlic powder
- ¼ teaspoon salt
- ¼ teaspoon pepper
- ⅓ cup seasoned bread crumbs
- 1 pound lean ground beef (90% lean)
- 4 whole wheat hamburger buns, split
- 4 slices provolone cheese
- 4 tablespoons pizza sauce

OPTIONAL TOPPINGS
  Sliced ripe olives, fresh mushrooms and/or green pepper rings

1. In a food processor, combine the vegetables, olives, pepperoni, tomato paste and seasonings; cover and pulse just until blended. Transfer to a large bowl; stir in bread crumbs. Crumble beef over mixture and mix well. Shape into four patties.
2. On a greased grill rack, grill burgers, covered, over medium heat or broil 4 in. from the heat for 5-7 minutes on each side or until a thermometer reads 160° and juices run clear.
3. Serve on buns with cheese and pizza sauce. Add toppings if desired.
PER SERVING *470 cal., 21g fat (9g sat. fat), 94mg chol., 1019mg sod., 35g carb. (7g sugars, 5g fiber), 36g pro.*

SIMPLE GRILLED STEAK FAJITAS

EAT SMART FAST FIX

SIMPLE GRILLED STEAK FAJITAS

Moving to a new state with two toddlers in tow, I needed some time-saving recipes. I came up with fajitas—an easy weeknight meal made on the grill or in a cast-iron skillet.

—SHANNEN MAHONEY ODESSA, MO

START TO FINISH: 30 MIN.
MAKES: 4 SERVINGS

- 1 beef top sirloin steak (¾ inch thick and 1 pound)
- 2 tablespoons fajita seasoning mix
- 1 large sweet onion, cut crosswise into ½-inch slices
- 1 medium sweet red pepper, halved
- 1 medium green pepper, halved
- 1 tablespoon olive oil
- 4 whole wheat tortillas (8 inches), warmed
  Optional ingredients: sliced avocado, chopped fresh cilantro and lime wedges

1. Rub steak with seasoning mix. Brush onion and peppers with oil.
2. Grill steak and vegetables, covered, over medium heat 4-6 minutes on each side or until meat reaches desired doneness (for medium-rare, a thermometer should read 145°; medium, 160°; well-done, 170°) and vegetables are tender. Remove from grill. Let steak stand, covered, 5 minutes before slicing.
3. Cut vegetables and steak into strips; serve in tortillas. If desired, top with avocado and cilantro and serve with lime wedges.
PER SERVING *363 cal., 13g fat (4g sat. fat), 54mg chol., 686mg sod., 34g carb. (6g sugars, 5g fiber), 27g pro.* **Diabetic Exchanges:** *3 lean meat, 2 starch, 1 vegetable, ½ fat.*

EGGS BENEDICT BURGERS

To feed my daughter's hungry cowboy friends after a rodeo, I created these burgers featuring bacon, eggs and hollandaise sauce. They were a huge hit!

—BONNIE GEAVARAS-BOOTZ
SCOTTSDALE, AZ

PREP: 25 MIN. • **GRILL:** 10 MIN.
MAKES: 4 SERVINGS

- 1½ **pounds ground beef**
- ½ **teaspoon salt**
- ¼ **teaspoon pepper**
- 4 **hamburger buns, split**
- 1 **envelope hollandaise sauce mix**
- 1½ **teaspoons stone-ground mustard**
- 4 **large eggs**
- 4 **lettuce leaves**
- 4 **slices tomato**
- 6 **bacon strips, halved and cooked**

1. In a large bowl, combine beef, salt and pepper, mixing lightly but thoroughly. Shape into four ½-in.-thick patties.

2. Grill burgers, covered, over medium heat 4-6 minutes on each side or until a thermometer reads 160°. Grill buns, cut side down, until toasted. Meanwhile, prepare sauce mix according to package directions using milk; stir in mustard. Keep warm.

3. Heat a large nonstick skillet coated with cooking spray over medium-high heat. Break eggs, one at a time, into pan; reduce heat to low. Cook until desired doneness, turning after whites are set.

4. Place lettuce, tomato and burgers on bottoms of buns; top with bacon, eggs and sauce. Replace tops.

PER SERVING *723 cal., 45g fat (19g sat. fat), 364mg chol., 1198mg sod., 30g carb. (7g sugars, 1g fiber), 48g pro.*

EGGS BENEDICT BURGERS

TEXAS-STYLE STEAK SANDWICHES

I love the bold flavor behind these hearty sandwiches. They grill up quickly and always taste great—whether they are topped with salsa, guacamole or both.
—LINDA STINSON NEW LONDON, MO

PREP: 10 MIN. + MARINATING • **GRILL:** 10 MIN.
MAKES: 2 SERVINGS

- 1 beef flank steak (½ pound)
- ⅓ cup finely chopped onion
- ¼ cup olive oil
- 2 tablespoons lime juice
- 2 tablespoons red wine vinegar
- 1 garlic clove, minced
- ½ to ¾ teaspoon chili powder
- ¼ to ½ teaspoon salt
- ⅛ to ¼ teaspoon ground cumin
- 2 French rolls, split and toasted
- ½ cup salsa or guacamole, optional

1. Pound steak to ¼-in. thickness. In a resealable plastic bag, combine the onion, oil, lime juice, vinegar, garlic, chili powder, salt and cumin; add beef. Seal bag and turn to coat; refrigerate for 8 hours or overnight.

2. Drain and discard marinade. Grill steak, uncovered, over medium heat or broil 4 in. from heat for 3-5 minutes on each side or until meat reaches desired doneness (for medium-rare steak, a thermometer should read 145°; medium, 160°; well-done, 170°). Slice meat across the grain. Serve on rolls. Top with salsa or guacamole if desired.

PER SERVING *423 cal., 20g fat (5g sat. fat), 54mg chol., 479mg sod., 32g carb., 2g fiber, 28g pro.*

TOP TIP

SERVING SUGGESTION
If sandwiches simply aren't your thing, serve slices of Texas-style flank steak over greens for a satisfying main dish.

BLUE CHEESE FLAT IRON STEAK

BLUE CHEESE FLAT IRON STEAK

The rich pairing of blue cheese with steak is a classic for a reason. I add a little butter to make the dish even more indulgent.
—AMANDA MARTIN MONSON, MA

PREP: 15 MIN. + MARINATING • **GRILL:** 10 MIN.
MAKES: 4 SERVINGS

- ¼ cup olive oil
- 2 tablespoons red wine vinegar
- 2 garlic cloves, minced
- 1 teaspoon dried oregano
- 1 teaspoon dried rosemary, crushed
- 1 teaspoon pepper
- ¼ teaspoon salt
- 1¼ pounds beef flat iron steak or top sirloin steak (1 inch thick)

BLUE CHEESE BUTTER

- ¼ cup crumbled blue cheese
- 3 tablespoons butter, softened
- 1 tablespoon minced fresh chives
- ⅛ teaspoon pepper

1. In a large resealable plastic bag, combine the first seven ingredients. Add beef; seal bag and turn to coat. Refrigerate 30 minutes.

2. In a small bowl, mix blue cheese, butter, chives and pepper; set aside. Drain beef, discarding marinade.

3. Grill steaks, covered, over medium heat or broil 4 in. from heat 5-7 minutes on each side or until the meat reaches desired doneness (for medium-rare, a thermometer should read 145°; medium, 160°; well-done, 170°). Serve with blue cheese butter.

PER SERVING *4 ounces cooked beef with 2 tablespoons cheese mixture: 483 cal., 39g fat (15g sat. fat), 120mg chol., 414mg sod., 2g carb. (0 sugars, 0 fiber), 29g pro.*

FILET MIGNON WITH RED WINE SAUCE

In this filet mignon recipe, it's all about the sauce. A buttery red wine reduction with fresh garlic takes this steak to the next level.

—**TARAH PESSEL** CLARKSTON, MI

PREP: 30 MIN. • **GRILL:** 15 MIN.
MAKES: 6 SERVINGS

- 1 **medium onion, thinly sliced**
- 3 **tablespoons butter, divided**
- 2 **garlic cloves, minced**
- ¾ **teaspoon salt, divided**
- ½ **teaspoon dried oregano**
- 2 **tablespoons tomato paste**
- 1¼ **cups dry red wine or beef broth**
- ½ **teaspoon pepper, divided**
- 6 **beef tenderloin steaks (4 to 6 ounces each)**
- 3 **tablespoons olive oil**

1. In a large saucepan, saute onion in 1 tablespoon butter until tender. Add garlic, ¼ teaspoon salt and oregano; cook and stir 1 minute. Add tomato paste; cook and stir 2 minutes longer.

2. Gradually whisk in wine. Bring to a boil. Reduce heat; simmer until reduced by half. Strain sauce and return to pan. Gradually stir in remaining butter until melted. Add ¼ teaspoon pepper. Remove from the heat; keep warm.

3. Sprinkle steaks with remaining salt and pepper. Drizzle with oil. Grill, covered, over medium heat or broil 4 in. from the heat for 6-8 minutes on each side or until meat reaches desired doneness (for medium-rare, a thermometer should read 145°; medium, 160°; well-done, 170°). Cover and let stand for 3-5 minutes. Serve with wine sauce.

PER SERVING *1 steak with 2 tablespoons sauce: 296 cal., 18g fat (6g sat. fat), 62mg chol., 331mg sod., 4g carb. (2g sugars, 1g fiber), 25g pro.*

GRILLED RIBEYES WITH GREEK RELISH

FAST FIX

GRILLED RIBEYES WITH GREEK RELISH

The classic Grecian flavors of olives, feta cheese and tomatoes are a surefire hit. Combine them to complement a perfectly grilled steak, and it's magic.

—**MARY LOU COOK** WELCHES, OR

START TO FINISH: 30 MIN.
MAKES: 4 SERVINGS

- 4 **plum tomatoes, seeded and chopped**
- 1 **cup chopped red onion**
- ⅔ **cup pitted Greek olives**
- ¼ **cup minced fresh cilantro**
- ¼ **cup lemon juice, divided**
- 2 **tablespoons olive oil**
- 2 **garlic cloves, minced**
- 2 **beef ribeye steaks (¾ pound each)**
- 1 **cup crumbled feta cheese**

1. For relish, combine tomatoes, onion, olives, cilantro, 2 tablespoons lemon juice, oil and garlic.

2. Drizzle remaining lemon juice over steaks. Grill steaks, covered, over medium heat or broil 4 in. from heat 5-7 minutes on each side or until the meat reaches desired doneness (for medium-rare, a thermometer should read 145°; medium, 160°; well-done, 170°). Let stand 5 minutes before cutting steaks in half. Serve with relish and cheese.

PER SERVING *4 ounces cooked beef with ⅔ cup relish and ¼ cup cheese: 597 cal., 44g fat (16g sat. fat), 115mg chol., 723mg sod., 11g carb. (4g sugars, 3g fiber), 37g pro.*

⑤ INGREDIENTS
TEXAS-STYLE BRISKET

This is the quintessential Texas-style brisket. Even my husband's sixth-generation Texas family is impressed! It tastes like a slice of heaven on a plate.
—**RENEE MORGAN** TAYLOR, TX

PREP: 35 MIN. + CHILLING
COOK: 6 HOURS + STANDING
MAKES: 20 SERVINGS

- 1 **whole fresh beef brisket (12 to 14 pounds)**
- ½ **cup pepper**
- ¼ **cup kosher salt**
  Large disposable foil pan
  About 6 cups wood chips, preferably oak

1. Trim fat on brisket to ½-inch thickness. Rub brisket with pepper and salt; place in a large disposable foil pan, fat side up. Refrigerate, covered, several hours or overnight. Meanwhile, soak wood chips in water.

2. To prepare grill for slow indirect cooking, adjust grill vents so top vent is half open and bottom vent is open only one-quarter of the way. Make two arrangements of 45 unlit coals on opposite sides of the grill, leaving the center of the grill open. Light 20 additional coals until ash-covered; distribute over unlit coals.

3. Sprinkle 2 cups soaked wood chips over lit coals. Close grill and allow temperature in grill to reach 275°, about 15 minutes.

4. Place foil pan with brisket in center of grill rack; cover grill and cook 3 hours (do not open grill). Check temperature of grill periodically to maintain a temperature of 275° throughout cooking. Heat level may be adjusted by opening vents to raise temperature and closing vents partway to decrease temperature.

5. Add an additional 10 unlit coals and 1 cup wood chips to each side of the grill. Cook brisket, covered, 3-4 hours longer or until fork tender (a thermometer inserted in brisket should read about 190°); add additional coals and wood chips as needed to maintain a grill temperature of 275°.

6. Remove from grill. Tightly cover pan with foil; let stand 30-60 minutes. Slice brisket across the grain.

PER SERVING *5 ounces: 351 cal., 12g fat (4g sat. fat), 116mg chol., 1243mg sod., 2g carb., 1g fiber, 56g pro.*

⑤ INGREDIENTS FAST FIX ▸
SIZZLING ANCHO RIBEYES (PICTURED ON PAGE 23)

We love the taste of chipotle peppers on just about anything. This delicious dinner proves that there might not be a better pairing than chipotle and grilled steak.
—**ANGELA SPENGLER** TAMPA, FL

START TO FINISH: 25 MIN.
MAKES: 6 SERVINGS

- 4 **teaspoons salt**
- 4 **teaspoons ground ancho chili pepper**
- 1 **teaspoon pepper**
- 6 **beef ribeye steaks (¾ pound each)**
- 6 **tablespoons butter, softened**
- 6 **chipotle peppers in adobo sauce**

1. In a small bowl, combine the salt, chili pepper and pepper; rub over steaks. In another small bowl, beat butter and chipotle peppers until blended.

2. Grill steaks, covered, over medium heat or broil 4 in. from the heat for 5-7 minutes on each side or until meat reaches desired doneness (for medium-rare, a thermometer should read 145°; medium, 160°; well-done, 170°). Serve with chipotle butter.

PER SERVING *1 steak with 1 tablespoon butter: 867 cal., 66g fat (29g sat. fat), 232mg chol., 1926mg sod., 2g carb. (1g sugars, 1g fiber), 61g pro.*

TEXAS-STYLE BRISKET

SUMMERTIME SPAGHETTI WITH GRILLED MEATBALLS

medium heat until sauce begins to simmer, about 10 minutes. Stir in basil.
4. Serve meatballs and sauce with spaghetti; top with shredded Parmesan.
PER SERVING *1 cup spaghetti with ½ cup sauce and 3 meatballs: 446 cal., 14g fat (5g sat. fat), 79mg chol., 470mg sod., 55g carb. (7g sugars, 4g fiber), 25g pro.*

EAT SMART **⑤INGREDIENTS** **FAST FIX** ▶

GRILLED SIRLOIN KABOBS WITH PEACH SALSA (PICTURED ON PAGE 23)

Having a new way to cook with salsa is just one of the perks of this quick and easy dish. Peaches three ways—fresh, preserved and in salsa—star in my signature grilled entree that also offers a blend of hot and sweet flavors.

—**BETH ROYALS** RICHMOND, VA

START TO FINISH: 25 MIN.
MAKES: 6 SERVINGS

- 3 **tablespoons peach preserves**
- 1 **tablespoon finely chopped seeded jalapeno pepper**
- 1 **beef top sirloin steak (1½ pounds), cut into 1-inch cubes**
- ½ **teaspoon salt**
- ¼ **teaspoon pepper**
- 3 **medium peaches, cut into sixths**
- 1½ **cups peach salsa**

1. In a small bowl, mix preserves and jalapeno. Season beef with salt and pepper. Alternately thread beef and peaches onto six metal or soaked wooden skewers.
2. Place kabobs on greased grill rack. Grill kabobs, covered, over medium heat or broil 4 in. from heat 6-8 minutes or until beef reaches desired doneness, turning occasionally. Remove from grill; brush with preserves mixture. Serve with salsa.
PER SERVING *1 kabob with ¼ cup salsa: 219 cal., 5g fat (2g sat. fat), 46mg chol., 427mg sod., 17g carb. (16g sugars, 3g fiber), 25g pro.* **Diabetic Exchanges:** *3 lean meat, ½ starch, ½ fruit.*

SUMMERTIME SPAGHETTI WITH GRILLED MEATBALLS

After Hurricane Sandy, we were without power for two weeks. I quickly learned just how much you can do on a grill!

—**ANDREA RIVERA** WESTBURY, NY

PREP: 25 MIN. • **COOK:** 10 MIN.
MAKES: 6 SERVINGS

- 12 **ounces uncooked spaghetti**

MEATBALLS
- ½ **cup finely chopped onion**
- ¼ **cup seasoned bread crumbs**
- 1 **large egg**
- 2 **tablespoons grated Parmesan cheese**
- 1 **tablespoon 2% milk**
- ½ **teaspoon garlic powder**
- ½ **teaspoon onion powder**
- 1 **pound ground beef**

TOMATO SAUCE
- 2 **pounds (4 to 5) large tomatoes, chopped**
- 3 **garlic cloves, minced**
- 1 **tablespoon olive oil**
- 1 **teaspoon sugar**
- ¾ **teaspoon salt**
- ½ **teaspoon dried oregano**
- ½ **teaspoon pepper**
- 2 **tablespoons minced fresh basil**

TOPPING
- **Shredded Parmesan cheese**

1. Cook spaghetti according to package directions; drain.
2. Meanwhile, combine onion, bread crumbs, egg, Parmesan, milk and seasonings. Add beef; mix lightly. With wet hands, shape into 1½-in. balls. Place meatballs on greased grill rack; grill, covered, over medium heat until cooked through, about 10 minutes.
3. For sauce, combine tomatoes, garlic, oil, sugar, salt, oregano and pepper in an 11x7x2-in. disposable foil pan. Grill over

STEAKS WITH CHERRY-CHIPOTLE GLAZE

This is a great way to take an inexpensive cut of meat and turn it into something special. My son, who claims to be a "meat-a-tarian," loves this and asks for it all year long.

—**CHERYL SNAVELY** HAGERSTOWN, MD

PREP: 15 MIN. + MARINATING • **GRILL:** 10 MIN.
MAKES: 4 SERVINGS

- ¼ cup sherry vinegar
- ¼ cup balsamic vinegar
- ¼ cup Worcestershire sauce
- ¼ cup olive oil
- 2 garlic cloves, minced
- 2 teaspoons Dijon mustard
- ¼ teaspoon salt
- ¼ teaspoon pepper
- 2 beef flat iron or top sirloin steaks (1 pound each)

GLAZE
- 2 tablespoons cherry preserves
- 1 tablespoon brown sugar
- 1 tablespoon olive oil
- 1 chipotle pepper in adobo sauce, minced

1. In a shallow bowl, combine the first eight ingredients. Add meat; turn to coat. Refrigerate at least 4 hours.

2. In a bowl, whisk glaze ingredients. Drain beef, discarding marinade. Grill, covered, over medium heat or broil 4 in. from heat until meat reaches desired doneness (for medium-rare steak, a thermometer should read 145°; medium, 160°; well-done, 170°), 4-6 minutes on each side. Baste with glaze during the last 2 minutes of cooking. Cut steaks in half to serve.

PER SERVING *7 ounces cooked beef: 510 cal., 31g fat (10g sat. fat), 146mg chol., 260mg sod., 12g carb. (11g sugars, 0 fiber), 43g pro.*

STEAKS WITH CHERRY-CHIPOTLE GLAZE

GRILLED ONION &
SKIRT STEAK TACOS

GRILLED ONION & SKIRT STEAK TACOS

I grew up watching my grandmother and mother in the kitchen. My grandparents came from Mexico, and this steak, marinated in beer and lime juice, honors their passion for full-flavored cooking.
—**ADAN FRANCO** MILWAUKEE, WI

PREP: 15 MIN. + MARINATING • **GRILL:** 5 MIN.
MAKES: 8 SERVINGS

- 2 **beef skirt or flank steaks (1 pound each)**
- 1 **bottle (12 ounces) beer**
- ¼ **cup lime juice**
- 3 **tablespoons olive oil, divided**
- 8 **spring onions**
- 1¼ **teaspoons salt, divided**
- ¾ **teaspoon pepper, divided**
  Corn tortillas, minced fresh cilantro and lime wedges

1. Pound beef with a meat mallet to tenderize. In a large bowl, mix beer, lime juice and 2 tablespoons oil until blended. Add beef to marinade; turn to coat. Refrigerate, covered, at least 30 minutes.
2. Meanwhile, cut partially through onions, leaving tops intact. Drizzle with remaining oil; sprinkle with ¼ teaspoon salt and ¼ teaspoon pepper.
3. Drain beef, discarding marinade; sprinkle with the remaining salt and pepper. On a greased grill rack, grill steaks and onions, covered, over medium heat or broil 4 in. from heat 2-4 minutes on each side or until meat reaches desired doneness (for medium-rare steak, a thermometer should read 145°; medium, 160°; well-done, 170°) and onions are crisp-tender. Cut steak diagonally across the grain into thin slices. Serve with corn tortillas, onions, cilantro and lime wedges.
PER SERVING *1 serving (calculated without tortillas, cilantro and lime wedges): 288 cal., 14g fat (5g sat. fat), 67mg chol., 458mg sod., 7g carb. (3g sugars, 1g fiber), 31g pro.*

GRILLED STEAKS WITH CILANTRO SAUCE

(PICTURED ON PAGE 22)
Fresh herbs made into a zesty sauce help make these steaks the star of our favorite summer grilling menu.
—**LYNNE KEAST** MONTE SERENO, CA

PREP: 25 MIN. • **GRILL:** 15 MIN.
MAKES: 8 SERVINGS (3 CUPS SAUCE)

- 2 **cups fresh parsley leaves**
- 2 **cups fresh cilantro leaves**
- 1 **cup fresh mint leaves**
- 8 **garlic cloves, chopped**
- 1¾ **teaspoons kosher salt, divided**
- ½ **teaspoon plus ¾ teaspoon freshly ground pepper, divided**
- 2 **cups olive oil**
- ⅔ **cup red wine vinegar**
- 2 **tablespoons lemon juice**
- ½ **teaspoon crushed red pepper flakes**
- 4 **pounds beef flat iron steaks or top sirloin steaks (1 inch thick)**

1. Place herbs, garlic, 1 teaspoon salt and ½ teaspoon pepper in a food processor; pulse until herbs are chopped. Gradually add oil, vinegar, lemon juice and pepper flakes, processing just until blended.
2. Sprinkle steaks with remaining salt and pepper. Grill, covered, over medium heat or broil 4 in. from heat 6-8 minutes on each side or until meat reaches desired doneness (for medium-rare steaks, a thermometer should read 145°; medium, 160°; well-done, 170°). Cut steaks into ¼-in. slices; serve with sauce.
PER SERVING *6 ounces cooked beef with ⅓ cup sauce: 901 cal., 78g fat (17g sat. fat), 146mg chol., 567mg sod., 5g carb. (0 sugars, 2g fiber), 45g pro.*

SOUTHWEST FLANK STEAK

EAT SMART **FAST FIX**
SOUTHWEST FLANK STEAK

Marinades are great, but they can be time-consuming when you've got a hungry crowd to feed. The perfectly balanced rub in this dish imparts deep flavors without all the muss and fuss.
—**KENNY FISHER** CIRCLEVILLE, OH

START TO FINISH: 25 MIN.
MAKES: 6 SERVINGS

- 3 **tablespoons brown sugar**
- 3 **tablespoons chili powder**
- 4½ **teaspoons ground cumin**
- 1 **tablespoon garlic powder**
- 1 **tablespoon cider vinegar**
- 1½ **teaspoons Worcestershire sauce**
- ½ **teaspoon cayenne pepper**
- 1 **beef flank steak (1½ pounds)**

1. In a small bowl, combine the first seven ingredients; rub over steak.
2. On a greased grill rack, grill steak, covered, over medium heat or broil 4 in. from the heat for 6-8 minutes on each side or until meat reaches desired doneness (for medium-rare, a thermometer should read 145°; medium, 160°; well-done, 170°).
3. Let stand for 5 minutes. To serve, thinly slice across the grain.
PER SERVING *3 ounces cooked beef: 219 cal., 9g fat (4g sat. fat), 54mg chol., 127mg sod., 11g carb. (7g sugars, 2g fiber), 23g pro.* **Diabetic Exchanges:** *3 lean meat, 1 starch.*

BURGER AMERICANA

BURGER AMERICANA

Here's a good basic burger your family will love. Grill the patties and load them sky-high with everyone's favorite toppings. Cheese, lettuce and tomato are classics, but you could also go for bacon and blue cheese.

—**SUSAN MAHANEY** NEW HARTFORD, NY

START TO FINISH: 25 MIN.
MAKES: 4 SERVINGS

- ½ **cup seasoned bread crumbs**
- 1 **large egg, lightly beaten**
- ½ **teaspoon salt**
- ½ **teaspoon pepper**
- 1 **pound ground beef**
- 1 **tablespoon olive oil**
- 4 **sesame seed hamburger buns, split**
  Toppings of your choice

1. In a large bowl, combine bread crumbs, egg, salt and pepper. Add beef; mix lightly but thoroughly. Shape into four ½-in.-thick patties. Press a shallow indentation in the center of each with your thumb. Brush both sides of patties with oil.

2. Grill burgers, covered, over medium heat or broil 4 in. from heat 4-5 minutes on each side or until a thermometer reads 160°. Serve on buns with toppings.

PER SERVING *1 burger (calculated without toppings): 429 cal., 20g fat (6g sat. fat), 123mg chol., 796mg sod., 32g carb. (3g sugars, 1g fiber), 28g pro.*

TOP TIP

SIMPLE SUBSTITUTIONS

This is my kind of recipe—easy and tasty! I used ground turkey and Worcestershire burger seasoning instead of the ground beef, pepper and salt.

—**IMMANDA**
TASTEOFHOME.COM

SESAME BEEF SKEWERS

(PICTURED ON PAGE 23)

A bottle of sesame-ginger dressing makes this amazing dish doable on any weeknight. We live in the South—where people grill all year long—but you can broil the beef if you don't have that luxury. My pineapple-y salad finishes off the dinner.

—**JANICE ELDER** CHARLOTTE, NC

START TO FINISH: 30 MIN.
MAKES: 4 SERVINGS

- 1 **pound beef top sirloin steak, cut into 1-inch cubes**
- 6 **tablespoons sesame ginger salad dressing, divided**
- 1 **tablespoon reduced-sodium soy sauce**

SALAD
- 1 **tablespoon sweet chili sauce**
- 1 **tablespoon lime juice**
- ¼ **teaspoon pepper**
- 2 **medium apples, chopped**
- 2 **cups chopped fresh pineapple**
- 1 **tablespoon sesame seeds, toasted**

1. In a bowl, toss beef with 3 tablespoons dressing and the soy sauce; let stand 10 minutes. Meanwhile, in a large bowl, mix chili sauce, lime juice and pepper; gently stir in apples and pineapple.

2. Thread beef on four metal or soaked wooden skewers; discard remaining marinade. Grill kabobs, covered, over medium heat or broil 4 in. from heat for 7-9 minutes or until desired doneness, turning occasionally; brush generously with remaining dressing during the last 3 minutes. Sprinkle with sesame seeds. Serve with salad.

PER SERVING *1 kabob with 1 cup salad: 311 cal., 11g fat (3g sat. fat), 46mg chol., 357mg sod., 28g carb. (21g sugars, 3g fiber), 25g pro.* **Diabetic Exchanges:** *3 lean meat, 1 starch, 1 fruit, ½ fat.*

FAJITA IN A BOWL

FAJITA IN A BOWL

Pull out the skewers and take a stab at grilling peppers, onions and corn for an awesome steak salad that's all summer and smoke.

—**PEGGY WOODWARD** SHULLSBURG, WI

START TO FINISH: 30 MIN.
MAKES: 4 SERVINGS

- 1 **tablespoon brown sugar**
- 1 **tablespoon chili powder**
- ½ **teaspoon salt**
- 1 **beef flank steak (1 pound)**
- 12 **miniature sweet peppers, halved and seeded**
- 1 **medium red onion, cut into thin wedges**
- 2 **cups cherry tomatoes**
- 2 **medium ears sweet corn, husks removed**

SALAD
- 12 **cups torn mixed salad greens**
- 1 **cup fresh cilantro leaves**
- ½ **cup reduced-fat lime vinaigrette**
  Optional ingredients: cotija cheese, lime wedges and tortillas

1. In a small bowl, mix brown sugar, chili powder and salt. Rub onto both sides of steak.

2. Place peppers and onion on a grilling grid; place on grill rack over medium heat. Grill, covered, 9-11 minutes or until crisp-tender, stirring occasionally; add tomatoes during the last 2 minutes. Remove from grill.

3. Place steak and corn directly on grill rack; close lid. Grill steak 8-10 minutes on each side or until a thermometer reads 145° for medium rare; grill corn 10-12 minutes or until lightly charred, turning occasionally.

4. Divide greens and cilantro among four bowls. Cut corn from cobs and thinly slice steak across the grain; place in bowls. Top with vegetables; drizzle with vinaigrette. If desired, serve with cheese, lime and tortillas.

PER SERVING *1 serving (calculated without optional ingredients): 351 cal., 14g fat (5g sat. fat), 54mg chol., 862mg sodium, 33g carb. (16g sugars, 7g fiber), 28g pro.*

BALSAMIC STEAK WITH RED GRAPE RELISH

Steak marinated in balsamic vinaigrette goes so well with a relish of red grapes and blue cheese. Everything looks just gorgeous on the plate, and it tastes wonderful!

—**NAYLET LAROCHELLE** MIAMI, FL

START TO FINISH: 25 MIN.
MAKES: 4 SERVINGS

- 1 **beef top sirloin steak (¾ inch thick and 1 pound)**
- ¾ **cup reduced-fat balsamic vinaigrette, divided**

- 2½ **cups seedless red grapes, halved**
- 4 **green onions, chopped (about ½ cup)**
- ½ **cup crumbled blue cheese**
- ¼ **teaspoon salt**
- ¼ **teaspoon coarsely ground pepper**

1. Place steak in a large resealable plastic bag; add ½ cup vinaigrette. Seal bag and turn to coat; let stand for 10 minutes. Meanwhile, in a small bowl, toss grapes with green onions and cheese.

2. Drain beef, discarding marinade. Sprinkle steak with salt and pepper. Grill steak, covered, over medium heat or broil 4 in. from heat 4-7 minutes on each side or until meat reaches desired doneness (for medium-rare, a thermometer should read 145°; medium, 160°; well-done, 170°).

3. Cut steak into thin slices. Serve with grape relish and remaining vinaigrette.

PER SERVING *3 ounces cooked beef with ¾ cup relish and 1 tablespoon vinaigrette: 332 cal., 14g fat (6g sat. fat), 59mg chol., 659mg sod., 22g carb. (18g sugars, 1g fiber), 28g pro.*

BALSAMIC STEAK WITH RED GRAPE RELISH

BARBECUE SLIDERS

GRILLED BEEF TERIYAKI

Pineapple juice and soy sauce combine in my robust Asian-style marinade.
—**LOU DUBRULE** EL PASO, TX

PREP: 20 MIN. + MARINATING • **GRILL:** 20 MIN.
MAKES: 6 SERVINGS

- 1 **beef flank steak (1½ pounds)**
- ¾ **cup beef broth**
- ½ **cup unsweetened pineapple juice**
- ¼ **cup reduced-sodium soy sauce**
- 1 **tablespoon lemon juice**
- 1 **tablespoon honey**
- ¼ **teaspoon ground ginger**
- 2 **large onions, cut into ¼-in. slices**

1. Score surface of steak, making shallow diagonal cuts. In a bowl, combine the broth, pineapple juice, soy sauce, lemon juice, honey and ginger.

2. Pour 1 cup marinade into a large resealable plastic bag; add steak. Seal bag and turn to coat; refrigerate for 8 hours or overnight, turning once or twice. Add onion to remaining marinade; cover and refrigerate for 4-6 hours, stirring often.

3. Drain and discard marinade. On a greased grill rack, grill steak, covered, over medium heat for 8-10 minutes on each side or until meat reaches desired doneness (for medium-rare, a meat thermometer should read 145°; medium, 160°; well-done, 170°).

4. Meanwhile, place onion slices on a grilling grid lightly coated with cooking oil; place on a grill rack. Grill, covered, over medium heat for 6 minutes on each side or until tender. Thinly slice steak across the grain; serve with grilled onion.

NOTE *If you do not have a grilling grid, use a disposable foil pan. Poke holes in the bottom of the pan with a meat fork to allow liquid to drain.*

PER SERVING *3 ounces: 196 cal., 8g fat (4g sat. fat), 54mg chol., 210mg sod., 6g carb. (5g sugars, 1g fiber), 23g pro.*
Diabetic Exchanges: *3 lean meat, 1 vegetable.*

⑤ INGREDIENTS **FAST FIX**

BARBECUE SLIDERS

When company dropped in by surprise, the only things I had defrosted were sausage and ground beef. We combined the two for juicy burgers on the grill, and were thrilled with the results. See for yourself!
—**BJ LARSEN** ERIE, CO

START TO FINISH: 25 MIN.
MAKES: 8 SERVINGS

- 1 **pound ground beef**
- 1 **pound bulk pork sausage**
- 1 **cup barbecue sauce, divided**
- 16 **Hawaiian sweet rolls, split**
  Optional toppings: lettuce leaves, sliced plum tomatoes and red onion

1. In a large bowl, mix beef and sausage lightly but thoroughly. Shape into sixteen ½-in.-thick patties.

2. Grill patties, covered, over medium heat or broil 4-5 in. from heat 3-4 minutes on each side or until a thermometer reads 160°; brush with ¼ cup sauce during the last 2 minutes of cooking. Serve on rolls with remaining barbecue sauce; top as desired.

FREEZE OPTION *Place patties on a plastic wrap-lined baking sheet; wrap and freeze until firm. Remove from pan and transfer to a large resealable plastic bag; return to freezer. To use, grill frozen patties as directed, increasing time as necessary.*

NOTE *Make these with 90 percent lean ground beef and turkey breakfast sausage and you'll save nearly 100 calories and more than half the fat .*

PER SERVING *2 sliders: 499 cal., 24g fat (9g sat. fat), 96mg chol., 885mg sod., 47g carb. (23g sugars, 2g fiber), 24g pro.*

SKILLET BBQ BEEF
POT PIE, PAGE 50

ONE-POT
CHILIGHETTI, PAGE 56

STOVETOP GREATS

When it's time to set a **hot and hearty** meal on the table, turn to these meaty family favorites. Not only do most of them come together in **30 minutes or less,** but these skillet sensations whip up with items you likely already have in your kitchen. What are you waiting for? Try any of these **24 sizzling suppers** tonight.

BASIL-BUTTER STEAKS
WITH ROASTED
POTATOES, PAGE 57

ITALIAN-STYLE SALISBURY STEAKS, PAGE 45

BEEF TERIYAKI NOODLES

(5)INGREDIENTS FAST FIX
BEEF TERIYAKI NOODLES

At our house, we love to combine fresh ingredients with convenience products. This version starts with beef, mushrooms and stir-fry veggies since we always have them on hand, but feel free to make the dish your own. Use what's in your pantry to bring out your inner chef!

—**RICHARD ROBINSON** PARK FOREST, IL

START TO FINISH: 20 MIN.
MAKES: 4 SERVINGS

- 1 envelope (4.6 ounces) lo mein noodles and teriyaki sauce mix
- 1 pound beef flat iron steak or top sirloin steak, cut into bite-size pieces
- ¼ teaspoon salt
- ¼ teaspoon pepper
- 2 tablespoons canola oil, divided
- 2 cups frozen pepper and onion stir-fry blend
- 1 cup sliced fresh mushrooms

1. Prepare noodle mix according to package directions.
2. Meanwhile, sprinkle beef with salt and pepper. In a large skillet, heat 1 tablespoon oil over medium-high heat. Add beef; stir-fry 6-8 minutes or until no longer pink. Remove from pan; discard drippings.
3. Stir-fry vegetable blend and mushrooms in remaining oil for 3-4 minutes or until vegetables are tender.
4. Return beef to pan. Stir in noodle mixture; heat through.

PER SERVING *1 cup: 403 cal., 20g fat (5g sat. fat), 73mg chol., 541mg sod., 28g carb. (3g sugars, 2g fiber), 24g pro.*

FAST FIX
GREEK RAVIOLI SKILLET

Looking to please picky little palates? One tester loved this simple skillet entree so much, she made it at home for her 2-year-old daughter, who said *Mmm!* after every single bite.

—*TASTE OF HOME* TEST KITCHEN

START TO FINISH: 30 MIN.
MAKES: 6 SERVINGS

- 1 package (20 ounces) refrigerated cheese ravioli
- 1 pound ground beef
- 1 medium zucchini, sliced
- 1 small red onion, chopped
- 3 cups marinara or spaghetti sauce
- ½ cup water
- ¼ teaspoon pepper
- 2 medium tomatoes, chopped
- ½ cup cubed feta cheese
- ½ cup pitted Greek olives, halved
- 2 tablespoons minced fresh basil, divided

1. Cook ravioli according to package directions. Meanwhile, in a large skillet, cook the beef, zucchini and onion over medium heat until meat is no longer pink; drain.
2. Drain ravioli; add to skillet. Stir in the marinara sauce, water and pepper. Bring to a boil. Reduce heat; simmer, uncovered, for 5 minutes. Add the tomatoes, cheese, olives and 1 tablespoon basil. Sprinkle with remaining basil.

PER SERVING *1½ cups: 543 cal., 20g fat (8g sat. fat), 89mg chol., 917mg sod., 58g carb. (13g sugars, 6g fiber), 32g pro.*

SOUTHWESTERN GOULASH

EAT SMART FAST FIX
SOUTHWESTERN GOULASH

I had some extra cilantro in the fridge and didn't want to throw it away, so I came up with this delightful and filling family recipe. Everyone just loved it!

—**VIKKI REBHOLZ** WEST CHESTER, OH

START TO FINISH: 25 MIN.
MAKES: 6 SERVINGS

- 1 cup uncooked elbow macaroni
- 1 pound lean ground beef (90% lean)
- 1 medium onion, chopped
- 1 can (28 ounces) diced tomatoes, undrained
- 1 can (8 ounces) tomato sauce
- ⅔ cup frozen corn
- 1 can (4 ounces) chopped green chilies
- ½ teaspoon ground cumin
- ½ teaspoon pepper
- ¼ teaspoon salt
- ¼ cup minced fresh cilantro

1. Cook macaroni according to package directions; drain. Meanwhile, in a 6-qt. stockpot, cook and crumble beef with onion over medium heat until meat is no longer pink, 6-8 minutes; drain.
2. Stir in tomatoes, tomato sauce, corn, chilies and dry seasonings; bring to a boil. Reduce heat; simmer, uncovered, until flavors are blended, about 5 minutes. Stir in macaroni and cilantro.

PER SERVING *1⅓ cups: 224 cal., 6g fat (2g sat. fat), 37mg chol., 567mg sod., 24g carb., 4g fiber, 19g pro.* **Diabetic Exchanges:** *2 lean meat, 2 vegetable, 1 starch.*

TOP TIP

TIPS FOR BEEF TERIYAKI NOODLES

This was excellent. I marinated the steak in soy sauce. Cutting against the steak's grain helps make it tender. I splashed the veggies and meat with a little teriyaki while cooking, too. It came out great. I'll definitely make this again.

—**JSWINN** TASTEOFHOME.COM

CILANTRO BEEF TACOS

FAST FIX ▶

CILANTRO BEEF TACOS

Whenever I have steak on hand, it's time to make tacos. Set out bowls of toppings such as lettuce, tomatoes, sour cream, avocado and salsa. Now that's a fiesta!

—**PATTI ROSE** TINLEY PARK, IL

START TO FINISH: 30 MIN.
MAKES: 4 SERVINGS

- 1 **beef flank steak (1 pound)**
- ½ **teaspoon salt**
- ¼ **teaspoon pepper**
- 4 **teaspoons olive oil, divided**
- 1 **medium onion, halved and sliced**
- 1 **jalapeno pepper, seeded and finely chopped**
- 1 **garlic clove, minced**
- ½ **cup salsa**
- ¼ **cup minced fresh cilantro**
- 2 **teaspoons lime juice**
  Dash hot pepper sauce
- 8 **flour tortillas (6 inches), warmed**
  Optional toppings: salsa, cilantro, shredded lettuce and sour cream

1. Sprinkle steak with salt and pepper. In a large skillet, heat 2 teaspoons oil over medium-high heat. Add steak; cook for 5-7 minutes on each side or until meat reaches desired doneness (for medium-rare, a thermometer should read 145°; medium, 160°; well-done, 170°). Remove from pan.

2. In same skillet, heat remaining oil over medium heat. Add onion; cook and stir 4-5 minutes or until tender. Add jalapeno and garlic; cook 2 minutes longer. Stir in salsa, cilantro, lime juice and pepper sauce; heat through.

3. Thinly slice steak across the grain; stir into onion mixture. Serve in tortillas; top as desired.

NOTE *Wear disposable gloves when cutting hot peppers; the oils can burn skin. Avoid touching your face.*

PER SERVING *2 tacos (calculated without toppings): 451 cal., 20g fat (7g sat. fat), 54mg chol., 884mg sod., 38g carb. (3g sugars, 4g fiber), 27g pro.*

ITALIAN-STYLE SALISBURY STEAKS (PICTURED ON PAGE 41)

This is my husband's favorite recipe. If you like, you can top each serving with mozzarella or Parmesan cheese.

—**HEATHER NALLEY** EASLEY, SC

START TO FINISH: 25 MIN.
MAKES: 4 SERVINGS

- 1 **large egg, beaten**
- 1 **teaspoon Worcestershire sauce**
- ½ **cup seasoned bread crumbs**
- ½ **teaspoon garlic powder**
- ½ **teaspoon pepper**
- 1 **pound ground beef**
- 1 **tablespoon canola oil**
- 1 **can (14½ ounces) diced tomatoes with basil, oregano and garlic, undrained**
- 1 **can (8 ounces) Italian tomato sauce**

1. In a large bowl, combine the first five ingredients. Crumble beef over mixture and mix well. Shape into four oval patties. In a large skillet, brown patties in oil on both sides. Drain.

2. In a small bowl, combine diced tomatoes and tomato sauce. Pour over patties. Bring to a boil. Reduce heat; cover and simmer for 10-15 minutes or until meat is no longer pink.

FREEZE OPTION *Freeze individual cooled steaks with some tomato mixture in resealable freezer bags. To use, partially thaw in refrigerator overnight. Microwave, covered, on high until heated through, gently stirring and adding a little water if necessary.*

PER SERVING *1 patty with ½ cup sauce: 359 cal., 20g fat (6g sat. fat), 123mg chol., 1104mg sod., 21g carb. (7g sugars, 2g fiber), 26g pro.*

SAUCY SKILLET LASAGNA

SAUCY SKILLET LASAGNA

Thanks to the no-cook noodles, this skillet lasagna makes a fast and filling Italian entree.

—**MEGHAN CRIHFIELD** RIPLEY, WV

START TO FINISH: 30 MIN.
MAKES: 8 SERVINGS

- 1 **pound ground beef**
- 1 **can (14½ ounces) diced tomatoes, undrained**
- 2 **large eggs, lightly beaten**
- 1½ **cups ricotta cheese**
- 4 **cups marinara sauce**
- 1 **package (9 ounces) no-cook lasagna noodles**
- 1 **cup shredded part-skim mozzarella cheese, optional**

1. In a large skillet, cook beef over medium heat 6-8 minutes or until no longer pink, breaking into crumbles; drain. Transfer to a large bowl; stir in tomatoes. In a small bowl, combine eggs and ricotta cheese.

2. Return 1 cup meat mixture to the skillet; spread evenly. Layer with 1 cup ricotta mixture, 1½ cups marinara sauce and half of the noodles, breaking noodles to fit as necessary. Repeat layers. Top with remaining marinara sauce.

3. Bring to a boil. Reduce heat; simmer, covered, 15-17 minutes or until noodles are tender. Remove from heat. If desired, sprinkle with mozzarella cheese. Let stand 2 minutes or until cheese is melted.

PER SERVING *430 cal., 18g fat (8g sat. fat), 108mg chol., 750mg sod., 41g carb. (11g sugars, 4g fiber), 27g pro.*

SOUTHWEST FRITO PIE

I got a real culture shock when we moved to New Mexico several years ago, but we grew to love the food. Now back in South Carolina, we still crave Southwestern dishes, and this is one of my favorites.

—JANET SCOGGINS NORTH AUGUSTA, SC

PREP: 20 MIN. • **COOK:** 25 MIN.
MAKES: 6 SERVINGS

- 2 pounds lean ground beef (90% lean)
- 3 tablespoons chili powder
- 2 tablespoons all-purpose flour
- 1 teaspoon salt
- 1 teaspoon garlic powder
- 2 cups water
- 1 can (15 ounces) pinto beans, rinsed and drained, optional
- 4½ cups Fritos corn chips
- 2 cups shredded lettuce
- 1½ cups shredded cheddar cheese
- ¾ cup chopped tomatoes
- 6 tablespoons finely chopped onion
  Sour cream and minced fresh cilantro, optional

1. In a 6-qt. stockpot, cook beef over medium heat until no longer pink, breaking into crumbles; drain. Stir in chili powder, flour, salt and garlic powder until blended. Gradually stir in water and, if desired, beans.

2. Bring to a boil. Reduce heat; simmer, uncovered, 12-15 minutes or until thickened, stirring occasionally.

3. To serve, divide chips among six serving bowls. Top with beef mixture, lettuce, cheese, tomatoes and onion. If desired, top with sour cream and cilantro.

PER SERVING (calculated without beans and sour cream): 615 cal., 38g fat (16g sat. fat), 143mg chol., 915mg sod., 25g carb. (2g sugars, 3g fiber), 43g pro.

BEEF & PEPPER SKILLET

FAST FIX

BEEF & PEPPER SKILLET

I love Mexican-inspired food. I also enjoy experimenting with recipes like this one and making them as healthy and downright good as can be!

—JENNY DUBINSKY INWOOD, WV

START TO FINISH: 30 MIN.
MAKES: 6 SERVINGS

- 1 pound lean ground beef (90% lean)
- 1 can (14½ ounces) diced tomatoes with mild green chilies, undrained
- 1 can (14½ ounces) beef broth
- 1 tablespoon chili powder
- ¼ teaspoon salt
- ⅛ teaspoon garlic powder
- 2 cups instant brown rice
- 1 medium sweet red pepper, sliced
- 1 medium green pepper, sliced
- 1 cup shredded Colby-Monterey Jack cheese

1. In a large skillet, cook beef over medium heat 6-8 minutes or until no longer pink, breaking into crumbles; drain.

2. Add tomatoes, broth, chili powder, salt and garlic powder; bring to a boil. Stir in rice and peppers. Reduce heat; simmer, covered, 8-10 minutes or until liquid is absorbed. Remove from heat; sprinkle with cheese. Let stand, covered, until cheese is melted.

FREEZE OPTION Before adding cheese, cool beef mixture. Freeze beef mixture and cheese separately in freezer containers. To use, partially thaw in refrigerator overnight. Heat through in a saucepan, stirring occasionally and adding a little broth if necessary. Sprinkle with cheese.

PER SERVING 1½ cups: 340 cal., 13g fat (7g sat. fat), 64mg chol., 807mg sod., 31g carb. (5g sugars, 4g fiber), 23g pro.

MY BEST SPAGHETTI & MEATBALLS

I remember as a kid going to the Old Spaghetti Factory and getting a big plate of cheesy spaghetti, meatballs and garlic bread. My recipe brings back those memories and satiates everyone's appetite for Italian food.

—ERIKA MONROE-WILLIAMS
SCOTTSDALE, AZ

PREP: 1 HOUR • **COOK:** 50 MIN.
MAKES: 10 SERVINGS (2½ QUARTS)

- ¾ cup soft bread crumbs
- ½ cup grated Parmesan cheese
- ¼ cup 2% milk
- 1 large egg, beaten
- 3 tablespoons minced fresh Italian flat-leaf parsley
- 3 garlic cloves, minced
- ¾ teaspoon salt
- ½ teaspoon coarsely ground pepper
- ½ pound ground beef
- ½ pound ground pork
- ½ pound ground veal or additional ground beef
- 2 tablespoons canola oil

SAUCE

- 2 tablespoons canola oil
- 1 medium onion, finely chopped
- 2 garlic cloves, minced
- 1 can (6 ounces) tomato paste
- ¾ cup dry red wine or beef broth
- 2 cans (28 ounces each) crushed tomatoes
- ¼ cup minced fresh parsley
- 2 teaspoons sugar
- 1½ teaspoons salt
- ¼ teaspoon coarsely ground pepper
- ¼ teaspoon crushed red pepper flakes
- 4 fresh basil leaves, torn into small pieces
  Hot cooked spaghetti
  Additional grated Parmesan cheese

1. In a large bowl, combine the first eight ingredients. Add beef, pork and veal; mix lightly but thoroughly. Shape into 1-in. balls. In a large skillet, heat oil over medium heat. Brown meatballs in batches; drain.

2. In a 6-qt. stockpot, heat oil over medium heat. Add onion; cook and stir 3-5 minutes or until tender. Add garlic; cook and stir 2 minutes. Add tomato paste; cook and stir 3-5 minutes or until paste darkens. Add wine; cook and stir 2 minutes to dissolve any browned tomato paste.

3. Stir in tomatoes, parsley, sugar, salt, pepper and pepper flakes. Bring to a boil. Reduce heat; simmer, uncovered, 15-20 minutes or until thickened, stirring occasionally. Add basil and meatballs; cook 20-25 minutes longer or until meatballs are cooked through, stirring occasionally. Serve meatballs and sauce with spaghetti. Sprinkle with the additional cheese.

NOTE *To make soft bread crumbs, tear bread into pieces and place in a food processor or blender. Cover and pulse until crumbs form. One slice of bread yields ½ to ¾ cup crumbs.*

PER SERVING *1 cup (calculated without pasta and additional cheese): 290 cal., 15g fat (4g sat. fat), 65mg chol., 974mg sod., 20g carb. (10g sugars, 4g fiber), 18g pro.*

MY BEST SPAGHETTI
& MEATBALLS

TOP TIP

TASTY THREESOME

The secret to these incredible meatballs is the combination of ground beef, pork and veal. Feel free to get creative, however. Substitute the veal with ground chicken, or use pizza-seasoned ground beef for the pork. You can also customize the sauce by stirring in oregano, sliced mushrooms or even a little bit of Parmesan or mozzarella cheese.

EAT SMART FAST FIX

WEEKNIGHT BEEF SKILLET

This hearty family fare is chock-full of veggies and good nutrition. It just might become one of your family's favorites!

—CLARA COULSON MINNEY
WASHINGTON COURT HOUSE, OH

START TO FINISH: 25 MIN.
MAKES: 4 SERVINGS

- 3 cups uncooked yolk-free whole wheat noodles
- 1 pound lean ground beef (90% lean)
- 1 medium green pepper, finely chopped
- 1 can (15 ounces) tomato sauce
- 1 tablespoon Worcestershire sauce
- 1½ teaspoons Italian seasoning
- 1 teaspoon sugar, optional
- 1 package (16 ounces) frozen mixed vegetables, thawed and drained
- ¼ cup minced fresh parsley

1. Cook noodles according to package directions; drain. Meanwhile, in a large nonstick skillet, cook beef and pepper over medium heat 5-7 minutes or until beef is no longer pink, breaking up beef into crumbles; drain.

2. Add tomato sauce, Worcestershire sauce, Italian seasoning and, if desired, sugar to beef mixture; bring to a boil. Stir in vegetables; heat through. Serve with noodles; sprinkle with parsley.

FREEZE OPTION *Do not cook noodles. Freeze cooled meat mixture in a freezer container. To use, partially thaw in refrigerator overnight. Cook noodles according to package directions. Place meat mixture in a large saucepan; heat through, stirring occasionally and adding a little broth or water if necessary. Serve as directed.*

PER SERVING *1¼ cups beef mixture with ¾ cup noodles : 400 cal., 11g fat (4g sat. fat), 71mg chol., 638mg sod., 48g carb. (8g sugars, 11g fiber), 31g pro.* **Diabetic Exchanges:** *3 starch, 3 lean meat, 1 vegetable.*

WEEKNIGHT BEEF SKILLET

ULTIMATE STEAK DE BURGO

You'll love this traditional beef entree seasoned with butter, herbs and garlic. There's lots of gravy, so it's great to serve with mashed potatoes or crusty bread for dipping. French onion soup is also a delicious accompaniment.

—HOLLIS MONROE AMES, IA

START TO FINISH: 30 MIN.
MAKES: 4 SERVINGS

- 1 garlic clove, minced
- ¾ teaspoon salt, divided
- 4 beef tenderloin steaks (1-inch thick and 4 ounces each)
- ¼ teaspoon pepper
- 1 tablespoon butter
- ½ cup butter, cubed
- ½ cup half-and-half cream
- 2 tablespoons sweet white wine
- ½ teaspoon minced fresh oregano or ⅛ teaspoon dried oregano
- ½ teaspoon minced fresh basil or ⅛ teaspoon dried basil

1. Place garlic on a cutting board; sprinkle with ¼ teaspoon salt. Mash garlic with flat side of the knife blade, forming a smooth paste. Sprinkle steaks with pepper and remaining salt.
2. In a large skillet, heat 1 tablespoon butter over medium heat. Add steaks; cook 4-6 minutes on each side or until meat reaches desired doneness (for medium-rare, a thermometer should read 145°; medium, 160°; well-done, 170°). Remove from pan; keep warm.
3. In same skillet, melt ½ cup butter over medium heat. Whisk in garlic paste, cream and wine; heat through. Serve over steaks; sprinkle with herbs.
PER SERVING *1 steak with ¼ cup sauce: 440 cal., 36g fat (21g sat. fat), 133mg chol., 663mg sod., 2g carb. (1g sugars, 0 fiber), 25g pro.*

DIJON BEEF TENDERLOIN

⑤ INGREDIENTS FAST FIX

DIJON BEEF TENDERLOIN

I like having an ace recipe up my sleeve, and this tenderloin with Dijon is my go-to for birthdays, buffets and holidays.

—DONNA LINDECAMP MORGANTON, NC

START TO FINISH: 20 MIN.
MAKES: 4 SERVINGS

- 4 beef tenderloin steaks (1 inch thick and 4 ounces each)
- ½ teaspoon salt
- ¼ teaspoon pepper
- 5 tablespoons butter, divided
- 1 large onion, halved and thinly sliced
- 1 cup beef stock
- 1 tablespoon Dijon mustard

1. Sprinkle steaks with salt and pepper. In a large skillet, heat 2 tablespoons butter over medium-high heat. Add steaks; cook 4-6 minutes on each side or until meat reaches desired doneness (for medium-rare, a thermometer should read 145°; medium, 160°; well-done, 170°). Remove from pan; keep warm.
2. In same pan, heat 1 tablespoon butter over medium heat. Add onion; cook and stir 4-6 minutes or until tender. Stir in stock; bring to a boil. Cook 1-2 minutes or until liquid is reduced by half. Stir in mustard; remove from heat. Cube the remaining butter; stir into sauce just until blended. Serve with steaks.
PER SERVING *3 ounces cooked beef with ¼ cup sauce: 317 cal., 21g fat (12g sat. fat), 88mg chol., 626mg sod., 5g carb. (2g sugars, 1g fiber), 26g pro.*

MOM'S SWEDISH MEATBALLS

3. Reduce heat to medium-low; return meatballs to pan. Cook, uncovered, 15-20 minutes longer or until meatballs are cooked through, stirring occasionally.

4. Meanwhile, cook noodles according to package directions. Drain; toss with butter. Serve with meatball mixture; sprinkle with parsley.

PER SERVING *6 meatballs with 1¾ cups noodles and about ⅓ cup sauce: 837 cal., 33g fat (14g sat. fat), 256mg chol., 1744mg sod., 82g carb. (10g sugars, 4g fiber), 50g pro.*

FAST FIX

SKILLET BBQ BEEF POT PIE (PICTURED ON PAGE 40)

Beef potpie is a classic comfort food, but who's got time to see it through? My crowd-pleaser is not only speedy; it uses up leftover stuffing.

—PRISCILLA YEE CONCORD, CA

START TO FINISH: 25 MIN.
MAKES: 4 SERVINGS

- 1 **pound lean ground beef (90% lean)**
- ⅓ **cup thinly sliced green onions, divided**
- 2 **cups frozen mixed vegetables, thawed**
- ½ **cup salsa**
- ½ **cup barbecue sauce**
- 3 **cups cooked cornbread stuffing**
- ½ **cup shredded cheddar cheese**
- ¼ **cup chopped sweet red pepper**

1. In a large skillet, cook beef and ¼ cup green onions over medium heat 6-8 minutes or until beef is no longer pink, breaking into crumbles; drain. Stir in mixed vegetables, salsa and barbecue sauce; cook, covered, over medium-low heat 4-5 minutes or until heated through.

2. Layer stuffing over beef; sprinkle with cheese, red pepper and remaining green onion. Cook, covered, 3-5 minutes longer or until heated through and cheese is melted.

PER SERVING *1½ cups: 634 cal., 27g fat (9g sat. fat), 85mg chol., 1372mg sod., 62g carb. (19g sugars, 9g fiber), 33g pro.*

MOM'S SWEDISH MEATBALLS

Mom fixed these meatballs for all sorts of family dinners, potluck suppers and PTA meetings. After smelling the aromas of browning meat and caramelized onions, everyone will be ready to eat.

—MARYBETH MANK MESQUITE, TX

PREP: 30 MIN. • **COOK:** 40 MIN.
MAKES: 6 SERVINGS

- ¾ **cup seasoned bread crumbs**
- 1 **medium onion, chopped**
- 2 **large eggs, lightly beaten**
- ⅓ **cup minced fresh parsley**
- 1 **teaspoon coarsely ground pepper**
- ¾ **teaspoon salt**
- 2 **pounds ground beef**

GRAVY

- ½ **cup all-purpose flour**
- 2¾ **cups 2% milk**
- 2 **cans (10½ ounces each) condensed beef consomme, undiluted**
- 1 **tablespoon Worcestershire sauce**
- 1 **teaspoon coarsely ground pepper**
- ¾ **teaspoon salt**

NOODLES

- 1 **package (16 ounces) egg noodles**
- ¼ **cup butter, cubed**
- ¼ **cup minced fresh parsley**

1. In a large bowl, combine the first six ingredients. Add beef; mix lightly but thoroughly. Shape into 1½-in. meatballs (about 36). In a large skillet over medium heat, brown meatballs in batches. Using a slotted spoon, remove to paper towels to drain, reserving drippings in pan.

2. For gravy, stir flour into drippings; cook over medium-high heat until light brown (do not burn). Gradually whisk in milk until smooth. Stir in the consomme, Worcestershire sauce, pepper and salt. Bring to a boil over medium-high heat; cook and stir for 2 minutes or until thickened.

EAT SMART **FAST FIX**

ONE-POT MEATY SPAGHETTI

I used to help my mom make this when I was growing up, and the recipe stuck. It was a beloved comfort food at college, and is now a weeknight staple for my fiance and me.

—**KRISTIN MICHALENKO** SEATTLE, WA

START TO FINISH: 30 MIN.
MAKES: 6 SERVINGS

- 1 **pound extra-lean ground beef (95% lean)**
- 2 **garlic cloves, minced**
- 1 **teaspoon sugar**
- 1 **teaspoon dried basil**
- ½ **teaspoon dried oregano**
- ¼ **teaspoon salt**
- ¼ **teaspoon paprika**
- ¼ **teaspoon pepper**
- 1 **can (28 ounces) diced tomatoes, undrained**
- 1 **can (15 ounces) tomato sauce**
- 2 **cups water**
- ¼ **cup chopped fresh parsley**
- 8 **ounces uncooked whole wheat spaghetti, broken in half**
- ¼ **cup grated Parmesan cheese**
  Additional chopped parsley

1. In a 6-qt. stockpot, cook and crumble beef with garlic over medium heat until no longer pink, 5-7 minutes; drain. Stir in sugar and seasonings. Add tomatoes, tomato sauce, water and ¼ cup parsley; bring to a boil. Reduce heat; simmer, covered, 5 minutes.

2. Stir in spaghetti, a little at a time; return to a boil. Reduce heat to medium-low; cook, uncovered, until spaghetti is al dente, 8-10 minutes, stirring occasionally. Stir in cheese. Sprinkle with additional parsley.

PER SERVING *1⅓ cups: 292 cal., 6g fat (2g sat. fat), 46mg chol., 737mg sod., 40g carb. (6g sugars, 8g fiber), 24g pro.* ***Diabetic Exchanges:*** *3 starch, 2 lean meat.*

ONE-POT MEATY SPAGHETTI

FETA STEAK TACOS

FETA STEAK TACOS

These tacos have the perfect combination of Mexican and Mediterranean flavors. They're a big hit with my family.

—**DEBBIE REID** CLEARWATER, FL

START TO FINISH: 30 MIN.
MAKES: 8 SERVINGS

- 1 **beef flat iron steak or top sirloin steak (1¼ pounds), cut into thin strips**
- ¼ **cup Greek vinaigrette**
- ½ **cup fat-free plain Greek yogurt**
- 2 **teaspoons lime juice**
- 1 **tablespoon oil from sun-dried tomatoes**
- 1 **small green pepper, cut into thin strips**
- 1 **small onion, cut into thin strips**
- ¼ **cup chopped oil-packed sun-dried tomatoes**
- ¼ **cup sliced Greek olives**
- 8 **whole wheat tortillas (8 inches), warmed**
- ¼ **cup crumbled garlic and herb feta cheese**
  Lime wedges

1. In a large bowl, toss beef with vinaigrette; let stand 15 minutes. In a small bowl, mix yogurt and lime juice.
2. In a large skillet, heat oil from sun-dried tomatoes over medium-high heat. Add pepper and onion; cook and stir 3-4 minutes or until crisp-tender. Remove to a small bowl; stir in sun-dried tomatoes and olives.
3. Place same skillet over medium-high heat. Add beef; cook and stir 2-3 minutes or until no longer pink. Remove from pan.
4. Serve steak and pepper mixture in tortillas; top with cheese. Serve with yogurt mixture and lime wedges.
PER SERVING *1 taco with 1 tablespoon yogurt mixture: 317 cal., 15g fat (4g sat. fat), 48mg chol., 372mg sod., 25g carb. (2g sugars, 3g fiber), 20g pro.* **Diabetic Exchanges:** *3 lean meat, 2 fat, 1½ starch.*

STEAK FRIED RICE

STEAK FRIED RICE

Perfect for an end-of-the-week meal, this sensational dish comes together quickly with leftover rice. I learned a great tip for the steak recently: Partially freeze it, and it will be easier to cut into thin slices.

—**SIMONE GARZA** EVANSVILLE, IN

START TO FINISH: 30 MIN.
MAKES: 4 SERVINGS

- 2 **large eggs, lightly beaten**
- 2 **teaspoons olive oil**
- 1 **beef top sirloin steak (¾ pound), cut into thin strips**
- 4 **tablespoons reduced-sodium soy sauce, divided**
- 1 **package (12 ounces) broccoli coleslaw mix**
- 1 **cup frozen peas**
- 2 **tablespoons grated fresh gingerroot**
- 3 **garlic cloves, minced**
- 2 **cups cooked brown rice**
- 4 **green onions, sliced**

1. In a large nonstick skillet coated with cooking spray, cook and stir eggs over medium heat until no liquid egg remains, breaking up eggs into small pieces. Remove from pan; wipe skillet clean if necessary.
2. In same pan, heat oil over medium-high heat. Add beef; stir-fry 1-2 minutes or until no longer pink. Stir in 1 tablespoon soy sauce; remove from pan.
3. Add coleslaw mix, peas, ginger and garlic to the pan; cook and stir until coleslaw mix is crisp-tender. Add rice and remaining soy sauce, tossing to combine rice with vegetable mixture; heat through. Stir in cooked eggs, beef and green onions; heat through.
PER SERVING *1½ cups: 346 cal., 9g fat (3g sat. fat), 140mg chol., 732mg sod., 36g carb. (5g sugars, 6g fiber), 29g pro.* **Diabetic Exchanges:** *3 lean meat, 2 starch, 1 vegetable, ½ fat.*

TENDERLOIN STEAK DIANE

TENDERLOIN STEAK DIANE

FAST FIX

TENDERLOIN STEAK DIANE

My son loves mushrooms, so I'll often toss a few extra into this dish. They are fantastic with the steak.
—**CAROLYN TURNER** RENO, NV

START TO FINISH: 30 MIN.
MAKES: 4 SERVINGS

- 4 **beef tenderloin steaks (6 ounces each)**
- 1 **teaspoon steak seasoning**
- 2 **tablespoons butter**
- 1 **cup sliced fresh mushrooms**
- ½ **cup reduced-sodium beef broth**
- ¼ **cup heavy whipping cream**
- 1 **tablespoon steak sauce**
- 1 **teaspoon garlic salt with parsley**
- 1 **teaspoon minced chives**

1. Sprinkle steaks with steak seasoning. In a large skillet, heat butter over medium heat. Add steaks; cook 4-5 minutes on each side or until meat reaches desired doneness. Remove steaks from pan.
2. Add mushrooms to skillet; cook and stir over medium-high heat until tender. Add broth, stirring to loosen browned bits from pan. Stir in cream, steak sauce and garlic salt. Bring to a boil; cook and stir 1-2 minutes or until sauce is slightly thickened.
3. Return steaks to pan; turn to coat and heat through. Stir in chives.
PER SERVING *1 steak with 2 tablespoons sauce: 358 cal., 21g fat (11g sat. fat), 111mg chol., 567mg sod., 2g carb. (1g sugars, 0 fiber), 37g pro.*

EAT SMART **FAST FIX**

TAKEOUT BEEF FRIED RICE

Transform last night's supper into tonight's dinner for six. Hoisin-flavored chuck roast works wonders in this recipe, but you can use flank steak, as well.

—*TASTE OF HOME* TEST KITCHEN

START TO FINISH: 30 MIN.
MAKES: 6 SERVINGS

- 4 teaspoons canola oil, divided
- 3 large eggs
- 1 can (11 ounces) mandarin oranges
- 2 medium sweet red peppers, chopped
- 1 cup fresh sugar snap peas, trimmed
- 1 small onion, thinly sliced
- 3 garlic cloves, minced
- ½ teaspoon crushed red pepper flakes
- 4 cups cold cooked rice
- 2 cups cooked beef, sliced across grain into bite-sized pieces
- 1 cup beef broth
- ¼ cup reduced-sodium soy sauce
- ½ teaspoon salt
- ¼ teaspoon ground ginger

1. In a large skillet, heat 1 tablespoon oil over medium-high heat. Whisk eggs until blended; pour into skillet. Mixture should set immediately at edge. As eggs set, push cooked portions toward center, letting uncooked portions flow underneath. When eggs are thickened and no liquid egg remains, remove to a cutting board and chop. Meanwhile, drain oranges, reserving 2 tablespoons juice.

2. In same skillet, heat remaining oil over medium-high heat. Add peppers, sugar snap peas and onion; cook and stir until crisp-tender, 1-2 minutes. Add garlic and pepper flakes; cook 1 minute longer. Add remaining ingredients and reserved juice; heat through. Gently stir in eggs and drained oranges.

PER SERVING *1⅓ cups: 367 cal., 9g fat (2g sat. fat), 136mg chol., 793mg sod., 45g carb., 3g fiber, 26g pro.* **Diabetic Exchanges:** *3 starch, 3 lean meat, 1 fat.*

HEARTY VEGETABLE BEEF RAGOUT

EAT SMART **FAST FIX**

HEARTY VEGETABLE BEEF RAGOUT

With this pasta ragout, I can have a hearty meal on the table in 30 minutes. It's a dish my children gobble up. If you're not fond of kale, stir in baby spinach or even chopped broccoli instead.

—KIM VAN DUNK CALDWELL, NJ

START TO FINISH: 30 MIN.
MAKES: 8 SERVINGS

- 4 cups uncooked whole wheat spiral pasta
- 1 pound lean ground beef (90% lean)
- 1 large onion, chopped
- 3 garlic cloves, minced
- 2 cans (14½ ounces each) Italian diced tomatoes, undrained
- 1 jar (24 ounces) meatless spaghetti sauce
- 2 cups finely chopped fresh kale
- 1 package (9 ounces) frozen peas, thawed
- ¾ teaspoon garlic powder
- ¼ teaspoon pepper
  Grated Parmesan cheese, optional

1. Cook pasta according to package directions; drain. Meanwhile, in a Dutch oven, cook beef, onion and garlic over medium heat 6-8 minutes or until beef is no longer pink, breaking up beef into crumbles; drain.

2. Stir in tomatoes, spaghetti sauce, kale, peas, garlic powder and pepper. Bring to a boil. Reduce heat; simmer, uncovered, 8-10 minutes or until kale is tender. Stir pasta into sauce. If desired, serve with cheese.

PER SERVING *1½ cups (calculated without cheese): 302 cal., 5g fat (2g sat. fat), 35mg chol., 837mg sod., 43g carb. (15g sugars, 7g fiber), 20g pro.* **Diabetic Exchanges:** *2 starch, 2 lean meat, 2 vegetable.*

SKILLET NACHOS

FAST FIX ▶
ONE-POT CHILIGHETTI (PICTURED ON PAGE 41)

Grab your stockpot for my meal-in-one chili and spaghetti. I've got a large family, and this beefy pasta takes care of everybody.

—**JENNIFER TRENHAILE** EMERSON, NE

START TO FINISH: 30 MIN.
MAKES: 8 SERVINGS

- 1½ **pounds ground beef**
- 1 **large onion, chopped**
- 1 **can (46 ounces) tomato juice**
- 1 **cup water**
- 2 **tablespoons Worcestershire sauce**
- 4 **teaspoons chili powder**
- ½ **teaspoon salt**
- ½ **teaspoon ground cumin**
- ½ **teaspoon pepper**
- 1 **package (16 ounces) spaghetti, broken into 2-inch pieces**
- 2 **cans (16 ounces each) kidney beans, rinsed and drained**
  Sour cream and shredded cheddar cheese

1. In a 6-qt. stockpot, cook beef and onion over medium-high heat 8-10 minutes or until beef is no longer pink and onion is tender, breaking up beef into crumbles; drain.

2. Stir in tomato juice, water, Worcestershire sauce and seasonings; bring to a boil. Add spaghetti. Reduce heat; simmer, covered, 9-11 minutes or until pasta is tender. Stir in beans; heat through. Top servings with sour cream and cheese.

FREEZE OPTION *Freeze cooled pasta mixture in freezer containers. To use, partially thaw in refrigerator overnight. Heat through in a saucepan, stirring occasionally and adding a little water if necessary.*

PER SERVING *1½ cups (calculated without sour cream and cheese): 508 cal., 12g fat (4g sat. fat), 53mg chol., 903mg sod., 70g carb. (9g sugars, 9g fiber), 32g pro.*

FAST FIX ▶
SKILLET NACHOS

My mother gave me a cookbook from a fundraiser, and the recipe I've used most is for skillet nachos. My whole family is on board. For toppings, think sour cream, tomatoes, jalapeno and red onion.

—**JUDY HUGHES** WAVERLY, KS

START TO FINISH: 30 MIN.
MAKES: 6 SERVINGS

- 1 **pound ground beef**
- 1 **can (14½ ounces) diced tomatoes, undrained**
- 1 **cup fresh or frozen corn, thawed**
- ¾ **cup uncooked instant rice**
- ½ **cup water**
- 1 **envelope taco seasoning**
- ½ **teaspoon salt**
- 1 **cup shredded Colby-Monterey Jack cheese**
- 1 **package (16 ounces) tortilla chips**
  Optional toppings: sour cream, sliced fresh jalapenos, shredded lettuce and lime wedges

1. In a large skillet, cook beef over medium heat 6-8 minutes or until no longer pink, breaking into crumbles; drain. Stir in tomatoes, corn, rice, water, taco seasoning and salt. Bring to a boil. Reduce heat; simmer, covered, 8-10 minutes until rice is tender and mixture is slightly thickened.

2. Remove from heat; sprinkle with cheese. Let stand, covered, 5 minutes or until cheese is melted. Divide tortilla chips among six plates; spoon beef mixture over chips. Serve with toppings as desired.

PER SERVING *(calculated without optional toppings): 676 cal., 31g fat (10g sat. fat), 63mg chol., 1293mg sod., 74g carb. (4g sugars, 4g fiber), 25g pro.*

⑤ INGREDIENTS FAST FIX

ASIAN BEEF & NOODLES

I created this dish on a whim to feed my hungry teenagers. It's since become a dinnertime staple. Now, two of my grandkids make it in their own kitchens.
—**JUDY BATSON** TAMPA, FL

START TO FINISH: 25 MIN.
MAKES: 4 SERVINGS

- 1 **beef top sirloin steak (1 pound), cut into ¼-inch-thick strips**
- 6 **tablespoons reduced-sodium teriyaki sauce, divided**
- 8 **ounces uncooked whole grain thin spaghetti**
- 2 **tablespoons canola oil, divided**
- 3 **cups broccoli coleslaw mix**
- 1 **medium onion, halved and thinly sliced**
  Chopped fresh cilantro, optional

1. Toss beef with 2 tablespoons marinade. Cook spaghetti according to package directions; drain.
2. In a large skillet, heat 1 tablespoon oil over medium-high heat; stir-fry beef until browned, 2-3 minutes. Remove from pan.
3. In same skillet, heat remaining oil over medium-high heat; stir-fry coleslaw mix and onion until crisp-tender, 3-5 minutes. Add spaghetti and remaining marinade; toss and heat through. Stir in beef. If desired, sprinkle with cilantro.

ASIAN BEEF & NOODLES

PER SERVING *2 cups: 462 cal., 13g fat (2g sat. fat), 46mg chol., 546mg sod., 52g carb., 8g fiber, 35g pro.*

⑤ INGREDIENTS FAST FIX

BASIL-BUTTER STEAKS WITH ROASTED POTATOES (PICTURED ON PAGE 41)

A few ingredients and 30 minutes are all you'll need for this incredibly satisfying meal. A simple basil butter gives these steaks a very special flavor.
—*TASTE OF HOME* TEST KITCHEN

START TO FINISH: 30 MIN.
MAKES: 4 SERVINGS

- 1 **package (15 ounces) frozen Parmesan and roasted garlic red potato wedges**
- 4 **beef tenderloin steaks (1¼ inches thick and 6 ounces each)**
- ½ **teaspoon salt**
- ½ **teaspoon pepper**
- 5 **tablespoons butter, divided**
- 2 **cups grape tomatoes**
- 1 **tablespoon minced fresh basil**

1. Bake potato wedges according to package directions.
2. Meanwhile, sprinkle steaks with salt and pepper. In a 10-in. cast-iron skillet, brown steaks in 2 tablespoons butter. Add tomatoes to skillet. Bake, uncovered, at 425° for 15-20 minutes or until meat reaches desired doneness (for medium-rare, a thermometer should read 145°; medium, 160°; well-done, 170°).
3. In a small bowl, combine basil and remaining butter. Spoon over steaks and serve with potatoes.
PER SERVING *538 cal., 29g fat (13g sat. fat), 112mg chol., 740mg sod., 27g carb. (2g sugars, 3g fiber), 41 pro.*

BEEFY FRENCH
ONION POTPIE, PAGE 75

EASY BEEF PIES, PAGE 64

ROASTS & OVEN ENTREES

Juicy prime rib, tangy brisket, cheesy casseroles, **meal-in-one pot roasts,** popular pizzas...these mouthwatering entrees **make dinnertime special** any night of the week. From classic to casual, the meaty recipes in this section offer the **perfect main courses** for any menu.

DOUBLE-CRUST PIZZA CASSEROLE, PAGE 69

ITALIAN CRUMB-CRUSTED BEEF ROAST, PAGE 72

OVEN-BAKED BRISKET

OVEN-BAKED BRISKET

Texans like brisket cooked on the smoker, but this recipe offers convenient prep in the oven. Sometimes I make extra sauce to serve on the side. Round out the meal with potato salad and some slaw.
—KATIE FERRIER HOUSTON, TX

PREP: 15 MIN. + MARINATING • **BAKE:** 4¼ HOURS
MAKES: 8 SERVINGS

- 1 fresh beef brisket (4 to 5 pounds)
- 2 tablespoons Worcestershire sauce
- 2 tablespoons soy sauce
- 1 tablespoon onion salt
- 1 tablespoon liquid smoke
- 2 teaspoons salt
- 2 teaspoons pepper
  Dash hot pepper sauce

SAUCE
- ½ cup ketchup
- 3 tablespoons brown sugar
- 1 tablespoon lemon juice
- 1 tablespoon soy sauce
- 1 teaspoon ground mustard
- 3 drops hot pepper sauce
  Dash ground nutmeg

1. Place brisket, fat side down, in a 13x9-in. baking dish. In a small bowl, mix Worcestershire sauce, soy sauce, onion salt, liquid smoke, salt, pepper and pepper sauce; pour over brisket. Turn brisket fat side up; refrigerate, covered, overnight.
2. Remove brisket from refrigerator. Preheat oven to 300°. Bake, covered, 4 hours. In a small bowl, combine sauce ingredients. Spread over brisket. Bake, uncovered, 15-30 minutes longer or until tender. Cut diagonally across the grain into thin slices.
NOTE *This is a fresh beef brisket, not corned beef.*
PER SERVING *6 ounces cooked beef: 334 cal., 10g fat (4g sat. fat), 97mg chol., 1922mg sod., 11g carb. (10g sugars, 0 fiber), 48g pro.*

BEEF

FAST FIX ▶

MEATBALL SUBMARINE CASSEROLE

We were hosting a bunch of friends for game night, and after a comedy of errors, I had to come up with a plan B for dinner. We turned meatball subs into this hearty casserole, and it was a resounding success.

—**RICK FRIEDMAN** PALM SPRINGS, CA

START TO FINISH: 30 MIN.
MAKES: 4 SERVINGS

- 1 package (12 ounces) frozen fully cooked Italian meatballs
- 4 slices sourdough bread
- 1½ teaspoons olive oil
- 1 garlic clove, halved
- 1½ cups pasta sauce with mushrooms
- ½ cup shredded part-skim mozzarella cheese, divided
- ½ cup grated Parmesan cheese, divided

1. Preheat broiler. Microwave meatballs, covered, on high until heated through, 4-6 minutes. Meanwhile, place bread on an ungreased baking sheet; brush one side of bread with oil. Broil 4-6 in. from heat until golden brown, 1-2 minutes. Rub bread with cut surface of garlic; discard garlic. Tear bread into bite-size pieces; transfer to a greased 11x7-in. baking dish. Reduce oven setting to 350°.

2. Add pasta sauce, ¼ cup mozzarella cheese and ¼ cup Parmesan cheese to meatballs; toss to combine. Pour mixture over bread pieces; sprinkle with the remaining cheeses. Bake, uncovered, until cheeses are melted, 15-18 minutes.

PER SERVING *1 serving: 417 cal., 28g fat (13g sat. fat), 59mg chol., 1243mg sod., 22g carb. (8g sugars, 3g fiber), 23g pro.*

BAKED BEEF TACOS

BAKED BEEF TACOS

Give tacos a fresh approach by baking the shells upright in refried beans and tomatoes. The base gets soft, and the top stays crisp and crunchy.

—**PATRICIA STAGICH** ELIZABETH, NJ

PREP: 15 MIN. • **BAKE:** 20 MIN.
MAKES: 12 SERVINGS

- 1½ pounds ground beef
- 1 envelope taco seasoning
- 2 cans (10 ounces each) diced tomatoes and green chilies, divided
- 1 can (16 ounces) refried beans
- 2 cups Mexican cheese blend, divided
- ¼ cup chopped fresh cilantro
- 1 teaspoon hot pepper sauce, optional
- 12 taco shells
  Chopped green onions

1. Preheat oven to 425°. In a large skillet, cook beef over medium heat 6-8 minutes or until no longer pink, breaking into crumbles; drain. Stir in taco seasoning and 1 can of undrained tomatoes; heat through.

2. Meanwhile, in a bowl, mix beans, ½ cup cheese, cilantro, remaining can of undrained tomatoes and, if desired, pepper sauce. Spread onto bottom of a greased 13x9-in. baking dish.

3. Stand taco shells upright over bean mixture. Fill each with 1 tablespoon cheese and about ⅓ cup beef mixture. Bake, covered, 15 minutes.

4. Uncover; sprinkle with remaining cheese. Bake, uncovered, 5-7 minutes or until cheese is melted and shells are lightly browned. Sprinkle with green onions.

PER SERVING *1 taco with ¼ cup bean mixture: 277 cal., 15g fat (7g sat. fat), 52mg chol., 836mg sod., 17g carb. (0 sugars, 3g fiber), 17g pro.*

SPAGHETTI
MEATBALL
BAKE

SPAGHETTI MEATBALL BAKE

On some nights, we're really in the mood for pasta and it seems nothing else will do. I came up with this saucy, meaty dish to satisfy our cravings.

—KIM FORNI LACONIA, NH

PREP: 45 MIN. • **BAKE:** 30 MIN.
MAKES: 10 SERVINGS

- 1½ cups dry bread crumbs, divided
- 3 large eggs, lightly beaten
- 1½ cups cooked spaghetti (3 ounces uncooked), coarsely chopped
- 2 garlic cloves, minced
- 2 teaspoons dried basil
- ¾ teaspoon salt
- 1 teaspoon dried oregano
- 1 teaspoon pepper
- 2 pounds ground beef

SAUCE

- 2 jars (24 ounces each) meatless pasta sauce
- 1 small onion, finely chopped
- 2 garlic cloves, minced
- 2 teaspoons dried basil
- 1 teaspoon dried oregano
- 2 cups shredded part-skim mozzarella cheese

1. Preheat oven to 375°. Place 1 cup bread crumbs in a shallow bowl. In a large bowl, combine eggs, chopped spaghetti, garlic, seasonings and remaining bread crumbs. Add beef; mix lightly but thoroughly. Shape into 1½-in. balls.

2. Roll meatballs in bread crumbs; place in a greased 13x9-in. baking dish. Bake 15-20 minutes or until cooked through.

3. In a large saucepan, combine pasta sauce, onion, garlic and seasonings; bring to a boil over medium heat, stirring occasionally. Pour over meatballs; sprinkle with cheese. Bake 15-20 minutes longer or until cheese is lightly browned.

PER SERVING *4 meatballs with ½ cup sauce: 390 cal., 17g fat (7g sat. fat), 124mg chol., 1074mg sodium, 29g carb. (10g sugars, 3g fiber), 29g pro.*

SALT-ENCRUSTED RIB ROAST

⑤INGREDIENTS

SALT-ENCRUSTED RIB ROAST

A rib roast is a big part of our holiday dinner traditions. We love the flavor that yellow mustard adds, but use your favorite—Dijon and others are fair game.

—REBECCA WIRTZBERGER YUMA, AZ

PREP: 15 MIN. • **BAKE:** 2½ HOURS + STANDING
MAKES: 10 SERVINGS

- 1 bone-in beef rib roast (about 6 pounds)
- ½ cup yellow mustard
- 3 cups kosher salt (about 1½ pounds)
- ½ cup water

1. Preheat oven to 450°. Place rib roast in a roasting pan, fat side up; spread all sides with mustard. In a bowl, mix salt and water to make a dry paste (mixture should be just moist enough to pack); press onto top and sides of roast.

2. Roast 15 minutes. Reduce oven setting to 325°. Roast 2¼-2¾ hours longer or until a thermometer inserted in beef reaches 135° for medium-rare; 150° for medium. (Temperature of roast will continue to rise about 10° upon standing.) Let stand 20 minutes before serving.

3. Remove and discard salt crust. Carve roast into slices.

PER SERVING *5 ounces cooked beef: 320 cal., 18g fat (7g sat. fat), 0 chol., 997mg sodium, 1g carb. (0 sugars, 0 fiber), 37g pro.*

FAST FIX ▶
EASY BEEF PIES
(PICTURED ON PAGE 59)

We make a lot of French dips and always have leftover roast beef—I put it to good use in these pies. Use any veggies you like. They're extra awesome drenched in cheese sauce.
—**JENNIE WEBER** PALMER, AK

START TO FINISH: 30 MIN.
MAKES: 4 SERVINGS

- 1 package (15 ounces) refrigerated beef roast au jus
- 1 tablespoon canola oil
- ¼ cup finely chopped onion
- ¼ cup finely chopped green pepper
- 1 garlic clove, minced
- 1 package (14.1 ounces) refrigerated pie pastry
- 1 cup shredded Mexican cheese blend
  Salsa con queso dip, optional

1. Preheat oven to 425°. Drain beef, reserving ¼ cup juices; shred meat with two forks. In a large skillet, heat oil over medium-high heat. Add onion and pepper; cook and stir 1-2 minutes or until tender. Add garlic; cook 30 seconds longer. Remove from heat; stir in beef and reserved juices.

2. Unroll one pastry sheet; cut in half. Layer ¼ cup shredded cheese and about ⅓ cup beef mixture over half of each pastry to within ½ in. of edge. Fold pastry over filling; press edges with a fork to seal. Place on a greased baking sheet. Repeat with remaining pastry and filling.

3. Bake 15-18 minutes or until golden brown. If desired, serve with queso dip.

FREEZE OPTION *Freeze cooled pastries in a resealable plastic freezer bag. To use, reheat pastries on a greased baking sheet in a preheated 350° oven until heated through.*

PER SERVING *1 pie (calculated without queso dip): 752 cal., 46g fat (19g sat. fat), 108mg chol., 921mg sod., 53g carb. (7g sugars, 0 fiber), 31g pro.*

GARLIC & HERB STEAK PIZZA

FAST FIX ▶
GARLIC & HERB STEAK PIZZA

We love pizza that's super fast, cheesy and original. This one, with steak and veggies, is for folks who like pies with everything on top.
—**JADE FEARS** GRAND RIDGE, FL

START TO FINISH: 30 MIN.
MAKES: 6 SERVINGS

- 1 beef top sirloin steak (¾ inch thick and 1 pound)
- ¾ teaspoon salt
- ¾ teaspoon pepper
- 1 tablespoon olive oil
- 1 prebaked 12-inch thin pizza crust
- ½ cup garlic-herb spreadable cheese (about 3 ounces)
- 2 cups chopped fresh spinach
- 1 cup sliced red onion
- 1 cup sliced fresh mushrooms
- 1½ cups shredded part-skim mozzarella cheese

1. Preheat oven to 450°. Season steak with salt and pepper. In a large skillet, heat oil over medium heat. Add steak; cook 5-6 minutes on each side or until a thermometer reads 145° for medium-rare doneness. Remove from pan.

2. Meanwhile, place pizza crust on an ungreased baking sheet; spread with garlic-herb cheese. Top with spinach and onion.

3. Cut steak into slices; arrange on pizza. Top with mushrooms and cheese. Bake 8-10 minutes or until cheese is melted. Cut into 12 pieces.

PER SERVING *2 pieces: 440 cal., 23g fat (11g sat. fat), 72mg chol., 926mg sod., 29g carb. (3g sugars, 2g fiber), 30g pro.*

EAT SMART

VEGETABLE & BEEF STUFFED RED PEPPERS

I adore this recipe because it's one of the few ways I can get my husband to eat veggies. For a meatless version, replace the beef with eggplant and add more vegetables, such as mushrooms or squash. You can also replace the rice with barley, couscous or orzo.

—**JENNIFER ZIMMERMAN** AVONDALE, AZ

PREP: 35 MIN. • **BAKE:** 40 MIN.
MAKES: 6 SERVINGS

- 6 medium sweet red peppers
- 1 pound lean ground beef (90% lean)
- 1 tablespoon olive oil
- 1 medium zucchini, chopped
- 1 medium yellow summer squash, chopped
- 1 medium onion, finely chopped
- ⅓ cup finely chopped green pepper
- 2 cups coarsely chopped fresh spinach
- 4 garlic cloves, minced
- 1 cup ready-to-serve long grain and wild rice
- 1 can (8 ounces) tomato sauce
- ½ cup shredded part-skim mozzarella cheese
- ¼ teaspoon salt
- 3 slices reduced-fat provolone cheese, halved

1. Preheat oven to 350°. Cut and discard tops from red peppers; remove seeds. In a 6-qt. stockpot, cook peppers in boiling water 3-5 minutes or until crisp-tender; drain and rinse in cold water.

2. In a large skillet, cook beef over medium heat 6-8 minutes or until no longer pink, breaking into crumbles. Drain and remove from pan. In same pan, heat oil over medium heat. Add zucchini, squash, onion and green pepper; cook and stir 4-5 minutes or until tender. Add spinach and garlic; cook and stir 1 minute longer or until wilted. Stir in cooked beef, rice, tomato sauce, shredded mozzarella and salt.

3. Place red peppers in a greased 8-in. square baking dish. Fill with meat mixture. Bake, covered, 35-40 minutes or until peppers are tender. Top each pepper with a halved cheese slice; bake, uncovered, 5 minutes or until cheese is melted. Let stand 5 minutes before serving.

PER SERVING *1 stuffed pepper: 287 cal., 13g fat (5g sat. fat), 57mg chol., 555mg sod., 21g carb. (8g sugars, 5g fiber), 23g pro.* **Diabetic Exchanges:** *3 lean meat, 2 vegetable, 1 fat, ½ starch.*

VEGETABLE & BEEF STUFFED RED PEPPERS

TOP TIP

SIMPLE SWAP

I substituted chopped fresh mushrooms for the spinach in this recipe without a problem. You may want to add additional sauce.

—**MARILYNRAZA**
TASTEOFHOME.COM

CHILI MAC & CHEESE

The Southwestern flair of my comforting casserole gives it mass appeal. It rates high on flavor and low on the difficulty scale.

—**MARY AGUILAR** SHELBY, OH

PREP: 30 MIN. • **BAKE:** 20 MIN.
MAKES: 8 SERVINGS

- 2 **packages (7¼ ounces each) macaroni and cheese dinner mix**
- 2 **pounds ground beef**
- 1 **small onion, chopped**
- 1 **can (14½ ounces) diced tomatoes, undrained**
- 1 **can (10 ounces) diced tomatoes and green chilies, undrained**
- 1 **can (8 ounces) tomato sauce**
- 2 **tablespoons chili powder**
- 1 **teaspoon garlic salt**
- ½ **teaspoon ground cumin**
- ¼ **teaspoon crushed red pepper flakes**
- ¼ **teaspoon pepper**
- 2 **cups (16 ounces) sour cream**
- 1½ **cups shredded Mexican cheese blend, divided**

1. Preheat oven to 350°. Set aside cheese packets from dinner mixes. In a large saucepan, bring 2 quarts water to a boil. Add macaroni; cook 8-10 minutes or until tender.

2. Meanwhile, in a Dutch oven, cook and stir beef and onion over medium heat 8-10 minutes or until beef is no longer pink; drain. Stir in tomatoes, tomatoes and green chilies, tomato sauce and seasonings. Drain macaroni; add to beef mixture. Stir in contents of cheese packets, sour cream and 1 cup cheese.

3. Transfer to a greased 13x9-in. baking dish; top with remaining cheese. Bake, uncovered, 20-25 minutes or until bubbly.

PER SERVING *1½ cups: 631 cal., 35g fat (17g sat. fat), 105mg chol., 1286mg sod., 22g carb. (10g sugars, 3g fiber), 35g pro.*

CHILI MAC & CHEESE

FAST FIX ▶

BACON-WRAPPED FILETS WITH SCOTCHED MUSHROOMS

I got the idea for this recipe when I came across bacon-wrapped filets on sale in the grocery store. The rest was inspired by my husband because he once made a sauce with scotch and ginger ale. This recipe is for two, but it can easily be doubled.

—**MARY KAY LABRIE** CLERMONT, FL

START TO FINISH: 30 MIN.
MAKES: 2 SERVINGS

- 2 bacon strips
- 2 beef tenderloin steaks (5 ounces each)
- ¼ teaspoon salt
- ¼ teaspoon coarsely ground pepper
- 3 teaspoons olive oil, divided
- 2 cups sliced baby portobello mushrooms
- ¼ teaspoon dried thyme
- 2 tablespoons butter, divided
- ¼ cup Scotch whiskey
- ½ cup diet ginger ale
- 1 tablespoon brown sugar
- 1½ teaspoons reduced-sodium soy sauce
- ¼ teaspoon rubbed sage

1. In a small skillet, cook bacon over medium heat until partially cooked but not crisp. Remove to paper towels to drain.

2. Preheat oven to 375°. Sprinkle steaks with salt and pepper; wrap a strip of bacon around the sides of each steak and secure with toothpicks.

3. In a small ovenproof skillet coated with cooking spray, cook steaks in 1½ teaspoons oil over medium-high heat 2 minutes on each side.

4. Bake, uncovered, 8-12 minutes or until meat reaches desired doneness (for medium-rare, a thermometer should read 145°; medium, 160°; well-done, 170°).

5. Meanwhile, in a large skillet, saute mushrooms and thyme in 1 tablespoon butter and remaining oil until tender; remove from heat. Add whiskey, stirring to loosen the browned bits from the pan. Stir in the ginger ale, brown sugar, soy sauce and sage.

6. Bring to a boil. Reduce heat; simmer, uncovered, 3-5 minutes or until reduced by half. Stir in remaining butter. Serve with steaks.

PER SERVING *1 filet with ⅓ cup mushroom mixture: 581 cal., 37g fat (15g sat. fat), 108mg chol., 729mg sod., 10g carb. (8g sugars, 1g fiber), 35g pro.*

ULTIMATE POT ROAST

When a juicy pot roast simmers in garlic, onions and veggies, everyone comes running to find out when dinner will be ready. The answer? Just wait—it'll be worth it!

—*TASTE OF HOME* TEST KITCHEN

PREP: 55 MIN. • **BAKE:** 2 HOURS
MAKES: 8 SERVINGS

- 1 boneless beef chuck-eye or other chuck roast (3 to 4 pounds)
- 2 teaspoons pepper
- 2 teaspoons salt, divided
- 2 tablespoons canola oil
- 2 medium onions, cut into 1-inch pieces
- 2 celery ribs, chopped
- 3 garlic cloves, minced
- 1 tablespoon tomato paste
- 1 tablespoon minced fresh thyme or 1 teaspoon dried thyme
- 2 bay leaves
- 1 cup dry red wine or reduced-sodium beef broth
- 2 cups reduced-sodium beef broth
- 1 pound small red potatoes, quartered
- 4 medium parsnips, peeled and cut into 2-inch pieces
- 6 medium carrots, cut into 2-inch pieces
- 1 tablespoon red wine vinegar
- 2 tablespoons minced fresh parsley
  Salt and pepper to taste

1. Preheat oven to 325°. Pat roast dry with a paper towel; tie at 2-in. intervals with kitchen string. Sprinkle roast with pepper and 1½ teaspoons salt. In a Dutch oven, heat oil over medium-high heat. Brown roast on all sides. Remove from the pan.

ULTIMATE POT ROAST

2. Add onions, celery and ½ teaspoon salt to the same pan; cook and stir over medium heat 8-10 minutes or until onions are browned. Add garlic, tomato paste, thyme and bay leaves; cook and stir 1 minute longer.

3. Add wine, stirring to loosen browned bits from pan; stir in broth. Return roast to pan. Arrange potatoes, parsnips and carrots around roast; bring to a boil. Bake, covered, until the meat is fork-tender, 2-2½ hours.

4. Remove roast and vegetables from pan; keep warm. Discard bay leaves; skim fat from cooking juices. On stovetop, bring juices to a boil; cook until liquid is reduced by half (about 1½ cups), 10-12 minutes. Stir in vinegar and parsley; season with salt and pepper to taste.

5. Remove string from roast. Serve with vegetables and sauce.

PER SERVING *3 ounces cooked beef with 1 cup vegetables and 3 tablespoons sauce; 459 cal., 20g fat (7g sat. fat), 112mg chol., 824mg sod., 32g carb. (8g sugars, 6g fiber), 37g pro.*

INDIVIDUAL
SHEPHERD'S PIES

INDIVIDUAL SHEPHERD'S PIES

These comforting little pies make a fun St. Patrick's Day surprise for the family or a comforting bite any time of the year. Leftovers are easy to freeze and eat later on busy weeknights.
—**ELLEN OSBORNE** CLARKSVILLE, TN

PREP: 30 MIN. • **BAKE:** 20 MIN.
MAKES: 5 SERVINGS

- 1 **pound ground beef**
- 3 **tablespoons chopped onion**
- ½ **teaspoon minced garlic**
- ⅓ **cup chili sauce or ketchup**
- 1 **tablespoon cider vinegar**
- 2 **cups hot mashed potatoes (with added milk and butter)**
- 3 **ounces cream cheese, softened**
- 1 **tube (12 ounces) refrigerated buttermilk biscuits**
- ½ **cup crushed potato chips**
    Paprika, optional

1. Preheat oven to 375°. In a large skillet, cook beef and onion over medium heat 5-7 minutes or until beef is no longer pink, breaking up beef into crumbles. Add garlic; cook 1 minute or until tender. Drain. Stir in chili sauce and vinegar.
2. In a small bowl, mix mashed potatoes and cream cheese until blended. Press one biscuit dough onto bottom and up sides of each of 10 greased muffin cups. Fill with beef mixture. Spread potato mixture over tops. Sprinkle with potato chips, pressing down lightly.
3. Bake 20-25 minutes or until golden brown. If desired, sprinkle with paprika.
FREEZE OPTION *Freeze cooled shepherd's pies in a single layer in freezer containers. To use, partially thaw in refrigerator overnight. Bake on a baking sheet in a preheated 375° oven 15-18 minutes or until heated through.*
PER SERVING *2 mini pies: 567 cal., 30g fat (12g sat. fat), 84mg chol., 1378mg sod., 51g carb. (9g sugars, 2g fiber), 23g pro.*

DOUBLE-CRUST PIZZA CASSEROLE (PICTURED ON PAGE 59)

When my husband and I first married, this biscuit pizza solved the what's-for-dinner problem. As our family grew, I just made bigger and bigger batches.

—PAT CRANE PINE CITY, NY

PREP: 20 MIN. • **BAKE:** 20 MIN.
MAKES: 12 SERVINGS

- 2 pounds lean ground beef (90% lean)
- 2 cans (15 ounces each) pizza sauce, divided
- 2 teaspoons dried oregano
- 3 cups biscuit/baking mix
- 1¼ cups 2% milk
- 1 large egg, lightly beaten
- 2 cups shredded part-skim mozzarella cheese
- 1 cup sliced fresh mushrooms
- 1 medium green pepper, chopped
- 1 medium onion, chopped
- ¼ cup grated Parmesan cheese
- 1 plum tomato, chopped

1. Preheat oven to 400°. In a large skillet, cook beef over medium heat 8-10 minutes or until no longer pink, breaking into crumbles; drain. Stir in 1 can pizza sauce and oregano. Bring to a boil. Reduce heat; simmer, uncovered, 5-6 minutes or until slightly thickened, stirring occasionally. Remove from heat.

2. In a large bowl, combine biscuit mix, milk and egg; stir just until moistened. Spread half of the batter onto bottom of a greased 13x9-in. baking pan. Spread with the remaining pizza sauce. Top with mozzarella cheese, mushrooms, pepper, onion and beef mixture. Spoon remaining batter over top; sprinkle with Parmesan cheese.

3. Bake, uncovered, 20-25 minutes or until golden brown. Sprinkle with tomato. Let stand 5 minutes before serving.

PER SERVING *1 piece: 369 cal., 16g fat (7g sat. fat), 78mg chol., 710mg sod., 30g carb. (4g sugars, 3g fiber), 26g pro.*

RESTAURANT-STYLE PRIME RIB

RESTAURANT-STYLE PRIME RIB

I have served this recipe to people visiting us from all over the world and to dear friends, family and neighbors. It is enjoyed and raved about by all, and makes an excellent main dish for a special-occasion feast.

—KELLY WILLIAMS FORKED RIVER, NJ

PREP: 10 MIN. • **COOK:** 2 HOURS + STANDING
MAKES: 8 SERVINGS

- 1 bone-in beef rib roast (4 to 5 pounds)
- ¼ cup kosher salt
- 2 tablespoons garlic powder
- 2 tablespoons dried rosemary, crushed
- 2 tablespoons wasabi powder
- 2 tablespoons butter, softened
- 1 tablespoon coarsely ground pepper
- 1 teaspoon herbes de Provence

1. Preheat oven to 350°. Place roast, fat side up, on a rack in a foil-lined roasting pan. In a small bowl, mix salt, garlic powder, rosemary, wasabi powder, butter, pepper and herbes de Provence; pat onto all sides of roast.

2. Roast 2-2½ hours or until meat reaches desired doneness (for medium-rare, a thermometer should read 145°; medium, 160°; well-done, 170°). Remove roast from oven; tent with foil. Let stand 15 minutes before carving.

PER SERVING *5 ounces cooked beef: 311 cal., 18g fat (8g sat. fat), 8mg chol., 1624mg sod., 5g carb. (0 sugars, 1g fiber), 31g pro.*

BEEF SHORT RIBS IN
BURGUNDY SAUCE

BEEF SHORT RIBS IN BURGUNDY SAUCE

My stepdad—an Army general—got this recipe from his aide, who said it was his mother's best Sunday meal. It's now a mouthwatering favorite in our family, too.
—**JUDY BATSON** TAMPA, FL

PREP: 35 MIN. • **COOK:** 2¼ HOURS
MAKES: 6 SERVINGS

- 3 **pounds bone-in beef short ribs**
- 3 **tablespoons butter**
- 1 **large sweet onion, halved and sliced**
- 2 **celery ribs, thinly sliced**
- 1 **medium carrot, thinly sliced**
- 1 **garlic clove, minced**
  Dash dried thyme
- 2 **tablespoons all-purpose flour**
- 1 **cup water**
- 1 **cup dry red wine or beef broth**
- 1 **beef bouillon cube or 1 teaspoon beef bouillon granules**
- 2 **tablespoons minced fresh parsley**
- ½ **teaspoon Worcestershire sauce**
- ¼ **teaspoon salt**
- ¼ **teaspoon browning sauce, optional**
- ⅛ **teaspoon pepper**

1. Preheat oven to 450°. Place short ribs on a rack in a shallow roasting pan. Roast 30-40 minutes or until browned, turning once.
2. Meanwhile, in a Dutch oven, heat butter over medium heat. Add onion, celery and carrot; cook and stir 10-12 minutes or until tender. Add garlic and thyme; cook 1 minute longer. Stir in flour until blended; gradually stir in water and wine. Add bouillon and parsley, stirring to dissolve bouillon.
3. Transfer ribs to Dutch oven; bring to a boil. Reduce heat; simmer, covered, 2-2½ hours or until meat is tender.
4. Remove short ribs; keep warm. Skim fat from sauce; stir in the remaining ingredients. Serve with ribs.

PER SERVING *1 serving: 264 cal., 17g fat (8g sat. fat), 70mg chol., 855mg sod., 8g carb. (4g sugars, 1g fiber), 19g pro.*

TACO CORN BREAD CASSEROLE

TACO CORN BREAD CASSEROLE

A whole can of chiles adds fire to this corn bread casserole. For less heat, use just enough of the chilies for your taste.
—**LISA PAUL** TERRE HAUTE, IN

PREP: 15 MIN. • **BAKE:** 1 HOUR
MAKES: 8 SERVINGS

- 2 **pounds ground beef**
- 2 **envelopes taco seasoning**
- 2 **cans (14½ ounces each) diced tomatoes, drained**
- 1 **cup water**
- 1 **cup cooked rice**
- 1 **can (4 ounces) chopped green chilies**
- 2 **packages (8½ ounces each) corn bread/muffin mix**
- 1 **can (8¾ ounces) whole kernel corn, drained**
- 1 **cup (8 ounces) sour cream**
- 2 **cups corn chips**
- 2 **cups shredded Mexican or cheddar cheese, divided**
- 1 **can (2¼ ounces) sliced ripe olives, drained**
  Shredded lettuce and chopped tomatoes, optional

1. Preheat oven to 400°. In a Dutch oven, cook beef over medium heat 8-10 minutes or until no longer pink, breaking into crumbles, drain. Stir in taco seasoning. Add tomatoes, water, rice and green chilies and heat through, stirring occasionally.
2. Meanwhile, prepare corn bread mix according to package directions; stir in corn. Pour half of the batter into a greased 13x9-in. baking dish. Layer with half of the meat mixture, all the sour cream, half of the corn chips and 1 cup cheese. Top with remaining batter, remaining meat mixture, olives and remaining corn chips.
3. Bake, uncovered, 55-60 minutes or until corn bread is cooked through. Sprinkle with remaining cheese; bake 3-5 minutes longer or until cheese is melted. If desired, serve with lettuce and chopped tomatoes.

PER SERVING *1½ cups (calculated without lettuce and tomatoes): 817 cal., 40g fat (17g sat. fat), 183mg chol., 1982mg sod., 74g carb. (20g sugars, 4g fiber), 36g pro.*

BEEF & MUSHROOM BRAISED STEW

Freeze cooled stew in freezer containers. To use, partially thaw in refrigerator overnight. Heat through in a saucepan, stirring occasionally and adding a little broth or water if necessary.
PER SERVING *1⅓ cup (calculated without mashed potatoes): 395 cal., 22g fat (7g sat. fat), 98mg chol., 761mg sod., 12g carb. (4g sugars, 2g fiber), 34g pro.*

⑤ INGREDIENTS

ITALIAN CRUMB-CRUSTED BEEF ROAST (PICTURED ON PAGE 59)

Italian-style panko crumbs and seasoning give this roast beef a special touch. It's a nice, effortless weeknight meal. Just set it in the oven and let it cook to perfection.

—MARIA REGAKIS SAUGUS, MA

PREP: 10 MIN. • **BAKE:** 1¾ HOURS + STANDING
MAKES: 8 SERVINGS

- 1 **beef sirloin tip roast (3 pounds)**
- ¼ **teaspoon salt**
- ¾ **cup Italian-style panko (Japanese) bread crumbs**
- ¼ **cup mayonnaise**
- 3 **tablespoons dried minced onion**
- ½ **teaspoon Italian seasoning**
- ¼ **teaspoon pepper**

1. Preheat oven to 325°. Place roast on a rack in a shallow roasting pan; sprinkle with salt. In a small bowl, mix remaining ingredients; press onto top and sides of roast.

2. Roast 1¾-2¼ hours or until meat reaches desired doneness (for medium-rare, a thermometer should read 145°; medium, 160°; well-done, 170°). Remove roast from oven; tent with foil. Let stand 10 minutes before slicing.

PER SERVING *5 ounces cooked beef: 319 cal., 15g fat (3g sat. fat), 111mg chol., 311mg sod., 7g carb. (0 sugars, 0 fiber), 35g pro.* **Diabetic Exchanges:** *5 lean meat, 1 fat, ½ starch.*

BEEF & MUSHROOM BRAISED STEW

Every spring, my family heads out to collect morel mushrooms and then we cook up this stew. We use the morels, of course, but baby portobellos or button mushrooms will work just as well.

—AMY WERTHEIM ATLANTA, IL

PREP: 35 MIN. • **BAKE:** 1½ HOURS
MAKES: 6 SERVINGS

- 1 **boneless beef chuck roast (2 to 3 pounds), cut into 1-inch cubes**
- ¼ **teaspoon salt**
- ¼ **teaspoon pepper**
- 3 **tablespoons olive oil**
- 1 **pound sliced fresh mushrooms**
- 2 **medium onions, sliced**
- 2 **garlic cloves, minced**
- 1 **carton (32 ounces) beef broth**
- 1 **cup dry red wine or additional beef broth**
- ½ **cup brandy**
- 1 **tablespoon tomato paste**
- ¼ **teaspoon each dried parsley flakes, rosemary, sage leaves, tarragon and thyme**
- 3 **tablespoons all-purpose flour**
- 3 **tablespoons water**
  Hot mashed potatoes

1. Preheat oven to 325°. Sprinkle beef with salt and pepper. In an ovenproof Dutch oven, heat oil over medium heat; brown beef in batches. Remove from pan.

2. Add mushrooms and onions to pan; cook and stir until tender. Add garlic; cook 1 minute longer. Stir in broth, red wine, brandy, tomato paste and herbs. Return beef to pan. Bring to a boil.

3. Bake, covered, 1 hour. In a small bowl, mix the flour and water until smooth; gradually stir into stew. Bake, covered, 30 minutes longer or until stew is thickened and beef is tender. Skim fat. Serve stew with mashed potatoes.

⑤INGREDIENTS FAST FIX

SMOTHERED BURRITOS

My brother-in-law joked that I knew how to make only five things using ground beef. I had to prove him wrong, so I came up with these savory burritos.

—**KIM KENYON** GREENWOOD, MO

START TO FINISH: 25 MIN.
MAKES: 4 SERVINGS

- 1 **can (10 ounces) green enchilada sauce**
- ¾ **cup salsa verde**
- 1 **pound ground beef**
- 4 **flour tortillas (10 inches)**
- 1½ **cups shredded cheddar cheese, divided**

1. Preheat oven to 375°. In a small bowl, mix enchilada sauce and salsa verde.
2. In a large skillet, cook beef over medium heat 8-10 minutes or until no longer pink, breaking into crumbles; drain. Stir in ½ cup sauce mixture.
3. Spoon ⅔ cup beef mixture across center of each tortilla; top each with 3 tablespoons cheese. Fold bottom and sides of tortilla over filling and roll up.
4. Place in a greased 11x7-in. baking dish. Pour remaining sauce mixture over top; sprinkle with remaining ¾ cup cheese. Bake, uncovered, 10-15 minutes or until cheese is melted.
PER SERVING *1 burrito: 624 cal., 33g fat (15g sat. fat), 115mg chol., 1470mg sod., 44g carb. (6g sugars, 2g fiber), 36g pro.*

TOP TIP

CHICKEN BURRITOS

I followed this recipe but used shredded chicken breast instead of beef. They were fantastic! Even better than the chicken enchiladas I usually make. They freeze well, too. We all loved them.

—**LOVEPIGGS**
TASTEOFHOME.COM

SMOTHERED BURRITOS

MINI REUBEN CASSEROLES

These cute and creamy individual roast beef casseroles have the classic flavors of a Reuben sandwich in a brand-new dish.

—TASTE OF HOME TEST KITCHEN

PREP: 20 MIN. • **BAKE:** 20 MIN.
MAKES: 4 SERVINGS

- 1 medium onion, chopped
- 1 medium green pepper, chopped
- 2 teaspoons olive oil
- 2 cups cubed cooked beef roast
- 1 can (14 ounces) sauerkraut, rinsed and well drained
- 1 can (10¾ ounces) condensed cream of chicken soup, undiluted
- 1¼ cups shredded Swiss cheese, divided
- ⅓ cup 2% milk
- ½ cup Thousand Island salad dressing
- 2 slices rye bread, cubed
- 1 tablespoon butter, melted
- ½ teaspoon onion powder

1. Preheat oven to 350°. In a large skillet, saute onion and pepper in oil until tender. Stir in meat, sauerkraut, soup, 1 cup cheese, milk and salad dressing; heat through. Transfer to four greased 10-oz. ramekins or custard cups. Place ramekins on a baking sheet.

2. In a small bowl, toss bread cubes with butter and onion powder. Arrange over tops. Bake, uncovered, 15 minutes. Sprinkle with remaining cheese. Bake 5-10 minutes longer or until cheese is melted.

PER SERVING 650 cal., 41g fat (15g sat. fat), 130mg chol., 1782mg sod., 31g carb. (12g sugars, 5g fiber), 37g pro.

MINI REUBEN CASSEROLES

NANA'S ITALIAN ROULADE

⑤ INGREDIENTS FAST FIX ▶

BEEFY FRENCH ONION POTPIE (PICTURED ON PAGE 58)

I came up with this dish knowing my husband loves French onion soup. It makes a perfect base for this hearty, beefy potpie.
—**SARA HUTCHENS** DU QUOIN, IL

PREP: 10 MIN. • **BAKE:** 20 MIN.
MAKES: 4 SERVINGS

- 1 **pound ground beef**
- 1 **small onion, chopped**
- 1 **can (10½ ounces) condensed French onion soup**
- 1½ **cups shredded part-skim mozzarella cheese**
- 1 **tube (12 ounces) refrigerated buttermilk biscuits**

1. Preheat oven to 350°. In a large skillet, cook beef and onion over medium heat 6-8 minutes or until beef is no longer pink, breaking beef into crumbles; drain. Stir in soup; bring to a boil.

2. Transfer to an ungreased 9-in. deep-dish pie plate; sprinkle with cheese. Bake 5 minutes or until cheese is melted. Top with biscuits. Bake 15-20 minutes longer or until biscuits are golden brown.

PER SERVING *1 serving: 553 cal., 23g fat (10g sat. fat), 98mg chol., 1550mg sod., 47g carb. (4g sugars, 1g fiber), 38g pro.*

NANA'S ITALIAN ROULADE

This cherished family recipe was passed down by my great-aunt from Sicily—it holds so many precious memories! Use as much sauce as you like; the only requirement is that the meat is covered during cooking.
—**ROSEANNE MCDONLAD** DAYS CREEK, OR

PREP: 30 MIN. • **COOK:** 1½ HOURS
MAKES: 8 SERVINGS

- 6 **bacon strips**
- 2 **garlic cloves, minced**
- ¾ **teaspoon Italian seasoning**
- ½ **teaspoon salt**
- ½ **teaspoon pepper**
- 1 **beef flank steak (1½ to 2 pounds)**
- ¼ **cup grated Parmesan cheese**
- 3 **hard-cooked large eggs, sliced**
- ¼ **cup minced fresh parsley**
- 2 **tablespoons olive oil**
- 3 **jars (24 ounces each) meatless pasta sauce**
  Hot cooked spaghetti
  Additional minced fresh parsley

1. Preheat oven to 350°. Place bacon on a microwave-safe plate lined with paper towels. Cover with additional paper towels; microwave on high 3-5 minutes or until partially cooked but not crisp. In a small bowl, mix garlic, Italian seasoning, salt and pepper.

2. Starting at one long side, cut steak horizontally in half to within ½ in. of opposite side. Open steak flat; cover with plastic wrap. Pound with a meat mallet to ¼-in. thickness; remove plastic.

3. Spread garlic mixture over steak; sprinkle with cheese. Layer with eggs and bacon to within 1 in. of edges; sprinkle with parsley. Starting with a long side of the steak, roll up jelly-roll style (along the grain); tie at 1½-in. intervals with kitchen string.

4. In a Dutch oven, heat oil over medium-high heat. Brown roulade on all sides. Pour pasta sauce over top. Bake, covered, 1½-1¾ hours or until meat is tender.

5. Remove roulade from pot; remove string and cut into slices. Serve with sauce over spaghetti. Sprinkle with additional parsley.

PER SERVING *1 slice with ¾ cup sauce (calculated without spaghetti): 331 cal., 15g fat (5g sat. fat), 119mg chol., 1491mg sod., 24g carb. (17g sugars, 4g fiber), 26g pro.*

GUINNESS CORNED BEEF AND CABBAGE, PAGE 87

BEEF & VEGGIE
SLOPPY JOES, PAGE 79

SIMPLY SLOW-COOKED

Plug in the slow cooker, load it up with **meaty favorites** and relax as dinner simmers to a **savory perfection** on its own. You'll be surprised at the **stick-to-your-ribs goodness** these slow-cooked entrees deliver, so what are you waiting for? Turn the page and simmer a winner tonight!

SWEET PEPPER
STEAK, PAGE 82

FRESH SPINACH TAMALE PIE, PAGE 88

CUBAN
ROPA VIEJA

CUBAN ROPA VIEJA

This entree offers a great authentic Mexican flavor that can be prepared at home. I love having this recipe in my back pocket—it's a great go-to dish for weeknight meals.
—**MELISSA PELKEY HASS** WALESKA, GA

PREP: 25 MIN. • **COOK:** 7 HOURS
MAKES: 8 SERVINGS

- 6 bacon strips, chopped
- 2 beef flank steaks (1 pound each), cut in half
- 1 can (28 ounces) crushed tomatoes
- 2 cups beef stock
- 1 can (6 ounces) tomato paste
- 5 garlic cloves, minced
- 1 tablespoon ground cumin
- 2 teaspoons dried thyme
- ¾ teaspoon salt
- ½ teaspoon pepper
- 1 medium onion, thinly sliced
- 1 medium sweet red pepper, sliced
- 1 medium green pepper, sliced
- ¼ cup minced fresh cilantro
  Hot cooked rice

1. In a large skillet, cook bacon over medium heat until crisp, stirring occasionally. Remove with a slotted spoon; drain on paper towels.
2. In same skillet, heat drippings over medium-high heat; brown steak in batches. Transfer meat and bacon to a 5- or 6-qt. slow cooker. In a large bowl, combine tomatoes, beef stock, tomato paste, garlic, seasonings and vegetables; pour over meat. Cook, covered, on low 7-9 hours or until meat is tender. Shred beef with two forks; return to slow cooker. Stir in cilantro. Remove with a slotted spoon; serve with rice.
FREEZE OPTION *Freeze cooled meat mixture in freezer containers. To use, partially thaw in refrigerator overnight. Microwave, covered, on high in a microwave-safe dish until heated through, gently stirring and adding a little stock or water if necessary.*
PER SERVING *1⅓ cups (calculated without rice): 335 cal., 17g fat (6g sat. fat), 68mg chol., 765mg sod., 17g carb. (9g sugars, 4g fiber), 29g pro.*

GREEN CHILI BEEF BURRITOS

The shredded beef in this recipe has a luscious slow-cooked flavor that we can't get anywhere else, and it gets rave reviews every time make it.
—**JENNY FLAKE** NEWPORT BEACH, CA

PREP: 30 MIN. • **COOK:** 9 HOURS
MAKES: 12 SERVINGS

- 1 boneless beef chuck roast (3 pounds)
- 1 can (14½ ounces) beef broth
- 2 cups green enchilada sauce
- 1 can (4 ounces) chopped green chilies
- ½ cup Mexican-style hot tomato sauce
- ½ teaspoon salt
- ½ teaspoon garlic powder
- ½ teaspoon pepper
- 12 flour tortillas (12 inches)
  Optional toppings: shredded lettuce, chopped tomatoes, shredded cheddar cheese and sour cream

1. Cut roast in half and place in a 3- or 4-qt. slow cooker. Add broth. Cover and cook on low for 8-9 hours or until the meat is tender.
2. Remove beef. When cool enough to handle, shred meat with two forks. Skim fat from cooking liquid; reserve ½ cup liquid. Return shredded beef and reserved liquid to the slow cooker. Stir in the enchilada sauce, green chilies, tomato sauce, salt, garlic powder and pepper.
3. Cover and cook on low for 1 hour or until heated through. Spoon beef mixture down the center of tortillas; add toppings of your choice. Roll up.
NOTE *This recipe was tested with El Pato brand Mexican-style hot tomato sauce. If you cannot find Mexican-style hot tomato sauce, you may substitute ½ cup tomato sauce, 1 teaspoon hot pepper sauce, ⅛ teaspoon onion powder and ⅛ teaspoon chili powder.*
PER SERVING *419 cal., 17g fat (6g sat. fat), 74mg chol., 1175mg sod., 36g carb. (2g sugars, 5g fiber), 29g pro.*

EAT SMART
BEEF & VEGGIE SLOPPY JOES

I'm always looking for ways to serve my family healthy and delicious food, so I started experimenting with my favorite veggies and ground beef. Now my kids actually request this creation!

—MEGAN NIEBUHR YAKIMA, WA

PREP: 35 MIN. • **COOK:** 5 HOURS
MAKES: 10 SERVINGS

- 4 **medium carrots, shredded**
- 1 **medium yellow summer squash, shredded**
- 1 **medium zucchini, shredded**
- 1 **medium sweet red pepper, finely chopped**
- 2 **medium tomatoes, seeded and chopped**
- 1 **small red onion, finely chopped**
- ½ **cup ketchup**
- 3 **tablespoons minced fresh basil or 3 teaspoons dried basil**
- 3 **tablespoons molasses**
- 2 **tablespoons cider vinegar**
- 2 **garlic cloves, minced**
- ½ **teaspoon salt**
- ½ **teaspoon pepper**
- 2 **pounds lean ground beef (90% lean)**
- 10 **whole wheat hamburger buns, split**

1. In a 5- or 6-qt. slow cooker, combine the first 13 ingredients. In a large skillet, cook beef over medium heat 8-10 minutes or until no longer pink, breaking into crumbles. Drain; transfer beef to slow cooker. Stir to combine.

2. Cook, covered, on low 5-6 hours or until heated through and vegetables are tender. Using a slotted spoon, serve beef mixture on buns.

PER SERVING *316 cal., 10g fat (3g sat. fat), 57mg chol., 565mg sod., 36g carb. (15g sugars, 5g fiber), 22g pro.* **Diabetic Exchanges:** *2 starch, 2 lean meat, 1 vegetable.*

BEEF & VEGGIE SLOPPY JOES

MEXICAN SHREDDED
BEEF WRAPS

MEXICAN SHREDDED BEEF WRAPS

The first time I served these meaty wraps was at the party following my son's baptism. I made a double batch and fed a crowd!
—**AMY LENTS** GRAND FORKS, ND

PREP: 20 MIN. • **COOK:** 6 HOURS
MAKES: 6 SERVINGS

- 1 **small onion, finely chopped**
- 1 **jalapeno pepper, seeded and minced**
- 3 **garlic cloves, minced**
- 1 **boneless beef chuck roast (2 to 3 pounds)**
- ½ **teaspoon salt**
- ½ **teaspoon pepper**
- 1 **can (8 ounces) tomato sauce**
- ¼ **cup lime juice**
- 1 **tablespoon chili powder**
- 1 **teaspoon ground cumin**
- ¼ **teaspoon cayenne pepper**
- 6 **flour or whole wheat tortillas (8 inches)**
  Optional toppings: torn romaine, chopped tomatoes and sliced avocado

1. Place onion, jalapeno and garlic in a 4-qt. slow cooker. Sprinkle roast with salt and pepper; place over vegetables. In a small bowl, mix tomato sauce, lime juice, chili powder, cumin and cayenne; pour over roast.
2. Cook, covered, on low 6-8 hours or until meat is tender. Remove roast; cool slightly. Shred meat with two forks; return to slow cooker. Serve beef on tortillas with toppings of your choice.
NOTE *Wear disposable gloves when cutting hot peppers; the oils can burn skin. Avoid touching your face.*
PER SERVING *1 wrap (calculated without optional toppings): 428 cal., 18g fat (6g sat. fat), 98mg chol., 696mg sod., 31g carb. (2g sugars, 1g fiber), 35g pro. Diabetic Exchanges: 5 lean meat, 2 starch.*

SHORT RIB POUTINE

SHORT RIB POUTINE

This dish combines the hearty, spicy flavors of my beloved slow cooker short ribs with my all-time favorite comfort food: fries and gravy. With a little prep in the morning, it's just about ready when I come home from work—plus, the kitchen smells amazing! If you are sensitive to heat from spices, reduce the amount of Sriracha chili sauce.
—**ERIN DEWITT** LONG BEACH, CA

PREP: 45 MIN. • **COOK:** 6 HOURS
MAKES: 4 SERVINGS

- 1 **pound well-trimmed boneless beef short ribs**
- 3 **tablespoons all-purpose flour**
- ½ **teaspoon pepper**
- 2 **tablespoons olive oil**
- 1 **medium onion, coarsely chopped**
- 4 **garlic cloves, minced**
- 1½ **cups beef stock, divided**
- ¼ **cup Sriracha Asian hot chili sauce**
- 3 **tablespoons ketchup**
- 2 **tablespoons Worcestershire sauce**
- 1 **tablespoon packed brown sugar**
- 3 **cups frozen french-fried potatoes (about 11 ounces)**
- 1 **cup cheese curds or 4 ounces white cheddar cheese, broken into small chunks**

1. Toss short ribs with flour and pepper, shaking off excess; reserve remaining flour mixture. In a large skillet, heat oil over medium-high heat; brown ribs on all sides. Transfer to a 3-qt. slow cooker, reserving drippings.
2. In the same skillet, saute onion in drippings over medium heat until tender, 2-3 minutes. Add garlic; cook and stir 1 minute. Stir in 1 cup stock; bring to a boil, stirring to loosen browned bits from pan.
3. In a small bowl, whisk the reserved flour mixture, chili sauce, ketchup, Worcestershire sauce, brown sugar and remaining stock until smooth; stir into onion mixture. Pour over ribs.
4. Cook, covered, on low until ribs are tender, 6-8 hours. Remove ribs; shred with two forks and keep warm. Skim fat from onion mixture; puree using an immersion blender. (Or cool slightly and puree in a blender; return to slow cooker to heat through.)
5. Cook potatoes according to package directions. Serve beef over potatoes; top with gravy and cheese
PER SERVING *560 cal., 31g fat (12g sat. fat), 80mg chol., 1,453mg sod., 39g carb., 3g fiber, 28g pro.*

SWEET PEPPER STEAK (PICTURED ON PAGE 77)

Pepper steak is one of my favorite dishes, but I was always disappointed with beef that was too tough. This recipe solves the tenderness problem! Store leftovers in individual portions for quick lunches or in one big resealable bag.

—JULIE RHINE ZELIENOPLE, PA

PREP: 30 MIN. • **COOK:** 6¼ HOURS
MAKES: 12 SERVINGS

- 1 beef top round roast (3 pounds)
- 1 large onion, halved and sliced
- 1 large green pepper, cut into ½-inch strips
- 1 large sweet red pepper, cut into ½-inch strips
- 1 cup water
- 4 garlic cloves, minced
- ⅓ cup cornstarch
- ½ cup reduced-sodium soy sauce
- 2 teaspoons sugar
- 2 teaspoons ground ginger
- 8 cups hot cooked brown rice

1. Place roast, onion and peppers in a 5-qt. slow cooker. Add water and garlic. Cook, covered, on low 6-8 hours or until meat is tender.
2. Remove beef to a cutting board. Transfer vegetables and cooking juices to a large saucepan. Bring to a boil. In a small bowl, mix cornstarch, soy sauce, sugar and ginger until smooth; stir into vegetable mixture. Return to a boil and stir constantly 1-2 minutes or until thickened.
3. Cut beef into slices. Stir gently into sauce; heat through. Serve with rice.

FREEZE OPTION *Freeze cooled beef mixture in freezer containers. To use, partially thaw in refrigerator overnight. Heat through in a saucepan, stirring occasionally and adding a little water if necessary.*

PER SERVING *322 cal., 5g fat (1g sat. fat), 64mg chol., 444mg sod., 38g carb. (3g sugars, 3g fiber), 30g pro.* **Diabetic Exchanges:** *3 lean meat, 2 starch.*

SLOW COOKER POT ROAST

SLOW COOKER POT ROAST

I work full time but love to make home-cooked meals for my husband and son. It's a comfort to walk in the door to the smell of this simmering roast and know that it will be fall-apart tender and delicious when I put it on the table.

—GINA JACKSON OGDENSBURG, NY

PREP: 15 MIN. • **COOK:** 6 HOURS
MAKES: 6 SERVINGS

- 1 cup warm water
- 1 tablespoon beef base
- ½ pound sliced fresh mushrooms
- 1 large onion, coarsely chopped
- 3 garlic cloves, minced
- 1 boneless beef chuck roast (3 pounds)
- ½ teaspoon pepper
- 1 tablespoon Worcestershire sauce
- ¼ cup butter, cubed
- ⅓ cup all-purpose flour
- ¼ teaspoon salt

1. In a 5- or 6-qt. slow cooker, whisk water and beef base; add mushrooms, onion and garlic. Sprinkle roast with pepper; transfer to slow cooker. Drizzle with the Worcestershire sauce. Cook, covered, on low 6-8 hours or until meat is tender.
2. Remove roast to a serving platter; tent with foil. Strain cooking juices, reserving vegetables. Skim fat from cooking juices. In a large saucepan, melt butter over medium heat. Stir in flour and salt until smooth; gradually whisk in cooking juices. Bring to a boil, stirring constantly for 1-2 minutes or until thickened. Stir in cooked vegetables. Serve with roast.

NOTE *Look for beef base near the broth and bouillon.*

PER SERVING *6 ounces cooked meat with ⅔ cup gravy: 507 cal., 30g fat (13g sat. fat), 168mg chol., 623mg sod., 11g carb. (3g sugars, 1g fiber), 47g pro.*

SLOW COOKER LASAGNA

Lasagna is a popular meal, but it's hard to find time to fix it. This slow cooker version will allow you to enjoy time with your family and still put an elegant dinner on the table.

—KATHRYN CONRAD MILWAUKEE, WI

PREP: 25 MIN. • **COOK:** 4 HOURS + STANDING
MAKES: 8 SERVINGS

- 1 pound ground beef
- 1 tablespoon olive oil
- ½ cup chopped onion
- ½ cup chopped zucchini
- ½ cup chopped carrot
- 1 jar (24 ounces) marinara sauce
- 2 teaspoons Italian seasoning
- ½ teaspoon crushed red pepper flakes, optional
- 2 cartons (15 ounces each) part-skim ricotta cheese
- 1 cup grated Parmesan cheese
- 4 large eggs
- ½ cup loosely packed basil leaves, chopped
- 12 no-cook lasagna noodles
- 3 cups shredded part-skim mozzarella cheese
    Quartered grape tomatoes and additional chopped fresh basil, optional

1. Cut three 25x3-in. strips of heavy-duty foil; crisscross so they resemble spokes of a wheel. Place strips on bottom and up sides of a 5-qt. slow cooker. Coat strips with cooking spray.

2. In a 6-qt. stockpot, cook beef over medium heat 6-8 minutes or until beef is no longer pink; drain. Set beef aside.

3. In same pot, heat oil over medium-high heat. Add onion, zucchini and carrot; cook and stir 2-3 minutes or until just tender. Transfer beef mixture back to pot. Stir in marinara sauce, Italian seasoning and, if desired, crushed red pepper. In a large bowl, combine ricotta, Parmesan, eggs and basil.

4. Spread ½ cup meat sauce into the bottom of the slow cooker. Layer with four noodles, breaking as needed to fit.

Top with 1½ cups meat mixture, 1⅔ cups cheese mixture and 1 cup mozzarella cheese. Repeat layers twice. Cook, covered, on low 4 hours or until noodles are tender. Let stand for 30 minutes. If desired, sprinkle with grape tomatoes and additional basil.

PER SERVING *1 slice: 631 cal., 32g fat (15g sat. fat), 199mg chol., 1074mg sod., 40g carb. (8g sugars, 3g fiber), 43g pro.*

HEARTY BUSY-DAY STEW

When I was living in Missouri, a friend gave me her family cookbooks. I got the idea for this easy stew from one of them. The taco seasoning adds just the right touch.

—KRISTEN HILLS LAYTON, UT

PREP: 10 MIN. • **COOK:** 7½ HOURS
MAKES: 6 SERVINGS

- 1½ pounds beef stew meat
- 1½ pounds potatoes (about 3 medium), peeled and cut into 1-inch cubes
- 1 can (14½ ounces) diced tomatoes, undrained
- 1 can (14½ ounces) beef broth
- 2½ cups fresh baby carrots (about 12 ounces)
- 1 large tomato, chopped
- 1 medium onion, chopped
- 2 tablespoons taco seasoning
- 2 garlic cloves, minced
- ½ teaspoon salt
- 2 tablespoons cornstarch
- 2 tablespoons cold water

1. In a 5- or 6-qt. slow cooker, combine the first ten ingredients. Cook, covered, on low 7-9 hours or until the beef and vegetables are tender.

2. In a small bowl, mix cornstarch and water until smooth; gradually stir into stew. Cook, covered, on high 30-45 minutes longer or until stew is slightly thickened.

PER SERVING *1¾ cups: 303 cal., 8g fat (3g sat. fat), 71mg chol., 986mg sod., 32g carb. (8g sugars, 4g fiber), 25g pro.*

SLOW COOKER LASAGNA

SLOW-COOKED TEX-MEX FLANK STEAK

This flavorful, tender beef dish has been a go-to recipe for many years; it's a lifesaver on nights I know I'll be getting home late.
—**ANNE MERRILL** CROGHAN, NY

PREP: 20 MIN. • **COOK:** 6 HOURS
MAKES: 4 SERVINGS

- 1 tablespoon canola oil
- 1 beef flank steak (1½ pounds)
- 1 large onion, sliced
- ⅓ cup water
- 1 can (4 ounces) chopped green chilies
- 2 tablespoons cider vinegar
- 2 to 3 teaspoons chili powder
- 1 teaspoon garlic powder
- 1 teaspoon sugar
- ½ teaspoon salt
- ⅛ teaspoon pepper

1. In a large skillet, heat the oil over medium-high heat; brown steak on both sides. Transfer to a 3-qt. slow cooker.
2. Add onion to same skillet; cook and stir 1-2 minutes or until crisp-tender. Add water to pan; cook 30 seconds, stirring to loosen browned bits from pan. Stir in remaining ingredients; return to a boil. Pour over steak.
3. Cook, covered, on low 6-8 hours or until meat is tender. Slice steak across the grain; serve with onion mixture.
PER SERVING *4 ounces cooked beef with ½ cup sauce: 316 cal., 16g fat (6g sat. fat), 81mg chol., 524mg sod., 7g carb. (3g sugars, 2g fiber), 34g pro.*

SLOW-COOKED TEX-MEX FLANK STEAK

TOP TIP

BROWNING IS KEY

Why brown beef on the stovetop before cooking it in the slow cooker? Browning the meat helps seal in the juices and gives meat an attractive color and shine that slow cooking simply cannot.

EAT SMART
PUMPKIN HARVEST BEEF STEW

By the time this stew is done simmering and a batch of bread finishes baking, our house smells absolutely wonderful.
—**MARCIA O'NEIL** CEDAR CREST, NM

PREP: 25 MIN. • **COOK:** 6½ HOURS
MAKES: 6 SERVINGS

- 1 tablespoon canola oil
- 1 beef top round steak (1½ pounds), cut into 1-inch cubes
- 1½ cups cubed peeled pie pumpkin or sweet potatoes
- 3 small red potatoes, peeled and cubed
- 1 cup cubed acorn squash
- 1 medium onion, chopped
- 2 cans (14½ ounces each) reduced-sodium beef broth
- 1 can (14½ ounces) diced tomatoes, undrained
- 2 bay leaves
- 2 garlic cloves, minced
- 2 teaspoons reduced-sodium beef bouillon granules
- ½ teaspoon chili powder
- ½ teaspoon pepper
- ¼ teaspoon ground allspice
- ¼ teaspoon ground cloves
- ¼ cup water
- 3 tablespoons all-purpose flour

1. In a large skillet, heat the oil over medium-high heat. Brown beef in batches; remove with a slotted spoon to a 4- or 5-qt. slow cooker. Add the pumpkin, potatoes, squash and onion. Stir in the broth, tomatoes and seasonings. Cover and cook on low for 6-8 hours or until meat is tender.
2. Remove bay leaves. In a small bowl, mix water and flour until smooth; gradually stir into stew. Cover and cook on high for 30 minutes or until liquid is thickened.
PER SERVING *1⅔ cups: 258 cal., 6g fat (1g sat. fat), 67mg chol., 479mg sod., 21g carb. (6g sugars, 4g fiber), 29g pro. Diabetic Exchanges: 3 lean meat, 1 starch, 1 vegetable, ½ fat.*

FESTIVE
SLOW-COOKED
BEEF TIPS

FESTIVE SLOW-COOKED BEEF TIPS

We once owned an organic greenhouse and produce business. Weekends were hectic, so I made no-fuss meals like yummy beef tips to fortify us at day's end.
—**SUE GRONHOLZ** BEAVER DAM, WI

PREP: 45 MIN. • **COOK:** 6 HOURS
MAKES: 8 SERVINGS

- 1 boneless beef chuck roast (about 2 pounds), cut into 2-inch pieces
- 1 teaspoon salt
- ¼ teaspoon pepper
- 2 tablespoons canola oil
- 1 medium onion, coarsely chopped
- 1 celery rib, coarsely chopped
- 6 garlic cloves, halved
- 2 cups beef broth
- 1½ cups dry red wine
- 1 fresh rosemary sprig
- 1 bay leaf
- 2 cans (4 ounces each) sliced mushrooms
- 2 tablespoons cornstarch
- ½ cup water
- 1 tablespoon balsamic vinegar
  Hot cooked egg noodles

1. Sprinkle beef with salt and pepper. In a large skillet, heat oil over medium-high heat. Brown beef in batches. Remove with a slotted spoon to a 3- or 4-qt. slow cooker.
2. In same pan, add onion and celery; cook and stir 6-8 minutes or until tender. Add garlic; cook 1 minute longer. Add broth, wine, rosemary and bay leaf. Bring to a boil; cook 8-10 minutes or until liquid is reduced to about 2 cups.
3. Pour over beef in slow cooker; stir in mushrooms. Cook, covered, on low 6-8 hours or until meat is tender. Remove rosemary and bay leaf.
4. In a small bowl, mix cornstarch, water and vinegar until smooth; gradually stir into beef mixture. Serve with noodles.
PER SERVING *1 cup (calculated without noodles): 290 cal., 15g fat (4g sat. fat), 74mg chol., 69mg sod., 7g carb. (2g sugars, 1g fiber), 24g pro.*

EAT SMART
SLOW COOKER BEEF VEGETABLE STEW

Come home to warm comfort food! This is based on my mom's wonderful recipe. Add a sprinkle of Parmesan for a finishing touch.
—**MARCELLA WEST** WASHBURN, IL

PREP: 20 MIN. • **COOK:** 6½ HOURS
MAKES: 8 SERVINGS (3 QUARTS)

- 1½ **pounds boneless beef chuck roast, cut into 1-inch cubes**
- 3 **medium potatoes, peeled and cubed**
- 3 **cups water**
- 1½ **cups fresh baby carrots**
- 1 **can (10¾ ounces) condensed tomato soup, undiluted**
- 1 **medium onion, chopped**
- 1 **celery rib, chopped**
- 2 **tablespoons Worcestershire sauce**
- 1 **tablespoon browning sauce, optional**
- 2 **teaspoons beef bouillon granules**
- 1 **garlic clove, minced**
- 1 **teaspoon sugar**
- ¾ **teaspoon salt**
- ¼ **teaspoon pepper**
- ¼ **cup cornstarch**
- ¾ **cup cold water**
- 2 **cups frozen peas, thawed**

1. Place the beef, potatoes, water, carrots, soup, onion, celery, Worcestershire sauce, browning sauce of desired, bouillon granules, garlic, sugar, salt and pepper in a 5- or 6-qt. slow cooker. Cover; cook on low for 6-8 hours or until meat is tender.

2. Combine cornstarch and cold water in a small bowl until smooth; gradually stir into stew. Stir in peas. Cover and cook on high for 30 minutes or until thickened.

PER SERVING *1½ cups (calculated without browning sauce):* 287 cal., 9g fat (3g sat. fat), 55mg chol., 705mg sod., 31g carb. (9g sugars, 4g fiber), 20g pro. *Diabetic Exchanges: 2 starch, 2 lean meat.*

SLOW COOKER BEEF VEGETABLE STEW

GUINNESS CORNED BEEF AND CABBAGE (PICTURED ON PAGE 76)

A dear friend of my mother's shared this recipe with her years ago. My husband and kids request it for special occasions like birthdays and, of course, St. Patrick's Day.
—**KARIN BRODBECK** RED HOOK, NY

PREP: 20 MIN. • **COOK:** 8 HOURS
MAKES: 9 SERVINGS

- 2 **pounds red potatoes, quartered**
- 1 **pound carrots, cut into 3-inch pieces**
- 2 **celery ribs, cut into 3-inch pieces**
- 1 **small onion, quartered**
- 1 **corned beef brisket with spice packet (3 to 3½ pounds)**
- 8 **whole cloves**
- 6 **whole peppercorns**
- 1 **bay leaf**
- 1 **bottle (12 ounces) Guinness stout or reduced-sodium beef broth**
- ½ **small head cabbage, thinly sliced**
  Prepared horseradish

1. In a 6-qt. slow cooker, combine potatoes, carrots, celery and onion. Add corned beef (discard spice packet or save for another use).

2. Place cloves, peppercorns and bay leaf on a double thickness of cheesecloth. Gather corners of cloth to enclose seasonings; tie securely with string. Place in slow cooker. Pour stout over top.

3. Cook, covered, on low 8-10 hours or until meat and vegetables are tender, adding cabbage during the last hour of cooking. Discard spice bag.

4. Cut beef diagonally across the grain into thin slices. Serve beef with vegetables and horseradish.

PER SERVING *3 ounces cooked beef with ¾ cup vegetables (calculated without horseradish): 374 cal., 20g fat (7g sat. fat), 104mg chol., 1256mg sod., 25g carb. (5g sugars, 4g fiber), 22g pro.*

DELUXE WALKING NACHOS

DELUXE WALKING NACHOS

My slow cooker chili makes an awesome filling for a hand-held bag of walk-around nachos. Cut the bag lengthwise to make it easier to load up your fork.
—**MALLORY LYNCH** MADISON, WI

PREP: 20 MIN. • **COOK:** 6 HOURS
MAKES: 18 SERVINGS

- 1 **pound lean ground beef (90% lean)**
- 1 **large sweet onion, chopped**
- 3 **garlic cloves, minced**
- 2 **cans (14½ ounces each) diced tomatoes with mild green chilies**
- 2 **cans (15 ounces each) pinto beans, rinsed and drained**
- 2 **cans (15 ounces each) black beans, rinsed and drained**
- 2 **to 3 tablespoons chili powder**
- 2 **teaspoons ground cumin**
- ½ **teaspoon salt**
- 18 **packages (1 ounce each) nacho-flavored tortilla chips**
  Optional toppings: shredded cheddar cheese, sour cream, chopped tomatoes and pickled jalapeno slices

1. In a large skillet, cook beef, onion and garlic over medium heat 6-8 minutes or until beef is no longer pink, breaking up beef into crumbles; drain.

2. Transfer beef mixture to a 5-qt. slow cooker. Drain one can tomatoes, discarding liquid; add to slow cooker. Stir in beans, chili powder, cumin, salt and remaining tomatoes. Cook, covered, on low 6-8 hours to allow flavors to blend. Mash beans to desired consistency.

3. Just before serving, cut open tortilla chip bags. Divide chili among bags; add toppings as desired.

FREEZE OPTION *Freeze cooled chili in a freezer container. To use, partially thaw in refrigerator overnight. Heat through in a saucepan, stirring occasionally and adding a little water if necessary.*

PER SERVING *1 nacho bag (calculated without optional toppings): 282 cal., 10g fat (2g sat. fat), 16mg chol., 482mg sod., 36g carb. (5g sugars, 6g fiber), 12g pro.*

FRESH SPINACH TAMALE PIE

BEEF & TORTELLINI MARINARA

This hearty pasta dish made with fresh green beans is a meal in itself. It's great served with crusty Italian bread to dip in the sauce and a nice big green salad.
—**JOYCE FREY** MACKSVILLE, KS

PREP: 30 MIN. • **COOK:** 6½ HOURS
MAKES: 11 SERVINGS

- 1 **pound beef stew meat**
- 2 **tablespoons olive oil**
- 2 **garlic cloves, minced**
- 1 **jar (26 ounces) marinara or spaghetti sauce**
- 2 **cups dry red wine or beef broth**
- 1 **pound fresh green beans, trimmed**
- 1 **can (14½ ounces) Italian diced tomatoes, undrained**
- ½ **pound small fresh mushrooms**
- 2 **envelopes thick and zesty spaghetti sauce mix**
- 2 **tablespoons minced fresh parsley**
- 1 **tablespoon dried minced onion**
- 2 **teaspoons minced fresh rosemary**
- 1 **teaspoon coarsely ground pepper**
- ¼ **teaspoon salt**
- 1 **package (9 ounces) refrigerated cheese tortellini**

1. In a large skillet, brown beef in oil until no longer pink. Add garlic; cook 1 minute longer. Transfer mixture to a 5- or 6-qt. slow cooker.
2. Stir in the marinara sauce, wine, green beans, tomatoes, mushrooms, sauce mix, parsley, onion, rosemary, pepper and salt. Cover and cook on low for 6-8 hours or until meat is tender.
3. Stir in tortellini. Cover and cook on high for 30 minutes or until tortellini are heated through.
PER SERVING *1 cup: 310 cal., 10g fat (3g sat. fat), 37mg chol., 1118mg sod., 29g carb. (11g sugars, 3g fiber), 14g pro.*

FRESH SPINACH TAMALE PIE

I got this recipe from my mother, who loved quick and easy meals for dinner. I made a few variations by adding spinach, bell peppers and fresh corn. The changes were well worth it—my family and friends love this dish!
—**NANCY HEISHMAN** LAS VEGAS, NV

PREP: 20 MIN. • **COOK:** 3 HOURS
MAKES: 10 SERVINGS

- 8 **frozen beef tamales, thawed**
- 2 **cans (15 ounces each) pinto beans, rinsed and drained**
- 2 **cups fresh or frozen corn**
- 4 **green onions, chopped**
- 1 **can (2¼ ounces) sliced ripe olives, drained**
- ½ **teaspoon garlic powder**
- ¾ **cup chopped sweet red pepper**
- ¾ **cup sour cream**
- 1 **can (4 ounces) whole green chilies, drained and chopped**
- 3 **cups chopped fresh spinach**
- 12 **bacon strips, cooked and crumbled**
- 2 **cups shredded cheddar cheese**
  Additional green onions, chopped

1. Place tamales in a single layer in a greased 6-qt. slow cooker. In a large bowl, combine beans, corn, onions, olives and garlic powder; spoon over tamales. In same bowl, combine pepper, sour cream and chilies; spoon over bean mixture. Top with spinach.
2. Cook, covered, on low 3-4 hours or until heated through. Sprinkle with bacon, cheese and additional green onions.
PER SERVING *459 cal., 24g fat (9g sat. fat), 49mg chol., 1013mg sod., 40g carb. (4g sugars, 7g fiber), 23g pro.*

FARM-STYLE BBQ RIBS

I got this recipe from a newspaper, and it was an instant hit with my husband and my friends. I originally prepared this meal in the oven, but I've since discovered how easy it is to make in the slow cooker.

—BETTE JO WELTON EUGENE, OR

PREP: 20 MIN. • **COOK:** 6 HOURS
MAKES: 4 SERVINGS

- 4 pounds bone-in beef short ribs
- 1 can (15 ounces) thick and zesty tomato sauce
- 1½ cups water
- 1 medium onion, chopped
- 1 can (6 ounces) tomato paste
- ⅓ cup packed brown sugar
- 3 tablespoons cider vinegar
- 3 tablespoons Worcestershire sauce
- 2 tablespoons chili powder
- 4 garlic cloves, minced
- 2 teaspoons ground mustard
- 1½ teaspoons salt

Place ribs in a 5- or 6-qt. slow cooker. In a large saucepan, combine the remaining ingredients. Bring to a boil. Reduce heat; simmer, uncovered, 5 minutes or until slightly thickened. Pour over ribs; cook, covered, on low 6-8 hours or until tender.
PER SERVING *578 cal., 24g fat (9g sat. fat), 110mg chol., 2503mg sod., 46g carb. (32g sugars, 7g fiber), 44g pro.*

TOP TIP

EASY ADDITIONS

Round out Farm-Style BBQ Ribs with frozen veggies that steam to perfection in the microwave; consider broccoli or corn alongside this entree. Buttered noodles, mashed potatoes or corn bread also make tasty menu companions for the saucy main course.

FARM-STYLE BBQ RIBS

SLOW COOKER
SPAGHETTI &
MEATBALLS

SLOW COOKER SPAGHETTI & MEATBALLS

I've been cooking 50 years and this dish is still the one guests ask for. The meatballs also make amazing hero sandwiches, and the sauce works wonderfully with any pasta.
—**JANE WHITTAKER** PENSACOLA, FL

PREP: 50 MIN. • **COOK:** 5 HOURS
MAKES: 12 SERVINGS
(ABOUT 3½ QUARTS SAUCE)

- 1 cup seasoned bread crumbs
- 2 tablespoons grated Parmesan and Romano cheese blend
- 1 teaspoon pepper
- ½ teaspoon salt
- 2 large eggs, lightly beaten
- 2 pounds ground beef

SAUCE

- 1 large onion, finely chopped
- 1 medium green pepper, finely chopped
- 3 cans (15 ounces each) tomato sauce
- 2 cans (14½ ounces each) diced tomatoes, undrained
- 1 can (6 ounces) tomato paste
- 6 garlic cloves, minced
- 2 bay leaves
- 1 teaspoon each dried basil, oregano and parsley flakes
- 1 teaspoon salt
- ½ teaspoon pepper
- ¼ teaspoon crushed red pepper flakes
  Hot cooked spaghetti

1. In a large bowl, mix bread crumbs, cheese, pepper and salt; stir in eggs. Add beef; mix lightly but thoroughly. Shape into 1½-in. balls. In a large skillet, brown meatballs in batches over medium heat; drain.
2. Place the first five sauce ingredients in a 6-qt. slow cooker; stir in garlic and seasonings. Add meatballs, stirring gently to coat. Cook, covered, on low 5-6 hours or until meatballs are cooked through.
3. Remove bay leaves. Serve sauce with spaghetti.
PER SERVING *1 cup (calculated without spaghetti): 254 cal., 11g fat (4g sat. fat), 79mg chol., 1133mg sod., 20g carb. (7g sugars, 3g fiber), 20g pro.*

CHEDDAR-TOPPED BARBECUE MEAT LOAF

CHEDDAR-TOPPED BARBECUE MEAT LOAF

My family loves the bold barbecue flavor of this tender meat loaf. I love that it's such an easy recipe to prepare in the slow cooker.
—**DAVID SNODGRASS** COLUMBIA, MO

PREP: 20 MIN. • **COOK:** 3¼ HOURS
MAKES: 8 SERVINGS

- 3 large eggs, lightly beaten
- ¾ cup old-fashioned oats
- 1 large sweet red or green pepper, chopped (about 1½ cups)
- 1 small onion, finely chopped
- 1 envelope onion soup mix
- 3 garlic cloves, minced
- ½ teaspoon salt
- ¼ teaspoon pepper
- 2 pounds lean ground beef (90% lean)
- 1 cup ketchup
- 2 tablespoons brown sugar
- 1 tablespoon barbecue seasoning
- 1 teaspoon ground mustard
- 1 cup shredded cheddar cheese

1. Cut three 18x3-in. strips of heavy-duty foil; crisscross so they resemble spokes of a wheel. Place strips on bottom and up sides of a 3-qt. slow cooker. Coat strips with cooking spray.
2. In a large bowl, combine eggs, oats, chopped pepper, onion, soup mix, garlic, salt and pepper. Add beef; mix lightly but thoroughly. Shape into a 7-in. round loaf. Place loaf in center of strips in slow cooker. Cook, covered, on low 3-4 hours or until a thermometer reads at least 160°.
3. In a small bowl, mix ketchup, brown sugar, barbecue seasoning and mustard; pour over meat loaf and sprinkle with cheese. Cook, covered, on low 15 minutes longer or until cheese is melted. Let stand 5 minutes. Using foil strips as handles, remove meat loaf to a platter.
PER SERVING *356 cal., 17g fat (7g sat. fat), 154mg chol., 1358mg sod., 22g carb. (13g sugars, 2g fiber), 29g pro.*

ROUND STEAK ROLL-UPS

Since I'm a working mom, I like to assemble these tasty steak rolls the night before and pop them in the slow cooker the next morning before we're all out the door. They make a great meal after a long day.

—KIMBERLY ALONGE WESTFIELD, NY

PREP: 20 MIN. • **COOK:** 6 HOURS
MAKES: 6 SERVINGS

- 2 pounds beef top round steak
- ½ cup grated carrot
- ⅓ cup chopped zucchini
- ¼ cup chopped sweet red pepper
- ¼ cup chopped green pepper
- ¼ cup sliced green onions
- 2 tablespoons grated Parmesan cheese
- 1 tablespoon minced fresh parsley or 1 teaspoon dried parsley flakes
- 1 garlic clove, minced
- ¼ teaspoon salt
- ¼ teaspoon pepper
- 2 tablespoons canola oil
- 1 jar (14 ounces) meatless spaghetti sauce
   Hot cooked spaghetti
   Additional Parmesan cheese, optional

1. Cut meat into six serving-size pieces; pound to ¼-in. thickness. Combine the vegetables, cheese and seasonings; place ⅓ cup in the center of each piece. Roll meat up around filing; secure with toothpicks.

2. In a large skillet, brown roll-ups in oil over medium-high heat. Transfer to a 5-qt. slow cooker; top with spaghetti sauce. Cover and cook on low for 6-8 hours or until meat is tender.

3. Discard toothpicks. Serve roll-ups and sauce with spaghetti. If desired, sprinkle with additional cheese.

PER SERVING *289 cal., 11g fat (3g sat. fat), 96mg chol., 500mg sod., 9g carb. (0 sugars, 2g fiber), 38g pro.* **Diabetic Exchanges:** *4 lean meat, 2 vegetable.*

SLOW COOKER BEEF TOSTADAS

SLOW COOKER BEEF TOSTADAS

My husband, an Italian man, can't get enough Mexican food. He loves these slow-simmered tostadas. Pile on your best toppings!

—TERESA DEVONO RED LION, PA

PREP: 20 MIN. • **COOK:** 6 HOURS
MAKES: 6 SERVINGS

- 1 large onion, chopped
- ¼ cup lime juice
- 1 jalapeno pepper, seeded and minced
- 1 serrano pepper, seeded and minced
- 1 tablespoon chili powder
- 3 garlic cloves, minced
- ½ teaspoon ground cumin
- 1 beef top round steak (about 1½ pounds)
- 1 teaspoon salt
- ½ teaspoon pepper
- ¼ cup chopped fresh cilantro
- 12 corn tortillas (6 inches)
   Cooking spray

TOPPINGS
- 1½ cups shredded lettuce
- 1 medium tomato, finely chopped
- ¾ cup shredded sharp cheddar cheese
- ¾ cup reduced-fat sour cream, optional

1. Place the first seven ingredients in a 3- or 4-qt. slow cooker. Cut steak in half and sprinkle with salt and pepper; add to slow cooker. Cook, covered, on low 6-8 hours or until meat is tender.

2. Remove meat; cool slightly. Shred meat with two forks. Return beef to slow cooker and stir in cilantro; heat through. Spritz both sides of tortillas with cooking spray. Place in a single layer on baking sheets; broil 1-2 minutes on each side or until crisp. Spoon beef mixture over tortillas; top with lettuce, tomato, cheese and, if desired, sour cream.

NOTE *Wear disposable gloves when cutting hot peppers; the oils can burn skin. Avoid touching your face.*

PER SERVING *2 tostadas: 372 cal., 13g fat (6g sat. fat), 88mg chol., 602mg sod., 30g carb. (5g sugars, 5g fiber), 35g pro.* **Diabetic Exchanges:** *4 lean meat, 2 starch, ½ fat.*

MOROCCAN POT ROAST

I love veggies and my husband loves meat, so we're both happy with this twist on pot roast. With lots of chickpeas, eggplant, honey and mint, it's like something you might enjoy at a Marrakech bazaar.

—CATHERINE DEMPSEY CLIFTON PARK, NY

PREP: 25 MIN. • **COOK:** 7 HOURS
MAKES: 8 SERVINGS

- 2 tablespoons olive oil
- 3 small onions, chopped
- 3 tablespoons paprika
- 1 tablespoon plus ½ teaspoon garam masala, divided
- 1¼ teaspoons salt, divided
- ¼ teaspoon cayenne pepper
- 2 tablespoons tomato paste
- 1 can (15 ounces) chickpeas or garbanzo beans, rinsed and drained
- 1 can (14½ ounces) beef broth
- ¼ teaspoon pepper
- 1 boneless beef chuck roast (3 pounds)
- 4 medium carrots, cut diagonally into ¾-inch pieces
- 1 small eggplant, cubed
- 2 tablespoons honey
- 2 tablespoons minced fresh mint
  Hot cooked couscous or flatbreads, optional

1. In a large skillet, heat oil over medium heat; saute onions with the paprika, 1 tablespoon garam masala, ½ teaspoon salt and cayenne until tender, 4-5 minutes. Stir in tomato paste; cook and stir 1 minute. Stir in chickpeas and broth; transfer to a 5- or 6-qt. slow cooker.

2. Mix pepper and the remaining ½ teaspoon garam masala and ¾ teaspoon salt; rub over roast. Place in slow cooker. Add carrots and eggplant. Cook, covered, until meat and vegetables are tender, 7-9 hours.

3. Remove roast from slow cooker; break into pieces. Remove vegetables with a slotted spoon; skim fat from cooking juices. Stir in honey. Return beef and vegetables to slow cooker and heat through. Sprinkle with mint. If desired, serve with couscous.

FREEZE OPTION *Freeze cooled beef and vegetable mixture in freezer containers. To use, partially thaw in refrigerator overnight. Microwave, covered, on high in a microwave-safe dish until heated through, stirring gently.*

PER SERVING *435 cal., 21g fat (7g sat. fat), 111mg chol., 766mg sod., 23g carb., 6g fiber, 38g pro.*

MOROCCAN POT ROAST

TOP TIP

GARAM MASALA

The ground Indian spice blend garam masala is typically a combination of cloves, cinnamon, mace, cumin, and black and white peppercorns. It lends a wonderfully warm flavor to beef, chicken and lamb as well as potatoes and rice. Look for it in the spice aisle of your grocery store.

MEATY SLOPPY JOE POCKETS, PAGE 106

ITALIAN VEGGIE
BEEF SOUP, PAGE 100

BEEFY SANDWICHES, SOUPS & MORE

Ready for quick comfort? Sink your teeth into any of these sandwiches **piled high with flavor,** enjoy no-fuss wraps guaranteed to please or savor the **comfort of beefy stews** and fast soups. Nothing beats the classic pairing of **soup and sandwich,** so turn here for hearty meals that always **satisfy in a hurry.**

TEX-MEX CHEESESTEAK
SANDWICHES, PAGE 96

ONE-POT SPINACH BEEF SOUP, PAGE 103

TEX-MEX CHEESESTEAK SANDWICHES

TEX-MEX CHEESESTEAK SANDWICHES

We adore cheesesteaks and anything with Southwestern flavor, so I combined the two. If you crave even more firepower, add some chopped jalapenos.

—JOAN HALLFORD
NORTH RICHLAND HILLS, TX

START TO FINISH: 25 MIN.
MAKES: 4 SERVINGS

- 1 package (15 ounces) refrigerated beef tips with gravy
- 1 tablespoon canola oil
- 1 medium onion, halved and thinly sliced
- 1 banana pepper, cut into strips
- ⅛ teaspoon salt
- ⅛ teaspoon pepper
- 4 whole wheat hoagie buns, split
- ¼ cup mayonnaise
- ⅛ teaspoon chili powder, optional
- 8 slices pepper jack cheese

1. Preheat broiler. Heat beef tips with gravy according to package directions. Meanwhile, in a small skillet, heat oil over medium-high heat. Add the onion and pepper; cook and stir 4-6 minutes or until tender. Stir in salt and pepper.
2. Place buns on a baking sheet, cut side up. Mix mayonnaise and, if desired, chili powder; spread on roll bottoms. Layer with beef tips, onion mixture and cheese. Broil 3-4 in. from heat 1-2 minutes or until cheese is melted and buns are toasted.
PER SERVING *600 cal., 36g fat (11g sat. fat), 90mg chol., 1312mg sod., 42g carb. (9g sugars, 7g fiber), 32g pro.*

MEATBALL & PASTA SOUP

When I serve this power-packed soup, my son eats his spinach and actually likes it. We add French bread or dinner rolls so that we can soak up every drop.

—LAURA GREENBERG LAKE BALBOA, CA

START TO FINISH: 30 MIN.
MAKES: 8 SERVINGS

- 8 **cups vegetable stock**
- 1 **garlic clove, minced**
- 1 **teaspoon salt, divided**
- 1 **large egg**
- ½ **cup dry bread crumbs**
- ¼ **cup 2% milk**
- 2 **tablespoons ketchup**
- 2 **teaspoons Worcestershire sauce**
- 1 **teaspoon onion powder**
- ½ **teaspoon pepper**
- 1 **pound lean ground beef (90% lean)**
- 4 **medium carrots, chopped**
- 1 **cup uncooked orzo pasta**
- 1 **package (6 ounces) fresh baby spinach**

1. In a 6-qt. stockpot, bring stock, garlic and ¾ teaspoon salt to a boil. Meanwhile, in a large bowl, mix egg, bread crumbs, milk, ketchup, Worcestershire sauce, onion powder, pepper and remaining salt. Add beef; mix lightly but thoroughly. Shape into 1-in. balls.

2. Add carrots, pasta and meatballs to boiling stock. Reduce heat; simmer, uncovered, 10-12 minutes or until meatballs are cooked through and pasta is tender, stirring occasionally. Stir in spinach until wilted.

FREEZE OPTION *Freeze cooled soup in freezer containers. To use, partially thaw in refrigerator overnight. Heat through in a saucepan, stirring occasionally and adding a little water if necessary.*

PER SERVING *1½ cups: 254 cal., 6g fat (2g sat. fat), 59mg chol., 1058mg sod., 31g carb. (4g sugars, 2g fiber), 17g pro.*

AUTUMN SLOW-COOKED BEEF STEW

AUTUMN SLOW-COOKED BEEF STEW

If any dish could taste like a holiday, it's this one with beef, pears, walnuts and sweet dried apricots. We recommend a leafy salad and rolls to complete the masterpiece.

—AMY DODSON DURANGO, CO

PREP: 35 MIN. • **COOK:** 6 HOURS
MAKES: 8 SERVINGS

- 2 **pounds boneless beef chuck roast, cubed**
- ½ **teaspoon garlic salt**
- ½ **teaspoon pepper**
- 2 **tablespoons olive oil**
- 2 **cups dry red wine or reduced-sodium beef broth**
- 1 **cup reduced-sodium beef broth**
- 4 **garlic cloves, minced**
- 1 **teaspoon rubbed sage**
- 1 **teaspoon dried thyme**
- ½ **teaspoon salt**
- 2½ **pounds small red potatoes (about 20)**
- 4 **medium carrots, cut into 1-inch pieces**
- 1 **large onion, halved and sliced**
- 2 **medium pears, quartered**
- 1 **cup walnut halves**
- 1 **cup dried apricots**
- 2 **tablespoons cornstarch**
- 3 **tablespoons cold water**

1. Sprinkle beef with garlic salt and pepper. In a large skillet, heat oil over medium-high heat. Brown beef in batches. Remove with a slotted spoon; transfer to a 6-qt. slow cooker.

2. In a large bowl, combine wine, broth, garlic, sage, thyme and salt; pour over beef. Top with potatoes, carrots, onion, pears, walnuts and apricots. Cook, covered, on low 6-8 hours or until meat is tender; skim fat.

3. In a small bowl, mix cornstarch and water until smooth; gradually stir into stew. Cook, covered, on high 20-30 minutes or until sauce is thickened.

PER SERVING *1¾ cups: 522 cal., 23g fat (5g sat. fat), 74mg chol., 394mg sod., 51g carb. (17g sugars, 8g fiber), 29g pro.*

REUBEN
CALZONES

GRILLED BEEF & BLUE CHEESE SANDWICHES

⑤ INGREDIENTS FAST FIX ▶

REUBEN CALZONES

I love a Reuben sandwich, so I tried the fillings in a pizza pocket instead of on rye bread. This hand-held dinner is always a big-time winner at our house. Check out the spinach version as well.

—NICKIE FRYE EVANSVILLE, IN

START TO FINISH: 30 MIN.
MAKES: 4 SERVINGS

- 1 tube (13.8 ounces) refrigerated pizza crust
- 4 slices Swiss cheese
- 1 cup sauerkraut, rinsed and well drained
- ½ pound sliced cooked corned beef
  Thousand Island salad dressing

1. Preheat oven to 400°. On a lightly floured surface, unroll pizza crust dough and pat into a 12-in. square. Cut into four squares. Layer a fourth of the cheese, sauerkraut and corned beef diagonally over half of each square to within ½ in. of edges. Fold one corner over filling to the opposite corner, forming a triangle; press edges with a fork to seal. Place on greased baking sheets.
2. Bake 15-18 minutes or until golden brown. Serve with salad dressing.

FOR SAUSAGE & SPINACH CALZONES
Substitute mozzarella for Swiss cheese. Cook and drain ½ pound bulk Italian sausage; add 3 cups fresh baby spinach and cook until wilted. Stir in ½ cup part-skim ricotta cheese and ¼ teaspoon each salt and pepper. Proceed as directed. Serve with marinara sauce if desired.

PER SERVING *1 Reuben calzone (calculated without salad dressing): 430 cal., 17g fat (6g sat. fat), 66mg chol., 1607mg sod., 49g carb. (7g sugars, 2g fiber), 21g pro.*

⑤ INGREDIENTS FAST FIX ▶

GRILLED BEEF & BLUE CHEESE SANDWICHES

Roast beef, red onion and blue cheese really amp up this deluxe grilled sandwich. If you like a little spice, mix some horseradish into the simple spread.

—BONNIE HAWKINS ELKHORN, WI

START TO FINISH: 25 MIN.
MAKES: 4 SERVINGS

- 2 ounces cream cheese, softened
- 2 ounces crumbled blue cheese
- 8 slices sourdough bread
- ¾ pound thinly sliced deli roast beef
- ½ small red onion, thinly sliced
- ¼ cup olive oil

1. In a small bowl, mix cream cheese and blue cheese until blended. Spread over bread slices. Layer four of the slices with roast beef and onion; top with remaining bread slices.
2. Brush outsides of sandwiches with oil. In a large skillet, toast sandwiches over medium heat 4-5 minutes on each side or until golden brown.

PER SERVING *471 cal., 27g fat (9g sat. fat), 72mg chol., 1021mg sod., 31g carb. (4g sugars, 1g fiber), 27g pro.*

FAST FIX ▶

BISTRO BEEF SANDWICH

Red pepper lends a nice crunch to this satisfying roast beef sandwich. You'll love the zing added by the garlic-herb spread.

—DAVID LOCKE WOBURN, MA

START TO FINISH: 15 MIN.
MAKES: 1 SERVING

- 2 slices rye bread
- 1 tablespoon garlic-herb spreadable cheese
- 3 slices deli roast beef
- 2 slices tomato
- 1 romaine leaf
- ¼ cup julienned sweet red pepper
- 2 teaspoons French salad dressing

Spread one bread slice with spreadable cheese. Layer with beef, tomato, lettuce and red pepper. Spread remaining bread with salad dressing; place on top.

PER SERVING *362 cal., 16g fat (6g sat. fat), 53mg chol., 957mg sod., 37g carb. (7g sugars, 5g fiber), 20g pro.*

EAT SMART FAST FIX ▶
ITALIAN VEGGIE BEEF SOUP (PICTURED ON PAGE 95)

My sweet father-in-law would bring this chunky soup to our house when we were under the weather. We like it so well, we take it to our own friends who need comfort. It always does the trick.
—**SUE WEBB** REISTERSTOWN, MD

START TO FINISH: 30 MIN.
MAKES: 12 SERVINGS (4 QUARTS)

- 1½ **pounds lean ground beef (90% lean)**
- 2 **medium onions, chopped**
- 4 **cups chopped cabbage**
- 1 **package (16 ounces) frozen mixed vegetables**
- 1 **can (28 ounces) crushed tomatoes**
- 1 **bay leaf**
- 3 **teaspoons Italian seasoning**
- 1 **teaspoon salt**
- ½ **teaspoon pepper**
- 2 **cartons (32 ounces each) reduced-sodium beef broth**

1. In a 6-qt. stockpot, cook ground beef and onions over medium-high heat 6-8 minutes or until beef is no longer pink, breaking up beef into crumbles; drain.
2. Add cabbage, mixed vegetables, tomatoes, seasonings and broth; bring to a boil. Reduce heat; simmer, uncovered, 10-15 minutes or until cabbage is crisp-tender. Remove bay leaf.

FREEZE OPTION *Freeze cooled soup in freezer containers. To use, partially thaw in refrigerator overnight. Heat through in a saucepan, stirring occasionally and adding a little broth if necessary.*

PER SERVING *1⅓ cups: 159 cal., 5g fat (2g sat. fat), 38mg chol., 646mg sod., 14g carb. (6g sugars, 4g fiber), 15g pro.* **Diabetic Exchanges:** *2 lean meat, 1 vegetable, ½ starch.*

WEST COAST SNAPPY JOES

EAT SMART FAST FIX ▶
WEST COAST SNAPPY JOES

Meet my California-inspired sloppy joe! Load it up with whatever taco toppings you like. The meat filling is also incredible served over mac and cheese.
—**DEVON DELANEY** WESTPORT, CT

START TO FINISH: 30 MIN.
MAKES: 6 SERVINGS

- 1 **pound lean ground beef (90% lean)**
- 1 **medium onion, chopped**
- 1 **garlic clove, minced**
- 1 **can (8 ounces) tomato sauce**
- ⅓ **cup soft sun-dried tomato halves (not packed in oil), chopped**
- ⅓ **cup chopped roasted sweet red peppers**
- 2 **tablespoons chopped pickled jalapeno peppers**
- 2 **tablespoons tomato paste**
- 1 **tablespoon brown sugar**
- 1 **tablespoon balsamic vinegar**
- ½ **teaspoon Montreal steak seasoning**
- ½ **teaspoon pepper**
- 6 **hamburger buns, split**
  Optional toppings: chopped avocado, sour cream, shredded cheddar cheese and chopped green onions

1. In a large skillet, cook beef, onion and garlic over medium heat 6-8 minutes or until beef is no longer pink, breaking up beef into crumbles; drain.
2. Stir in tomato sauce, sun-dried tomatoes, roasted peppers, jalapenos, tomato paste, brown sugar, vinegar, steak seasoning and pepper. Bring to a boil. Reduce heat; simmer, uncovered, 4-6 minutes or until thickened, stirring occasionally. Serve on buns with toppings as desired.

FREEZE OPTION *Freeze cooled meat mixture in freezer containers. To use, partially thaw in refrigerator overnight. Heat through in a saucepan, stirring occasionally and adding a little water if necessary.*

NOTE *This recipe was tested with sun-dried tomatoes that are ready to use without soaking. When using other sun-dried tomatoes that are not oil-packed, cover with boiling water and let stand until soft. Drain before using.*

PER SERVING *1 sandwich (calculated without optional toppings): 288 cal., 8g fat (3g sat. fat), 47mg chol., 575mg sod., 32g carb. (10g sugars, 3g fiber), 20g pro.* **Diabetic Exchanges:** *2 starch, 2 lean meat.*

BEEF BARLEY SOUP WITH ROASTED VEGETABLES

The beauty of this soup is that I can roast the vegetables in the oven while the soup simmers on the stovetop. Then I simply add them during the last minutes of cooking.
—**GAYLA SCOTT** WEST JEFFERSON, NC

PREP: 25 MIN. • **COOK:** 1 HOUR
MAKES: 8 SERVINGS

- ¼ cup all-purpose flour
- 1 teaspoon salt
- ½ teaspoon pepper
- 1 pound beef stew meat (¾-inch cubes)
- 5 tablespoons olive oil, divided
- 1 large portobello mushroom, stem removed, chopped
- 1 medium onion, chopped
- 1 fennel bulb, chopped
- 1 garlic clove, minced
- 8 cups beef stock
- 2 cups water
- 2 cups cubed peeled butternut squash
- 1 large baking potato, peeled and cubed
- 2 large carrots, cut into ½-inch slices
- ⅔ cup quick-cooking barley
- 2 teaspoons minced fresh thyme
  Dash ground nutmeg
- ¼ cup minced fresh parsley

1. In a small bowl, mix the flour, salt and pepper; sprinkle over beef and toss to coat. In a Dutch oven, heat 2 tablespoons oil over medium heat. Add beef; brown evenly. Remove from the pan.

2. In the same pan, heat 1 tablespoon oil over medium-high heat. Add the mushroom, onion and fennel; cook and stir for 4-5 minutes or until tender. Stir in garlic; cook 1 minute longer. Add stock and water, stirring to loosen browned bits from pan. Return beef to pan. Bring to a boil; reduce heat. Cover and simmer for 40-60 minutes or until meat is tender.

3. Meanwhile, place the squash, potato and carrots on a greased 15x10x1-in. baking pan; drizzle with remaining oil and toss to coat. Bake at 425° for 20-25 minutes or until vegetables are almost tender, stirring twice.

4. Add barley, thyme, nutmeg and roasted vegetables to soup; return to a boil. Reduce heat; cover and simmer for 10-12 minutes or until barley is tender. Sprinkle with parsley.

FREEZE OPTION *Freeze cooled soup in freezer containers. To use, partially thaw in refrigerator overnight. Heat through in a saucepan, stirring occasionally and adding a little broth or water if necessary.*

PER SERVING *1½ cups: 339 cal., 13g fat (3g sat. fat), 35mg chol., 855mg sod., 37g carb. (7g sugars, 6g fiber), 20g pro.*

BEEF BARLEY SOUP WITH ROASTED VEGETABLES

---

⑤INGREDIENTS FAST FIX

TROPICAL BEEF WRAP

For my finicky little ones, I create fast, tasty recipes like this tropical sandwich wrap. It's nice for using up leftover roast beef in a pinch.
—**AMY TONG** ANAHEIM, CA

START TO FINISH: 15 MIN
MAKES: 4 SERVINGS

- 1 carton (8 ounces) spreadable pineapple cream cheese
- 4 flour tortillas (10 inches)
- 4 cups fresh baby spinach (about 4 ounces)
- ¾ pound thinly sliced deli roast beef
- 1 medium mango, peeled and sliced

Spread cream cheese over tortillas to within 1 in. of edges. Layer with spinach, roast beef and mango. Roll up tightly and serve.

PER SERVING *522 cal., 20g fat (10g sat. fat), 100mg chol., 1211mg sod., 58g carb. (21g sugars, 4g fiber), 26g pro.*

FAJITA
BURGER
WRAPS

FAJITA BURGER WRAPS

This combo gives you a tender burger, crisp veggies and a crunchy shell—plus fajita flavor. Kids love it.

—**ANTONIO SMITH** CANAL WINCHESTER, OH

START TO FINISH: 30 MIN.
MAKES: 4 SERVINGS

- 1 **pound lean ground beef (90% lean)**
- 2 **tablespoons fajita seasoning mix**
- 2 **teaspoons canola oil**
- 1 **medium green pepper, cut into thin strips**
- 1 **medium red sweet pepper, cut into thin strips**
- 1 **medium onion, halved and sliced**
- 4 **flour tortillas (10 inches)**
- ¾ **cup shredded cheddar cheese**

1. In a large bowl, combine beef and seasoning mix, mixing lightly but thoroughly. Shape into four ½-in.-thick patties.

2. In a large skillet, heat oil over medium heat. Add burgers; cook 4 minutes on each side. Remove from pan. In the same skillet, add peppers and onion; cook and stir 5-7 minutes or until lightly browned and tender.

3. On the center of each tortilla, place ½ cup pepper mixture, one burger and 3 tablespoons cheese. Fold sides of tortilla over burger; fold top and bottom to close, forming a square.

4. Wipe skillet clean. Place wraps in skillet, seam side down. Cook on medium heat 1-2 minutes on each side or until golden brown and a thermometer inserted in beef reads 160°.

PER SERVING *533 cal., 23g fat (9g sat. fat), 92mg chol., 1190mg sod., 45g carb. (5g sugars, 3g fiber), 34g pro.*

ONE-POT SPINACH BEEF SOUP (PICTURED ON PAGE 95)

My idea of a winning weeknight meal is this beefy soup that simmers in one big pot. Grate some Parmesan and pass the saltines!

—**JULIE DAVIS** JACKSONVILLE, FL

START TO FINISH: 30 MIN.
MAKES: 8 SERVINGS

- 1 **pound ground beef**
- 3 **garlic cloves, minced**
- 2 **cartons (32 ounces each) reduced-sodium beef broth**
- 2 **cans (14½ ounces each) diced tomatoes with green pepper, celery and onion, undrained**
- 1 **teaspoon dried basil**
- ½ **teaspoon pepper**
- ¼ **teaspoon dried oregano**
- ¼ **teaspoon salt**
- 3 **cups uncooked bow tie pasta**
- 4 **cups fresh spinach, coarsely chopped Grated Parmesan cheese**

1. In a 6-qt. stockpot, cook beef and garlic over medium heat 6-8 minutes or until beef is no longer pink, breaking up beef into crumbles; drain. Stir in broth, tomatoes and seasonings; bring to a boil. Stir in pasta; return to a boil. Cook, uncovered, 7-9 minutes or until the pasta is tender.
2. Stir in spinach until wilted. Sprinkle servings with cheese.

PER SERVING 1⅓ cups (calculated without cheese): 258 cal., 7g fat (3g sat. fat), 40mg chol., 909mg sod., 30g carb. (8g sugars, 3g fiber), 17g pro.

SWAP IN SAUSAGE

This soup is very tasty and filling. Made this a second time using Italian sausage instead of the ground beef. It added extra flavor.

—**JARVISFAMILY** TASTEOFHOME.COM

BEEF STROGANOFF SANDWICHES

BEEF STROGANOFF SANDWICHES

For a new take on a classic comfort food, we turn beef stroganoff into open-faced sandwiches. They come together fast and our family always devours them.

—**ALISON GARCIA** BEATRICE, NE

START TO FINISH: 25 MIN.
MAKES: 6 SERVINGS

- 1 **pound ground beef**
- 1 **cup sliced fresh mushrooms**
- 1 **small green pepper, finely chopped**
- 1 **small onion, finely chopped**
- 1 **envelope ranch dip mix**
- ¾ **cup sour cream**
- 1 **loaf (about 8 ounces) French bread**
- 2 **cups shredded part-skim mozzarella cheese**

1. Preheat broiler. In a large skillet, cook beef, mushrooms, pepper and onion over medium-high heat 8-10 minutes or until beef is no longer pink, breaking up beef into crumbles; drain. Stir in dip mix and sour cream.
2. Cut French bread horizontally in half; place halves on a baking sheet, cut side up. Broil 3-4 in. from heat 1-2 minutes or until lightly toasted. Remove from broiler.
3. Spoon beef mixture over bread. Sprinkle with cheese. Broil 1-2 minutes longer or until cheese is lightly browned. To serve, cut each into three pieces.

PER SERVING 443 cal., 22g fat (11g sat. fat), 87mg chol., 1124mg sod., 28g carb. (3g sugars, 1g fiber), 29g pro.

**MOROCCAN
APPLE BEEF STEW**

FREEZE OPTION *Freeze cooled stew in freezer containers. To use, partially thaw in refrigerator overnight. Heat through in a saucepan, stirring occasionally and adding a little broth if necessary.*
PER SERVING *1 cup (calculated without rice): 339 cal., 13g fat (4g sat. fat), 88mg chol., 905mg sod., 24g carb. (14g sugars, 2g fiber), 29g pro.*

(5) INGREDIENTS FAST FIX

BROCCOLI-CHEDDAR BEEF ROLLS

My grandma taught me how to make these rolls—although I've condensed the recipe a bit over the years. Try making them with ham or just veggies instead of ground beef. They freeze well and reheat well in the microwave.
—**KENT CALL** RIVERSIDE, UT

START TO FINISH: 30 MIN.
MAKES: 6 SERVINGS

- ½ **pound lean ground beef (90% lean)**
- 2 **cups chopped fresh broccoli**
- 1 **small onion, chopped**
- ½ **teaspoon salt**
- ¼ **teaspoon pepper**
- 6 **hard rolls**
- 2 **cups shredded cheddar cheese, divided**

1. Preheat to 325°. In a large skillet, cook and crumble beef with broccoli and onion over medium heat until no longer pink, 4-6 minutes. Stir in salt and pepper.

2. Cut one third off the top of each roll; discard or save for another use. Hollow out bottoms, leaving ½-in.-thick shells; place on a baking sheet.

3. Tear bread removed from centers into ½-in. pieces and place in a bowl. Stir in 1½ cups cheese and beef mixture. Spoon into bread shells. Sprinkle with remaining cheese. Bake until heated through and cheese is melted, 10-15 minutes.

PER SERVING *394 cal., 18g fat (9g sat. fat), 61mg chol., 783mg sod., 34g carb. (2g sugars, 2g fiber), 23g pro.*

MOROCCAN APPLE BEEF STEW

I love the mix of sweet and savory flavors in this stew. It's the perfect blend of adventurous and comforting, and it's a fun dish to share with friends and family.
—**TRISHA KRUSE** EAGLE, ID

PREP: 20 MIN. • **COOK:** 2 HOURS
MAKES: 8 SERVINGS

- 1¼ **teaspoons salt**
- ½ **teaspoon ground cinnamon**
- ½ **teaspoon pepper**
- ¼ **teaspoon ground allspice**
- 2½ **pounds beef stew meat, cut into 1-inch pieces**
- 2 **to 3 tablespoons olive oil**
- 1 **large onion, chopped (about 2 cups)**
- 3 **garlic cloves, minced**
- 1 **can (15 ounces) tomato sauce**
- 1 **can (14½ ounces) beef broth**
- 1 **cup pitted dried plums, coarsely chopped**
- 1 **tablespoon honey**
- 2 **medium Fuji or Gala apples, peeled and cut into 1½-inch pieces**
  Hot cooked rice or couscous, optional

1. Mix salt, cinnamon, pepper and allspice; sprinkle over beef and toss to coat. In a Dutch oven, heat 2 tablespoons oil over medium heat. Brown beef in batches, adding additional oil as necessary. Remove the beef with a slotted spoon.

2. Add onion to same pan; cook and stir 6-8 minutes or until tender. Add garlic; cook 1 minute longer. Stir in tomato sauce, broth, dried plums and honey. Return beef to pan; bring to a boil. Reduce heat; simmer, covered, 1½ hours.

3. Add apples; cook, covered, 30-45 minutes longer or until beef and apples are tender. Skim fat. If desired, serve stew with rice.

FAST FIX ▸

CURRIED BEEF PITAS WITH CUCUMBER SAUCE

A good friend gave me this recipe when I first got married. Because some of the ingredients weren't familiar to me, I was apprehensive about trying it...but years later, it remains a family favorite!

—SHANNON KOENE BLACKSBURG, VA

START TO FINISH: 25 MIN.
MAKES: 4 SERVINGS (1½ CUPS SAUCE)

- 1 **cup fat-free plain Greek yogurt**
- 1 **cup finely chopped peeled cucumber**
- 1 **tablespoon minced fresh mint**
- 2 **garlic cloves, minced**
- 2 **teaspoons snipped fresh dill**
- 2 **teaspoons lemon juice**
- ¼ **teaspoon salt**

PITAS

- 1 **pound lean ground beef (90% lean)**
- 1 **small onion, chopped**
- 1 **medium Golden Delicious apple, finely chopped**
- ¼ **cup raisins**
- 2 **teaspoons curry powder**
- ¼ **teaspoon salt**
- 8 **whole wheat pita pocket halves**

1. In a small bowl, mix the first seven ingredients. Refrigerate until serving.
2. In a large skillet, cook beef and onion over medium heat 6-8 minutes or until beef is no longer pink, breaking up beef into crumbles; drain. Add apple, raisins, curry powder and salt; cook until apple is tender, stirring occasionally. Serve in pita halves with sauce.

PER SERVING *2 filled pita halves with ⅓ cup sauce: 429 cal., 11g fat (4g sat. fat), 71mg chol., 686mg sod., 50g carb. (13g sugars, 6g fiber), 36g pro.*

**CURRIED BEEF PITAS
WITH CUCUMBER SAUCE**

MEATY SLOPPY JOE POCKETS

It's easy to turn sloppy joes into hearty hot pocket snacks. I make the filling ahead and use refrigerated biscuits for all the goodness of sloppy joes in a neat, hand-held pocket!
—**SHELLY FLYE** ALBION, ME

PREP: 45 MIN. + COOLING • **BAKE:** 20 MIN.
MAKES: 8 SERVINGS

- 1   pound lean ground beef (90% lean)
- ¼   cup finely chopped onion
- ¼   cup finely chopped celery
- ¼   cup shredded carrot
- 1   can (8 ounces) tomato sauce
- ¼   cup ketchup
- 2   tablespoons brown sugar
- 1   tablespoon red wine vinegar
- 1   tablespoon Worcestershire sauce
- 1   tablespoon tomato paste
- 1   tube (16.3 ounces) large refrigerated buttermilk biscuits
- ½   cup shredded cheddar cheese, optional

1. In a large skillet, cook beef, onion, celery and carrot over medium heat 6-8 minutes or until beef is no longer pink and vegetables are tender, breaking up beef into crumbles; drain.

2. Stir in tomato sauce, ketchup, brown sugar, vinegar, Worcestershire sauce and tomato paste. Bring to a boil. Reduce heat; simmer, uncovered, 10-15 minutes or until thickened, stirring occasionally. Cool completely.

3. Preheat oven to 350°. On a lightly floured surface, pat or roll each biscuit into a 6-in. circle. Spoon scant ⅓ cup beef mixture over half of each circle to within ½ in. of edge. If desired, sprinkle with cheese. Fold dough over filling; press edge with a fork to seal.

4. Place on an ungreased baking sheet. Cut three slits in top of each pocket. Bake 18-20 minutes or until golden brown.

PER SERVING *1 pocket (calculated without cheese): 294 cal., 11g fat (4g sat. fat), 35mg chol., 909mg sod., 33g carb. (9g sugars, 1g fiber), 15g pro.*

MEATY SLOPPY JOE POCKETS

MOM'S DYNAMITE SANDWICHES

Whenever we had a big family get-together, my mom would make her delicious dynamite sandwiches. These are a staple in the area where I grew up—what cheesesteaks are to Philadelphia, dynamites are to Woonsocket, Rhode Island!

—**KATHY HEWITT** CRANSTON, RI

PREP: 15 MIN. • **COOK:** 1 HOUR 20 MIN.
MAKES: 16 SERVINGS

- 2½ **pounds ground beef**
- 5 **medium green peppers, finely chopped**
- 4 **large onions, chopped (6 cups)**
- 1 **can (28 ounces) crushed tomatoes in puree**
- 1 **can (16 ounces) tomato sauce**
- 1 **can (12 ounces) tomato paste**
- 1 **cup water**
- 2 **tablespoons sugar**
- 2 **tablespoons garlic powder**
- 1 **tablespoon Italian seasoning**
- 1 **tablespoon dried oregano**
- 2¼ **teaspoons salt**
- 2 **teaspoons hot pepper sauce**
- 1½ **teaspoons pepper**
- ½ **teaspoon crushed red pepper flakes, optional**
- 16 **hoagie buns or other sandwich rolls, split**

1. In a Dutch oven, cook beef over medium-high heat 8-10 minutes or until no longer pink, breaking into crumbles; drain.

2. Stir in all remaining ingredients except buns. Bring to a boil. Reduce heat; simmer, uncovered, 1 hour or until desired consistency and flavors are blended, stirring occasionally. Serve on buns.

PER SERVING *414 cal., 13g fat (4g sat. fat), 44mg chol., 1003mg sod., 52g carb. (14g sugars, 5g fiber), 24g pro.*

FAMILY-FAVORITE ITALIAN BEEF SANDWICHES

EAT SMART

FAMILY-FAVORITE ITALIAN BEEF SANDWICHES

With only a few ingredients, this roast beef is a snap to throw together in the slow cooker.

—**LAUREN ADAMSON** LAYTON, UT

PREP: 10 MIN. • **COOK:** 8 HOURS
MAKES: 12 SERVINGS

- 1 **jar (16 ounces) sliced pepperoncini, undrained**
- 1 **can (14½ ounces) diced tomatoes, undrained**
- 1 **medium onion, chopped**
- ½ **cup water**
- 2 **packages Italian salad dressing mix**
- 1 **teaspoon dried oregano**
- ½ **teaspoon garlic powder**
- 1 **beef rump roast or bottom round roast (3 to 4 pounds)**
- 12 **Italian rolls, split**

1. In a bowl, mix the first seven ingredients. Place roast in a 5- or 6-qt. slow cooker. Pour pepperoncini mixture over top. Cook, covered, on low 8-10 hours or until meat is tender.

2. Remove roast; cool slightly. Skim fat from cooking juices. Shred beef with two forks. Return beef and cooking juices to slow cooker; heat through. Serve on rolls.

TO MAKE AHEAD *In a large resealable plastic freezer bag, combine the first seven ingredients. Add roast; seal bag and freeze. To use, place filled freezer bag in refrigerator for 48 hours or until roast is completely thawed. Cook and serve as directed. Freeze option: Freeze cooled, cooked beef mixture in freezer containers. To use, partially thaw in refrigerator overnight. Heat through in a saucepan, stirring occasionally and adding a little water if necessary.*

PER SERVING *278 cal., 7g fat (2g sat. fat), 67mg chol., 735mg sod., 24g carb. (3g sugars, 2g fiber), 26g pro.* **Diabetic Exchanges:** *3 lean meat, 2 starch.*

When it comes to family-favorite dinners, you just can't beat the flavor, convenience and versatility of chicken. From grilled greats to Southern-fried classics, these dishes are all winners.

CHICKEN

CHICKEN [101]

For a fast and easy dinner solution, chicken is an all-time lifesaver.

Winner, winner, chicken dinner! Cook up a meal that delivers thumbs-up approval when you make chicken the main ingredient. Easy to prepare and fast to cook up, chicken dishes are versatile enough to satisfy all of your culinary cravings.

Slather chicken with barbecue sauce, simmer it in a soup, stir-fry it with veggies or roast it for a Sunday dinner you'll never forget. Read the following tips, then get cooking!

A BIRD IN THE HAND

- Buy chicken that is fresh and moist. The color of the skin indicates the chicken's diet, not its freshness.

- Check to be sure the package is free of tears and holes. Avoid packages with excessive liquid.

- If the sell-by date is the same day you're purchasing the chicken, either use the poultry that day or freeze it for later.

THE HEN HOUSE

- A whole broiler/fryer chicken weighs up to 4.5 pounds. You can also find broiler/fryer chickens that have been sectioned into breast halves, thighs, drumsticks and wings. These chickens are great for grilling, roasting and frying.

- A roaster chicken is similar to a broiler/fryer chicken, but it is older and heavier. It is ideal for roasting, as it's less likely to dry out.

- Drumsticks are the lower portions of the leg. Chicken legs are the attached drumstick and thigh. Drumettes are the first sections of the wings.

- Organic poultry labels mean that a producer certified by USDA's National Organic Program raised the chicken. Natural poultry labels indicate that the chicken does not contain artificial or synthetic flavors or ingredients.

BARBECUED STRAWBERRY CHICKEN, PAGE 175

RULE THE ROOST

The great thing about cooking with chicken is that nearly any cut or type works well with just about any cooking method—from grilling to roasting. Stick to boneless breasts, however, when preparing chicken on the stovetop, and remember that cut parts of the bird work best when deep-frying.

When baking, roasting or grilling a whole chicken, follow the recipe's directions closely. Always use an instant-read thermometer to ensure the meat is cooked properly.

A THERMOMETER INSERTED IN THE THICKEST PART OF THE THIGH OF A WHOLE CHICKEN SHOULD READ 170° to 175° for proper food safety.

SMOKED MOZZARELLA CHICKEN WITH PASTA, PAGE 158

SPICY BBQ CHICKEN WINGS, PAGE 122

Neck
Back
Tail
Wing
Breast
Leg
Thigh

[CHICKEN LITTLE]

Whether you're an experienced cook or just learning your way around the kitchen, chicken offers the versatility and ease folks look for when it's time to prepare a meal. For busy weeknights and special celebrations, chicken is a natural choice. Turn the page and cook up a winner tonight!

BUFFALO WING DIP, PAGE 122

JALAPENO POPPER POCKET, PAGE 121

EASY APPETIZERS

Think beyond wings! Chicken is a tasty, versatile ingredient that can make an entire buffet of appetizers. **Dips, sliders, nachos, meatballs, pizza** and all kinds of finger food— something for every taste. And of course there are wings, too, because **wings are awesome!** Check out these sure-to-be new favorites!

PINEAPPLE CHICKEN SLIDERS, PAGE 115

RICH CHICKEN ALFREDO PIZZA, PAGE 117

GRILLED CHERRY-GLAZED CHICKEN WINGS

GRILLED CHERRY-GLAZED CHICKEN WINGS

When I bring these grilled wings to a party, there are never any leftovers. The cherry glaze transforms regular chicken wings into something special.

—ASHLEY GABLE ATLANTA, GA

PREP: 20 MIN. • **GRILL:** 15 MIN.
MAKES: 1 DOZEN

- 12 **chicken wings (about 3 pounds)**
- 3 **tablespoons canola oil, divided**
- 1 **garlic clove, minced**
- 1 **cup ketchup**
- ½ **cup cider vinegar**
- ½ **cup cherry preserves**
- 2 **tablespoons Louisiana-style hot sauce**
- 1 **tablespoon Worcestershire sauce**
- 3 **teaspoons coarse salt, divided**
- 1 **teaspoon coarsely ground pepper, divided**

1. Using a sharp knife, cut through the two wing joints; discard wing tips. In a small saucepan, heat 1 tablespoon oil over medium heat. Add garlic; cook and stir 1 minute. Stir in ketchup, vinegar, preserves, hot sauce, Worcestershire sauce, 1 teaspoon salt and ½ teaspoon pepper. Cook and stir until heated through. Brush wings with remaining oil; sprinkle with remaining salt and pepper.
2. Grill, covered, over medium heat for 15-18 minutes or until juices run clear, turning occasionally and brushing with glaze during the last 5 minutes of grilling. Serve with the remaining glaze.
PER SERVING *1 chicken wing: 214 cal., 12g fat (3g sat. fat), 36mg chol., 867mg sod., 15g carb. (14g sugars, 0 fiber), 12g pro.*

PINEAPPLE CHICKEN SLIDERS (PICTURED ON PAGE 113)

For fun appetizers that tide over even the hungriest guests, try these mini sandwiches. My youngest daughter likes their small size and the tangy sweetness of the pineapple.

—MARIA VASSEUR VALENCIA, CA

PREP: 25 MIN. • **BROIL:** 10 MIN.
MAKES: 8 SERVINGS

- 1 can (8 ounces) unsweetened crushed pineapple
- ¼ cup shredded carrot
- 2 tablespoons grated onion
- 1 tablespoon plus ½ teaspoon reduced-sodium soy sauce, divided
- ¼ teaspoon garlic powder
- 1 pound ground chicken
- 8 whole wheat dinner rolls, split
- ¼ cup reduced-fat sour cream
- 2 tablespoons mayonnaise
- ¼ teaspoon ground ginger
- 1 cup shredded lettuce

1. Drain the pineapple, reserving 2 teaspoons juice. In a large bowl, combine carrot, onion, 1 tablespoon soy sauce, garlic powder and drained pineapple. Add chicken; mix lightly but thoroughly. Shape into eight ½-in.-thick patties.
2. Place rolls on a greased 15x10x1-in. baking pan, cut side up. Broil 4 in. from heat 30-60 seconds or until toasted. Remove from pan; keep warm.
3. Add burgers to same pan. Broil 4 in. from heat for 4-6 minutes on each side or until a thermometer reads 165°.
4. Meanwhile, in a small bowl, mix sour cream, mayonnaise, ginger, remaining soy sauce and reserved pineapple juice. Serve burgers on rolls with lettuce and sauce.
PER SERVING *1 slider: 223 cal., 9g fat (2g sat. fat), 39mg chol., 331mg sod., 24g carb. (8g sugars, 3g fiber), 13g pro.*

BUFFALO CHICKEN POTATO SKINS

BUFFALO CHICKEN POTATO SKINS

Take two popular restaurant nibbles, put them together and you'll have an unforgettable appetizer for the next get-together.

—BRIDGET O'CONNOR
ROUND LAKE BEACH, IL

PREP: 70 MIN. • **BAKE:** 15 MIN.
MAKES: 2 DOZEN

- 12 small red potatoes (about 1½ pounds)
- 2 teaspoons canola oil
- 1½ cups refrigerated shredded chicken
- ⅓ cup Buffalo wing sauce
- 1½ cups shredded cheddar cheese
- 1⅓ cups crumbled cooked bacon
- 1⅓ cups sour cream
- 1 cup shredded carrots
  Green onions, thinly sliced

1. Preheat oven to 400°. Scrub the potatoes; pierce several times with a fork. Rub potatoes with oil. Place in a 13x9-in. baking pan. Bake 50-55 minutes or until tender.
2. When cool enough to handle, cut each potato crosswise in half. Scoop out the pulp, leaving ⅛-in.-thick shells (save removed pulp for another use).
3. In a large bowl, combine chicken and Buffalo sauce. Spoon the chicken mixture into potatoes. Top with cheese and bacon. Return potatoes to baking pan. Bake, skin side down, 15-18 minutes or until cheese is melted. Serve with sour cream, carrots and green onions.
PER SERVING *1 filled potato skin: 122 cal., 7g fat (3g sat. fat), 17mg chol., 404mg sod., 9g carb. (3g sugars, 1g fiber), 7g pro.*

BUFFALO CHICKEN
POCKETS

⑤ INGREDIENTS FAST FIX

BUFFALO CHICKEN POCKETS

Here's my idea of pub food made easy: biscuits flavored with Buffalo wing sauce and blue cheese. They're my Friday night favorite.
—**MARIA REGAKIS** SAUGUS, MA

START TO FINISH: 30 MIN.
MAKES: 8 SERVINGS

- ¾ **pound ground chicken**
- ⅓ **cup Buffalo wing sauce**
- 1 **tube (16.3 ounces) large refrigerated buttermilk biscuits**
- ½ **cup shredded cheddar cheese**
  Blue cheese salad dressing, optional

1. Preheat oven to 375°. In a large skillet, cook the chicken over medium heat for 5-7 minutes or until no longer pink, breaking into crumbles; drain. Remove from heat; stir in wing sauce.
2. On a lightly floured surface, roll each biscuit into a 6-in. circle; top each with ¼ cup chicken mixture and 2 tablespoons cheese. Fold dough over filling; pinch edge to seal.
3. Transfer to an ungreased baking sheet. Bake for 12-14 minutes or until golden brown. If desired, serve with blue cheese dressing.
FREEZE OPTION *Freeze cooled pockets in a resealable plastic freezer bag. To use, reheat pockets on an ungreased baking sheet in a preheated 375° oven until heated through.*
PER SERVING *1 pocket (calculated without blue cheese dressing): 258 cal., 12g fat (5g sat. fat), 35mg chol., 987mg sod., 25g carb. (3g sugars, 1g fiber), 12g pro.*

RICH CHICKEN ALFREDO PIZZA (PICTURED ON PAGE 113)

After a busy day, settle in for this appetizing homemade pizza. With a prebaked crust and simple Alfredo sauce, it's easy and delicious.
—**TAMMY HANKS** GAINSVILLE, FL

PREP: 30 MIN. • **BAKE:** 15 MIN.
MAKES: 1 PIZZA (12 APPETIZER SLICES OR 8 MAIN DISH)

- 2½ **teaspoons butter**
- 1 **garlic clove, minced**
- 1½ **cups heavy whipping cream**
- 3 **tablespoons grated Parmesan cheese**
- ½ **teaspoon salt**
- ¼ **teaspoon pepper**
- 1 **tablespoon minced fresh parsley**
- 1 **prebaked 12-inch thin pizza crust**
- 1 **cup cubed cooked chicken breast**
- 1 **cup thinly sliced baby portobello mushrooms**
- 1 **cup fresh baby spinach**
- 2 **cups shredded part-skim mozzarella cheese**

1. In a small saucepan over medium heat, melt butter. Add garlic; cook and stir for 1 minute. Add cream; cook until liquid is reduced by half, about 15-20 minutes. Add Parmesan cheese, salt and pepper; cook and stir until thickened. Remove from heat; stir in parsley. Cool slightly.
2. Place crust on an ungreased baking sheet; spread with cream mixture. Top with chicken, mushrooms, spinach and mozzarella cheese. Bake at 450° for 15-20 minutes or until cheese is melted and crust is golden brown.
PER SERVING *1 slice: 391 cal., 26g fat (15g sat. fat), 87mg chol., 612mg sod., 21g carb. (3g sugars, 1g fiber), 18g pro.*

BBQ CHICKEN WAFFLE FRIES

BBQ CHICKEN WAFFLE FRIES

This dish sounds so wrong but tastes so right! Trust me: Barbecue chicken leftovers are fantastic with fries. We add lettuce, tomato and pickle, but you can add anything you like.
—**JANET TELLEEN** RUSSELL, IA

PREP: 10 MIN. • **BAKE:** 25 MIN.
MAKES: 8 SERVINGS

- 1 **package (22 ounces) frozen waffle-cut fries**
- 12 **ounces refrigerated shredded barbecued chicken (1½ cups)**
- 1 **cup shredded Colby-Monterey Jack cheese**
- ¼ **cup chopped red onion**
- ½ **cup shredded lettuce**
- 1 **medium tomato, chopped**
- ¼ **cup chopped dill pickle**
  Pickled banana peppers

Bake waffle fries according to package directions. Transfer to a 10-in. ovenproof skillet. Top with chicken, cheese and onion. Bake 5 minutes longer or until cheese is melted. Top with lettuce, tomato and pickle; serve with peppers.
PER SERVING *⅔ cup: 243 cal., 11g fat (5g sat. fat), 29mg chol., 476mg sod., 28g carb. (6g sugars, 2g fiber), 10g pro.*

TOP TIP

KEEP CHICKEN WINGS ON HAND

Wings are always a hit when we entertain; planning ahead makes prep so much easier. I buy whole wings in bulk, cut them into three pieces, discard the tips and freeze the pieces in freezer bags. Preparing appetizers on party day is a snap!
—**LORRAINE CALAND** THUNDER BAY, ON

WARM CHICKEN FIESTA DIP

This crowd-pleasing dip is always a success, whether I follow the recipe as written or if I substitute shredded pork and stir in chopped fresh mushrooms.

—SHANNON COPLEY PICKERINGTON, OH

PREP: 25 MIN. • **BAKE:** 25 MIN.
MAKES: 8 CUPS

- 1 medium green pepper, chopped
- 1 medium onion, chopped
- 1 tablespoon olive oil
- ½ teaspoon chili powder
- ¼ teaspoon salt
- ¼ teaspoon pepper
- ¼ teaspoon ground cumin
- 1 package (8 ounces) cream cheese, softened
- 1 can (10¾ ounces) condensed cream of chicken soup, undiluted
- 1 can (10 ounces) diced tomatoes and green chilies, undrained
- 1 jalapeno pepper, finely chopped
- 4 cups shredded rotisserie chicken
- 2 cups shredded Mexican cheese blend, divided
- 1 green onion, thinly sliced
  Tortilla or corn chips

1. In a large skillet, saute green pepper and onion in oil until tender. Add the chili powder, salt, pepper and cumin; cook 1 minute longer. Remove from the heat and set aside.

2. In a large bowl, beat cream cheese until smooth. Add the soup, tomatoes and jalapeno. Stir in the chicken, 1 cup cheese blend and green pepper mixture. Transfer to a greased 11x7-in. baking dish. Sprinkle with sliced green onion and remaining cheese blend.

3. Bake, uncovered, at 350° for 25-30 minutes or until bubbly. Let stand for 5 minutes. Serve with chips.

NOTE *Wear disposable gloves when cutting hot peppers; the oils can burn skin. Avoid touching your face.*

PER SERVING *¼ cup: 103 cal., 7g fat (4g sat. fat), 30mg chol., 209mg sod., 2g carb. (0 sugars, 0 fiber), 8g pro.*

BUFFALO CHICKEN MEATBALLS

⑤ INGREDIENTS

BUFFALO CHICKEN MEATBALLS

I like to make these meatballs as a game-day appetizer with blue cheese or ranch salad dressing for dipping. If I make them for a meal, I'll skip the dressing and serve the meatballs with blue cheese polenta on the side. Yum!

—AMBER MASSEY ARGYLE, TX

PREP: 15 MIN. • **BAKE:** 20 MIN.
MAKES: 2 DOZEN

- ¾ cup panko (Japanese) bread crumbs
- ⅓ cup plus ½ cup Louisiana-style hot sauce, divided
- ¼ cup chopped celery
- 1 large egg white
- 1 pound lean ground chicken
  Reduced-fat blue cheese or ranch salad dressing, optional

1. Preheat oven to 400°. In a large bowl, combine the bread crumbs, ⅓ cup hot sauce, celery and egg white. Add chicken; mix lightly but thoroughly.

2. Shape into twenty-four 1-in. balls. Place on a greased rack in a shallow baking pan. Bake for 20-25 minutes or until cooked through.

3. Toss the meatballs with the remaining hot sauce. If desired, drizzle with salad dressing just before serving.

PER SERVING *1 meatball: 35 cal., 1g fat (0 sat. fat), 14mg chol., 24mg sod., 2g carb. (0 sugars, 0 fiber), 4g pro.*

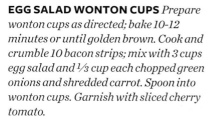

⑤ INGREDIENTS FAST FIX

CHICKEN CHILI WONTON BITES

Everyone needs a surefire, grab-and-go tailgate or picnic recipe. Wonton wrappers filled with chicken and spices make these bites flavorful and fun on the run.

—HEIDI JOBE CARROLLTON, GA

START TO FINISH: 30 MIN.
MAKES: 3 DOZEN

- 36 **wonton wrappers**
- ½ **cup buttermilk ranch salad dressing**
- 1 **envelope reduced-sodium chili seasoning mix**
- 1½ **cups shredded rotisserie chicken**
- 1 **cup shredded sharp cheddar cheese**
  Sour cream and sliced green onions, optional

1. Preheat oven to 350°. Press wonton wrappers into greased miniature muffin cups. Bake 4-6 minutes or until lightly browned.

2. In a small bowl, mix salad dressing and seasoning mix; add chicken and toss to coat. Spoon 1 tablespoon filling into each wonton cup. Sprinkle with cheese.

3. Bake 8-10 minutes longer or until heated through and wrappers are golden brown. Serve warm. If desired, top with sour cream and green onions before serving.

MINI REUBEN CUPS *Prepare and bake wonton cups as directed. Mix ½ pound chopped deli corned beef, ½ cup sauerkraut (rinsed and well drained), and ½ cup Thousand Island salad dressing; spoon into wonton cups. Sprinkle with 1 cup shredded Swiss cheese. Bake as directed.*

EGG SALAD WONTON CUPS *Prepare wonton cups as directed; bake 10-12 minutes or until golden brown. Cook and crumble 10 bacon strips; mix with 3 cups egg salad and ⅓ cup each chopped green onions and shredded carrot. Spoon into wonton cups. Garnish with sliced cherry tomato.*

CHICKEN POPPER CUPS *Prepare and bake wonton cups as directed. Mix 1½ cups shredded cooked chicken, 8 ounces cream cheese, ½ cup shredded Parmesan, ⅓ cup mayonnaise, a 4-ounce can of chopped green chilies (undrained), and 1 minced jalapeno pepper. Spoon into wonton cups; bake as directed.*

PER SERVING *1 chicken chili appetizer (calculated without sour cream): 67 cal., 3g fat (1g sat. fat), 10mg chol., 126mg sod., 6g carb. (0 sugars, 0 fiber), 3g pro.*

CHICKEN CHILI WONTON BITES

CURRIED CHICKEN CHEESE LOG

Curry and cooked chicken team up to make this unique cheese log. The seasoning is mild, so even people who don't generally care for curry still enjoy this spread.

—KAREN OWEN RISING SUN, IN

PREP: 25 MIN. + CHILLING
MAKES: 3 CUPS

- 2 **packages (8 ounces each) cream cheese, softened**
- 1½ **cups finely chopped cooked chicken**
- ⅓ **cup finely chopped celery**
- 2 **tablespoons minced fresh parsley**
- 1 **tablespoon steak sauce**
- ½ **teaspoon curry powder**
- ½ **cup sliced almonds, toasted and coarsely chopped**
  Ritz crackers

In a large bowl, beat cream cheese until smooth. Stir in the chicken, celery, parsley, steak sauce and curry powder. Shape into a 9-in. log. Roll in almonds. Wrap in plastic; refrigerate for at least 2 hours. Serve with crackers.

PER SERVING *2 tablespoons: 95 cal., 8g fat (4g sat. fat), 29mg chol., 77mg sod., 1g carb. (0 sugars, 0 fiber), 4g pro.*

(5)INGREDIENTS FAST FIX

BBQ CHICKEN BITES

Chicken bites wrapped in bacon get a kick from Montreal seasoning and sweetness from barbecue sauce. We love the mix of textures.

—**KATHRYN DAMPIER** QUAIL VALLEY, CA

START TO FINISH: 25 MIN.
MAKES: 1½ DOZEN

- 6 **bacon strips**
- ¾ **pound boneless skinless chicken breasts, cut into 1-inch cubes (about 18)**
- 3 **teaspoons Montreal steak seasoning**
- 1 **teaspoon prepared horseradish, optional**
- ½ **cup barbecue sauce**

1. Preheat oven to 400°. Cut bacon crosswise into thirds. Place bacon on a microwave-safe plate lined with paper towels. Cover with additional paper towels; microwave on high 3-4 minutes or until partially cooked but not crisp.
2. Place chicken in a small bowl; sprinkle with steak seasoning and toss to coat. Wrap a bacon piece around each chicken cube; secure with a toothpick. Place on a parchment paper-lined baking sheet.
3. Bake 10 minutes. If desired, add horseradish to the barbecue sauce; brush sauce over wrapped chicken. Bake 5-10 minutes longer or until chicken is no longer pink and bacon is crisp.
PER SERVING *1 appetizer: 47 cal., 2g fat (0 sat. fat), 13mg chol., 249mg sod., 3g carb. (3g sugars, 0 fiber), 5g pro.*

BBQ CHICKEN BITES

JALAPENO POPPER POCKET (PICTURED ON PAGE 113)

For a fresh take on fried jalapeno poppers, we stuff chicken, cheeses and jalapenos inside puff pastry and bake.

—**SALLY SIBTHORPE** SHELBY TOWNSHIP, MI

PREP: 15 MIN. • **BAKE:** 20 MIN. + STANDING
MAKES: 12 SERVINGS

- 2 **cups chopped rotisserie chicken**
- 1 **carton (8 ounces) spreadable chive and onion cream cheese**
- 1 **cup shredded pepper jack or Monterey Jack cheese**
- 1 **can (4 ounces) diced jalapeno peppers**
- 1 **sheet frozen puff pastry, thawed**
- 1 **large egg, lightly beaten**

1. Preheat oven to 425°. In a bowl, mix chicken, cream cheese, pepper jack cheese and peppers.
2. On a lightly floured surface, unfold puff pastry; roll into a 13-in. square. Place on a parchment paper-lined baking sheet. Spread one half with chicken mixture to within ½ in. of edges. Fold remaining half over filling; press edges with a fork to seal.
3. Brush lightly with beaten egg. Cut slits in pastry. Bake 20-25 minutes or until golden brown. Let stand 10 minutes before cutting.
PER SERVING *1 piece: 237 cal., 15g fat (6g sat. fat), 58mg chol., 252mg sod., 13g carb. (1g sugars, 2g fiber), 12g pro.*

TOP TIP

HOW LONG IS SAFE?

Food shouldn't sit out at room temperature for more than two hours. For a party that goes on longer, set dishes of cold apps in a bowl of ice, and serve hot dishes from a slow cooker. Or, set out smaller portions and replenish from stores kept in the fridge (for cold apps) or in a 200-250° oven (for hot).

CURRIED CHICKEN MEATBALL WRAPS

EAT SMART

CURRIED CHICKEN MEATBALL WRAPS

My strategy to get my picky kids to eat healthy is to let them assemble their dinner at the table. They love these easy meatball wraps topped with crunchy vegetables and a creamy dollop of yogurt.

—**JENNIFER BECKMAN** FALLS CHURCH, VA

PREP: 25 MIN. • **BAKE:** 20 MIN.
MAKES: 2 DOZEN

- 1 **large egg, lightly beaten**
- 1 **small onion, finely chopped**
- ½ **cup Rice Krispies**
- ¼ **cup golden raisins**
- ¼ **cup minced fresh cilantro**
- 2 **teaspoons curry powder**
- ½ **teaspoon salt**
- 1 **pound lean ground chicken**

SAUCE
- 1 **cup (8 ounces) plain yogurt**
- ¼ **cup minced fresh cilantro**

WRAPS
- 24 **small Bibb or Boston lettuce leaves**
- 1 **medium carrot, shredded**
- ½ **cup golden raisins**
- ½ **cup chopped salted peanuts**
  Additional minced fresh cilantro

1. Preheat oven to 350°. In a large bowl, combine the first seven ingredients. Add chicken; mix lightly but thoroughly. With wet hands, shape mixture into 24 balls (about 1¼ in.).
2. Place meatballs on a greased rack in a 15x10x1-in. baking pan. Bake for 17-20 minutes or until cooked through.
3. In a small bowl, mix the sauce ingredients. To serve, place 1 teaspoon sauce and one meatball in each lettuce leaf; top with remaining ingredients.
PER SERVING *1 appetizer: 72 cal., 3g fat (1g sat. fat), 22mg chol., 89mg sod., 6g carb. (4g sugars, 1g fiber), 6g pro. Diabetic Exchanges: 1 lean meat, ½ starch.*

SPICY BBQ
CHICKEN WINGS

2. Preheat oven to 375°. In a deep skillet, heat 1 in. oil to 375°. Fry wings, a few at a time, 3-4 minutes on each side or until golden brown. Drain on paper towels; cool 10 minutes.

3. Meanwhile, in a small saucepan over medium heat, cook and stir the barbecue sauces, honey and jalapeno. Bring to a boil; reduce heat and simmer, stirring occasionally, to allow flavors to blend, 10-15 minutes.

4. Dip wings in sauce; place on greased foil-lined baking pans. Bake until glazed, about 10 minutes.

PER SERVING *2 pieces: 317 cal., 19g fat (3g sat. fat), 36mg chol., 816mg sod., 23g carb. (16g sugars, 0 fiber), 12g pro.*

BUFFALO WING DIP
(PICTURED ON PAGE 112)

If you love spicy wings, you'll love this dip. It's super cheesy, full of rich flavor and tastes just like buffalo wings!

—*TASTE OF HOME* TEST KITCHEN

PREP: 20 MIN. • **COOK:** 2 HOURS
MAKES: 6 CUPS

- 2 packages (8 ounces each) cream cheese, softened
- ½ cup ranch salad dressing
- ½ cup sour cream
- 5 tablespoons crumbled blue cheese
- 2 cups shredded cooked chicken
- ½ cup Buffalo wing sauce
- 2 cups shredded cheddar cheese, divided
- 1 green onion, sliced
  Tortilla chips

1. In a small bowl, combine the cream cheese, dressing, sour cream and blue cheese. Transfer to a 3-qt. slow cooker. Layer with chicken, wing sauce and 1 cup cheese. Cover and cook on low for 2-3 hours or until heated through.

2. Sprinkle with remaining cheese and onion. Serve with tortilla chips.

PER SERVING *¼ cup dip (calculated without chips): 167 cal., 14g fat (8g sat. fat), 47mg chol., 348mg sod., 2g carb. (0 sugars, 0 fiber), 8g pro.*

SPICY BBQ CHICKEN WINGS

For zesty appetizers that win big every time, we glaze chicken wings with barbecue sauce, a little heat and a good team of spices. Whether you're tailgating on the frozen tundra or watching the game from the comfort of the couch, these wings will keep you warm from the inside.

—PACKERS WOMEN'S ASSOCIATION
GREEN BAY, WI

PREP: 25 MIN. + CHILLING • **COOK:** 45 MIN.
MAKES: 16 SERVINGS

- 4 pounds chicken wings
- 2 cups white vinegar
- 2 cups water
- 1 cup all-purpose flour
- 1 tablespoon adobo seasoning
- 1 teaspoon garlic salt
- 1 teaspoon coarsely ground pepper
- 1 teaspoon kosher salt
- 1 teaspoon onion powder
  Canola oil for frying
- 1 cup honey barbecue sauce
- 1 cup hickory smoke-flavored barbecue sauce
- ¼ cup honey
- 1 jalapeno pepper, seeded and minced

1. Using a sharp knife, cut through the two wing joints; discard wing tips. Place wings in a large bowl; add vinegar and water. Refrigerate, covered, 45 minutes. Drain and rinse, discarding the vinegar mixture. Combine flour and seasonings; add chicken, tossing to coat.

SMOKY CHICKEN NACHOS

This recipe combines layers of crunchy tortilla chips and black beans with a creamy, smoky chicken mixture that takes it from a simple snack to a can't-stop-munching treat. Whenever we entertain on game day, these nachos are gone by halftime.

—WHITNEY SMITH WINTER HAVEN, FL

PREP: 20 MIN. • **BAKE:** 15 MIN.
MAKES: 12 SERVINGS

- 1 **pound ground chicken**
- ⅔ **cup water**
- 1 **envelope taco seasoning**
- ¼ **cup cream cheese, softened**
- 3 **tablespoons minced fresh chives**
- 2 **tablespoons plus 1½ teaspoons 2% milk**
- 2 **tablespoons dry bread crumbs**
- 1 **teaspoon prepared mustard**
- ½ **teaspoon paprika**
- ¾ **teaspoon liquid smoke, optional**
- 6 **cups tortilla chips**
- 1 **can (15 ounces) black beans, rinsed and drained**
- 1 **cup shredded cheddar-Monterey Jack cheese**
  Optional toppings: chopped tomatoes and sliced ripe olives

1. In a large skillet over medium heat, cook chicken until no longer pink; drain. Add water and taco seasoning; bring to a boil. Reduce heat and simmer for 5 minutes. Combine the cream cheese, chives, milk, bread crumbs, mustard, paprika and liquid smoke if desired; stir into chicken mixture until blended.
2. In an ungreased 13x9-in. baking dish, layer half of the chips, chicken mixture, beans and cheese. Repeat layers.
3. Bake at 350° for 15-20 minutes or until cheese is melted. Serve with tomatoes and olives if desired.
PER SERVING *195 cal., 10g fat (5g sat. fat), 41mg chol., 224mg sod., 14g carb. (1g sugars, 2g fiber), 11g pro.*

SMOKY CHICKEN NACHOS

SPICY
LEMON
CHICKEN
KABOBS,
PAGE 133

MARGHERITA CHICKEN, PAGE 128

GRILLED TO PERFECTION

Fire up the grill—it's time to sink your teeth in to one of these **mouthwatering chicken** recipes! No matter the season, grilled chicken always makes for a **fresh, quick meal** that's loaded with flavor and family appeal. So hit the grill grates and baste your way to a **lip-smacking** supper tonight!

BEER CAN CHICKEN, PAGE 135

GRILLED CHICKEN WITH BLACK BEAN SALSA, PAGE 130

DAD'S LEMONY
GRILLED CHICKEN

DAD'S LEMONY GRILLED CHICKEN

Lemon juice, onions and garlic add tangy flavor to my grilled chicken.

—MIKE SCHULZ TAWAS CITY, MI

PREP: 20 MIN. + MARINATING • **GRILL:** 30 MIN.
MAKES: 8 SERVINGS

- 1 **cup olive oil**
- ⅔ **cup lemon juice**
- 6 **garlic cloves, minced**
- 1 **teaspoon salt**
- ½ **teaspoon pepper**
- 2 **medium onions, chopped**
- 8 **chicken drumsticks (2 pounds)**
- 8 **bone-in chicken thighs (2 pounds)**

1. In a small bowl, whisk the first five ingredients until blended; stir in onions. Pour 1½ cups marinade into a large resealable plastic bag. Add the chicken; seal the bag and turn to coat. Refrigerate overnight. Cover and refrigerate the remaining marinade.

2. Prepare grill for indirect heat. Drain chicken, discarding the marinade in bag. Place chicken on grill rack, skin side up. Grill, covered, over indirect medium heat for 15 minutes. Turn; grill 15-20 minutes longer or until a thermometer reads 170°-175°, basting occasionally with the reserved marinade.

PER SERVING *1 chicken drumstick and thigh: 528 cal., 39g fat (8g sat. fat), 129mg chol., 318mg sod., 6g carb. (3g sugars, 1g fiber), 38g pro.*

STRAWBERRY MINT CHICKEN

TOP TIP

MARINATE ONCE

Always marinate in the refrigerator in a glass container or resealable plastic bag. Don't reuse marinades, especially when working with poultry, pork or seafood. If a marinade is also to be used as a basting or dipping sauce, reserve a portion before adding the uncooked food to the marinade.

EAT SMART **FAST FIX** ▶

STRAWBERRY MINT CHICKEN

I hand-pick wild strawberries for this saucy chicken dish. We love it with fresh spring greens and a sweet white wine.

—ALICIA DUERST MENOMONIE, WI

START TO FINISH: 30 MIN.
MAKES: 4 SERVINGS

- 1 **tablespoon cornstarch**
- 1 **tablespoon sugar**
- ⅛ **teaspoon ground nutmeg**
- ⅛ **teaspoon pepper**
- ½ **cup water**
- 1 **cup fresh strawberries, coarsely chopped**
- ½ **cup white wine or white grape juice**
- 2 **teaspoons minced fresh mint**

CHICKEN
- 4 **boneless skinless chicken breast halves (6 ounces each)**
- ½ **teaspoon salt**
- ¼ **teaspoon pepper**
  Sliced green onion

1. In a small saucepan, mix the first five ingredients until smooth; stir in the strawberries and wine. Bring to a boil. Reduce heat; simmer, uncovered, for 3-5 minutes or until thickened and the strawberries are softened, stirring occasionally. Remove from heat; stir in the mint.

2. Sprinkle chicken with salt and pepper. On a lightly greased grill rack, grill the chicken, covered, over medium heat for 5-7 minutes on each side or until a thermometer reads 165°; brush occasionally with ¼ cup sauce during the last 4 minutes. Serve with remaining sauce. Sprinkle with green onion.

PER SERVING *1 chicken breast half with ¼ cup sauce: 224 cal., 4g fat (1g sat. fat), 94mg chol., 378mg sod., 8g carb. (5g sugars, 1g fiber), 35g pro.* **Diabetic Exchanges:** *5 lean meat, ½ starch.*

SPICE-RUBBED
CHICKEN THIGHS

MARGHERITA CHICKEN (PICTURED ON PAGE 125)

Fresh basil gets all the respect in this super supper—even forks will stand at attention when it hits the table.

—JUDY ARMSTRONG PRAIRIEVILLE, LA

PREP: 25 MIN. + MARINATING ● **GRILL:** 10 MIN.
MAKES: 4 SERVINGS

- 4 boneless skinless chicken breast halves (6 ounces each)
- ½ cup reduced-fat balsamic vinaigrette
- 3 garlic cloves, minced
- ½ teaspoon salt
- ¼ teaspoon pepper
- ¼ cup marinara sauce
- 16 fresh basil leaves
- 2 plum tomatoes, thinly sliced lengthwise
- 1 cup frozen artichoke hearts, thawed and chopped
- 3 green onions, chopped
- ¼ cup shredded part-skim mozzarella cheese

1. Flatten each chicken piece to ½-in. thickness. In a large resealable plastic bag, combine the vinaigrette and garlic. Add the chicken; seal bag and turn to coat. Refrigerate for 30 minutes. Drain and discard marinade. Sprinkle chicken with salt and pepper.

2. On a lightly greased grill rack, grill chicken, covered, over medium heat or broil 4 in. from heat for 5 minutes. Turn chicken; top with marinara sauce, basil, tomatoes, artichokes, onions and cheese. Cover and cook for 5-6 minutes or until the chicken is no longer pink and cheese is melted.

PER SERVING *1 chicken breast: 273 cal., 8g fat (2g sat. fat), 98mg chol., 606mg sod., 10g carb. (4g sugars, 3g fiber), 38g pro. **Diabetic Exchanges:** 5 lean meat, 1 vegetable, ½ fat.*

SPICE-RUBBED CHICKEN THIGHS

Our go-to meal has always been baked chicken thighs. This easy grilled version takes the cooking outside with a zesty rub of turmeric, paprika and chili powder.

—BILL STALEY MONROEVILLE, PA

START TO FINISH: 20 MIN.
MAKES: 6 SERVINGS

- 1 teaspoon salt
- 1 teaspoon garlic powder
- 1 teaspoon onion powder
- 1 teaspoon dried oregano
- ½ teaspoon ground turmeric
- ½ teaspoon paprika
- ¼ teaspoon chili powder
- ¼ teaspoon pepper
- 6 boneless skinless chicken thighs (about 1½ pounds)

1. In a small bowl, mix the first eight ingredients. Sprinkle over both sides of the chicken.

2. On a lightly greased grill rack, grill chicken, covered, over medium heat or broil 4 in. from heat 6-8 minutes on each side or until a thermometer reads 170°.

PER SERVING *1 chicken thigh: 169 cal., 8g fat (2g sat. fat), 76mg chol., 460mg sod., 1g carb. (0 sugars, 0 fiber), 21g pro. **Diabetic Exchange:** 3 lean meat.*

FAST FIX

ITALIAN SAUSAGE AND PROVOLONE SKEWERS

My husband made these sausage and veggie kabobs when we didn't have buns to make classic sausage bombers. Grill 'em up, then add cheese cubes.

—CINDY HILLIARD KENOSHA, WI

START TO FINISH: 30 MIN.
MAKES: 8 SERVINGS

- 1 large onion
- 1 large sweet red pepper
- 1 large green pepper
- 2 cups cherry tomatoes
- 1 tablespoon olive oil
- ½ teaspoon pepper
- ¼ teaspoon salt
- 2 packages (12 ounces each) fully cooked Italian chicken sausage links, cut into 1¼-inch slices
- 16 cubes provolone cheese (¾ inch each)

1. Cut onion and peppers into 1-in. pieces; place in a large bowl. Add the tomatoes, oil, pepper and salt; toss to coat. On 16 metal or soaked wooden skewers, alternately thread sausage and vegetables.
2. Grill, covered, over medium heat for 8-10 minutes or until the sausage is heated through and the vegetables are tender, turning occasionally. Remove kabobs from grill; thread one cheese cube onto each kabob.
PER SERVING *2 kabobs: 220 cal., 13g fat (5g sat. fat), 75mg chol., 682mg sod., 7g carb. (3g sugars, 2g fiber), 20g pro.*
Diabetic Exchanges: 3 medium-fat meat, 1 vegetable.

ITALIAN SAUSAGE AND PROVOLONE SKEWERS

GRILLED CHICKEN WITH BLACK BEAN SALSA

(PICTURED ON PAGE 125)

I like to slice this chicken and serve it over a long grain and wild rice mix.
—**TERRI CLOUSE** CONNOQUENESSING, PA

PREP: 15 MIN. + MARINATING • **GRILL:** 10 MIN.
MAKES: 5 SERVINGS

- 1 **cup lime juice**
- 2 **tablespoons olive oil**
- 2 **teaspoons ground cumin**
- 1 **teaspoon salt**
- 1 **teaspoon dried oregano**
- ½ **teaspoon pepper**
- 5 **boneless skinless chicken breast halves (4 ounces each)**

BLACK BEAN SALSA

- 1 **can (15 ounces) black beans, rinsed and drained**
- 1 **mango, peeled and cubed**
- ¼ **cup minced fresh cilantro**
- 3 **tablespoons lime juice**
- 1 **tablespoon olive oil**
- 2 **teaspoons brown sugar**
- 1 **teaspoon minced jalapeno pepper**

1. In a small bowl, whisk the first six ingredients. Pour ⅔ cup marinade into a large resealable plastic bag. Add chicken; seal bag and turn to coat. Refrigerate for 1-2 hours. Reserve remaining marinade for basting. In a small bowl, combine the salsa ingredients; toss to combine.

2. Drain chicken, discarding marinade. Grill, covered, over medium heat or broil 4 in. from heat 5-6 minutes on each side or until a thermometer reads 165°, basting occasionally with reserved marinade during the last 4 minutes. Serve with salsa.

NOTE *Wear disposable gloves when cutting hot peppers; the oils can burn skin. Avoid touching your face.*

PER SERVING *1 chicken breast half with ½ cup salsa: 266 cal., 7g fat (1g sat. fat), 63mg chol., 339mg sod., 23g carb. (9g sugars, 4g fiber), 27g pro.* **Diabetic Exchanges:** *3 lean meat, 1½ starch, 1 fat.*

TANDOORI CHICKEN THIGHS

TANDOORI CHICKEN THIGHS

I spent some time in India and I love reminders of this vibrant culture, so serving this tandoori chicken makes me happy. Paired with warmed naan bread and a cool tomato and cucumber salad, it makes a whole meal.
—**CLAIRE ELSTON** SPOKANE, WA

START TO FINISH: 30 MIN.
MAKES: 4 SERVINGS

- 1 **cup (8 ounces) reduced-fat plain yogurt**
- 1 **tablespoon minced fresh gingerroot**
- 1 **teaspoon ground cumin**
- 1 **garlic clove, minced**
- ¾ **teaspoon kosher salt**
- ½ **teaspoon curry powder**
- ½ **teaspoon pepper**
- ¼ **teaspoon cayenne pepper**
- 4 **boneless skinless chicken thighs (about 1 pound)**

1. In a small bowl, mix the first eight ingredients until blended. Add chicken to marinade; turn to coat. Let stand for 10 minutes.

2. Place chicken on greased grill rack. Grill, covered, over medium heat for 6-8 minutes on each side or until a thermometer reads 170°.

PER SERVING *1 chicken thigh: 193 cal., 9g fat (3g sat. fat), 78mg chol., 333mg sod., 4g carb. (3g sugars, 0 fiber), 23g pro.* **Diabetic Exchanges:** *3 lean meat, ½ fat.*

EAT SMART **FAST FIX**

CHICKEN WITH PEACH-CUCUMBER SALSA

To keep our kitchen cool in the summer, we grill chicken outdoors and serve it with minty peach salsa that can easily be made ahead.

—JANIE COLLE HUTCHINSON, KS

START TO FINISH: 25 MIN.
MAKES: 4 SERVINGS

- 1½ **cups chopped peeled fresh peaches (about 2 medium)**
- ¾ **cup chopped cucumber**
- 4 **tablespoons peach preserves, divided**
- 3 **tablespoons finely chopped red onion**
- 1 **teaspoon minced fresh mint**
- ¾ **teaspoon salt, divided**
- 4 **boneless skinless chicken breast halves (6 ounces each)**
- ¼ **teaspoon pepper**

1. For salsa, in a small bowl, combine peaches, cucumber, 2 tablespoons of the preserves, onion, mint and ¼ teaspoon of the salt.

2. Sprinkle chicken with pepper and the remaining salt. On a lightly greased grill rack, grill chicken, covered, over medium heat 5 minutes. Turn; grill 7-9 minutes longer or until a thermometer reads 165°, brushing the tops occasionally with the remaining preserves. Serve with salsa.

PER SERVING *1 chicken breast half with ½ cup salsa: 261 cal., 4g fat (1g sat. fat), 94mg chol., 525mg sod., 20g carb. (17g sugars, 1g fiber), 35g pro.* **Diabetic Exchanges:** *5 lean meat, ½ starch, ½ fruit.*

CHICKEN WITH PEACH-CUCUMBER SALSA

EAT SMART **FAST FIX** ▶
GRILLED CHICKEN CHOPPED SALAD

Layered desserts always grab my family's attention, but salads? Not so much. I wondered whether presenting a healthy salad in an eye-catching way could get everyone on board. I'm happy to report that it worked!

—CHRISTINE HADDEN WHITMAN, MA

START TO FINISH: 30 MIN.
MAKES: 4 SERVINGS

- **1 pound chicken tenderloins**
- **6 tablespoons zesty Italian salad dressing, divided**
- **2 medium zucchini, quartered lengthwise**
- **1 medium red onion, quartered**
- **2 medium ears sweet corn, husks removed**
- **1 bunch romaine, chopped**
- **1 medium cucumber, chopped**
  Additional salad dressing, optional

1. In a bowl, toss the chicken with 4 tablespoons dressing. Brush zucchini and onion with remaining 2 tablespoons of dressing.

2. Place corn, zucchini and onion on a grill rack over medium heat; close lid. Grill corn 10-12 minutes or until tender, turning occasionally. Grill zucchini and onion for 2-3 minutes on each side or until tender.

3. Drain chicken, discarding marinade. Grill chicken, covered, over medium heat for 3-4 minutes on each side or until no longer pink.

4. Cut corn from cobs; cut zucchini, onion and chicken into bite-size pieces. In a 3-qt. trifle bowl or other glass bowl, layer romaine, cucumber, grilled vegetables and chicken. If desired, serve with additional dressing.

PER SERVING *3 cups: 239 cal., 5g fat (0 sat. fat), 56mg chol., 276mg sod., 21g carb. (9g sugars, 5g fiber), 32g pro.*
Diabetic Exchanges: *3 lean meat, 2 vegetable, ½ starch, ½ fat.*

GRILLED CHICKEN CHOPPED SALAD

GRILLED HULI HULI CHICKEN

SPICY LEMON CHICKEN KABOBS (PICTURED ON PAGE 124)

When I see Meyer lemons in the store, I know that spring has arrived. I like using them for these easy, smoky chicken kabobs, but regular grilled lemons can also get the job done.
—**TERRI CRANDALL** GARDNERVILLE, NV

PREP: 15 MIN. + MARINATING • **GRILL:** 10 MIN.
MAKES: 6 SERVINGS

- ¼ cup lemon juice
- 4 tablespoons olive oil, divided
- 3 tablespoons white wine
- 1½ teaspoons crushed red pepper flakes
- 1 teaspoon minced fresh rosemary or ¼ teaspoon dried rosemary, crushed
- 1½ pounds boneless skinless chicken breasts, cut into 1-inch cubes
- 2 medium lemons, halved
  Minced chives

1. In a large resealable plastic bag, combine lemon juice, 3 tablespoons oil, wine, pepper flakes and rosemary. Add chicken; seal bag and turn to coat. Refrigerate up to 3 hours.
2. Drain chicken, discarding marinade. Thread chicken onto six metal or soaked wooden skewers. Grill, covered, over medium heat 10-12 minutes or until no longer pink, turning once.
3. Place lemons on grill, cut side down. Grill 8-10 minutes or until lightly browned. Squeeze lemon halves over chicken. Drizzle with remaining oil; sprinkle with chives.
PER SERVING *1 kabob: 182 cal., 8g fat (2g sat. fat), 63mg chol., 55mg sodium, 2g carb. (1g sugars, 1g fiber), 23g pro. Diabetic Exchanges: 3 lean meat, 1 fat.*

GRILLED HULI HULI CHICKEN

When I lived in Hawaii, a friend gave me the recipe for this ginger-soy-flavored dish. *Huli* means "turn" in Hawaiian and refers to turning the meat on the grill.
—**SHARON BOLING** SAN DIEGO, CA

PREP: 15 MIN. + MARINATING • **GRILL:** 15 MIN.
MAKES: 12 SERVINGS

- 1 cup packed brown sugar
- ¾ cup ketchup
- ¾ cup reduced-sodium soy sauce
- ⅓ cup sherry or chicken broth
- 2½ teaspoons minced fresh gingerroot
- 1½ teaspoons minced garlic
- 24 boneless skinless chicken thighs (about 5 pounds)

1. In a bowl, mix the first six ingredients. Reserve 1⅓ cups for basting; cover and refrigerate. Divide remaining marinade between two large resealable plastic bags. Add 12 chicken thighs to each; seal bags and turn to coat. Refrigerate for 8 hours or overnight.
2. Drain and discard marinade from chicken. Moisten a paper towel with cooking oil; using long-handled tongs, lightly coat the grill rack.
3. Grill chicken, covered, over medium heat for 6-8 minutes on each side or until no longer pink; baste occasionally with reserved marinade during the last 5 minutes.
PER SERVING *2 chicken thighs: 391 cal., 16g fat (5g sat. fat), 151mg chol., 651mg sod., 15g carb. (14g sugars, 0 fiber), 43g pro.*

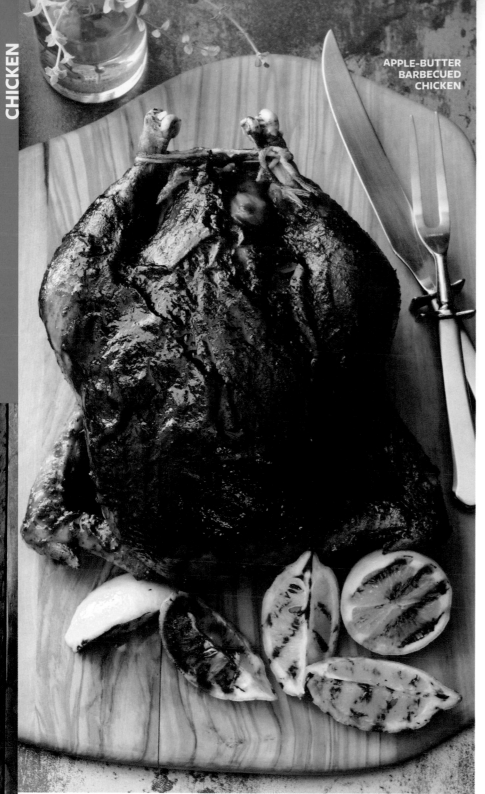

APPLE-BUTTER
BARBECUED
CHICKEN

APPLE-BUTTER BARBECUED CHICKEN

I love cooking so much that I sometimes think of recipes in my sleep and wake up to write them down. This dream-inspired dish is my family's most-requested chicken recipe.
—**HOLLY KILBEL** AKRON, OH

PREP: 15 MIN. • **GRILL:** 1½ HOURS + STANDING
MAKES: 6-8 SERVINGS

- 1 **teaspoon salt**
- ¾ **teaspoon garlic powder**
- ¼ **teaspoon pepper**
- ⅛ **teaspoon cayenne pepper**
- 1 **roasting chicken (6 to 7 pounds)**
- 1 **can (11½ ounces) unsweetened apple juice**
- ½ **cup apple butter**
- ¼ **cup barbecue sauce**

1. Combine salt, garlic powder, pepper and cayenne; sprinkle over the chicken.
2. Prepare grill for indirect heat, using a drip pan. Pour half of the apple juice into another container and save for future use. With a can opener, poke additional holes in the top of the can. Holding the chicken with legs pointed down, lower chicken over the can so the can fills the body cavity. Place the chicken on grill rack over drip pan.
3. Grill chicken, covered, over indirect medium heat for 1½-2 hours or until a thermometer reads 180°. Combine apple butter and barbecue sauce; baste chicken occasionally during the last 30 minutes. Remove chicken from gill; cover and let stand for 10 minutes. Remove can from chicken before carving.
PER SERVING *6 ounces: 441 cal., 24g fat (7g sat. fat), 134mg chol., 489mg sod., 11g carb. (10g sugars, 0 fiber), 43g pro.*

BEER CAN CHICKEN

(PICTURED ON PAGE 125)

You'll be proud to serve this stand-up chicken at any family gathering. Treated to a savory rub, then roasted over a beer can for added moisture, it's so tasty you may want to call dibs on the leftovers now!

—SHIRLEY WARREN THIENSVILLE, WI

PREP: 20 MIN. • **GRILL:** 1¼ HOURS + STANDING
MAKES: 4 SERVINGS

- 4 teaspoons chicken seasoning
- 2 teaspoons sugar
- 2 teaspoons chili powder
- 1½ teaspoons paprika
- 1¼ teaspoons dried basil
- ¼ teaspoon pepper
- 1 broiler/fryer chicken (3-4 pounds)
- 1 tablespoon canola oil
- 2 lemon slices
- 1 can (12 ounces) beer or nonalcoholic beer

1. In a small bowl, combine the first six ingredients. Gently loosen skin from the chicken. Brush chicken with oil. Sprinkle 1 teaspoon of spice mixture into cavity. Rub the remaining spice mixture over and under the skin. Place lemon slices in neck cavity. Tuck the wing tips behind the back.

2. Prepare grill for indirect heat, using a drip pan. Pour out half of the beer, reserving for future use. Poke additional holes in top of the can with a can opener. Holding the chicken with legs pointed down, lower it over the can so the can fills the body cavity.

3. Place chicken over drip pan; grill, covered, over indirect medium heat for 1¼-1½ hours or until a thermometer reads 180°. Remove chicken from grill; cover and let stand 10 minutes. Remove can from chicken before carving.

PER SERVING *7 ounces cooked chicken: 415 cal., 25g fat (6g sat. fat), 131mg chol., 366mg sod., 3g carb. (2g sugars, 1g fiber), 42g pro.*

CHICKEN WITH CITRUS CHIMICHURRI SAUCE

CHICKEN WITH CITRUS CHIMICHURRI SAUCE

Chimichurri is a green sauce from South America that is served with grilled meats. My citrus version brightens up grilled chicken, which gets its juiciness from brining.

—TYFFANIE PEREZ SPRINGVILLE, UT

PREP: 20 MIN. + MARINATING • **GRILL:** 10 MIN.
MAKES: 4 SERVINGS

- 4 cups water
- ¼ cup kosher salt
- 1 tablespoon honey
- 1 teaspoon grated lemon peel
- 1 teaspoon grated orange peel
- 4 boneless skinless chicken breast halves (6 ounces each)

CHIMICHURRI SAUCE
- ½ cup olive oil
- ¼ cup packed fresh parsley sprigs
- 1 tablespoon minced fresh thyme
- 1 tablespoon lemon juice
- 1 tablespoon orange juice
- 1 garlic clove, peeled
- ¼ teaspoon salt
- ⅛ teaspoon pepper

1. In a large bowl, whisk water, salt, honey and citrus peels until salt is dissolved. Add chicken, making sure it's submerged. Refrigerate up to 2 hours.

2. Pulse sauce ingredients in a food processor until smooth. Reserve ½ cup sauce for serving.

3. Remove chicken; rinse and pat dry. Brush chicken with chimichurri sauce. Grill, covered, over medium-high heat or broil 4 in. from heat until a thermometer reads 165°, 4-6 minutes on each side. Serve with reserved sauce.

PER SERVING *1 chicken breast half with 2 tablespoons sauce: 427 cal., 31g fat (5g sat. fat), 94mg chol., 279mg sod., 1g carb. (1g sugars, 0 fiber), 35g pro.*

SAUCY BARBECUE DRUMSTICKS

SAUCY BARBECUE DRUMSTICKS

After searching high and low for an out-of-this-world bottled barbecue sauce, I threw in the towel and stirred up my own with ketchup, honey, brown mustard...the works.

—**KATHLEEN CRIDDLE** LAKE WORTH, FL

PREP: 25 MIN. • **GRILL:** 15 MIN.
MAKES: 8 SERVINGS (2 CUPS SAUCE)

- 2 **cups ketchup**
- ⅔ **cup honey**
- ⅓ **cup packed brown sugar**
- 2 **tablespoons finely chopped sweet onion**
- 2 **tablespoons spicy brown mustard**
- 4 **garlic cloves, minced**
- 1 **tablespoon Worcestershire sauce**
- 1 **tablespoon cider vinegar**
- 16 **chicken drumsticks**

1. In a large saucepan, mix the first eight ingredients; bring to a boil. Reduce heat; simmer, uncovered, for 15-20 minutes to allow flavors to blend, stirring sauce occasionally. Reserve 2 cups of the sauce for serving.

2. On a lightly greased grill rack, grill chicken, covered, over medium heat 15-20 minutes or until a thermometer reads 170°-175°, turning occasionally and brushing generously with remaining sauce during the last 5 minutes. Serve with reserved sauce.

PER SERVING *2 chicken drumsticks with ¼ cup sauce: 422 cal., 12g fat (3g sat. fat), 95mg chol., 909mg sod., 49g carb. (48g sugars, 0 fiber), 29g pro.*

GRILLED ORANGE CHICKEN THIGHS

FAST FIX ▶

GRILLED ORANGE CHICKEN THIGHS

This orangey chicken was the first meal I served my future husband. I chose it because it's easy, but he thought it was amazing and gobbled it up. We were married three months later, so I guess it worked!

—**LEAH HARVATH** HEBER CITY, UT

START TO FINISH: 30 MIN.
MAKES: 6 SERVINGS

- 1 **cup orange juice**
- ⅓ **cup sugar**
- ⅓ **cup packed light brown sugar**
- ¼ **teaspoon salt**
- 1 **tablespoon Dijon mustard**
- 2 **teaspoons grated orange peel**

CHICKEN

- 6 **boneless skinless chicken thighs (about 1½ pounds)**
- ½ **teaspoon lemon-pepper seasoning**

1. In a small saucepan, combine juice, sugars and salt; bring to a boil, stirring to dissolve sugar. Cook, uncovered, 10-15 minutes or until mixture reaches a glaze consistency. Remove from heat; stir in mustard and orange peel.

2. Sprinkle chicken with lemon pepper. On a lightly greased grill rack, grill the chicken, covered, over medium heat for 6-8 minutes on each side or until a thermometer reads 170°, brushing occasionally with some of the sauce during the last 5 minutes. Serve with remaining sauce.

PER SERVING *1 chicken thigh with about 1 tablespoon sauce: 277 cal., 8g fat (2g sat. fat), 76mg chol., 256mg sod., 29g carb. (27g sugars, 0 fiber), 21g pro.*

DR PEPPER DRUMSTICKS

APRICOT-GLAZED CHICKEN KABOBS

I have made this recipe for my family for years and it's still everyone's top pick. I like to serve it with rice on the side.

—AMY CHELLINO SHOREWOOD, IL

PREP: 20 MIN. + MARINATING • **GRILL:** 10 MIN.
MAKES: 4 SERVINGS

- ½ cup apricot spreadable fruit
- 3 tablespoons reduced-sodium soy sauce
- 1 tablespoon lemon juice
- 1 tablespoon honey
- 2 teaspoons Chinese five-spice powder
- ¼ teaspoon crushed red pepper flakes
- 1½ pounds boneless skinless chicken breasts, cut into 1-inch cubes
- 1 medium red onion, cut into 1-inch pieces
- 1 medium zucchini, cut into 1-inch pieces
- 1 medium yellow summer squash, cut into 1-inch pieces

1. In a small bowl, combine the first six ingredients. Pour ½ cup marinade into a large resealable plastic bag. Add chicken; seal bag and turn to coat. Refrigerate for at least 8 hours or overnight. Cover and refrigerate the remaining marinade.
2. Drain chicken and discard marinade in bag. On four metal or soaked wooden skewers, alternately thread the chicken, onion, zucchini and summer squash.
3. On a lightly greased grill rack, grill kabobs, covered, over medium heat or broil 4 in. from the heat 10-15 minutes or until juices run clear, turning and basting occasionally with reserved marinade.
PER SERVING *1 kabob: 268 cal., 4g fat (1g sat. fat), 94mg chol., 341mg sod., 20g carb. (14g sugars, 2g fiber), 36g pro.*
Diabetic Exchanges: *5 lean meat, 1 starch, 1 vegetable.*

DR PEPPER DRUMSTICKS

If you love Dr Pepper as much as I do, try it in this barbecue sauce for grilled chicken. It adds just the right zip to the ketchup, bourbon and barbecue seasoning.

—SHANNON HOLLE-FUNK VENEDY, IL

PREP: 20 MIN. • **GRILL:** 30 MIN.
MAKES: 6 SERVINGS

- 1 cup ketchup
- ⅔ cup Dr Pepper
- 2 tablespoons brown sugar
- 2 tablespoons bourbon
- 4 teaspoons barbecue seasoning
- 1 tablespoon Worcestershire sauce
- 2 teaspoons dried minced onion
- ⅛ teaspoon salt
- ¼ teaspoon celery salt, optional
- 12 chicken drumsticks

1. In a small saucepan, combine the first eight ingredients; if desired, stir in celery salt. Bring to a boil. Reduce heat; simmer, uncovered, 8-10 minutes or until slightly thickened, stirring frequently.
2. On an oiled grill, cook the chicken, covered, over medium-low heat for 15 minutes. Turn; grill 15-20 minutes longer or until a thermometer reads 170°-175°, brushing occasionally with sauce mixture.
PER SERVING *2 drumsticks: 316 cal., 12g fat (3g sat. fat), 95mg chol., 1289mg sod., 19g carb. (19g sugars, 0 fiber), 29g pro.*

TANDOORI-STYLE CHICKEN WITH CUCUMBER MELON RELISH

We all need a quick meal that's delicious and healthy. I get the chicken marinating before I leave for work; when I get home, I grill the chicken and make the relish. If you want a hotter dish, add more crushed red pepper flakes.

—NAYLET LAROCHELLE MIAMI, FL

PREP: 20 MIN. + MARINATING • **GRILL:** 15 MIN.
MAKES: 4 SERVINGS

- 1½ cups reduced-fat plain yogurt
- 2 tablespoons lemon juice, divided
- 1½ teaspoons garam masala or curry powder
- ½ teaspoon salt
- ¼ to ½ teaspoon crushed red pepper flakes
- 4 boneless skinless chicken breast halves (6 ounces each)
- 1½ cups chopped cantaloupe
- ½ cup chopped seeded peeled cucumber
- 2 green onions, finely chopped
- 2 tablespoons minced fresh cilantro
- 1 tablespoon minced fresh mint
- ¼ cup toasted sliced almonds, optional

1. In a small bowl, whisk the yogurt, 1 tablespoon lemon juice, garam masala, salt and pepper flakes until blended. Pour 1 cup marinade into a large resealable plastic bag. Add chicken; seal bag and turn to coat. Refrigerate up to 6 hours. Cover and refrigerate remaining marinade.

2. For relish, in a small bowl, mix cantaloupe, cucumber, green onions, cilantro, mint and remaining lemon juice.

3. On a lightly greased grill rack, grill chicken, covered, over medium heat or broil 4 in. from heat for 6-8 minutes on each side or until a thermometer reads 165°. Serve with relish and reserved marinade. Sprinkle with almonds.

NOTE *To toast nuts, bake in a shallow pan in a 350° oven for 5-10 minutes or cook in a skillet over low heat until lightly browned, stirring occasionally.*

PER SERVING (*calculated without almonds*): 247 cal., 5g fat (2g sat. fat), 98mg chol., 332mg sod., 10g carb. (9g sugars, 1g fiber), 38g pro. **Diabetic Exchanges:** 5 lean meat, ½ starch.

 GRILL SKILL ⎯⎯⎯⎯⎯

If you like to have professional-looking grill marks on your chicken, add a little honey to your marinade or sauce. The sugar in the honey caramelizes when heated on the grill, creating well-defined marks. You'll need about 1-3 teaspoons depending on the amount of marinade or sauce. It works on the stovetop, too: Brush chicken with honey and saute in a nonstick pan coated with cooking spray to give it a golden-brown color.

—LISA M. SPRING VALLEY, NY

TANDOORI-STYLE CHICKEN WITH CUCUMBER MELON RELISH

FAST FIX ▶

PEANUT BUTTER CHICKEN TENDERS

These chicken skewers are brushed with a delightful peanut butter and ginger-lime sauce, then grilled to tender perfection.

—BILLIE MOSS WALNUT CREEK, CA

START TO FINISH: 30 MIN.
MAKES: 2 SERVINGS

- ¼ cup water
- ¼ cup creamy peanut butter
- 1 tablespoon brown sugar
- 1 tablespoon lemon juice
- 1 tablespoon lime juice
- 1 tablespoon reduced-sodium soy sauce
- 2 garlic cloves, minced
- ½ teaspoon minced fresh gingerroot
- 2 boneless skinless chicken breast halves (6 ounces each)
- 1 cup shredded red cabbage
- 1 tablespoon finely chopped celery
- 1 tablespoon sunflower kernels

1. In a small saucepan, combine the first eight ingredients. Cook and stir over medium-high heat for 3 minutes or until smooth. Remove from the heat; set aside 2 tablespoons of the sauce for serving.
2. Slice the chicken lengthwise into 1-in. strips; thread onto metal or soaked wooden skewers. Grill, uncovered, over medium-high heat or broil 6 in. from the heat for 2 minutes; turn and brush with the remaining sauce. Continue turning and basting for 4-6 minutes or until no longer pink.
3. Place cabbage on a serving plate; top with skewers. Sprinkle with celery and sunflower kernels. Serve with the reserved sauce.
PER SERVING *1 chicken tender: 421 cal., 21g fat (4g sat. fat), 94mg chol., 518mg sod., 17g carb. (10g sugars, 3g fiber), 43g pro.*

HONEY BBQ CHICKEN

HONEY BBQ CHICKEN

I grill everything—veggies, oxtail, tofu—but this chicken is our favorite. I keep a ready supply of sauce and rub on hand, so the prep couldn't be easier.

—JERRY T. H. ROSIEK EUGENE, OR

PREP: 15 MIN. + CHILLING • **GRILL:** 40 MIN.
MAKES: 6 SERVINGS

- 6 chicken leg quarters

RUB
- ¼ cup packed brown sugar
- 1 tablespoon kosher salt
- ½ teaspoon garlic powder
- ⅛ teaspoon ground cinnamon

SAUCE
- 2 tablespoons butter
- ⅔ cup ketchup
- ½ cup honey
- 3 tablespoons balsamic vinegar
- 2 tablespoons yellow mustard
- 2 teaspoons reduced-sodium soy sauce
  Dash cayenne pepper, optional

1. Pat chicken dry. Combine rub ingredients. Rub over chicken pieces; refrigerate in a shallow dish for 2 hours.
2. Meanwhile, in a small saucepan over medium heat, combine sauce ingredients, adding cayenne if desired. Bring to a boil, stirring constantly; reduce the heat and simmer, uncovered, to allow the flavors to blend, 8-10 minutes.
3. On an oiled grill rack, grill chicken, covered, over indirect medium heat, turning frequently, until a thermometer reads 170°, 35-45 minutes. Remove.
4. Reduce heat to medium-low. Place the chicken on greased heavy-duty foil; brush with sauce, reserving ½ cup. Return to grill; cook, covered, until chicken pieces appear glazed, 4-6 minutes. Serve with the reserved sauce.
PER SERVING *1 chicken leg quarter equals 466 cal., 20g fat (7g sat. fat), 114mg chol., 1542mg sod., 42g carb., 0 fiber, 30g pro.*

GARLIC-GRILLED CHICKEN WITH PESTO ZUCCHINI RIBBONS

I first swapped zucchini noodles for pasta to reduce carbohydrates and calories. Now we just do it because we love their flavor and texture. For variety, try this dish with shrimp in place of the chicken—it's delicious!
—**SUZANNE BANFIELD** BASKING RIDGE, NJ

PREP: 35 MIN. • **GRILL:** 10 MIN.
MAKES: 4 SERVINGS

- 2 teaspoons grated lemon peel
- 2 tablespoons lemon juice
- 4 garlic cloves, minced
- ½ teaspoon coarsely ground pepper
- ¼ teaspoon salt
- 4 boneless skinless chicken breast halves (6 ounces each)

ZUCCHINI MIXTURE

- 4 large zucchini (about 2½ pounds)
- ¼ cup chopped oil-packed sun-dried tomatoes
- 1 teaspoon olive oil
- 2 garlic cloves, minced
- ¼ teaspoon salt
- ¼ teaspoon crushed red pepper flakes
- ¼ teaspoon coarsely ground pepper
- ¼ cup prepared pesto
- 4 ounces fresh mozzarella cheese, cut into ½-inch cubes

1. In a large bowl, mix the first five ingredients. Add chicken; turn to coat. Let stand 15 minutes.
2. Trim the ends of zucchini. Using a cheese slicer or vegetable peeler, cut zucchini lengthwise into long thin slices. Cut zucchini on all sides, as if peeling a carrot, until the seeds are visible. Discard the seeded portion or save for future use.
3. Grill chicken, covered, over medium heat or broil 4 in. from heat 4-5 minutes on each side or until a thermometer inserted in chicken reads 165°. Remove from grill; keep warm.
4. In a large nonstick skillet, heat the sun-dried tomatoes and olive oil over medium-high heat. Add the garlic, salt, pepper flakes and pepper; cook and stir 30 seconds. Add zucchini; cook and stir for 2-3 minutes or until crisp-tender. Remove from heat. Stir in pesto.
5. Cut chicken into slices. Serve with zucchini noodles. Top with mozzarella.
PER SERVING *1 chicken breast half with 1½ cup zucchini noodles: 397 cal., 18g fat (6g sat. fat), 116mg chol., 636mg sod., 14g carb. (7g sugars, 3g fiber), 44g pro. Diabetic Exchanges: 6 lean meat, 1½ fat, 1 vegetable.*

GARLIC-GRILLED CHICKEN WITH PESTO ZUCCHINI RIBBONS

---

⑤ INGREDIENTS FAST FIX ▸

SWEET AND SPICY GRILLED CHICKEN

This simple recipe has become my family's favorite way to eat chicken. The blend of sweet and spicy is perfect.
—**MELISSA BALL** PEARISBURG, VA

START TO FINISH: 20 MIN.
MAKES: 6 SERVINGS

- 2 tablespoons brown sugar
- 1 tablespoon paprika
- 2 teaspoons onion powder
- 1½ teaspoons salt
- 1 teaspoon chili powder
- 6 boneless skinless chicken breast halves (6 ounces each)

1. Combine the first five ingredients; rub over chicken.
2. On a lightly greased grill rack, grill the chicken, covered, over medium heat or broil 4 in. from heat 4-5 minutes on each side or until a thermometer reads 165°.
PER SERVING *207 cal., 4g fat (1g sat. fat), 94mg chol., 679mg sod., 6g carb. (5g sugars, 1g fiber), 35g pro. Diabetic Exchanges: 5 lean meat, ½ starch.*

ENCHILADA
CHICKEN, PAGE 151

CAESAR CHICKEN
WITH FETA, PAGE 150

CHICKEN IN A SKILLET

When it comes to quick, easy and fresh, **the top of the stove is tops!** From fried dishes and stovetop casseroles to meals with mouthwatering sauces, here's a fabulous collection of **fast, winning recipes** to make in the skillet and serve with confidence.

SKILLET CHICKEN
BURRITOS, PAGE 159

CHICKEN & GARLIC WITH FRESH HERBS, PAGE 145

CHICKEN TACOS WITH AVOCADO SALSA

CHICKEN TACOS WITH AVOCADO SALSA

My family has special dietary needs, and these zesty tacos suit everyone. For extra toppings, add cilantro, red onion, jalapeno, black olives and lettuce.

—CHRISTINE SCHENHER EXETER, CA

START TO FINISH: 30 MIN.
MAKES: 4 SERVINGS

- 1 pound boneless skinless chicken breasts, cut into ½-inch strips
- ⅓ cup water
- 1 teaspoon sugar
- 1 tablespoon chili powder
- 1 teaspoon onion powder
- 1 teaspoon dried oregano
- 1 teaspoon ground cumin
- 1 teaspoon paprika
- ½ teaspoon salt
- ½ teaspoon garlic powder
- 1 medium ripe avocado, peeled and cubed
- 1 cup fresh or frozen corn, thawed
- 1 cup cherry tomatoes, quartered
- 2 teaspoons lime juice
- 8 taco shells, warmed

1. Place a large nonstick skillet coated with cooking spray over medium-high heat. Brown chicken. Add water, sugar and seasonings. Cook 4-5 minutes or until the chicken is no longer pink, stirring occasionally.

2. Meanwhile, in a small bowl, gently mix avocado, corn, tomatoes and lime juice. Spoon the chicken mixture into the taco shells; top with avocado salsa.

FREEZE OPTION *Freeze cooled meat mixture in freezer containers. To use, partially thaw in refrigerator overnight. Heat through in a saucepan, stirring occasionally and adding a little water if necessary.*

PER SERVING *2 tacos: 354 cal., 15g fat (3g sat. fat), 63mg chol., 474mg sod., 30g carb. (4g sugars, 6g fiber), 27g pro.* **Diabetic Exchanges:** *3 lean meat, 2 starch, 1 fat.*

FAST FIX ▶

CHICKEN & GARLIC WITH FRESH HERBS

(PICTURED ON PAGE 143)

The key to this savory chicken dish is the combination of garlic, rosemary and thyme. Served with homemade bread or a side of mashed potatoes, it's a wonderful 30-minute dish.

—**JAN VALDEZ** LOMBARD, IL

START TO FINISH: 30 MIN.
MAKES: 6 SERVINGS

- 6 boneless skinless chicken thighs (about 1½ pounds)
- ½ teaspoon salt
- ¼ teaspoon pepper
- 1 tablespoon olive oil
- 10 garlic cloves, peeled and halved
- 2 tablespoons brandy or chicken stock
- 1 cup chicken stock
- 1 teaspoon minced fresh rosemary or ¼ teaspoon dried rosemary, crushed
- ½ teaspoon minced fresh thyme or ⅛ teaspoon dried thyme
- 1 tablespoon minced fresh chives

1. Sprinkle chicken with salt and pepper. In a large skillet, heat oil over medium-high heat. Brown the chicken on both sides. Remove from pan.

2. Remove skillet from heat; add halved garlic cloves and brandy. Return to heat; cook and stir over medium heat for 1-2 minutes or until liquid is almost evaporated.

3. Stir in stock, rosemary and thyme; return chicken to pan. Bring to a boil. Reduce heat; simmer, uncovered, for 6-8 minutes or until a thermometer reads 170°. Sprinkle with chives.

PER SERVING *1 chicken thigh with 2 tablespoons cooking juices: 203 cal., 11g fat (3g sat. fat), 76mg chol., 346mg sod., 2g carb. (0 sugars, 0 fiber), 22g pro. Diabetic Exchanges: 3 lean meat, ½ fat.*

CHEESY CHICKEN & BROCCOLI ORZO

⑤ INGREDIENTS **FAST FIX**

CHEESY CHICKEN & BROCCOLI ORZO

Broccoli and rice casserole tops my family's comfort food list, but when we need something fast, this is the stuff. Cooking chicken and veggie orzo on the stovetop speeds everything up.

—**MARY SHIVERS** ADA, OK

START TO FINISH: 30 MIN.
MAKES: 6 SERVINGS

- 1¼ cups uncooked orzo pasta
- 2 packages (10 ounces each) frozen broccoli with cheese sauce
- 2 tablespoons butter
- 1½ pounds boneless skinless chicken breasts, cut into ½-inch cubes
- 1 medium onion, chopped
- ¾ teaspoon salt
- ½ teaspoon pepper

1. Cook orzo according to the package directions. Meanwhile, heat broccoli with cheese sauce according to the package directions.

2. In a large skillet, heat butter over medium heat. Add chicken, onion, salt and pepper; cook and stir 6-8 minutes or until the chicken is no longer pink and the onion is tender. Drain orzo. Stir orzo and broccoli with cheese sauce into skillet; heat through.

PER SERVING *1 cup: 359 cal., 9g fat (4g sat. fat), 77mg chol., 655mg sod., 38g carb. (4g sugars, 3g fiber), 30g pro. Diabetic Exchanges: 3 lean meat, 2 starch, 1 vegetable, 1 fat.*

CHICKEN WITH FIRE-ROASTED TOMATOES

CHICKEN WITH FIRE-ROASTED TOMATOES

This chicken delivers the colors and flavors of Italy. The fire-roasted tomatoes sound complicated, but you just have to open a can!
—**MARGARET WILSON** SAN BERNARDINO, CA

START TO FINISH: 30 MIN.
MAKES: 4 SERVINGS

- 2 **tablespoons salt-free garlic herb seasoning blend**
- ½ **teaspoon salt**
- ¼ **teaspoon Italian seasoning**
- ¼ **teaspoon pepper**
- ⅛ **teaspoon crushed red pepper flakes, optional**

- 4 **boneless skinless chicken breast halves (6 ounces each)**
- 1 **tablespoon olive oil**
- 1 **can (14½ ounces) fire-roasted diced tomatoes, undrained**
- ¾ **pound fresh green beans, trimmed**
- 2 **tablespoons water**
- 1 **tablespoon butter**
  Hot cooked pasta, optional

1. Mix first five ingredients; sprinkle on both sides of chicken. In a large skillet, heat oil over medium heat. Brown chicken on both sides. Add tomatoes; bring to a boil. Reduce heat; simmer, covered, 10-12 minutes or until a thermometer inserted in chicken reads 165°.

2. Meanwhile, in a 2-qt. microwave-safe dish, combine green beans and water; microwave, covered, on high 3-4 minutes or just until tender. Drain.

3. Remove chicken from skillet; keep warm. Stir butter and beans into the tomato mixture. Serve with the chicken and, if desired, pasta.

PER SERVING *1 chicken breast half with 1 cup green bean mixture: 294 cal., 10g fat (3g sat. fat), 102mg chol., 681mg sod., 12g carb. (5g sugars, 4g fiber), 37g pro.* ***Diabetic Exchanges:*** *5 lean meat, 1 vegetable, 1 fat.*

⑤ INGREDIENTS FAST FIX ▶

MANGO CHUTNEY CHICKEN CURRY

My father dreamed up this curry and chutney combination. Now my family cooks it on road trips—in rain and sun, in the mountains, even on the beach. Adjust the curry for taste and your desired level of heat.

—DINA MORENO SEATTLE, WA

START TO FINISH: 25 MIN.
MAKES: 4 SERVINGS

- 1 tablespoon canola oil
- 1 pound boneless skinless chicken breasts, cubed
- 1 tablespoon curry powder
- 2 garlic cloves, minced
- ¼ teaspoon salt
- ¼ teaspoon pepper
- ½ cup mango chutney
- ½ cup half-and-half cream

1. In a large skillet, heat oil over medium-high heat; brown chicken. Stir in curry powder, garlic, salt and pepper; cook 1-2 minutes longer or until aromatic.
2. Stir in chutney and cream. Bring to boil. Reduce heat; simmer, uncovered, 4-6 minutes or until chicken is no longer pink, stirring occasionally.
PER SERVING ½ cup: 320 cal., 9g fat (3g sat. fat), 78mg chol., 558mg sod., 30g carb. (19g sugars, 1g fiber), 24g pro.

TOP TIP

HOME COOKS' SWAPS FOR MANGO CHUTNEY CHICKEN CURRY

I used creme fraiche instead of half-and-half and it was awesome.
—STEVO TASTEOFHOME.COM

We made this once with pineapple chutney and once with mango chutney and loved it each time.
—PIEHLAR TASTEOFHOME.COM

CHICKEN MARSALA WITH GORGONZOLA

CHICKEN MARSALA WITH GORGONZOLA

Chicken topped with melting Gorgonzola is quick enough for weeknight cooking and elegant enough for a dinner party. We live near the Faribault, Minnesota, caves that are used to age a lovely Gorgonzola cheese, so this is a favorite for us.

—JILL ANDERSON SLEEPY EYE, MN

PREP: 10 MIN. • **COOK:** 30 MIN.
MAKES: 4 SERVINGS

- 4 boneless skinless chicken breast halves (6 ounces each)
- ¼ teaspoon plus ⅛ teaspoon salt, divided
- ¼ teaspoon pepper
- 3 tablespoons olive oil, divided
- ½ pound sliced baby portobello mushrooms
- 2 garlic cloves, minced
- 1 cup Marsala wine
- ⅔ cup heavy whipping cream
- ½ cup crumbled Gorgonzola cheese, divided
- 2 tablespoons minced fresh parsley

1. Sprinkle chicken with ¼ teaspoon each salt and pepper. In a large skillet, cook chicken in 2 tablespoons oil over medium heat 6-8 minutes on each side or until a thermometer reads 165°. Remove and keep warm.
2. In same skillet, saute mushrooms in remaining oil until tender. Add garlic; cook 1 minute.
3. Add wine, stirring to loosen browned bits from pan. Bring to a boil; cook until liquid is reduced by a third. Stir in cream and remaining salt. Return to a boil; cook until slightly thickened.
4. Return chicken to pan; add ⅓ cup cheese. Cook until cheese is melted. Sprinkle with remaining cheese; garnish with parsley.
PER SERVING 514 cal., 33g fat (15g sat. fat), 161mg chol., 514mg sod., 8g carb. (3g sugars, 1g fiber), 40g pro.

CHICKEN BURRITO SKILLET

CHICKEN BURRITO SKILLET

We love Mexican night at our house, and I enjoy re-creating dishes from our favorite restaurants. This burrito-inspired main course is ready for the table in almost no time—give it a try tonight.

—KRISTA MARSHALL FORT WAYNE, IN

PREP: 15 MIN. • **COOK:** 30 MIN.
MAKES: 6 SERVINGS

- 1 **pound boneless skinless chicken breasts, cut into 1½-inch pieces**
- ⅛ **teaspoon salt**
- ⅛ **teaspoon pepper**
- 2 **tablespoons olive oil, divided**
- 1 **cup uncooked long grain rice**
- 1 **can (15 ounces) black beans, rinsed and drained**
- 1 **can (14½ ounces) diced tomatoes, drained**
- 1 **teaspoon ground cumin**
- ½ **teaspoon onion powder**
- ½ **teaspoon garlic powder**
- ½ **teaspoon chili powder**
- 2½ **cups reduced-sodium chicken broth**
- 1 **cup shredded Mexican cheese blend**
- 1 **medium tomato, chopped**
- 3 **green onions, chopped**

1. Toss chicken with salt and pepper. In a large skillet, heat 1 tablespoon oil over medium-high heat; saute the chicken until browned, about 2 minutes. Remove from pan.

2. In the same pan, heat the remaining oil over medium-high heat; saute rice until lightly browned, 1-2 minutes. Stir in beans, canned tomatoes, seasonings and broth; bring to a boil. Place chicken on top (do not stir into rice). Simmer, covered, until rice is tender and the chicken is no longer pink, 20-25 minutes.

3. Remove from heat; sprinkle with cheese. Let stand, covered, until cheese is melted. Top with tomato and green onions.

PER SERVING *1⅓ cups: 403 cal., 13g fat (4g sat. fat), 58mg chol., 690mg sod., 43g carb., 5g fiber, 27g pro.* **Diabetic Exchanges:** *3 starch, 3 lean meat, 1½ fat.*

FAMILY-FAVORITE FRIED CHICKEN

FAMILY-FAVORITE FRIED CHICKEN

I was never impressed with the fried chicken recipes I'd tried, but then I started to experiment and came up with one that my whole family loves. Once you taste it, you'll know why!

—SAMANTHA PAZDERNIK BRECKENRIDGE, MN

PREP: 20 MIN. • **COOK:** 10 MIN./BATCH
MAKES: 4 SERVINGS

- 1 **cup all-purpose flour**
- ½ **cup dry bread crumbs**
- 2 **tablespoons poultry seasoning**
- 1 **tablespoon paprika**
- ½ **teaspoon dried parsley flakes**
- ¼ **teaspoon salt**
- ¼ **teaspoon onion powder**
- ¼ **teaspoon garlic powder**
- ¼ **teaspoon pepper**
- 3 **large eggs**
- 1 **broiler/fryer chicken (3-4 pounds), cut up**
  Oil for deep-fat frying

1. In a shallow bowl, mix the first nine ingredients. In a separate shallow bowl, whisk eggs. Dip chicken pieces, one at a time, in the eggs; coat with flour mixture.

2. Heat oil to 375° in an electric skillet, deep-fat fryer or cast iron skillet. Fry chicken, a few pieces at a time, 4-5 minutes on each side or until golden brown and juices run clear. Drain on paper towels.

PRETZEL-CRUSTED FRIED CHICKEN:
Omit the first nine ingredients. Reduce eggs to 2. In a food processor, finely crush 2½ cups sourdough pretzel nuggets. In a shallow bowl, combine crushed pretzels with ½ cup flour. In another shallow bowl, beat 2 eggs with ¼ cup buttermilk, 2 minced garlic cloves and ⅛ teaspoon pepper. Coat and fry the chicken as the recipe directs. Serve with honey mustard if desired.

PER SERVING *7 ounces cooked chicken: 630 cal., 29g fat (8g sat. fat), 290mg chol., 414mg sod., 37g carb. (2g sugars, 2g fiber), 52g pro.*

CAESAR CHICKEN WITH FETA (PICTURED ON PAGE 143)

My tomato-y chicken is the perfect answer on those crazy days when supper has to be on the table in 30 minutes, tops. It doesn't hurt that it's delicious, too.
—**DENISE CHELPKA** PHOENIX, AZ

START TO FINISH: 10 MIN.
MAKES: 4 SERVINGS

- 4 boneless skinless chicken breast halves (4 ounces each)
- ½ teaspoon salt
- ¼ teaspoon pepper
- 2 teaspoons olive oil
- 1 medium tomato, chopped
- ¼ cup creamy Caesar salad dressing
- ½ cup crumbled feta cheese

Sprinkle chicken with salt and pepper. In a large skillet, heat oil over medium-high heat. Brown chicken on one side. Turn chicken; add tomato and salad dressing to skillet. Cook, covered, 6-8 minutes or until a thermometer inserted in chicken reads 165°. Sprinkle with cheese.

PER SERVING *1 chicken breast half with 3 tablespoons tomato mixture: 262 cal., 16g fat (4g sat. fat), 76mg chol., 664mg sod., 2g carb. (1g sugars, 1g fiber), 26g pro.*

TOP TIP

ADD A LITTLE COLOR

It's easy to add some color to this Parmesan Bow Tie Pasta dish. The recipe is delicious as is, but also makes a great base for all kinds of vegetables. Opt for zucchini instead of summer squash, or go for a mixture of both. Add some bell peppers: green, red, orange or a mixture of all three. Add fresh vegetables to the pan along with the squash and cook until tender.

PARMESAN BOW TIE PASTA WITH CHICKEN

FAST FIX

PARMESAN BOW TIE PASTA WITH CHICKEN

On lazy summer weekends, we like chicken and yellow squash tossed with bow tie pasta. Fresh grated Parmesan adds a special touch.
—**SARAH SMILEY** BANGOR, ME

START TO FINISH: 30 MIN.
MAKES: 6 SERVINGS

- 1 package (16 ounces) bow tie pasta
- 5 tablespoons butter, divided
- 1 pound boneless skinless chicken breasts, cut into 1-inch pieces
- 1 teaspoon salt, divided
- 1 teaspoon pepper, divided
- 2 medium yellow summer squash or zucchini, cut into 1-inch pieces
- 3 tablespoons all-purpose flour
- 2 garlic cloves, minced
- 1½ cups fat-free milk
- ¾ cup grated Parmesan cheese

1. In a 6-qt. stockpot, cook pasta according to the package directions.
2. In a large skillet, heat 1 tablespoon butter over medium heat. Add chicken; cook and stir for 7-9 minutes or until no longer pink. Add ¼ teaspoon each salt and pepper; remove chicken from pan. In the same pan, heat 1 tablespoon butter over medium heat. Add squash; cook and stir 3-5 minutes or until tender. Remove from heat.
3. In a small saucepan, melt remaining 3 tablespoons butter over medium heat. Stir in flour and garlic until blended; gradually whisk in milk. Bring to a boil, stirring constantly; cook and stir for 1-2 minutes or until thickened. Remove from heat; stir in cheese and remaining salt and pepper.
4. Drain pasta; return to pot. Add the chicken, squash and sauce; heat through, stirring to combine.

PER SERVING *1½ cups: 528 cal., 16g fat (9g sat. fat), 77mg chol., 690mg sod., 64g carb. (7g sugars, 4g fiber), 33g pro.*

ONE-PAN CHICKEN RICE CURRY

I've been loving the subtle spice from curry lately, so I incorporated it into this saucy chicken and rice dish. It's a one-pan meal that's become a go-to dinnertime favorite.
—**MARY LOU TIMPSON** COLORADO CITY, AZ

START TO FINISH: 30 MIN.
MAKES: 4 SERVINGS

- 2 **tablespoons butter, divided**
- 1 **medium onion, halved and thinly sliced**
- 2 **tablespoons all-purpose flour**
- 3 **teaspoons curry powder**
- ½ **teaspoon salt**
- ½ **teaspoon pepper**
- 1 **pound boneless skinless chicken breasts, cut into 1-inch pieces**
- 1 **can (14½ ounces) reduced-sodium chicken broth**
- 1 **cup uncooked instant rice**
  Chopped fresh cilantro leaves, optional

1. In a large nonstick skillet, heat 1 tablespoon butter over medium-high heat; saute onion until tender and lightly browned, 3-5 minutes. Remove from pan.

2. Mix flour and seasonings; toss with chicken. In same pan, heat remaining butter over medium-high heat. Add chicken; cook just until no longer pink, 4-6 minutes, turning occasionally.

3. Stir in broth and onion; bring to a boil. Stir in rice. Remove from heat; let stand, covered, 5 minutes (mixture will be saucy). If desired, sprinkle with cilantro.

PER SERVING *1 cup: 300 cal., 9g fat (4g sat. fat), 78mg chol., 658mg sod., 27g carb., 2g fiber, 27g pro.* ***Diabetic Exchanges:*** *3 lean meat, 2 starch, 1½ fat.*

EAT SMART
ENCHILADA CHICKEN
(PICTURED ON PAGE 142)

We enjoy Southwestern flavors, and this six-ingredient recipe never gets boring. The chicken sizzles in the skillet before going in the oven and comes out tender and juicy every time.
—**NANCY SOUSLEY** LAFAYETTE, IN

PREP: 15 MIN. • **BAKE:** 20 MIN.
MAKES: 4 SERVINGS

- 4 **boneless skinless chicken breast halves (6 ounces each)**
- 2 **teaspoons salt-free Southwest chipotle seasoning blend**
- 1 **tablespoon olive oil**
- ¼ **cup enchilada sauce**
- ½ **cup shredded sharp cheddar cheese**
- 2 **tablespoons minced fresh cilantro**

Sprinkle chicken with seasoning blend. In an ovenproof skillet, brown chicken in oil. Top with enchilada sauce, cheese and cilantro. Bake at 350° for 18-20 minutes or until a thermometer reads 170°.
PER SERVING *1 chicken breast half: 265 cal., 11g fat (5g sat. fat), 109mg chol., 252mg sod., 2g carb. (0 sugars, 0 fiber), 38g pro.* ***Diabetic Exchanges:*** *5 lean meat, 1 fat.*

ONE-PAN CHICKEN RICE CURRY

CHICKEN VEGGIE SKILLET

EAT SMART | FAST FIX ▶
CHICKEN VEGGIE SKILLET

I concocted this chicken and veggie dish to use up extra mushrooms and asparagus. My husband suggested I write it down because it's a keeper.

—REBEKAH BEYER SABETHA, KS

START TO FINISH: 30 MIN.
MAKES: 6 SERVINGS

- 1½ **pounds boneless skinless chicken breasts, cut into ½-inch strips**
- ½ **teaspoon salt**
- ¼ **teaspoon pepper**
- 6 **teaspoons olive oil, divided**
- ½ **pound sliced fresh mushrooms**
- 1 **small onion, halved and sliced**
- 2 **garlic cloves, minced**
- 1 **pound fresh asparagus, trimmed and cut into 1-inch pieces**
- ½ **cup sherry or chicken stock**
- 2 **tablespoons cold butter, cubed**

1. Sprinkle chicken with salt and pepper. In a large skillet, heat 1 teaspoon oil over medium-high heat. Add half of the chicken; cook and stir 3-4 minutes or until no longer pink. Remove from pan. Repeat with 1 teaspoon oil and remaining chicken.

2. In same pan, heat 2 teaspoons oil. Add mushrooms and onion; cook and stir 2-3 minutes or until tender. Add garlic; cook 1 minute longer. Add to chicken.

3. Heat remaining oil in pan. Add asparagus; cook 2-3 minutes or until crisp-tender. Add to chicken and mushrooms.

4. Add sherry to skillet, stirring to loosen browned bits from pan. Bring to a boil; cook 1-2 minutes or until liquid is reduced to 2 tablespoons. Return the chicken and vegetables to pan; heat through. Remove from heat; stir in butter, 1 tablespoon at a time.

PER SERVING *1 cup: 228 cal., 11g fat (4g sat. fat), 73mg chol., 384mg sod., 6g carb. (2g sugars, 1g fiber), 25g pro.* **Diabetic Exchanges:** *3 lean meat, 2 fat, 1 vegetable.*

FAST FIX ▶
CRISPY SAGE CHICKEN TENDERS

One of my mom's favorite chicken recipes used fresh sage. Her version was smothered with gravy, but we like these Panko-crusted tenders as they are.

—DEB PERRY TRAVERSE CITY, MI

START TO FINISH: 30 MIN.
MAKES: 4 SERVINGS

- ½ **cup buttermilk**
- ¾ **teaspoon salt**
- ¼ **teaspoon hot pepper sauce**
- ⅛ **teaspoon pepper**
- 1 **pound chicken tenderloins**
- 1 **cup panko (Japanese) bread crumbs**
- 2 **to 3 tablespoons fresh minced sage**
  Oil for frying
  Salt to taste
  Ranch salad dressing, optional

1. In a bowl, whisk buttermilk, salt, pepper sauce and pepper until blended. Add chicken, turning to coat; let stand 15 minutes. In a shallow bowl, toss bread crumbs with sage.

2. In a deep skillet, heat 1 in. oil to 365°. Dip chicken in crumb mixture to coat both sides, patting to help coating adhere. Fry 2-3 minutes on each side or until deep golden brown. Drain on paper towels. Sprinkle with additional salt to taste. If desired, serve with ranch dressing.

PER SERVING *227 cal., 11g fat (1g sat. fat), 67mg chol., 320mg sod., 6g carb. (1g sugars, 0 fiber), 27g pro.*

CRISPY SAGE CHICKEN TENDERS

(5) INGREDIENTS FAST FIX ▶

SUPER QUICK CHICKEN FRIED RICE

After my first child was born, I needed meals that were both satisfying and fast. This fried rice has become one of our routine dinners.
—**ALICIA GOWER** AUBURN, NY

START TO FINISH: 30 MIN.
MAKES: 6 SERVINGS

- 1 **package (12 ounces) frozen mixed vegetables**
- 2 **tablespoons olive oil, divided**
- 2 **large eggs, lightly beaten**
- 4 **tablespoons sesame oil, divided**
- 3 **packages (8.8 ounces each) ready-to-serve garden vegetable rice**
- 1 **rotisserie chicken, skin removed, shredded**
- ¼ **teaspoon salt**
- ¼ **teaspoon pepper**

1. Prepare frozen vegetables according to package directions. Meanwhile, in a large skillet, heat 1 tablespoon olive oil over medium-high heat. Pour in eggs; cook and stir until eggs are thickened and no liquid egg remains. Remove from pan.
2. In same skillet, heat 2 tablespoons sesame oil and the remaining olive oil over medium-high heat. Add rice; cook and stir 10-12 minutes or until the rice begins to brown.
3. Stir in chicken, salt and pepper. Add eggs and vegetables; heat through, breaking the eggs into small pieces and stirring to combine. Drizzle with the remaining sesame oil.
PER SERVING *1½ cups: 548 cal., 25g fat (5g sat. fat), 163mg chol., 934mg sod., 43g carb. (3g sugars, 3g fiber), 38g pro.*

SUPER QUICK CHICKEN FRIED RICE

QUICK CHICKEN &
BROCCOLI STIR-FRY

**APPLE-GLAZED
CHICKEN THIGHS**

EAT SMART FAST FIX ▶
QUICK CHICKEN & BROCCOLI STIR-FRY

This Asian stir-fry is a suppertime best bet. The spicy sauce works with beef, chicken, pork or seafood. Add whatever veggies you have on hand.

—KRISTIN RIMKUS SNOHOMISH, WA

START TO FINISH: 25 MIN.
MAKES: 4 SERVINGS

- 2 **tablespoons rice vinegar**
- 2 **tablespoons mirin (sweet rice wine)**
- 2 **tablespoons chili garlic sauce**
- 1 **tablespoon cornstarch**
- 1 **tablespoon reduced-sodium soy sauce**
- 2 **teaspoons fish sauce or additional soy sauce**
- ½ **cup reduced-sodium chicken broth, divided**
- 2 **cups instant brown rice**
- 2 **teaspoons sesame oil**
- 4 **cups fresh broccoli florets**
- 2 **cups cubed cooked chicken**
- 2 **green onions, sliced**

1. In a small bowl, mix the first six ingredients and ¼ cup chicken broth until smooth. Cook rice according to the package directions.
2. Meanwhile, in a large skillet, heat oil over medium-high heat. Add broccoli; stir-fry 2 minutes. Add the remaining broth; cook 1-2 minutes or until broccoli is crisp-tender. Stir sauce mixture and add to pan. Bring to a boil; cook and stir 1-2 minutes or until sauce is thickened.
3. Stir in chicken and green onions; heat through. Serve with rice.
PER SERVING *1 cup chicken mixture with ½ cup rice: 387 cal., 9g fat (2g sat. fat), 62mg chol., 765mg sod., 45g carb. (6g sugars, 4g fiber), 28g pro.* **Diabetic Exchanges:** *3 lean meat, 2½ starch, 1 vegetable, ½ fat.*

EAT SMART ⑤INGREDIENTS FAST FIX ▶
APPLE-GLAZED CHICKEN THIGHS

My child is choosy but willing to eat this chicken glazed with apple juice and thyme. I dish it up with mashed potatoes and beans.

—KERRY PICARD SPOKANE, WA

START TO FINISH: 25 MIN.
MAKES: 6 SERVINGS

- 6 **boneless skinless chicken thighs (1½ pounds)**
- ¾ **teaspoon seasoned salt**
- ¼ **teaspoon pepper**
- 1 **tablespoon canola oil**
- 1 **cup unsweetened apple juice**
- 1 **teaspoon minced fresh thyme or ¼ teaspoon dried thyme**

1. Sprinkle chicken with seasoned salt and pepper. In a large skillet, heat oil over medium-high heat. Brown chicken on both sides. Remove from pan.
2. Add juice and thyme to skillet. Bring to a boil, stirring to loosen browned bits from pan; cook until liquid is reduced by half. Return chicken to the pan; cook, covered, over medium heat 3-4 minutes longer or until a thermometer inserted in chicken reads 170°.
PER SERVING *1 chicken thigh with about 1 tablespoon glaze: 204 cal., 11g fat (2g sat. fat), 76mg chol., 255mg sod., 5g carb. (4g sugars, 0 fiber), 21g pro.* **Diabetic Exchanges:** *3 lean meat, ½ fat.*

BUFFALO CHICKEN TENDERS

These chicken tenders get a spicy kick thanks to homemade Buffalo sauce. They taste like they're from a restaurant, but are so easy to make at home. Blue cheese dipping sauce takes them over the top.

—**DAHLIA ABRAMS** DETROIT, MI

START TO FINISH: 20 MIN.
MAKES: 4 SERVINGS

- 1 **pound chicken tenderloins**
- 2 **tablespoons all-purpose flour**
- ¼ **teaspoon pepper**
- 2 **tablespoons butter, divided**
- ⅓ **cup Louisiana-style hot sauce**
- 1¼ **teaspoons Worcestershire sauce**
- 1 **teaspoon minced fresh oregano**
- ½ **teaspoon garlic powder**
  Blue cheese salad dressing, optional

1. Toss chicken with flour and pepper. In a large skillet, heat 1 tablespoon butter over medium heat. Add the chicken; cook until no longer pink, 4-6 minutes per side. Remove from pan.

2. Mix hot sauce, Worcestershire sauce, oregano and garlic powder. In the same skillet, melt the remaining butter; stir in sauce mixture. Add chicken; heat through, turning to coat. If desired, serve with blue cheese dressing.

PER SERVING *184 cal., 7g fat (4g sat. fat), 71mg chol., 801mg sod., 5g carb. (1g sugars, 0 fiber), 27g pro.* **Diabetic Exchanges:** *3 lean meat, 1½ fat.*

TOP TIP

CUT YOUR OWN TENDERS

Chicken tenders are the strips of meat that are attached to the underside of each breast half. You can buy tenders separately, but they cost more. Alternatively, cut regular boneless, skinless chicken breasts into strips; they'll cook up just like tenders, and they taste great, too.

BUFFALO CHICKEN TENDERS

FAST FIX ▶

SAGE & PROSCIUTTO CHICKEN SALTIMBOCCA

The Italian word *saltimbocca* means to jump into one's mouth. This wonderful dish fulfills the promise with prosciutto and fresh sage leaves. What a savory dinner!
—**TRISHA KRUSE** EAGLE, ID

START TO FINISH: 25 MIN.
MAKES: 4 SERVINGS

- ½ cup plus 2 teaspoons all-purpose flour, divided
- 4 boneless skinless chicken breast halves (6 ounces each)
- ½ teaspoon salt
- ¼ teaspoon pepper
- 8 fresh sage leaves
- 8 thin slices prosciutto or deli ham
- 2 tablespoons olive oil
- 1 tablespoon butter
- ½ cup chicken broth
- 2 tablespoons lemon juice
- 2 tablespoons white wine or additional chicken broth
  Lemon slices and fresh sage, optional

1. Place ½ cup flour in a shallow bowl; set aside. Flatten chicken breasts to ¼-in. thickness. Sprinkle both sides with salt and pepper; top each breast half with two sage leaves and two slices of prosciutto, pressing to adhere. Dip chicken sides only in flour to coat.

2. In a large skillet, heat oil and butter over medium heat; cook chicken for 3-4 minutes on each side or until lightly browned and chicken is no longer pink. Remove and keep warm.

3. In a small bowl, whisk the chicken broth, lemon juice, wine and remaining flour; add to the skillet, stirring to loosen browned bits from pan. Bring to a boil; cook and stir 1 minute or until thickened. Spoon over chicken. Top chicken with lemon slices and sage if desired.

PER SERVING *1 chicken breast half with 2 tablespoons sauce: 355 cal., 17g fat (5g sat. fat), 128mg chol., 1070mg sod., 5g carb. (0 sugars, 0 fiber), 43g pro.*

GARLIC CHICKEN RIGATONI

FAST FIX ▶

GARLIC CHICKEN RIGATONI

My family loves the scampi-inspired combination of garlic and olive oil in this delicious pasta. I love that it's guilt-free!
—**JUDY CRAWFORD** DEMING, NM

START TO FINISH: 30 MIN.
MAKES: 4 SERVINGS

- 8 ounces uncooked rigatoni or large tube pasta
- ¼ cup sun-dried tomatoes (not packed in oil)
- ½ cup boiling water
- ½ pound boneless skinless chicken breasts, cut into 1-inch cubes
- ¼ teaspoon garlic salt
- 2 tablespoons all-purpose flour
- 2 tablespoons olive oil, divided
- 1½ cups sliced fresh mushrooms
- 3 garlic cloves, minced
- ¼ cup reduced-sodium chicken broth
- ¼ cup white wine or additional reduced-sodium chicken broth
- 2 tablespoons minced fresh parsley
- ¼ teaspoon dried basil
- ⅛ teaspoon salt
- ⅛ teaspoon pepper
- ⅛ teaspoon crushed red pepper flakes
- ¼ cup grated Parmesan cheese

1. Cook rigatoni according to package directions. In a small bowl, combine tomatoes and boiling water; let stand for 5 minutes. Drain; chop tomatoes.

2. Sprinkle chicken with garlic salt; add flour and toss to coat. In a large skillet, heat 1 tablespoon oil over medium-high heat. Add the chicken; cook and stir for 4-5 minutes or until meat is no longer pink. Remove from pan.

3. In same skillet, heat remaining oil over medium-high heat. Add mushrooms and garlic; cook and stir until tender. Add broth, wine, parsley, seasonings and chopped tomatoes; bring to a boil. Stir in chicken; heat through.

4. Drain rigatoni; add to chicken mixture. Sprinkle with cheese and toss to coat.

PER SERVING *1½ cups: 398 cal., 11g fat (2g sat. fat), 36mg chol., 290mg sod., 50g carb. (5g sugars, 3g fiber), 23g pro.*

FAST FIX ▶

SMOKED MOZZARELLA CHICKEN WITH PASTA

Make chicken breasts extraordinary with just a few flavorful additions. Use prosciutto instead of ham to elevate the dish even further.
—NAYLET LAROCHELLE MIAMI, FL

START TO FINISH: 30 MIN.
MAKES: 4 SERVINGS

- 8 ounces uncooked angel hair pasta or thin spaghetti
- 4 boneless skinless chicken breast halves (6 ounces each)
- ½ teaspoon salt
- ¼ teaspoon pepper
- ⅔ cup seasoned bread crumbs
- 2 tablespoons olive oil
- 4 thin slices smoked deli ham
- 4 slices smoked mozzarella cheese
- ½ teaspoon dried sage leaves
- ½ cup prepared pesto
  Grated Parmesan cheese, optional

1. Cook pasta according to package directions. Drain; transfer to a large bowl.
2. Meanwhile, pound chicken breasts with a meat mallet to ½-in. thickness; sprinkle with salt and pepper. Place bread crumbs in a shallow bowl. Dip chicken in bread crumbs to coat both sides; shake off excess.

3. In a large skillet, heat oil over medium-high heat. Add chicken; cook 4 minutes. Turn; cook 2 minutes longer. Top with ham and mozzarella cheese; sprinkle with sage. Cook 1-2 minutes longer or until a thermometer inserted in chicken reads 165°. Remove from heat.
4. Add pesto to pasta and toss to coat. Serve chicken with pasta. If desired, sprinkle with Parmesan cheese.

PER SERVING *1 chicken breast half with ¾ cup pasta (calculated without Parmesan cheese): 694 cal., 28g fat (7g sat. fat), 122mg chol., 1184mg sod., 53g carb. (4g sugars, 3g fiber), 53g pro.*

SMOKED MOZZARELLA CHICKEN WITH PASTA

CHICKEN SAUSAGE & GNOCCHI SKILLET

EAT SMART **FAST FIX**

SKILLET CHICKEN BURRITOS (PICTURED ON PAGE 143)

Here's one of my go-to dishes when I'm in a rush to make dinner. Preparing the burritos in the skillet not only saves time, it gives them a crispy outside and ooey-gooey inside.
—**SCARLETT ELROD** NEWNAN, GA

START TO FINISH: 30 MIN.
MAKES: 8 SERVINGS

- 1 cup (8 ounces) reduced-fat sour cream
- ¼ cup chopped fresh cilantro
- 2 tablespoons chopped pickled jalapeno slices
- 2 teaspoons chopped onion
- 2 teaspoons Dijon mustard
- 1 teaspoon grated lime peel

BURRITOS

- 2 cups cubed cooked chicken breast
- 1 can (15 ounces) black beans, rinsed and drained
- 1 can (11 ounces) Mexicorn, drained
- 1 cup shredded reduced-fat cheddar cheese
- ¼ teaspoon salt
- 8 whole wheat tortillas (8 inches), warmed
  Cooking spray
  Salsa, optional

1. In a small bowl, combine the first six ingredients. In a large bowl, combine chicken, beans, corn, cheese, salt and ½ cup of the sour cream mixture. Spoon ½ cup chicken mixture onto each tortilla. Fold sides and ends over filling and roll up. Spritz both sides with cooking spray.
2. In a large nonstick skillet or griddle coated with cooking spray, cook burritos in batches over medium heat for 3-4 minutes on each side or until golden brown. Serve with remaining sour cream mixture and, if desired, salsa.
PER SERVING *1 burrito with 1 tablespoon sour cream mixture (calculated without salsa): 349 cal., 10g fat (4g sat. fat), 46mg chol., 770mg sod., 40g carb (6g sugars, 5g fiber), 23g pro.* **Diabetic Exchanges:** *3 lean meat, 2½ starch.*

FAST FIX

CHICKEN SAUSAGE & GNOCCHI SKILLET

I had a bunch of fresh veggies and combined them with sausage, gnocchi and goat cheese when I needed a quick dinner. Mix and match the ingredients you have on hand to give it your own spin.
—**DAHLIA ABRAMS** DETROIT, MI

START TO FINISH: 30 MIN.
MAKES: 4 SERVINGS

- 1 package (16 ounces) potato gnocchi
- 1 tablespoon butter
- 1 tablespoon olive oil
- 2 fully cooked Italian chicken sausage links (3 ounces each), sliced
- ½ pound sliced baby portobello mushrooms
- 1 medium onion, finely chopped
- 1 pound fresh asparagus, trimmed and cut into ½-inch pieces
- 2 garlic cloves, minced
- 2 tablespoons white wine or chicken broth
- 2 ounces herbed fresh goat cheese
- 2 tablespoons minced fresh basil or 2 teaspoons dried basil
- 1 tablespoon lemon juice
- ¼ teaspoon salt
- ⅛ teaspoon pepper
  Grated Parmesan cheese

1. Cook gnocchi according to package directions; drain. Meanwhile, in a large skillet, heat butter and oil over medium-high heat. Add sausage, mushrooms and onion; cook and stir until the sausage is browned and vegetables are tender. Add asparagus and garlic; cook and stir for 2-3 minutes longer.
2. Stir in wine. Bring to a boil; cook until the liquid is almost evaporated. Add goat cheese, basil, lemon juice, salt and pepper. Stir in gnocchi; heat through. Sprinkle with Parmesan cheese.
PER SERVING *1½ cups (calculated without Parmesan cheese): 454 cal., 15g fat (6g sat. fat), 58mg chol., 995mg sod., 56g carb. (11g sugars, 5g fiber), 21g pro.*

CITRUS-HERB ROASTED CHICKEN , PAGE 168

CAPRESE CHICKEN, PAGE 166

WINNER, WINNER, CHICKEN DINNER

When it comes to no-fail dinners the **whole family craves,** chicken is a natural choice. From roasted chicken to meal-in-one casseroles, the selection of **oven-baked dinners** offered here makes menu planning a snap. Preheat the oven and get ready to try some **winning dishes** sure to become new dinnertime favorites.

BARBECUE CHICKEN PIZZA, PAGE 163

CHICKEN TAMALE BAKE, PAGE 171

⑤INGREDIENTS

CONTEST-WINNING BROCCOLI CHICKEN CASSEROLE

All ages seem to appreciate this comforting, scrumptious meal-in-one. It takes a handful of ingredients and just minutes to put together. I've found that adding dried cranberries to the stuffing mix adds both flavor and color.

—JENNIFER SCHLACHTER BIG ROCK, IL

PREP: 15 MIN. • **BAKE:** 30 MIN.
MAKES: 6 SERVINGS

- 1 **package (6 ounces) chicken stuffing mix**
- 2 **cups cubed cooked chicken**
- 1 **cup frozen broccoli florets, thawed**
- 1 **can (10¾ ounces) condensed broccoli cheese soup, undiluted**
- 1 **cup shredded cheddar cheese**

1. Preheat oven to 350°. Prepare stuffing mix according to package directions, using 1½ cups water.

2. In a large bowl, combine chicken, broccoli and soup; transfer to a greased 11x7-in. baking dish. Top with stuffing; sprinkle with cheese. Bake, covered, 20 minutes. Uncover; bake 10-15 minutes longer or until heated through.

FREEZE OPTION *Transfer individual portions of cooled casserole to freezer containers; freeze. To use, partially thaw in refrigerator overnight. Transfer to a microwave-safe dish; microwave, covered, on high until a thermometer inserted in center reads 165°, stirring occasionally and adding a little broth if necessary.*

PER SERVING *1⅓ cups: 315 cal., 13g fat (6g sat. fat), 66mg chol., 1025mg sod., 25g carb. (4g sugars, 2g fiber), 23g pro.*

**CONTEST-WINNING
BROCCOLI CHICKEN
CASSEROLE**

BARBECUE CHICKEN PIZZA (PICTURED ON PAGE 161)

My husband and I love barbecue chicken pizza, but I took it up a notch by adding other toppings that we love, including smoky bacon and creamy Gorgonzola.

—MEGAN CROW LINCOLN, NE

PREP: 30 MIN. • **BAKE:** 15 MIN.
MAKES: 8 SERVINGS

- 2 tablespoons olive oil
- 1 medium red onion, sliced
- 1 tube (13.8 ounces) refrigerated pizza crust
- ¾ cup barbecue sauce
- 2 cups shredded cooked chicken breast
- 6 bacon strips, cooked and crumbled
- ¼ cup crumbled Gorgonzola cheese
- 2 jalapeno peppers, seeded and minced
- 1 teaspoon paprika
- 1 teaspoon garlic powder
- 2 cups shredded part-skim mozzarella cheese

1. Preheat oven to 425°. In a large skillet, heat oil over medium heat. Add onion; cook and stir for 4-6 minutes or until softened. Reduce heat to medium-low; cook 20-25 minutes or until deep golden brown, stirring occasionally.
2. Unroll and press dough onto bottom and ½ in. up sides of a greased 15x10x1-in. baking pan. Bake 8 minutes.
3. Spread barbecue sauce over dough; top with chicken, cooked onion, bacon, Gorgonzola cheese and minced jalapenos. Sprinkle with paprika and garlic powder; top with mozzarella cheese. Bake pizza 8-10 minutes or until crust is golden and cheese is melted.
FREEZE OPTION *Bake pizza crust as directed; cool. Top with all the ingredients as directed, then securely wrap and freeze unbaked pizza. To use, unwrap pizza; bake as directed, increasing time as necessary.*
NOTE *Wear disposable gloves when cutting hot peppers; the oils can burn skin. Avoid touching your face.*
PER SERVING *1 slice: 354 cal., 15g fat (5g sat. fat), 53mg chol., 851mg sod., 29g carb. (7g sugars, 2g fiber), 25g pro.*

CHICKEN CORDON BLEU CRESCENT RING

FAST FIX

CHICKEN CORDON BLEU CRESCENT RING

A classic Cordon Bleu has chicken, cheese and ham. To change it up, roll everything inside crescent dough for a speedy meal. It seems nobody can get enough of this dish!

—STELLA CULOTTA PASADENA, MD

START TO FINISH: 30 MIN.
MAKES: 6 SERVINGS

- 1 tube (8 ounces) refrigerated crescent rolls
- 2 cups shredded Swiss cheese
- 2 cups cubed cooked chicken
- ¾ cup mayonnaise
- ½ cup cubed fully cooked ham
- 2 tablespoons honey mustard

1. Preheat oven to 375°. Unroll crescent dough and separate into triangles. On an ungreased 12-in. pizza pan, arrange the triangles in a ring with points toward the outside and wide ends overlapping. Press overlapping dough to seal.
2. In a large bowl, mix the remaining ingredients. Spoon across wide ends of triangles. Fold pointed ends of triangles over filling, tucking points under to form a ring (filling will be visible).
3. Bake 15-20 minutes or until golden brown and heated through.
PER SERVING *1 slice: 603 cal., 45g fat (13g sat. fat), 91mg chol., 772mg sod., 19g carb. (6g sugars, 0 fiber), 29g pro.*

CHICKEN & SWISS
CASSEROLE

CHICKEN & SWISS CASSEROLE

I love the taste of roasted chicken, but with just me at home, I often have a lot of chicken left over. This casserole recipe was given to me by a deli worker along with my chicken one day and I've used it ever since.

—CHRISTINA PETRI ALEXANDRIA, MN

PREP: 30 MIN. • **BAKE:** 10 MIN.
MAKES: 8 SERVINGS

- 5½ cups uncooked egg noodles (about ½ pound)
- 3 tablespoons olive oil
- 3 shallots, chopped
- 3 small garlic cloves, minced
- ⅓ cup all-purpose flour
- 2 cups chicken broth
- ¾ cup 2% milk
- 1½ teaspoons dried thyme
- ¾ teaspoon grated lemon peel
- ½ teaspoon salt
- ¼ teaspoon ground nutmeg
- ¼ teaspoon pepper
- 5 cups cubed rotisserie chicken
- 1½ cups frozen peas
- 2 cups shredded Swiss cheese
- ¾ cup dry bread crumbs
- 2 tablespoons butter, melted

1. Preheat oven to 350°. Cook noodles according to package directions; drain. In a large skillet, heat oil over medium heat. Add the shallots and garlic; cook and stir 45 seconds. Stir in flour; cook and stir 1 minute. Add broth, milk, thyme, lemon peel, salt, nutmeg and pepper. Stir in chicken and peas; heat through. Stir in noodles and cheese.
2. Transfer to a greased 13x9-in. baking dish. In a small bowl, mix bread crumbs and butter; sprinkle over top. Bake 8-10 minutes or until top is browned.
PER SERVING *1¼ cups: 551 cal., 25g fat (10g sat. fat), 136mg chol., 661mg sod., 38g carb. (4g sugars, 3g fiber), 41g pro.*

CLASSIC CHICKEN
& WAFFLES

FAST FIX
CLASSIC CHICKEN & WAFFLES

A down-home diner special gets weeknight-easy with the help of rotisserie chicken. Want 'em even faster? Make the waffles ahead of time and freeze till dinner.

—LAUREN REIFF EAST EARL, PA

START TO FINISH: 30 MIN.
MAKES: 6 SERVINGS

- 3 tablespoons butter
- 3 tablespoons all-purpose flour
- ½ teaspoon salt
- ¼ teaspoon pepper
- ½ cup chicken broth
- 1¼ cups 2% milk
- 2 cups coarsely shredded rotisserie chicken

WAFFLES
- 2 cups all-purpose flour
- 2 tablespoons sugar
- 4 teaspoons baking powder
- ½ teaspoon salt
- 2 large eggs
- 1½ cups 2% milk
- 5 tablespoons butter, melted
  Sliced green onions, optional

1. In a large saucepan, melt butter over medium heat. Stir in flour, salt and pepper until smooth; gradually whisk in broth and milk. Bring to a boil, stirring constantly; cook and stir until thickened, 1-2 minutes. Stir in chicken; heat through. Keep warm.
2. Preheat waffle maker. Whisk together flour, sugar, baking powder and salt. In another bowl, whisk together eggs, milk and melted butter; add to dry ingredients, stirring just until moistened.
3. Bake waffles according to the manufacturer's directions until golden brown. Top waffles with chicken mixture and, if desired, green onions.
PER SERVING *2 waffles with ⅔ cup chicken mixture: 488 cal., 23g fat (13g sat. fat), 154mg chol., 981mg sod., 45g carb., 1g fiber, 24g pro.*

CAPRESE CHICKEN

(PICTURED ON PAGE 161)

I love a Caprese salad of tomatoes, basil and cheese, so why not use those items with chicken? You can grill this dish, but my family agrees it's juicier straight from the oven.
—**DANA JOHNSON** SCOTTSDALE, AZ

PREP: 10 MIN. + MARINATING • **BAKE:** 20 MIN.
MAKES: 4 SERVINGS

- ⅔ cup Italian salad dressing
- 2 teaspoons chicken seasoning
- 2 teaspoons Italian seasoning
- 4 boneless skinless chicken breast halves (6 ounces each)
- 2 tablespoons canola oil
- ½ pound fresh mozzarella cheese, cut into 4 slices
- 2 medium tomatoes, sliced
- 1 tablespoon balsamic vinegar or balsamic glaze
   Torn fresh basil leaves

1. In a large resealable plastic bag, combine salad dressing, chicken seasoning and Italian seasoning. Add chicken; seal bag and turn to coat. Refrigerate 4-6 hours. Drain chicken, discarding marinade.
2. Preheat oven to 450°. In an ovenproof skillet, heat oil over medium-high heat. Brown chicken on both sides. Transfer skillet to oven; bake 15-18 minutes or until a thermometer reads 165°.
3. Top chicken with cheese and tomato. Bake 3-5 minutes longer or until cheese is melted. Drizzle with vinegar; top with torn basil.

PER SERVING *1 chicken breast half: 525 cal., 34g fat (11g sat. fat), 139mg chol., 761mg sod., 5g carb. (4g sugars, 1g fiber), 45g pro.*

BAKED MONTEREY CHICKEN WITH ROASTED VEGGIES

BAKED MONTEREY CHICKEN WITH ROASTED VEGGIES

Everyone asks me for this baked chicken. Roasting the veggies adds extra flavor that tastes great with fettuccine, rice or mashed potatoes.
—**GLORIA BRADLEY** NAPERVILLE, IL

PREP: 15 MIN. • **BAKE:** 25 MIN.
MAKES: 6 SERVINGS

- 1 pound fresh asparagus, trimmed and cut into 2-inch pieces
- 2 large sweet red peppers, cut into strips
- 1 tablespoon olive oil
- 1½ teaspoons salt, divided
- ¾ teaspoon coarsely ground pepper, divided
- 6 boneless skinless chicken breast halves (6 ounces each)
- 5 tablespoons butter, divided
- ¼ cup all-purpose flour
- 1 cup chicken broth
- 1 cup heavy whipping cream
- ¼ cup white wine or additional chicken broth
- 1½ cups shredded Monterey Jack cheese, divided

1. Preheat oven to 400°. Place asparagus and red peppers in a greased 13x9-in. baking dish; toss with oil, ½ teaspoon salt and ¼ teaspoon pepper. Roast for 5-8 minutes or just until crisp-tender. Remove vegetables from dish.
2. Season chicken with the remaining salt and pepper. In a large skillet, heat 1 tablespoon butter over medium heat; brown 3 chicken breasts on both sides. Transfer to the same baking dish. Repeat with an additional 1 tablespoon butter and remaining chicken. Top chicken with roasted vegetables.
3. In same skillet, melt remaining butter over medium heat. Stir in flour until smooth; gradually whisk in broth, cream and wine. Bring to a boil over medium heat, stirring constantly; cook and stir 2-3 minutes or until thickened. Stir in 1 cup cheese until melted. Pour over chicken.
4. Bake, uncovered, 25-30 minutes or until a thermometer inserted in chicken reads 165°. Sprinkle with remaining cheese.

PER SERVING *1 chicken breast half: 581 cal., 40g fat (22g sat. fat), 200mg chol., 1093mg sod., 11g carb. (3g sugars, 2g fiber), 44g pro.*

CHICKEN RANCH MAC & CHEESE

Prep once and feed the family twice when you double this casserole and freeze half. I created this recipe for the people I love most, using the ingredients they love best.

—ANGELA SPENGLER TAMPA, FL

PREP: 15 MIN. • **BAKE:** 30 MIN.
MAKES: 8 SERVINGS

- 3 cups uncooked elbow macaroni
- 3 tablespoons butter
- 2 tablespoons all-purpose flour
- ½ teaspoon salt
- ¼ teaspoon pepper
- 1 cup 2% milk
- 1½ cups shredded cheddar cheese
- ½ cup grated Parmesan cheese
- ½ cup shredded Swiss cheese
- ¾ cup ranch salad dressing
- 1 cup coarsely chopped cooked chicken

TOPPING
- ⅓ cup seasoned bread crumbs
- 2 tablespoons butter, melted
- 10 bacon strips, cooked and crumbled
- 1 tablespoon minced fresh parsley

1. Preheat oven to 350°. In a 6-qt. stockpot, cook macaroni according to package directions for al dente; drain and return to pot.
2. Meanwhile, in a medium saucepan, melt butter over medium heat. Stir in flour, salt and pepper until smooth; gradually whisk in milk. Bring to a boil, stirring constantly; cook and stir 1-2 minutes or until thickened. Stir in cheeses until blended. Stir in dressing.
3. Add chicken and sauce to macaroni, tossing to combine. Transfer to a greased 13x9-in. baking dish.
4. Toss bread crumbs with melted butter; sprinkle over macaroni. Top with bacon. Bake, uncovered, 30-35 minutes or until topping is golden brown. Sprinkle with parsley.

FREEZE OPTION *Prepare recipe as directed, increasing milk to 1⅓ cups. Cool unbaked casserole; cover and freeze. To use, partially thaw in refrigerator overnight. Remove from refrigerator 30 minutes before baking. Preheat oven to 350°. Cover casserole with foil; bake 30 minutes. Uncover; continue baking as directed or until heated through and for a thermometer inserted in center to read 165°.*

PER SERVING *1 cup: 586 cal., 37g fat (15g sat. fat), 84mg chol., 889mg sod., 40g carb. (4g sugars, 2g fiber), 25g pro.*

CHICKEN RANCH MAC & CHEESE

TOP TIP

READER REVIEW AND HEALTHY SUBSTITUTION

Clever recipe! It has all the key ingredients that my family enjoys, all thrown into one dish. This will be a regular on our table. I used whole wheat macaroni in place of the regular macaroni. So good!

—ANGEL182009
TASTEOFHOME.COM

**CITRUS-HERB
ROAST CHICKEN**

2-2½ hours, sprinkling green onions over vegetables during the last 20 minutes. (Cover loosely with foil if chicken browns too quickly.)

4. Remove chicken from oven; tent with foil. Let stand 15 minutes before carving. Discard herbs. If desired, skim fat and thicken pan drippings for gravy. Serve with chicken and vegetables.

PER SERVING *7 ounces cooked chicken with 1¼ cups vegetables: 561 cal., 24g fat (7g sat. fat), 136mg chol., 826mg sod., 39g carb. (5g sugars, 5g fiber), 47g pro.*

⑤ INGREDIENTS

BACON CHICKEN ROLL-UPS

I get many requests for these cute roll-ups. I love the recipe because it's so simple but has a hearty flavor.

—SANDI GUETTLER BAY CITY, MI

PREP: 20 MIN. • **BAKE:** 35 MIN.
MAKES: 6 SERVINGS

- 12 **bacon strips**
- 6 **boneless skinless chicken breast halves (4 ounces each)**
- 1 **package (8 ounces) cream cheese, softened**
- 1 **medium sweet onion, halved and cut into slices**
- **Dash salt and pepper**

1. Preheat oven to 350°. In a large skillet, cook bacon over medium heat until cooked but not crisp. Remove to paper towels to drain.

2. Meanwhile, flatten chicken to ⅛-in. thickness. Spread cream cheese down the center of each chicken breast; top with onion. Roll up from a long side; tuck ends in. Sprinkle with salt and pepper. Wrap two bacon strips around each piece of chicken; secure with toothpicks.

3. Place in a greased 13x9-in. baking dish. Bake 35-40 minutes or until a thermometer reads 165°. Discard toothpicks.

PER SERVING *1 roll-up: 332 cal., 21g fat (11g sat. fat), 118mg chol., 484mg sod., 4g carb. (1g sugars, 0 fiber), 31g pro.*

CITRUS-HERB ROAST CHICKEN

This recipe is one of my all-time favorites. Flavorful, juicy chicken with the best flavors of spring: fresh herbs, lemon, and spring onions. It's the perfect one-pot meal.

—MEGAN FORDYCE FAIRCHANCE, PA

PREP: 25 MIN. • **BAKE:** 2 HOURS + STANDING
MAKES: 8 SERVINGS

- 6 **garlic cloves**
- 1 **roasting chicken (6 to 7 pounds)**
- 3 **pounds baby red potatoes, halved**
- 6 **medium carrots, halved lengthwise and cut into 1-inch pieces**
- 4 **fresh thyme sprigs**
- 4 **fresh dill sprigs**
- 2 **fresh rosemary sprigs**
- 1 **medium lemon**
- 1 **small navel orange**
- 1 **teaspoon salt**
- ½ **teaspoon pepper**
- 3 **cups chicken broth, warmed**
- 6 **green onions, cut into 2-inch pieces**

1. Preheat oven to 350°. Peel and cut garlic into quarters. Place chicken on a cutting board. Tuck wings under chicken. With a sharp paring knife, cut 24 small slits in breasts, drumsticks and thighs. Insert garlic in slits. Tie drumsticks together.

2. Place potatoes and carrots in a shallow roasting pan; top with herbs. Place chicken, breast side up, over vegetables and herbs. Cut lemon and orange in half; gently squeeze juices over chicken and vegetables. Place squeezed fruits inside chicken cavity. Sprinkle chicken with salt and pepper. Pour broth around chicken.

3. Roast until a thermometer inserted in thickest part of thigh reads 170°-175°,

EAT SMART
ARTICHOKE RATATOUILLE CHICKEN

I loaded all the fresh produce I could find into this speedy chicken dinner. Serve it on its own or over pasta.

—**JUDY ARMSTRONG** PRAIRIEVILLE, LA

PREP: 25 MIN. • **BAKE:** 1 HOUR
MAKES: 6 SERVINGS

- 3 Japanese eggplants (about 1 pound)
- 4 plum tomatoes
- 1 medium sweet yellow pepper
- 1 medium sweet red pepper
- 1 medium onion
- 1 can (14 ounces) water-packed artichoke hearts, drained and quartered
- 2 tablespoons minced fresh thyme
- 2 tablespoons capers, drained
- 2 tablespoons olive oil
- 2 garlic cloves, minced
- 1 teaspoon Creole seasoning, divided
- 1½ pounds boneless skinless chicken breasts, cubed
- 1 cup white wine or chicken broth
- ¼ cup grated Asiago cheese
  Hot cooked pasta, optional

1. Preheat oven to 350°. Cut eggplants, tomatoes, peppers and onion into ¾-in. pieces; transfer to a large bowl. Stir in artichoke hearts, thyme, capers, oil, garlic and ½ teaspoon Creole seasoning.

2. Sprinkle chicken with remaining Creole seasoning. Transfer chicken to a 13x9-in. baking dish coated with cooking spray; spoon vegetable mixture over top. Drizzle wine over vegetables.

3. Bake, covered, 30 minutes. Uncover; bake 30-45 minutes longer or until chicken is no longer pink and vegetables are tender. Sprinkle with cheese. If desired, serve with pasta.

PER SERVING 1⅔ cups (calculated without pasta): 252 cal., 9g fat (2g sat. fat), 67mg chol., 468mg sod., 15g carb. (4g sugars, 4g fiber), 28g pro. **Diabetic Exchanges:** 3 lean meat, 1 starch, 1 fat.

ARTICHOKE RATATOUILLE CHICKEN

CHICKEN TACO PIE

This family favorite comes to the rescue on busy nights when we've been rushing to soccer, swimming lessons or Scouts. I put it together in the morning and just pop it in the oven when we get home.

—**KAREN LATIMER** WINNIPEG, MB

PREP: 20 MIN. • **BAKE:** 30 MIN.
MAKES: 6 SERVINGS

- 1 **tube (8 ounces) refrigerated crescent rolls**
- 1 **pound ground chicken**
- 1 **envelope taco seasoning**
- 1 **can (4 ounces) chopped green chilies**
- ½ **cup water**
- ½ **cup salsa**
- ½ **cup shredded Mexican cheese blend**
- 1 **cup shredded lettuce**
- 1 **small sweet red pepper, chopped**
- 1 **small green pepper, chopped**
- 1 **medium tomato, seeded and chopped**
- 1 **green onion, thinly sliced**
- 2 **tablespoons pickled jalapeno slices**
  Sour cream and additional salsa

1. Preheat oven to 350°. Unroll crescent dough and separate into triangles. Press onto bottom of a greased 9-in. pie plate to form a crust, sealing seams well. Bake 18-20 minutes or until golden brown.

2. Meanwhile, in a large skillet, cook chicken over medium heat 6-8 minutes or until no longer pink, breaking into crumbles; drain. Stir in taco seasoning, green chilies, water and salsa; bring to a boil.

3. Spoon into crust; sprinkle with cheese. Bake 8-10 minutes or until cheese is melted.

4. Top with lettuce, peppers, tomato, green onion and pickled jalapeno. Serve with sour cream and additional salsa.

PER SERVING *1 piece (calculated without sour cream and additional salsa): 328 cal., 17g fat (6g sat. fat), 58mg chol., 1122mg sod., 25g carb. (5g sugars, 1g fiber), 17g pro.*

EASY CHICKEN ALFREDO LASAGNA

CHICKEN TAMALE BAKE (PICTURED ON PAGE 161)

When I serve this Mexican-style casserole, everyone scrapes their plates clean. Offer fresh toppings like green onions, tomatoes and avocado.

—JENNIFER STOWELL MONTEZUMA, IA

PREP: 10 MIN. • **BAKE:** 25 MIN. + STANDING
MAKES: 8 SERVINGS

- 1 **large egg, lightly beaten**
- 1 **can (14¾ ounces) cream-style corn**
- 1 **package (8½ ounces) corn bread/ muffin mix**
- 1 **can (4 ounces) chopped green chilies**
- ⅓ **cup 2% milk**
- ¼ **cup shredded Mexican cheese blend**

TOPPING

- 2 **cups coarsely shredded cooked chicken**
- 1 **can (10 ounces) enchilada sauce**
- 1 **teaspoon ground cumin**
- ½ **teaspoon onion powder**
- 1¾ **cups shredded Mexican cheese blend Chopped green onions, tomatoes and avocado, optional**

1. Preheat oven to 400°. In a large bowl, combine the first six ingredients; stir just until dry ingredients are moistened. Transfer to a greased 13x9-in. baking dish. Bake 15-18 minutes or until light golden brown and a toothpick inserted in center comes out clean.

2. In a large skillet, combine chicken, enchilada sauce, cumin and onion powder; bring to a boil, stirring occasionally. Reduce heat; simmer, uncovered, 5 minutes. Spread over corn bread layer; sprinkle with cheese.

3. Bake 10-12 minutes longer or until cheese is melted. Let stand 10 minutes before serving. If desired, top with green onions, tomatoes and avocado.

PER SERVING *1 piece (calculated without optional toppings): 364 cal., 17g fat (7g sat. fat), 81mg chol., 851mg sod., 35g carb. (9g sugars, 4g fiber), 21g pro.*

EASY CHICKEN ALFREDO LASAGNA

My family was growing tired of the traditional red sauce lasagna, so I created this delicious dish. Using rotisserie chicken is an easy and tasty time-saver.

—CAITLIN MACNEILLY UNCASVILLE, CT

PREP: 35 MIN. • **BAKE:** 45 MIN. + STANDING
MAKES: 12 SERVINGS

- 4 **ounces thinly sliced pancetta, cut into strips**
- 3 **ounces thinly sliced prosciutto or deli ham, cut into strips**
- 3 **cups shredded rotisserie chicken**
- 5 **tablespoons unsalted butter, cubed**
- ¼ **cup all-purpose flour**
- 4 **cups whole milk**
- 2 **cups shredded Asiago cheese, divided**
- 2 **tablespoons minced fresh parsley, divided**
- ¼ **teaspoon coarsely ground pepper Pinch ground nutmeg**
- 9 **no-cook lasagna noodles**
- 1½ **cups shredded part-skim mozzarella cheese**
- 1½ **cups shredded Parmesan cheese**

1. In a large skillet, cook pancetta and prosciutto over medium heat until browned. Drain on paper towels. Transfer to a large bowl; add chicken and toss to combine.

2. For sauce, in a large saucepan, melt butter over medium heat. Stir in flour until smooth; gradually whisk in milk. Bring to a boil, stirring constantly; cook and stir 1-2 minutes or until thickened. Remove from heat; stir in ½ cup Asiago cheese, 1 tablespoon parsley, pepper and nutmeg.

3. Preheat oven to 375°. Spread ½ cup sauce into a greased 13x9-in. baking dish. Layer with a third of each of the following: noodles, sauce, meat mixture, Asiago, mozzarella and Parmesan cheeses. Repeat layers twice.

4. Bake, covered, 30 minutes. Uncover; bake 15 minutes longer or until bubbly. Sprinkle with remaining parsley. Let stand 10 minutes before serving.

PER SERVING *421 cal., 25g fat (13g sat. fat), 99mg chol., 688mg sod., 18g carb. (5g sugars, 1g fiber), 31g pro.*

LEMONY CHICKEN & RICE

LEMONY CHICKEN & RICE

I couldn't say who loves this recipe best, because every time I serve it, it gets raves. Occasionally I even get a phone call or email from a friend requesting the recipe, and it's certainly a favorite for my grown children and 15 grandchildren.

—MARYALICE WOOD LANGLEY, BC

PREP: 15 MIN. + MARINATING • **BAKE:** 55 MIN.
MAKES: 2 CASSEROLES (4 SERVINGS EACH)

- 2 **cups water**
- ½ **cup reduced-sodium soy sauce**
- ¼ **cup lemon juice**
- ¼ **cup olive oil**
- 2 **garlic cloves, minced**
- 2 **teaspoons ground ginger**
- 2 **teaspoons pepper**
- 16 **bone-in chicken thighs, skin removed (about 6 pounds)**
- 2 **cups uncooked long grain rice**
- 4 **tablespoons grated lemon peel, divided**
- 2 **medium lemons, sliced**

1. In a large resealable plastic bag, combine the first seven ingredients. Add chicken; seal bag and turn to coat. Refrigerate 4 hours or overnight.

2. Preheat oven to 325°. Spread 1 cup rice into each of two greased 13x9-in. baking dishes. Top each with 1 tablespoon lemon peel, 8 chicken thighs and half of the marinade. Top with sliced lemons.

3. Bake, covered, 40 minutes. Bake, uncovered, 15-20 minutes longer or until a thermometer inserted in chicken reads 180°. Sprinkle with remaining lemon peel.

PER SERVING *2 chicken thighs with ¾ cup rice mixture: 624 cal., 26g fat (6g sat. fat), 173mg chol., 754mg sod., 41g carb. (1g sugars, 1g fiber), 53g pro.*

BLACK BEAN & CHICKEN ENCHILADA LASAGNA

CHICKEN PARMIGIANA

For years my husband ordered Chicken Parmigiana at restaurants. Then I found this recipe in our local newspaper, adjusted it for two and began making it at home. Now it's his favorite recipe. You can speed up prep a bit by eliminating the from-scatch sauce in favor of 2 cups of marinara sauce from a jar.

—IOLA BUTLER SUN CITY, CA

PREP: 25 MIN. • **COOK:** 15 MIN.
MAKES: 2 SERVINGS

- 1 can (15 ounces) tomato sauce
- 2 teaspoons Italian seasoning
- ½ teaspoon garlic powder
- 1 large egg
- ¼ cup seasoned bread crumbs
- 3 tablespoons grated Parmesan cheese
- 2 boneless skinless chicken breast halves (4 ounces each)
- 2 tablespoons olive oil
- 2 slices part-skim mozzarella cheese

1. In a small saucepan, combine the tomato sauce, Italian seasoning and garlic powder. Bring to a boil. Reduce heat; cover and simmer for 20 minutes.
2. Meanwhile, in a shallow bowl, lightly beat the egg. In another shallow bowl, combine bread crumbs and Parmesan cheese. Dip chicken in egg, then coat with crumb mixture.
3. In a large skillet, cook chicken in oil over medium heat for 5 minutes on each side or until a thermometer reads 170°. Top with mozzarella cheese. Cover and cook 3-4 minutes longer or until cheese is melted. Serve with the tomato sauce.
PER SERVING *1 chicken breast half: 444 cal., 26g fat (8g sat. fat), 166mg chol., 1496mg sod., 23g carb. (5g sugars, 3g fiber), 29g pro.*

BLACK BEAN & CHICKEN ENCHILADA LASAGNA

Twice a month I make lasagna-style chicken enchiladas. It's a regular with us because assembly is easy and my whole family gives it a thumb's up.

—CHERYL SNAVELY HAGERSTOWN, MD

PREP: 30 MIN. • **BAKE:** 25 MIN. + STANDING
MAKES: 8 SERVINGS

- 2 cans (10 ounces each) enchilada sauce
- 12 corn tortillas (6 inches)
- 2 cups coarsely shredded rotisserie chicken
- 1 small onion, chopped
- 1 can (15 ounces) black beans, rinsed and drained
- 3 cans (4 ounces each) whole green chilies, drained and coarsely chopped
- 3 cups crumbled queso fresco or shredded Mexican cheese blend
- 2 medium ripe avocados
- 2 tablespoons sour cream
- 2 tablespoons lime juice
- ½ teaspoon salt
   Chopped fresh tomatoes and cilantro

1. Preheat oven to 350°. Spread ½ cup enchilada sauce into a greased 13x9-in. baking dish; top with four tortillas, 1 cup chicken, ¼ cup onion, ¼ cup beans, ⅓ cup green chilies and 1 cup cheese. Repeat layers. Drizzle with ½ cup enchilada sauce; top with the remaining tortillas, onion, beans, chilies, sauce and cheese.
2. Bake, uncovered, 25-30 minutes or until bubbly and cheese is melted. Let stand 10 minutes before serving.
3. Meanwhile, quarter, peel and pit one avocado; place avocado in a food processor. Add sour cream, lime juice and salt; process until smooth. Peel, pit and cut remaining avocado into small cubes.
4. Top lasagna with tomatoes, cilantro and cubed avocado. Serve with avocado sauce.
PER SERVING *1 piece with 1 tablespoon sauce (calculated without tomatoes): 407 cal., 18g fat (7g sat. fat), 64mg chol., 857mg sod., 39g carb. (4g sugars, 8g fiber), 28g pro.*

MOM'S CHICKEN
TETRAZZINI

MOM'S CHICKEN TETRAZZINI

Rotisserie chicken turns this baked spaghetti into a warm, cozy meal our family craves.

—JENNIFER PETRINO NEWNAN, GA

PREP: 35 MIN. • **BAKE:** 25 MIN. + STANDING
MAKES: 6 SERVINGS

- 8 **ounces uncooked spaghetti**
- 2 **teaspoons plus 3 tablespoons butter, divided**
- 8 **bacon strips, chopped**
- 2 **cups sliced fresh mushrooms**
- 1 **small onion, chopped**
- 1 **small green pepper, chopped**
- ⅓ **cup all-purpose flour**
- ¼ **teaspoon salt**
- ¼ **teaspoon pepper**
- 3 **cups chicken broth**
- 3 **cups coarsely shredded rotisserie chicken**
- 2 **cups frozen peas (about 8 ounces)**
- 1 **jar (4 ounces) diced pimientos, drained**
- ½ **cup grated Romano or Parmesan cheese**

1. Preheat oven to 375°. Cook spaghetti according to package directions for al dente. Drain; transfer to a greased 13x9-in. baking dish. Add 2 teaspoons butter and toss to coat.

2. Meanwhile, in a large skillet, cook bacon over medium heat until crisp, stirring occasionally. Remove with a slotted spoon; drain on paper towels. Discard drippings, reserving 1 tablespoon in pan. Add mushrooms, onion and green pepper to drippings; cook and stir over medium-high heat 5-7 minutes or until tender. Remove from pan.

3. In same pan, heat remaining butter over medium heat. Stir in flour, salt and pepper until smooth; gradually whisk in chicken broth. Bring to a boil, stirring occasionally; cook and stir 3-5 minutes or until slightly thickened. Add chicken, peas, pimientos and mushroom mixture; heat through, stirring occasionally. Spoon over spaghetti. Sprinkle with the bacon and cheese.

4. Bake, uncovered, 25-30 minutes or until golden brown. Let stand 10 minutes before serving.

PER SERVING *1½ cups: 533 cal., 23g fat (10g sat. fat), 107mg chol., 1133mg sodium, 44g carb. (6g sugars, 4g fiber), 38g pro.*

BARBECUED STRAWBERRY CHICKEN

When it's time to impress family and friends, we serve barbecued chicken garnished with strawberries. It's easier than anyone would ever guess.

—BONNIE HAWKINS ELKHORN, WI

PREP: 25 MIN. • **BAKE:** 15 MIN.
MAKES: 4 SERVINGS

- 2 **tablespoons canola oil**
- 4 **boneless skinless chicken breast halves (6 ounces each)**
- 2 **tablespoons butter**
- ¼ **cup finely chopped red onion**
- 1 **cup barbecue sauce**
- 2 **tablespoons brown sugar**
- 2 **tablespoons balsamic vinegar**
- 2 **tablespoons honey**
- 1 **cup sliced fresh strawberries**

1. Preheat oven to 350°. In a large ovenproof skillet, heat oil over medium-high heat. Brown chicken on both sides. Remove from pan. In same pan, heat butter over medium-high heat. Add onion; cook and stir 1 minute or until tender.

2. Stir in barbecue sauce, brown sugar, vinegar and honey. Bring to a boil. Reduce heat; simmer, uncovered, 4-6 minutes or until thickened. Return the chicken to the pan. Bake 12-15 minutes or until a thermometer reads 165°. Stir in the strawberries.

PER SERVING *1 chicken breast half with ⅓ cup sauce: 495 cal., 17g fat (5g sat. fat), 109mg chol., 829mg sod., 49g carb. (4g sugars, 2g fiber), 35g pro.*

BARBECUED STRAWBERRY CHICKEN

CHICKEN CHILE RELLENO CASSEROLE

My husband likes Mexican food and casseroles, so I combined the two. This chicken with chilies satisfies our craving for Mexican restaurant-style dinners.

—**ERICA INGRAM** LAKEWOOD, OH

PREP: 20 MIN. • **BAKE:** 35 MIN. + STANDING
MAKES: 8 SERVINGS

- 2 **tablespoons butter**
- 2 **poblano peppers, seeded and coarsely chopped**
- 1 **small onion, finely chopped**
- 2 **tablespoons all-purpose flour**
- 1 **teaspoon ground cumin**
- 1 **teaspoon smoked paprika**
- ¼ **teaspoon salt**
- ⅔ **cup 2% milk**
- 1 **package (8 ounces) cream cheese, cubed**
- 2 **cups shredded pepper jack cheese**
- 2 **cups coarsely shredded rotisserie chicken**
- 1 **can (4 ounces) chopped green chilies**
- 2 **packages (8½ ounces each) corn bread/muffin mix**

1. Preheat oven to 350°. In a large skillet, heat butter over medium-high heat. Add peppers and onion; cook and stir 4-6 minutes or until peppers are tender.
2. Stir in flour and seasonings until blended; gradually stir in milk. Bring to a boil, stirring constantly; cook and stir until thickened, about 1 minute. Stir in cream cheese until blended. Add jack cheese, chicken and green chilies; heat through, stirring to combine. Transfer to a greased 11x7-in. baking dish.
3. Prepare corn muffin batter according to package directions. Spread over the chicken mixture. Bake, uncovered, for 35-40 minutes or until golden brown and a toothpick inserted in topping comes out clean. Let stand 10 minutes before serving.

PER SERVING *1 piece: 610 cal., 34g fat (16g sat. fat), 151mg chol., 987mg sod., 51g carb. (16g sugars, 5g fiber), 27g pro.*

TERIYAKI PINEAPPLE DRUMSTICKS

TERIYAKI PINEAPPLE DRUMSTICKS

We have a large family and love to throw big parties, so I look for ways to free my husband from the grill. My roasted drumsticks keep everyone happy.

—**ERICA ALLEN** TUCKERTON, NJ

PREP: 35 MIN. • **BAKE:** 1½ HOURS
MAKES: 12 SERVINGS

- 1 **tablespoon garlic salt**
- 1 **tablespoon minced chives**
- 1½ **teaspoons paprika**
- 1½ **teaspoons pepper**
- ½ **teaspoon salt**
- 24 **chicken drumsticks**
- ½ **cup canola oil**
- 1 **can (8 ounces) crushed pineapple**
- ½ **cup water**
- ¼ **cup packed brown sugar**
- ¼ **cup Worcestershire sauce**
- ¼ **cup yellow mustard**
- 4 **teaspoons cornstarch**
- 2 **tablespoons cold water**

1. Preheat oven to 350°. Mix the first five ingredients; sprinkle over chicken. In a large skillet, heat oil over medium-high heat. Brown drumsticks in batches. Transfer to a roasting pan.
2. Meanwhile, combine pineapple, ½ cup water, brown sugar, Worcestershire sauce and mustard; pour over chicken. Cover; bake until tender, 1½-2 hours, uncovering during the last 20-30 minutes of baking to let skin crisp.
3. Remove drumsticks to a platter; keep warm. Transfer cooking juices to a small saucepan; skim fat. Bring juices to a boil. In a small bowl, mix cornstarch and cold water until smooth; stir into cooking juices. Return to a boil; cook and stir 1-2 minutes or until thickened. Serve with drumsticks.

PER SERVING *2 drumsticks: 360 cal., 22g fat (4g sat. fat), 95mg chol., 540mg sod., 11g carb. (8g sugars, 1g fiber), 29g pro.*

PUFF PASTRY CHICKEN POTPIE

When we're craving comfort food, I whip up potpie. It delivers soul-satisfying flavor.
—**NICK IVERSON** MILWAUKEE, WI

PREP: 45 MIN. • **BAKE:** 45 MIN. + STANDING
MAKES: 8 SERVINGS

- 1 package (17.3 ounces) frozen puff pastry, thawed
- 2 pounds boneless skinless chicken breasts, cut into 1-inch pieces
- 1 teaspoon salt, divided
- 1 teaspoon pepper, divided
- 4 tablespoons butter, divided
- 1 large onion, chopped
- 2 garlic cloves, minced
- 1 teaspoon minced fresh thyme or ¼ teaspoon dried thyme
- 1 teaspoon fresh sage or ¼ teaspoon rubbed sage
- ½ cup all-purpose flour
- 2 cups chicken broth
- 1 cup plus 1 tablespoon half-and-half cream, divided
- 2 cups frozen mixed vegetables (about 10 ounces)
- 1 tablespoon lemon juice
- 1 large egg yolk

1. Preheat oven to 400°. On a lightly floured surface, roll each pastry sheet into a 12x10-in. rectangle. Cut one sheet crosswise into six 2-in. strips; cut the remaining sheet lengthwise into five 2-in. strips. On a baking sheet, closely weave strips to make a 12x10-in. lattice. Freeze while making filling.

2. Toss chicken with ½ teaspoon each salt and pepper. In a large skillet, heat 1 tablespoon butter over medium-high heat; saute chicken until browned, 5-7 minutes. Remove from pan.

3. In same skillet, heat remaining butter over medium-high heat; saute onion until tender, 5-7 minutes. Stir in garlic and herbs; cook 1 minute. Stir in flour until blended; cook and stir 1 minute. Gradually stir in broth and 1 cup cream. Bring to a boil, stirring constantly; cook and stir until thickened, about 2 minutes.

4. Stir in vegetables, lemon juice, chicken and the remaining salt and pepper; return to a boil. Transfer to a greased 2-qt. oblong baking dish. Top with lattice, trimming to fit.

5. Whisk together egg yolk and the remaining cream; brush over pastry. Bake, uncovered, until bubbly and golden brown, 45-55 minutes. Let stand 15 minutes before serving.

PER SERVING 523 cal., 25g fat (10g sat. fat), 118mg chol., 829mg sod., 42g carb. (4g sugars, 6g fiber), 30g pro.

PUFF PASTRY CHICKEN POTPIE

TOP TIP
LATTICE TOPPING

Weave the puff pastry strips together on a baking sheet, then set the sheet in the freezer while preparing the rest of the pie. When ready, the lattice topping will easily slip off the baking sheet and over the filling. Trim the lattice to fit the baking dish.

SLOW-ROASTED
CHICKEN WITH
VEGETABLES, PAGE 181

GREEK GARLIC
CHICKEN, PAGE 189

SLOW-COOKED SPECIALTIES

One of the most **versatile ingredients** meets one of the most convenient kitchen tools, and the results are magic. Casseroles, stews, sandwiches, lasagnas—even whole roast chickens—all **ready for you** at the end of a long day. And the rich flavors that come from slow cooking are **simply fantastic!**

HAM & SWISS CHICKEN
ROLL-UPS, PAGE 191

AUTUMN APPLE CHICKEN, PAGE 194

BBQ CHICKEN

BBQ CHICKEN

Of all the recipes I make in my slow cooker, this is my favorite. If you like your BBQ sweet with a little spice, this could be your new favorite, too.

—YVONNE MCKIM VANCOUVER, WA

PREP: 15 MIN. • **COOK:** 5 HOURS
MAKES: 12 SERVINGS

- 6 **chicken leg quarters, skin removed**
- ¾ **cup ketchup**
- ½ **cup orange juice**
- ¼ **cup packed brown sugar**
- ¼ **cup red wine vinegar**
- ¼ **cup olive oil**
- 4 **teaspoons minced fresh parsley**
- 2 **teaspoons Worcestershire sauce**
- 1 **teaspoon garlic salt**
- ½ **teaspoon pepper**
- 2 **tablespoons plus 2 teaspoons cornstarch**
- ¼ **cup water**

1. Using a sharp knife, cut through the joint of each leg quarter to separate into two pieces. Place the chicken in a 4-qt. slow cooker.
2. In a small bowl, mix ketchup, orange juice, brown sugar, vinegar, oil, parsley, Worcestershire sauce, garlic salt and pepper; pour over chicken. Cook, covered, on low 5-6 hours or until meat is tender.
3. Remove chicken to a serving platter; keep warm. Skim fat from the cooking juices; pour into a measuring cup to measure 2 cups. Transfer to a small saucepan; bring to a boil. In a small bowl, mix cornstarch and water until smooth; stir into cooking juices. Return to a boil, stirring constantly; cook and stir for 1-2 minutes or until thickened. Serve with chicken.
PER SERVING *179 cal., 9g fat (2g sat. fat), 45mg chol., 392mg sod., 12g carb. (9g sugars, 0 fiber), 13g pro.* **Diabetic Exchanges:** *2 lean meat, 1 starch, 1 fat.*

SLOW-ROASTED CHICKEN WITH VEGETABLES

(PICTURED ON PAGE 178)

The aroma of rosemary and garlic is mouthwatering and this recipe could not be easier. Just a few minutes of prep and you'll come home to a delicious dinner. Even if you're not an experienced cook, this will make you look like a pro.

—ANITA BELL HERMITAGE, TN

PREP: 15 MIN. • **COOK:** 6 HOURS + STANDING
MAKES: 6 SERVINGS

- 2 medium carrots, halved lengthwise and cut into 3-inch pieces
- 2 celery ribs, halved lengthwise and cut into 3-inch pieces
- 8 small red potatoes, quartered
- ¾ teaspoon salt, divided
- ⅛ teaspoon pepper
- 1 medium lemon, halved
- 2 garlic cloves, crushed
- 1 broiler/fryer chicken (3 to 4 pounds)
- 1 tablespoon dried rosemary, crushed
- 1 tablespoon lemon juice
- 1 tablespoon olive oil
- 2½ teaspoons paprika

1. Place carrots, celery and potatoes in a 6-qt. slow cooker; toss with ¼ teaspoon salt and the pepper. Place lemon halves and garlic in chicken cavity. Tuck wings under chicken; tie drumsticks together. Place chicken over vegetables in slow cooker, breast side up. Mix rosemary, lemon juice, oil, paprika and remaining salt; rub over chicken.

2. Cook, covered, on low 6-8 hours or until a thermometer inserted in thickest part of thigh reads 170°-175° and the vegetables are tender.

3. Remove chicken to a serving platter; tent with foil. Let stand 15 minutes before carving. Serve with vegetables.

PER SERVING *3 ounces cooked chicken with ⅔ cup vegetables: 329 cal., 17g fat (4g sat. fat), 88mg chol., 400mg sod., 14g carb. (2g sugars, 3g fiber), 29g pro.*

EASY CHICKEN TAMALE PIE

EASY CHICKEN TAMALE PIE

All you need are some simple ingredients from the pantry to put this together. I love that I can go fishing while it cooks.

—PETER HALFERTY CORPUS CHRISTI, TX

PREP: 20 MIN. • **COOK:** / HOURS
MAKES: 8 SERVINGS

- 1 pound ground chicken
- 1 teaspoon ground cumin
- 1 teaspoon chili powder
- ½ teaspoon salt
- ¼ teaspoon pepper
- 1 can (15 ounces) black beans, rinsed and drained
- 1 can (14½ ounces) diced tomatoes, undrained
- 1 can (11 ounces) whole kernel corn, drained
- 1 can (10 ounces) enchilada sauce
- 2 green onions, chopped
- ¼ cup minced fresh cilantro
- 1 package (8½ ounces) corn bread/muffin mix
- 2 large eggs, lightly beaten
- 1 cup shredded Mexican cheese blend
  Optional toppings: sour cream, salsa and minced fresh cilantro

1. In a large skillet, cook chicken over medium heat for 6-8 minutes or until no longer pink, breaking into crumbles. Stir in seasonings.

2. Transfer to a 4-qt. slow cooker. Stir in beans, tomatoes, corn, enchilada sauce, green onions and cilantro. Cook, covered, on low 6-8 hours or until heated through.

3. In a small bowl, combine muffin mix and eggs; spoon over chicken mixture. Cook, covered, on low for 1-1½ hours longer or until a toothpick inserted in corn bread layer comes out clean.

4. Sprinkle with cheese; let stand, covered, 5 minutes. If desired, serve with toppings.

PER SERVING *1¼ cups (calculated without optional toppings): 359 cal., 14g fat (5g sat. fat), 110mg chol., 1021mg sod., 40g carb. (11g sugars, 5g fiber), 20g pro.*

**AMAZING SLOW COOKER
ORANGE CHICKEN**

AMAZING SLOW COOKER ORANGE CHICKEN

Orange chicken is my favorite Chinese takeout food, but I know that it's very high in sodium and fat. So I set to work and created a healthier version. Now I have peace of mind, knowing that it's better for my family.
—**BARB MILLER** OAKDALE, MN

PREP: 25 MIN. • **COOK:** 4½ HOURS
MAKES: 8 SERVINGS

- 1 **cup chicken stock**
- 1 **cup orange juice**
- 1 **cup orange marmalade**
- ½ **cup ketchup**
- ¼ **cup Dijon mustard**
- 2 **tablespoons brown sugar**
- 2 **tablespoons rice vinegar**
- 2 **tablespoons reduced-sodium soy sauce**
- 1 **tablespoon minced fresh gingerroot**
- 1 **teaspoon garlic powder**
- ¾ **teaspoon crushed red pepper flakes**
- 2 **tablespoons molasses, optional**
- 2 **pounds boneless skinless chicken breasts, cut into ¾-inch pieces**
- ½ **cup cornstarch**
- ¾ **teaspoon salt**
- ½ **teaspoon pepper**
- 1 **large sweet red pepper, cut into 1-inch pieces**
- 2 **cups fresh broccoli florets**
  Hot cooked rice
  Optional toppings: chopped green onions, peanuts and fresh cilantro

1. In a small bowl, combine the first 11 ingredients; stir in molasses if desired. In a 4-qt. slow cooker, combine chicken, cornstarch, salt and pepper; toss to coat. Top with red pepper. Pour stock mixture over the top. Cover and cook on low for 4 hours or until chicken is tender.
2. Stir in broccoli. Cover and cook on high for 30-40 minutes longer or until broccoli is crisp-tender. Serve with rice. If desired, sprinkle with toppings of choice.
PER SERVING *1 cup (calculated without rice and toppings): 319 cal., 3g fat (1g sat. fat), 63mg chol., 891mg sod., 50g carb. (36g sugars, 1g fiber), 25g pro.*

APPLE BALSAMIC CHICKEN

APPLE BALSAMIC CHICKEN

I love the sweet and tart flavor that balsamic vinegar gives to this dish. It's easy to prepare, and after cooking in the slow cooker, the chicken thighs are tender and flavorful.
—**JULI SNAER** ENID, OK

PREP: 15 MIN. • **COOK:** 4 HOURS
MAKES: 4 SERVINGS

- 4 **bone-in chicken thighs (about 1½ pounds), skin removed**
- ½ **cup chicken broth**
- ¼ **cup apple cider or juice**
- ¼ **cup balsamic vinegar**
- 2 **tablespoons lemon juice**
- ½ **teaspoon salt**
- ½ **teaspoon garlic powder**
- ½ **teaspoon dried thyme**
- ½ **teaspoon paprika**
- ½ **teaspoon pepper**
- 2 **tablespoons butter**
- 2 **tablespoons all-purpose flour**

1. Place chicken in a 1½-qt. slow cooker. In a small bowl, combine broth, cider, vinegar, lemon juice and seasonings; pour over meat. Cover and cook on low for 4-5 hours or until the chicken is tender.
2. Remove chicken; keep warm. Skim fat from cooking liquid. In a small saucepan, melt butter; stir in flour until smooth. Gradually add the cooking liquid. Bring to a boil; cook and stir for 2-3 minutes or until thickened. Serve with chicken.
PER SERVING *1 chicken thigh with ⅓ cup sauce: 277 cal., 15g fat (6g sat. fat), 103mg chol., 536mg sod., 9g carb. (4g sugars, 0 fiber), 25g pro.*

LEMON DILL CHICKEN

The lemon and dill in this recipe give the chicken a bright, fresh taste. Pair it with a side of noodles or a mixed green salad.
—**LORI LOCKREY** PICKERING, ON

PREP: 20 MIN. • **COOK:** 4 HOURS + STANDING
MAKES: 6 SERVINGS

- 2 medium onions, coarsely chopped
- 2 tablespoons butter, softened
- ¼ teaspoon grated lemon peel
- 1 broiler/fryer chicken (4 to 5 pounds)
- ¼ cup chicken stock
- 4 sprigs fresh parsley
- 4 fresh dill sprigs
- 3 tablespoons lemon juice
- 1 teaspoon salt
- 1 teaspoon paprika
- ½ teaspoon dried thyme
- ¼ teaspoon pepper

1. Place onions on the bottom of a 6-qt. slow cooker. In a small bowl, mix butter and lemon peel.
2. Tuck wings under chicken; tie drumsticks together. With your fingers, carefully loosen skin from chicken breast; rub butter mixture under the skin. Secure skin to the underside of the breast with toothpicks. Place chicken over onions, breast side up. Add stock, parsley and dill.
3. Drizzle lemon juice over chicken; sprinkle with seasonings. Cook, covered, on low 4-5 hours (a thermometer inserted in thigh should read at least 170°).
4. Remove chicken from the slow cooker; tent with foil. Let stand for 15 minutes before carving.
PER SERVING *5 ounces cooked chicken: 366 cal., 23g fat (8g sat. fat), 127mg chol., 542mg sod., 1g carb. (0 sugars, 0 fiber), 37g pro.*

SLOW COOKER CHICKEN CACCIATORE

EAT SMART

SLOW COOKER CHICKEN CACCIATORE

Treat company to this perfect Italian meal. You'll have plenty of time to visit with guests as it cooks hands-free. I like to serve it with couscous, green beans and a dry red wine. *Mangia!*
—**MARTHA SCHIRMACHER** STERLING HEIGHTS, MI

PREP: 15 MIN. • **COOK:** 8½ HOURS
MAKES: 12 SERVINGS

- 12 boneless skinless chicken thighs (about 3 pounds)
- 2 medium green peppers, chopped
- 1 can (14½ ounces) diced tomatoes with basil, oregano and garlic, undrained
- 1 can (6 ounces) tomato paste
- 1 medium onion, sliced
- ½ cup reduced-sodium chicken broth
- ¼ cup dry red wine or additional reduced-sodium chicken broth
- 3 garlic cloves, minced
- ¾ teaspoon salt
- ⅛ teaspoon pepper
- 2 tablespoons cornstarch
- 2 tablespoons cold water

1. Place chicken in a 4- or 5-qt. slow cooker. In a medium bowl, combine green peppers, tomatoes, tomato paste, onion, broth, wine, garlic, salt and pepper; pour over chicken. Cook, covered, on low for 8-10 hours or until chicken is tender.
2. In a small bowl, mix cornstarch and water until smooth; gradually stir into slow cooker. Cook, covered, on high 30 minutes or until sauce is thickened.
PER SERVING *3 ounces cooked chicken with ½ cup sauce: 207 cal., 9g fat (2g sat. fat), 76mg chol., 410mg sod., 8g carb. (4g sugars, 1g fiber), 23g pro.* **Diabetic Exchanges:** *3 lean meat, 1 vegetable, ½ fat.*

MEDITERRANEAN CHICKEN IN EGGPLANT SAUCE

Spice-coated chicken thighs simmer in a rich eggplant-red pepper sauce. This savory entree is perfect for an everyday meal or potluck. It's an easy slow cooker dish to prepare in the morning so that dinner is ready at the end of the day.

—**JUDY ARMSTRONG** PRAIRIEVILLE, LA

PREP: 45 MIN. • **COOK:** 5 HOURS
MAKES: 8 SERVINGS

- ⅓ cup all-purpose flour
- 2 teaspoons paprika
- 2 teaspoons ground cumin
- 1 teaspoon salt
- 1 teaspoon freshly ground pepper
- 3 pounds boneless skinless chicken thighs, cut into 2-inch pieces
- 2 tablespoons olive oil
- 1¼ cups white wine or chicken broth
- 1 small eggplant (1 pound), peeled and cubed
- 1 jar (12 ounces) roasted sweet red peppers, drained
- 1 medium onion, chopped
- 1 jalapeno pepper, seeded and chopped
- 2 tablespoons tomato paste
- 1 tablespoon brown sugar
- 3 garlic cloves, minced
- 1 cup pitted ripe olives, halved
- ¼ cup minced fresh Italian parsley
- 1 cup crumbled feta cheese
- 8 naan flatbreads, quartered

1. In a large bowl, combine the first five ingredients. Add chicken; toss to coat. In a large skillet, brown chicken in oil in batches. Transfer to a 4-qt. slow cooker.

2. Add wine to the skillet, stirring to loosen browned bits from pan. Stir in the eggplant, red peppers, onion, jalapeno, tomato paste, brown sugar and garlic. Bring to a boil. Reduce heat; simmer, uncovered, for 5 minutes. Cool slightly. Transfer to a blender; cover and process until pureed. Pour over chicken.

3. Cover and cook on low for 5-6 hours or until chicken is tender, adding olives and parsley during the last 30 minutes. Just before serving, sprinkle with feta cheese. Serve with naan.

NOTE *Wear disposable gloves when cutting hot peppers; the oils can burn skin. Avoid touching your face.*

PER SERVING *1 cup chicken mixture with 4 pieces naan flatbread: 588 cal., 23g fat (7g sat. fat), 126mg chol., 1293mg sod., 44g carb. (10g sugars, 4g fiber), 40g pro.*

MEDITERRANEAN CHICKEN IN EGGPLANT SAUCE

> **TOP TIP**
>
> ### ABOUT EGGPLANT
> Choose an eggplant with smooth skin; avoid those with soft or brown spots. Refrigerate for up to five days in a plastic bag. To peel, cut off the stem end and a small slice from the bottom so that the eggplant can rest flat. Remove the peel with a vegetable peeler. Eggplant peel can be tough and bitter, and is best removed in most recipes. However, some small varieties are completely edible, including the peel.

MANGO-PINEAPPLE CHICKEN TACOS

3. Shred chicken with two forks. Return chicken and reserved mango mixture and cooking juices to the slow cooker; heat through. Serve in taco shells; sprinkle with cilantro.

FREEZE OPTION *Freeze cooled meat mixture in freezer containers. To use, partially thaw in refrigerator overnight. Heat through in a saucepan, stirring occasionally and adding a little broth if necessary.*

PER SERVING *2 tacos: 246 cal., 7g fat (2g sat. fat), 51mg chol., 582mg sod., 25g carb. (10g sugars, 2g fiber), 21g pro.* **Diabetic Exchanges:** *3 lean meat, 1½ starch.*

ROSEMARY MUSHROOM CHICKEN

A delicate hint of rosemary lightly seasons the rich, creamy mushroom gravy in this savory dish. Cooking the chicken and gravy together saves so much time during the dinner rush. Add noodles or rice for a complete supper.

—**GENNY MONCHAMP** REDDING, CA

PREP: 30 MIN. • **COOK:** 7 HOURS
MAKES: 6 SERVINGS

- 6 **chicken leg quarters, skin removed**
- 2 **cups sliced fresh mushrooms**
- 2 **cans (10¾ ounces each) condensed cream of mushroom soup, undiluted**
- ½ **cup white wine or chicken broth**
- 1 **teaspoon garlic salt**
- 1 **teaspoon dried rosemary, crushed**
- ½ **teaspoon paprika**
- ⅛ **teaspoon pepper**
  Hot cooked egg noodles

Place chicken in a 5- or 6-qt. slow cooker coated with cooking spray; top with mushrooms. Combine the soup, wine, garlic salt, rosemary, paprika and pepper; pour over top. Cover and cook on low for 7-9 hours or until chicken is tender. Serve with noodles.

PER SERVING *294 cal., 14g fat (3g sat. fat), 94mg chol., 1107mg sod., 9g carb. (1g sugars, 1g fiber), 28g pro.*

EAT SMART

MANGO-PINEAPPLE CHICKEN TACOS

I lived in the Caribbean as a child and the fresh tropical fruits in this delectable chicken entree take me back to my childhood.

—**LISSA NELSON** PROVO, UT

PREP: 25 MIN. • **COOK:** 5 HOURS
MAKES: 16 SERVINGS

- 2 **medium mangoes, peeled and chopped**
- 1½ **cups cubed fresh pineapple or canned pineapple chunks, drained**
- 2 **medium tomatoes, chopped**
- 1 **medium red onion, finely chopped**
- 2 **small Anaheim peppers, seeded and chopped**
- 2 **green onions, finely chopped**
- 1 **tablespoon lime juice**
- 1 **teaspoon sugar**
- 4 **pounds bone-in chicken breast halves, skin removed**
- 3 **teaspoons salt**
- ¼ **cup packed brown sugar**
- 32 **taco shells, warmed**
- ¼ **cup minced fresh cilantro**

1. In a large bowl, combine the first eight ingredients. Place chicken in a 6-qt. slow cooker; sprinkle with salt and brown sugar. Top with mango mixture. Cover and cook on low for 5-6 hours or until the chicken is tender.

2. Remove chicken; cool slightly. Strain cooking juices, reserving mango mixture and ½ cup juices. Discard the remaining juices. When cool enough to handle, remove chicken from bones; discard the bones.

ONE-DISH MOROCCAN CHICKEN

Spices really work their magic on chicken in this exciting dish. Dried fruit and couscous add an impressive touch.

—**KATHY MORGAN** RIDGEFIELD, WA

PREP: 20 MIN. • **COOK:** 6 HOURS
MAKES: 4 SERVINGS

- 4 medium carrots, sliced
- 2 large onions, halved and sliced
- 1 broiler/fryer chicken (3 to 4 pounds), cut up, skin removed
- ½ teaspoon salt
- ½ cup chopped dried apricots
- ½ cup raisins
- 1 can (14½ ounces) reduced-sodium chicken broth
- ¼ cup tomato paste
- 2 tablespoons all-purpose flour
- 2 tablespoons lemon juice
- 2 garlic cloves, minced
- 1½ teaspoons ground ginger
- 1½ teaspoons ground cumin
- 1 teaspoon ground cinnamon
- ¾ teaspoon pepper
  Hot cooked couscous

1. Place carrots and onions in a greased 5-qt. slow cooker. Sprinkle chicken with salt; add to slow cooker. Top with apricots and raisins. In a small bowl, whisk broth, tomato paste, flour, lemon juice, garlic and seasonings until blended; add to the slow cooker.

2. Cook, covered, on low for 6-7 hours or until chicken is tender. Serve with couscous.

PER SERVING (*calculated without couscous*): *435 cal., 9g fat (3g sat. fat), 110mg chol., 755mg sod., 47g carb. (27g sugars, 6g fiber), 42g pro.*

ONE-DISH
MOROCCAN
CHICKEN

CHICKEN MOLE

If you're not familiar with mole, don't be afraid of this versatile Mexican sauce. I love sharing this recipe because it's a great one to experiment with.

—DARLENE MORRIS FRANKLINTON, LA

PREP: 25 MIN. • **COOK:** 6 HOURS
MAKES: 12 SERVINGS

- 12 **bone-in chicken thighs (about 4½ pounds), skin removed**
- 1 **teaspoon salt**

MOLE SAUCE

- 1 **can (28 ounces) whole tomatoes, drained**
- 1 **medium onion, chopped**
- 2 **dried ancho chilies, stems and seeds removed**
- ½ **cup sliced almonds, toasted**
- ¼ **cup raisins**
- 3 **ounces bittersweet chocolate, chopped**
- 3 **tablespoons olive oil**
- 1 **chipotle pepper in adobo sauce**
- 3 **garlic cloves, peeled and halved**
- ¾ **teaspoon ground cumin**
- ½ **teaspoon ground cinnamon**
  Fresh cilantro leaves, optional

1. Sprinkle chicken with salt; place in a 5- or 6-qt. slow cooker. Place the tomatoes, onion, chilies, almonds, raisins, chocolate, oil, chipotle pepper, garlic, cumin and cinnamon in a food processor; cover and process until blended. Pour over the chicken.

2. Cover and cook on low for 6-8 hours or until chicken is tender; skim fat. Serve chicken with sauce; sprinkle with cilantro if desired.

FREEZE OPTION *Cool chicken in mole sauce. Freeze in freezer containers. To use, partially thaw in refrigerator overnight. Heat through slowly in a covered skillet or Dutch oven until a thermometer inserted in chicken reads 165°, stirring occasionally and adding a little broth or water if necessary.*

PER SERVING *1 chicken thigh with ⅓ cup sauce: 311 cal., 18g fat (5g sat. fat), 86mg chol., 378mg sod., 12g carb. (7g sugars, 3g fiber), 26g pro.*

CHICKEN MOLE

GREEK GARLIC CHICKEN (PICTURED ON PAGE 179)

Lively flavors of the Greek Isles come through in this chicken entree. I created it so that my husband and I could have a nice dinner after a busy day out and about.

—MARGEE BERRY WHITE SALMON, WA

PREP: 20 MIN. • **COOK:** 3½ HOURS
MAKES: 6 SERVINGS

- ½ cup chopped onion
- 1 tablespoon plus 1 teaspoon olive oil, divided
- 3 tablespoons minced garlic
- 2½ cups chicken broth, divided
- ¼ cup pitted Greek olives, chopped
- 3 tablespoons chopped sun-dried tomatoes (not packed in oil)
- 1 tablespoon quick-cooking tapioca
- 2 teaspoons grated lemon peel
- 1 teaspoon dried oregano
- 6 boneless skinless chicken breast halves (6 ounces each)
- 1¾ cups uncooked couscous
- ½ cup crumbled feta cheese

1. In a small skillet, saute onion in 1 tablespoon oil until crisp-tender. Add garlic; cook 1 minute longer.
2. Transfer to a 5-qt. slow cooker. Stir in ¾ cup broth, olives, tomatoes, tapioca, lemon peel and oregano. Add chicken. Cover and cook on low for 3½-4 hours or until chicken is tender.
3. In a large saucepan, bring remaining oil and broth to a boil. Stir in couscous. Cover and remove from the heat; let stand for 5 minutes or until the broth is absorbed. Serve with chicken; sprinkle with feta cheese.
PER SERVING *318 cal., 8g fat (2g sat. fat), 21mg chol., 625mg sod., 47g carb. (3g sugars, 3g fiber), 16g pro.*

TUSCAN-STYLE CHICKEN

TUSCAN-STYLE CHICKEN

I found this Italian-style chicken recipe in a magazine and tweaked it to suit my family's tastes. I have taken it to potlucks and served it at dinner parties. I serve my chicken entree with crusty bread and a spinach salad with lemon vinaigrette.

—MARY WATKINS LITTLE ELM, TX

PREP: 25 MIN. • **COOK:** 6 HOURS
MAKES: 4 SERVINGS

- 2 cans (14½ ounces each) Italian stewed tomatoes, undrained
- 10 small red potatoes (about 1 pound), quartered
- 1 medium onion, chopped
- 1 can (6 ounces) tomato paste
- 2 fresh rosemary sprigs
- 4 garlic cloves, minced
- 1 teaspoon olive oil
- ½ teaspoon dried basil
- 1 teaspoon Italian seasoning, divided
- 1 broiler/fryer chicken (3 to 4 pounds), cut up and skin removed
- ½ teaspoon salt
- ½ teaspoon pepper
- 1 jar (5¾ ounces) pimiento-stuffed olives, drained

1. In a 5-qt. slow cooker, combine the first eight ingredients. Stir in ½ teaspoon Italian seasoning. Place chicken on top. Sprinkle with salt, pepper and remaining Italian seasoning. Top with olives.
2. Cover and cook on low for 6-7 hours or until the chicken is tender. Discard the rosemary sprigs before serving.
PER SERVING *498 cal., 16g fat (3g sat. fat), 110mg chol., 1797mg sod., 47g carb. (17g sugars, 7g fiber), 43g pro.*

CHUNKY CHICKEN CACCIATORE

EAT SMART

EAT SMART

CHUNKY CHICKEN CACCIATORE

This recipe is just so versatile! Look in your fridge for anything else you want to throw in, like red pepper, mushrooms, extra zucchini—you name it. And if you're a vegetarian, go ahead and leave out the chicken.

—**STEPHANIE LOAIZA** LAYTON, UT

PREP: 10 MIN. • **COOK:** 4 HOURS
MAKES: 6 SERVINGS

- 6 **boneless skinless chicken thighs (about 1½ pounds)**
- 2 **medium zucchini, cut into 1-inch slices**
- 1 **medium green pepper, cut into 1-inch pieces**
- 1 **large sweet onion, coarsely chopped**
- ½ **teaspoon dried oregano**
- 1 **jar (24 ounces) garden-style spaghetti sauce**
  Hot cooked spaghetti
  Sliced ripe olives and shredded Parmesan cheese, optional

1. Place chicken and vegetables in a 3-qt. slow cooker; sprinkle with oregano. Pour sauce over top. Cook, covered, on low for 4-5 hours or until chicken is tender.
2. Remove chicken; break up slightly with two forks. Return to slow cooker. Serve with spaghetti. If desired, top with olives and cheese.

TO MAKE AHEAD *Place the first six ingredients in a large resealable plastic freezer bag; seal bag and freeze. To use, place filled freezer bag in refrigerator for 48 hours or until contents are completely thawed. Cook and serve as directed.*

PER SERVING *(calculated without spaghetti and optional ingredients): 285 cal., 11g fat (2g sat. fat), 76mg chol., 507mg sod., 21g carb. (14g sugars, 3g fiber), 24g pro.* **Diabetic Exchanges:** *3 lean meat, 1½ starch.*

HAM & SWISS CHICKEN ROLL-UPS (PICTURED ON PAGE 179)

White wine dresses up cream of chicken soup to make a lovely sauce for these chicken, ham and Swiss cheese roll-ups. This tried-and-true recipe comes from my mother.

—CAROL MCCOLLOUGH MISSOULA, MT

PREP: 25 MIN. + CHILLING • **COOK:** 4 HOURS
MAKES: 6 SERVINGS

- 6 **boneless skinless chicken breast halves (4 ounces each)**
- 6 **thin slices deli ham**
- 6 **slices Swiss cheese**
- ¼ **cup all-purpose flour**
- ¼ **cup grated Parmesan cheese**
- ½ **teaspoon salt**
- ¼ **teaspoon pepper**
- 2 **tablespoons canola oil**
- 1 **can (10¾ ounces) condensed cream of chicken soup, undiluted**
- ½ **cup dry white wine or chicken broth**
  Hot cooked rice

1. Flatten chicken to ¼-in. thickness. Top each piece with a slice of ham and cheese. Roll up tightly; secure with toothpicks. In a shallow bowl, combine flour, Parmesan cheese, salt and pepper. Roll each chicken bundle in the flour mixture; refrigerate for 1 hour.

2. In a large skillet, brown roll-ups in oil on all sides; transfer to a 3-qt. slow cooker. Combine the soup and wine or broth; pour over chicken.

3. Cover and cook on low 4-5 hours or until the chicken is longer pink. Remove roll-ups and stir sauce. Remove and discard the toothpicks. Serve with rice.

FREEZE OPTION *Freeze cooled chicken roll-ups and sauce in freezer containers. To use, partially thaw in refrigerator overnight. Heat through in a covered saucepan, gently stirring and adding a little broth or milk if necessary.*

PER SERVING *1 roll-up: 286 cal., 13g fat (3g sat. fat), 78mg chol., 867mg sod., 9g carb. (1g sugars, 1g fiber), 28g pro.*

SLOW COOKER CURRY CHICKEN

SLOW COOKER CURRY CHICKEN

My husband travels for business and has discovered that he likes Indian cuisine. This simple slow-cooked recipe has the flavors he really enjoys. Use parsley instead of cilantro if you prefer.

—KATIE SCHULTZ TEMPLE, GA

PREP: 15 MIN. • **COOK:** 3 HOURS
MAKES: 4 SERVINGS

- 2 **medium onions, cut into wedges**
- 2 **medium sweet red peppers, cut into 1-inch strips**
- 4 **boneless skinless chicken breast halves (6 ounces each)**
- 2 **tablespoons curry powder, divided**
- 1 **teaspoon salt, divided**
- 1 **cup light coconut milk**
- ½ **cup chicken broth**
- 3 **garlic cloves, minced**
- ½ **teaspoon pepper**
- 1 **cup chopped dried apricots (about 6 ounces)**
  Hot cooked rice and lime wedges
  Chopped cashews and minced fresh cilantro, optional

1. Place onions and peppers in a 4-qt. slow cooker. Sprinkle chicken with 1 tablespoon curry powder and ½ teaspoon salt; place over vegetables.

2. In a small bowl, whisk coconut milk, broth, garlic, pepper and the remaining curry powder and salt. Pour into slow cooker. Cook, covered, on low for 3-3½ hours or until chicken is tender (a thermometer should read at least 165°), adding apricots during the last 30 minutes of cooking.

3. Serve with rice and lime wedges. If desired, sprinkle with cashews and cilantro.

PER SERVING *1 chicken breast half with about 1 cup vegetable mixture (calculated without optional ingredients): 367 cal., 9g fat (4g sat. fat), 95mg chol., 824mg sod., 34g carb. (21g sugars, 6g fiber), 37g pro.*

SLOW COOKER
ROAST CHICKEN

SLOW COOKER ROAST CHICKEN

Roast chicken is easy to make in a slow cooker. We save the shredded chicken to use during busy weeks.

—COURTNEY STULTZ WEIR, KS

PREP: 20 MIN. • **COOK:** 4 HOURS + STANDING
MAKES: 6 SERVINGS

- 2 **medium carrots, cut into 1-inch pieces**
- 1 **medium onion, cut into 1-inch pieces**
- 2 **garlic cloves, minced**
- 2 **teaspoons olive oil**
- 1 **teaspoon dried parsley flakes**
- 1 **teaspoon pepper**
- ¾ **teaspoon salt**
- ½ **teaspoon dried oregano**
- ½ **teaspoon rubbed sage**
- ½ **teaspoon chili powder**
- 1 **broiler/fryer chicken (4 to 5 pounds)**

1. Place carrots and onion in a 6-qt. slow cooker. In a small bowl, mix garlic and oil. In another bowl, mix dry seasonings.
2. Tuck wings under chicken; tie the drumsticks together. With your fingers, carefully loosen skin from chicken breast; rub garlic mixture under the skin. Secure skin to the underside of the breast with toothpicks.
3. Place chicken in slow cooker over vegetables, breast side up; sprinkle with seasoning mixture. Cook, covered, on low 4-5 hours (a thermometer inserted in thigh should read at least 170°).
4. Remove chicken from slow cooker; tent with foil. Let chicken stand for 15 minutes before carving.
PER SERVING *5 ounces cooked chicken: 423 cal., 24g fat (6g sat. fat), 139mg chol., 439mg sod., 4g carb. (2g sugars, 1g fiber), 45g pro.*

CARIBBEAN CHICKEN STEW

EAT SMART

CARIBBEAN CHICKEN STEW

I lived with a West Indian family for a while and enjoyed watching them cook. I lightened up this recipe by leaving out the oil and sugar, removing the skin from the chicken and using chicken sausage.

—JOANNE IOVINO KINGS PARK, NY

PREP: 25 MIN. + MARINATING • **COOK:** 6 HOURS
MAKES: 8 SERVINGS

- ¼ **cup ketchup**
- 3 **garlic cloves, minced**
- 1 **tablespoon sugar**
- 1 **tablespoon hot pepper sauce**
- 1 **teaspoon browning sauce, optional**
- 1 **teaspoon dried basil**
- 1 **teaspoon dried thyme**
- 1 **teaspoon paprika**
- ½ **teaspoon salt**
- ½ **teaspoon dried oregano**
- ½ **teaspoon ground allspice**
- ½ **teaspoon pepper**
- 8 **bone-in chicken thighs (about 3 pounds), skin removed**
- 1 **pound fully cooked andouille chicken sausage links, sliced**
- 1 **medium onion, finely chopped**
- 2 **medium carrots, finely chopped**
- 2 **celery ribs, finely chopped**

1. In a large resealable plastic bag, combine ketchup, garlic, sugar, pepper sauce and, if desired, browning sauce; stir in seasonings. Add chicken thighs, sausage and vegetables. Seal bag and turn to coat. Refrigerate 8 hours or overnight.
2. Transfer contents of bag to a 4- or 5-qt. slow cooker. Cook, covered, on low for 6-8 hours or until the chicken is tender.
PER SERVING *309 cal., 14g fat (4g sat. fat), 131mg chol., 666mg sod., 9g carb. (6g sugars, 1g fiber), 35g pro.* **Diabetic Exchanges:** *5 lean meat, ½ starch.*

AUTUMN APPLE CHICKEN (PICTURED ON PAGE 179)

I'd just been apple picking and wanted to bake something new with the bounty. Slow-cooking chicken with apples and barbecue sauce filled my whole house with the most delicious smell. We couldn't wait to eat!

—**CAITLYN HAUSER** BROOKLINE, NH

PREP: 20 MIN. • **COOK:** 3½ HOURS
MAKES: 4 SERVINGS

- 1 tablespoon canola oil
- 4 bone-in chicken thighs (about 1½ pounds), skin removed
- ¼ teaspoon salt
- ¼ teaspoon pepper
- 2 medium Fuji or Gala apples, coarsely chopped
- 1 medium onion, chopped
- 1 garlic clove, minced
- ⅓ cup barbecue sauce
- ¼ cup apple cider or juice
- 1 tablespoon honey

1. In a large skillet, heat oil over medium heat. Brown chicken thighs on both sides; sprinkle with salt and pepper. Transfer to a 3-qt. slow cooker; top with apples.
2. Add onion to same skillet; cook and stir over medium heat 2-3 minutes or until tender. Add garlic; cook 1 minute longer. Stir in barbecue sauce, apple cider and honey; increase heat to medium-high. Cook 1 minute, stirring to loosen browned bits from pan. Pour over chicken and apples. Cook, covered, on low 3½-4½ hours or until chicken is tender.

FREEZE OPTION *Freeze cooled chicken mixture in freezer containers. To use, partially thaw in refrigerator overnight. Heat through in a covered saucepan, stirring occasionally.*

PER SERVING *1 chicken thigh with ½ cup apple mixture: 333 cal., 13g fat (3g sat. fat), 87mg chol., 456mg sod., 29g carb. (22g sugars, 3g fiber), 25g pro.* **Diabetic Exchanges:** *4 lean meat, 1½ starch, ½ fruit.*

MEDITERRANEAN CHICKEN ORZO

MEDITERRANEAN CHICKEN ORZO

Orzo pasta with chicken, olives and herbes de Provence has the bright flavors of Mediterranean cuisine. Here's a bonus: The leftovers reheat well.

—**THOMAS FAGLON** SOMERSET, NJ

PREP: 15 MIN. • **COOK:** 4 HOURS
MAKES: 6 SERVINGS

- 1½ pounds boneless skinless chicken thighs, cut into 1-inch pieces
- 2 cups reduced-sodium chicken broth
- 2 medium tomatoes, finely chopped
- 1 cup sliced pitted green olives
- 1 cup sliced pitted ripe olives
- 1 large carrot, finely chopped
- 1 small red onion, finely chopped
- 1 tablespoon grated lemon peel
- 3 tablespoons lemon juice
- 2 tablespoons butter
- 1 tablespoon herbes de Provence
- 1 cup uncooked orzo pasta

In a 3- or 4-qt. slow cooker, combine the first 11 ingredients. Cook, covered, on low 4-5 hours or until chicken, pasta and vegetables are tender, adding orzo during the last 30 minutes of cooking.

PER SERVING *1⅓ cups: 415 cal., 19g fat (5g sat. fat), 86mg chol., 941mg sod., 33g carb. (4g sugars, 3g fiber), 27g pro.*

CHICKEN CORN BREAD CASSEROLE

I love this super easy slow-cooked chicken because it tastes like Thanksgiving but comes without all the hassle. It's such a hearty, delicious meal for the fall or winter season.

—**NANCY BARKER** PEORIA, AZ

PREP: 40 MIN. • **COOK:** 3 HOURS
MAKES: 6 SERVINGS

- 5 **cups cubed corn bread**
- ¼ **cup butter, cubed**
- 1 **large onion, chopped (about 2 cups)**
- 4 **celery ribs, chopped (about 2 cups)**
- 3 **cups shredded cooked chicken**
- 1 **can (10¾ ounces) condensed cream of chicken soup, undiluted**
- 1 **can (10¾ ounces) condensed cream of mushroom soup, undiluted**
- ½ **cup reduced-sodium chicken broth**
- 1 **teaspoon poultry seasoning**
- ½ **teaspoon salt**
- ½ **teaspoon rubbed sage**
- ¼ **teaspoon pepper**

1. Preheat oven to 350°. Place bread cubes on an ungreased 15x10x1-in. baking pan. Bake 20-25 minutes or until toasted. Cool on baking pan.
2. In a large skillet, heat butter over medium-high heat. Add onion and celery; cook and stir 6-8 minutes or until tender. Transfer to a greased 4-qt. slow cooker. Stir in corn bread, chicken, soups, broth and seasonings.
3. Cook, covered, on low 3-4 hours or until heated through.

PER SERVING *1⅓ cups: 500 cal., 21g fat (8g sat. fat), 89mg chol., 1657mg sod., 48g carb. (5g sugars, 5g fiber), 27g pro.*

CHICKEN CORN BREAD CASSEROLE

SLOW COOKER ROTISSERIE-STYLE CHICKEN

You wouldn't believe this golden brown chicken was made in the slow cooker. Packed with flavor, the meat is moist, the carrots are tender and the juices would make a nice gravy, if you're so inclined.

—*TASTE OF HOME* TEST KITCHEN

PREP: 30 MIN. • **COOK:** 6 HOURS + STANDING
MAKES: 6 SERVINGS

- 4 **teaspoons seasoned salt**
- 4 **teaspoons poultry seasoning**
- 1 **tablespoon paprika**
- 1½ **teaspoons onion powder**
- 1½ **teaspoons brown sugar**
- 1½ **teaspoons salt-free lemon-pepper seasoning**
- ¾ **teaspoon garlic powder**
- 1 **broiler/fryer chicken (4 pounds)**
- 1 **pound carrots, halved lengthwise and cut into 1½-inch lengths**
- 2 **large onions, chopped**
- 2 **tablespoons cornstarch**

1. In a small bowl, combine the first seven ingredients. Carefully loosen skin from chicken breast; rub 1 tablespoon spice mixture under the skin. Rub remaining spice mixture over chicken. In another bowl, toss carrots and onions with cornstarch; transfer to a 6-qt. slow cooker. Place chicken on vegetables.
2. Cover and cook on low for 6-7 hours or until a thermometer inserted in the thigh reads 180°. Remove chicken and vegetables to a serving platter; cover and let stand for 15 minutes before carving. Skim fat from cooking juices. Serve juices with chicken and vegetables.

PER SERVING *402 cal., 19g fat (5g sat. fat), 117mg chol., 1169mg sod., 18g carb. (7g sugars, 4g fiber), 39g pro.*

SHREDDED CHICKEN GYROS, PAGE 206

CHICKEN PARMESAN
BURGERS, PAGE 199

SANDWICHES, SOUPS & MORE

Take a bite out of hunger with the **chicken specialties** found here. Whether you like your poultry **simmered in a stew,** piled onto a sandwich or wrapped into a handheld snack, this chapter is for you. From quick lunches to **casual dinners,** this colorful collection has you covered.

THAI CHICKEN LETTUCE WRAPS, PAGE 209

QUICK CHICKEN & WILD
RICE SOUP, PAGE 204

**CAROLINA-STYLE
VINEGAR BBQ CHICKEN**

CAROLINA-STYLE
VINEGAR BBQ CHICKEN

I live in Georgia but I appreciate the tangy, sweet and slightly spicy taste of Carolina vinegar chicken. I make my version in the slow cooker—and when you walk in the door after being gone all day, the aroma will knock you off your feet.

—RAMONA PARRIS CANTON, GA

PREP: 10 MIN. **• COOK:** 4 HOURS
MAKES: 6 SERVINGS

- 2 cups water
- 1 cup white vinegar
- ¼ cup sugar
- 1 tablespoon reduced-sodium chicken base
- 1 teaspoon crushed red pepper flakes
- ¾ teaspoon salt
- 1½ pounds boneless skinless chicken breasts
- 6 whole wheat hamburger buns, split, optional

1. In a small bowl, mix the first six ingredients. Place chicken in a 3-qt. slow cooker; add vinegar mixture. Cook, covered, on low 4-5 hours or until chicken is tender.

2. Remove chicken; cool slightly. Reserve 1 cup cooking juices; discard remaining juices. Shred chicken with two forks. Return meat and reserved cooking juices to slow cooker; heat through. If desired, serve chicken mixture on buns.

NOTE *Look for chicken base near the broth and bouillon.*

PER SERVING *½ cup (calculated without buns): 134 cal., 3g fat (1g sat. fat), 63mg chol., 228mg sod., 3g carb. (3g sugars, 0 fiber), 23g pro.* **Diabetic Exchange:** *3 lean meat.*

**CAROLINA-STYLE
VINEGAR BBQ CHICKEN**

EAT SMART **FAST FIX**

CHICKEN PARMESAN BURGERS (PICTURED ON PAGE 197)

We love chicken Parmesan and thought, *Why not make it a burger?* I like to use fresh mozzarella on these. I've also made the burgers with ground turkey.

—**CHARLOTTE GEHLE** BROWNSTOWN, MI

START TO FINISH: 30 MIN.
MAKES: 4 SERVINGS

- ½ cup dry bread crumbs
- ¼ cup grated Parmesan cheese
- 3 garlic cloves, minced
- 1 tablespoon minced fresh basil or 1 teaspoon dried basil
- ½ teaspoon dried oregano
- 1 pound lean ground chicken
- 1 cup meatless spaghetti sauce, divided
- 2 slices part-skim mozzarella cheese, cut in half
- 4 slices Italian bread (¾ inch thick)

1. In a large bowl, combine the first five ingredients. Add chicken; mix lightly but thoroughly. Shape into four ½-in.-thick oval patties.

2. Grill burgers, covered, over medium heat or broil 4 in. from heat 4-7 minutes on each side or until a thermometer reads 165°. Top burgers with ½ cup spaghetti sauce and cheese. Cover and grill 30-60 seconds longer or until cheese is melted.

3. Grill bread, uncovered, over medium heat or broil 4 in. from heat for 30-60 seconds on each side or until toasted. Top with remaining spaghetti sauce. Serve burgers on toasted bread.

FREEZE OPTION *Place patties on a plastic wrap-lined baking sheet; wrap and freeze until firm. Remove from pan and transfer to a resealable plastic freezer bag; return to freezer. To use, grill frozen patties as directed, increasing time as necessary for a thermometer to read 165°.*

PER SERVING *1 burger: 381 cal., 12g fat (5g sat. fat), 93mg chol., 784mg sod., 32g carb. (5g sugars, 3g fiber), 35g pro.*
Diabetic Exchanges: 3 lean meat, 2 starch, 1 fat.

SOUTHWESTERN CHICKEN & LIMA BEAN STEW

EAT SMART

SOUTHWESTERN CHICKEN & LIMA BEAN STEW

I always try to have my daughter, son-in-law and grandchildren over for this supper. They make me so happy by saying, "That was so good" or by just going to fill up their bowls a second time. This stew is a healthy hit.

—**PAM CORDER** MONROE, LA

PREP: 20 MIN. • **COOK:** 6 HOURS
MAKES: 6 SERVINGS

- 4 bone-in chicken thighs (1½ pounds), skin removed
- 2 cups frozen lima beans
- 2 cups frozen corn
- 1 large green pepper, chopped
- 1 large onion, chopped
- 2 cans (14 ounces each) fire-roasted diced tomatoes, undrained
- ¼ cup tomato paste
- 3 tablespoons Worcestershire sauce
- 3 garlic cloves, minced
- 1½ teaspoons ground cumin
- 1½ teaspoons dried oregano
- ¼ teaspoon salt
- ¼ teaspoon pepper
  Chopped fresh cilantro, optional

1. Place the first five ingredients in a 5-qt. slow cooker. In a large bowl, combine tomatoes, tomato paste, Worcestershire sauce, garlic and dry seasonings; pour over top.

2. Cook, covered, on low 6-8 hours or until chicken is tender. Remove chicken from slow cooker. When cool enough to handle, remove meat from bones; discard bones. Shred meat with two forks; return to slow cooker and heat through. If desired, sprinkle with cilantro.

PER SERVING *1½ cups: 312 cal., 7g fat (2g sat. fat), 58mg chol., 614mg sod., 39g carb. (9g sugars, 8g fiber), 24g pro.*
Diabetic Exchanges: 3 lean meat, 2 starch, 1 vegetable.

...LED CHICKEN

...a chipotle kick to it.
...when I'm looking for

...ANLIUS, NY

...: 3 HOURS

- 2 **cups ketchup**
- 1 **small onion, finely chopped**
- ¼ **cup Worcestershire sauce**
- 3 **tablespoons reduced-sodium soy sauce**
- 2 **tablespoons brown sugar**
- 2 **tablespoons cider vinegar**
- 3 **garlic cloves, minced**
- 1 **tablespoon molasses**
- 2 **teaspoons dried oregano**
- 2 **teaspoons minced chipotle pepper in adobo sauce plus 1 teaspoon sauce**
- 1 **teaspoon ground cumin**
- 1 **teaspoon smoked paprika**
- ¼ **teaspoon salt**
- ¼ **teaspoon crushed red pepper flakes**
- 2½ **pounds boneless skinless chicken breasts**
- 12 **sesame seed hamburger buns, split and toasted**

1. In a 3-qt. slow cooker, combine the first 14 ingredients; add chicken. Cook, covered, on low 3-4 hours or until chicken is tender (a thermometer should read at least 165°).

2. Remove chicken from slow cooker. Shred with two forks; return to slow cooker. Using tongs, place chicken mixture on bun bottoms. Replace tops.

FREEZE OPTION *Freeze cooled meat mixture and sauce in freezer containers. To use, partially thaw in refrigerator overnight. Heat through in a saucepan, stirring occasionally.*

PER SERVING *298 cal., 5g fat (2g sat. fat), 52mg chol., 1031mg sod., 39g carb. (18g sugars, 1g fiber), 24g pro.*

PECAN-CRUSTED CHICKEN WAFFLE SANDWICHES

FAST FIX

PECAN-CRUSTED CHICKEN WAFFLE SANDWICHES

Chicken and waffles is a Southern tradition. I turned it into a sandwich with crunchy pecans and a sweet and spicy mustard sauce to give it a kick.

—ELIZABETH DUMONT MADISON, MS

START TO FINISH: 30 MIN.
MAKES: 4 SERVINGS

- 4 **boneless skinless chicken breast halves (5 ounces each)**
- 1 **large egg**
- ½ **cup plus ⅓ cup maple syrup, divided**
- 1 **cup finely chopped pecans**
- ⅔ **cup dry bread crumbs**
- ¾ **teaspoon plus ⅛ teaspoon salt, divided**
- ½ **teaspoon plus ⅛ teaspoon pepper, divided**
- ¼ **cup canola oil**
- ¼ **cup spicy brown mustard**
- 1 **tablespoon white wine vinegar**
- 8 **frozen waffles, toasted**

1. Flatten chicken to ½-in. thickness. In a shallow bowl, whisk egg and ½ cup syrup. In another shallow bowl, combine the pecans, bread crumbs, ¾ teaspoon salt and ½ teaspoon pepper. Dip the chicken in egg mixture, then coat with the pecan mixture.

2. In a large skillet over medium heat, cook chicken in oil in batches for 5-6 minutes on each side or until no longer pink. Meanwhile, combine the mustard, vinegar and remaining syrup, salt and pepper.

3. Drizzle 1 tablespoon sauce mixture over each of four waffles; top with chicken and drizzle with remaining sauce mixture. Top with remaining waffles.

PER SERVING *796 cal., 38g fat (4g sat. fat), 123mg chol., 1095mg sod., 76g carb. (37g sugars, 4g fiber), 37g pro.*

SLOW-COOKED CHICKEN ENCHILADA SOUP

This soup delivers a big bowl of comfort. Toppings like avocado, sour cream and tortilla strips are a must. It's a great dish all year long!
—**HEATHER SEWELL** HARRISONVILLE, MO

PREP: 25 MIN. • **COOK:** 6 HOURS
MAKES: 8 SERVINGS

- 1 tablespoon canola oil
- 2 Anaheim or poblano peppers, finely chopped
- 1 medium onion, chopped
- 3 garlic cloves, minced
- 1 pound boneless skinless chicken breasts
- 1 carton (48 ounces) chicken broth
- 1 can (14½ ounces) Mexican diced tomatoes, undrained
- 1 can (10 ounces) enchilada sauce
- 2 tablespoons tomato paste
- 1 tablespoon chili powder
- 2 teaspoons ground cumin
- ½ teaspoon pepper
- ½ to 1 teaspoon chipotle hot pepper sauce, optional
- ⅓ cup minced fresh cilantro
  Optional toppings: shredded cheddar cheese, cubed avocado, sour cream and crispy tortilla strips

1. In a large skillet, heat oil over medium heat. Add peppers and onion; cook and stir 6-8 minutes or until tender. Add garlic; cook 1 minute longer. Transfer pepper mixture and chicken to a 5- or 6-qt. slow cooker. Stir in chicken broth, tomatoes, enchilada sauce, tomato paste, seasonings and, if desired, pepper sauce. Cook, covered, on low 6-8 hours or until chicken is tender (a thermometer should read at least 165°).

2. Remove chicken from slow cooker. Shred with two forks; return to slow cooker. Stir in cilantro. Serve with toppings as desired.

FREEZE OPTION *Freeze cooled soup in freezer containers. To use, partially thaw in refrigerator overnight. Heat through in a saucepan, stirring occasionally and adding a little water if necessary.*

PER SERVING *1½ cups (calculated without optional toppings): 125 cal., 4g fat (1g sat. fat), 35mg chol., 1102mg sod., 9g carb. (4g sugars, 3g fiber), 14g pro.*

SLOW-COOKED CHICKEN ENCHILADA SOUP

TOP TIP

ALL-TIME GREAT

Oh. My. Gosh. This soup is so tasty and easy to make, it will become a part of my permanent soup rotation. I suggest using poblanos and the mildest Mexican tomatoes. I topped it with a little cheese, sour cream and tortilla strips. I can't wait to make it again!
—**PAGERD**
TASTEOFHOME.COM

CHICKEN CAESAR PITAS

CHICKEN CAESAR PITAS

Hand-held and picnic friendly, these chicken-stuffed pockets pack a double dose of whole grains from brown rice and whole wheat pitas. The chicken can be made up to two days in advance for a fast-fix lunch.
—**TASTE OF HOME** TEST KITCHEN

PREP: 20 MIN. + CHILLING • **GRILL:** 10 MIN.
MAKES: 4 SERVINGS

- ¾ teaspoon dried oregano
- ½ teaspoon dried basil
- ¼ teaspoon onion powder
- ¼ teaspoon paprika
- ⅛ teaspoon dried mint
- 1 pound boneless skinless chicken breasts
- 2 cups torn romaine
- 1 cup ready-to-serve brown rice
- ½ cup reduced-fat Caesar vinaigrette
- 8 whole wheat pita pocket halves

1. In a spice grinder or with a mortar and pestle, combine the first five ingredients; grind until mixture becomes fine. Rub over chicken.

2. On a greased grill, cook chicken, covered, over medium heat or broil 4 in. from the heat for 4-5 minutes on each side or until a thermometer reads 170°. When cool enough to handle, cut into ½-in. strips. Refrigerate until chilled.

3. In a large bowl, combine the chicken, romaine and rice. Drizzle with Caesar vinaigrette; toss to coat. Serve in pitas.

PER SERVING 2 filled pita halves: 398 cal., 10g fat (2g sat. fat), 65mg chol., 919mg sod., 44g carb. (3g sugars, 5g fiber), 31g pro.

TOP TIP

NO GRILL?

We cooked the chicken on the stove instead of the grill and added shredded cheese. It was fabulous! The whole family agrees.

—**JOYFULKARA**
TASTEOFHOME.COM

COLD-DAY CHICKEN NOODLE SOUP

EAT SMART

COLD-DAY CHICKEN NOODLE SOUP

When I was sick, my mom would stir up a heartwarming chicken noodle soup. It's so soothing for colds and cold weather days.
—**ANTHONY GRAHAM** OTTAWA, IL

PREP: 15 MIN. • **COOK:** 25 MIN.
MAKES: 8 SERVINGS

- 1 tablespoon canola oil
- 2 celery ribs, chopped
- 2 medium carrots, chopped
- 1 medium onion, chopped
- 8 cups reduced-sodium chicken broth
- ½ teaspoon dried basil
- ¼ teaspoon pepper
- 3 cups uncooked whole wheat egg noodles (about 4 ounces)
- 3 cups coarsely chopped rotisserie chicken
- 1 tablespoon minced fresh parsley

1. In a 6-qt. stockpot, heat oil over medium-high heat. Add celery, carrots and onion; cook and stir 5-7 minutes or until tender.

2. Add broth, basil and pepper; bring to a boil. Stir in noodles; cook 12-14 minutes or until al dente. Stir in chicken and parsley; heat through.

PER SERVING 1½ cups: 195 cal., 6g fat (1g sat. fat), 47mg chol., 639mg sod., 16g carb. (2g sugars, 3g fiber), 21g pro. *Diabetic Exchanges:* 2 lean meat, 1 starch, ½ fat.

CHICKEN 🐓 SANDWICHES, SOUPS & MORE   203

**SLOW-COOKED
CHICKEN CHILI**

4. Place tortilla strips on a baking sheet coated with cooking spray. Bake at 400° for 8-10 minutes or until crisp. Serve chili with sour cream and tortilla strips.
PER SERVING *1¼ cups with 10 tortilla strips and 1 tablespoon sour cream: 356 cal., 14g fat (3g sat. fat), 55mg chol., 644mg sod., 39g carb. (5g sugars, 8g fiber), 21g pro.* **Diabetic Exchanges:** *2 starch, 2 lean meat, 2 vegetable, 1 fat.*

FAST FIX ▸

QUICK CHICKEN & WILD RICE SOUP (PICTURED ON PAGE 197)

My mother-in-law raves about the chicken-and-rice soup we serve at our house. I tweaked the recipe several times to get it just right. This version is ready in half an hour!
—TERESA JACOBSON ST JOHNS, FL

START TO FINISH: 30 MIN.
MAKES: 4 SERVINGS

- 1 **package (6.2 ounces) fast-cooking long grain and wild rice mix**
- 2 **tablespoons butter**
- 1 **small onion, finely chopped**
- 1 **celery rib, finely chopped**
- 1 **medium carrot, finely chopped**
- 1 **garlic clove, minced**
- 2 **tablespoons all-purpose flour**
- 3 **cups 2% milk**
- 1½ **cups chicken broth**
- 2 **cups cubed cooked chicken**

1. Cook rice mix according to package directions.
2. Meanwhile, in a large saucepan, heat butter over medium-high heat. Add the onion, celery and carrot; cook and stir 6-8 minutes or until tender. Add garlic; cook 1 minute longer. Stir in flour until blended; gradually whisk in milk and broth. Bring to a boil, stirring constantly; cook and stir 1-2 minutes or until slightly thickened.
3. Stir in chicken and rice mix; heat through.
PER SERVING *2 cups: 465 cal., 15g fat (7g sat. fat), 94mg chol., 1095mg sod., 50g carb. (12g sugars, 2g fiber), 32g pro.*

SLOW-COOKED CHICKEN CHILI

Lime juice gives this chili a zesty twist, while canned tomatoes and beans make prep work a breeze. It's fun to serve with toasted tortilla strips, and it's great on a buffet.
—DIANE RANDAZZO SINKING SPRING, PA

PREP: 25 MIN. • **COOK:** 4 HOURS
MAKES: 6 SERVINGS

- 1 **medium onion, chopped**
- 1 **each medium sweet yellow, red and green peppers, chopped**
- 2 **tablespoons olive oil**
- 3 **garlic cloves, minced**
- 1 **pound ground chicken**
- 2 **cans (14½ ounces each) diced tomatoes, undrained**
- 1 **can (15 ounces) cannellini beans, rinsed and drained**
- ¼ **cup lime juice**
- 1 **tablespoon all-purpose flour**
- 1 **tablespoon baking cocoa**
- 1 **tablespoon ground cumin**
- 1 **tablespoon chili powder**
- 2 **teaspoons ground coriander**
- 1 **teaspoon grated lime peel**
- ½ **teaspoon salt**
- ½ **teaspoon garlic pepper blend**
- ¼ **teaspoon pepper**
- 2 **flour tortillas (8 inches), cut into ¼-inch strips**
- 6 **tablespoons reduced-fat sour cream**

1. In a large skillet, saute onion and peppers in oil for 7-8 minutes or until crisp-tender. Add garlic; cook 1 minute longer. Add chicken; cook and stir over medium heat for 8-9 minutes or until meat is no longer pink.
2. Transfer to a 3-qt. slow cooker. Stir in the tomatoes, beans, lime juice, flour, cocoa, cumin, chili powder, coriander, lime peel, salt, garlic pepper and pepper.
3. Cover and cook on low for 4-5 hours or until heated through.

EAT SMART **FAST FIX**

FETA CHICKEN BURGERS

My friends always request these quick chicken burgers. Sometimes I make them on the grill; other times I add olives to punch up the flavor. Try them with the cucumber mayo or get creative with toppings.

—ANGELA ROBINSON FINDLAY, OH

START TO FINISH: 30 MIN.
MAKES: 6 SERVINGS

- ¼ cup finely chopped cucumber
- ¼ cup reduced-fat mayonnaise

BURGERS

- ½ cup chopped roasted sweet red pepper
- 1 teaspoon garlic powder
- ½ teaspoon Greek seasoning
- ¼ teaspoon pepper
- 1½ pounds lean ground chicken
- 1 cup crumbled feta cheese
- 6 whole wheat hamburger buns, split and toasted
  Lettuce leaves and tomato slices, optional

1. Preheat broiler. Mix cucumber and mayonnaise. For burgers, mix red pepper and seasonings. Add chicken and cheese; mix lightly but thoroughly (mixture will be sticky). Shape into six ½-in.-thick patties.

2. Broil burgers 4 in. from heat until a thermometer reads 165°, 3-4 minutes per side. Serve in buns with cucumber sauce. If desired, top with lettuce and tomato.

FREEZE OPTION *Place uncooked patties on a plastic wrap-lined baking sheet; wrap and freeze until firm. Remove from pan and transfer to a large resealable plastic bag; return to freezer. To use, broil frozen patties as directed.*

PER SERVING *1 burger with 1 tablespoon sauce: 356 cal., 14g fat (5g sat. fat), 95mg chol., 703mg sod., 25g carb., 4g fiber, 31g pro.* **Diabetic Exchanges:** *5 lean meat, 2 starch, ½ fat.*

FETA CHICKEN BURGERS

SHREDDED CHICKEN GYROS (PICTURED ON PAGE 196)

We go to the annual Greek Festival in Salt Lake City for the awesome food. This chicken, with lemon and spices, is a tasty reminder of the fest. It is a great way to mix up our menu, and my kids are big fans.

—**CAMILLE BECKSTRAND** LAYTON, UT

PREP: 20 MIN. • **COOK:** 3 HOURS
MAKES: 8 SERVINGS

- 2 medium onions, chopped
- 6 garlic cloves, minced
- 1 teaspoon lemon-pepper seasoning
- 1 teaspoon dried oregano
- ½ teaspoon ground allspice
- ½ cup water
- ½ cup lemon juice
- ¼ cup red wine vinegar
- 2 tablespoons olive oil
- 2 pounds boneless skinless chicken breasts
- 8 whole pita breads
  Toppings: tzatziki sauce, torn romaine and sliced tomato, cucumber and onion

1. In a 3-qt. slow cooker, combine first nine ingredients; add chicken. Cook, covered, on low 3-4 hours or until chicken is tender (a thermometer should read at least 165°).

2. Remove chicken from slow cooker. Shred with two forks; return to slow cooker. Using tongs, place chicken mixture on pita breads. Serve with toppings.

PER SERVING *1 gyro (calculated without toppings): 337 cal., 7g fat (1g sat. fat), 63mg chol., 418mg sod., 38g carb. (2g sugars, 2g fiber), 29g pro.* **Diabetic Exchanges:** *3 lean meat, 2½ starch, ½ fat.*

CHICKEN STEW

CHICKEN STEW

Rely on this slow-cooked stew on busy weekends when you'd rather not be in the kitchen. Chicken, vegetables and seasonings give this dish great flavor, and it's lower in fat than most stews.

—**LINDA EMERY** BEARDEN, AR

PREP: 10 MIN. • **COOK:** 4½ HOURS
MAKES: 10 SERVINGS

- 2 pounds boneless skinless chicken breasts, cut into 1-inch cubes
- 2 cans (14½ ounces each) reduced-sodium chicken broth
- 3 cups cubed peeled potatoes
- 1 cup chopped onion
- 1 cup sliced celery
- 1 cup thinly sliced carrots
- 1 teaspoon paprika
- ½ teaspoon pepper
- ½ teaspoon rubbed sage
- ½ teaspoon dried thyme
- 1 can (6 ounces) no-salt-added tomato paste
- ¼ cup cold water
- 3 tablespoons cornstarch
  Shredded Parmesan cheese, optional

1. In a 5-qt. slow cooker, combine the first 11 ingredients; cover and cook on high for 4 hours.

2. Mix water and cornstarch until smooth; stir into stew. Cook, covered, 30 minutes more or until the vegetables are tender. If desired, sprinkle with Parmesan cheese.

PER SERVING *1 cup: 193 cal., 3g fat (0 sat. fat), 59mg chol., 236mg sod., 16g carb. (0 sugars, 0 fiber), 24g pro.* **Diabetic Exchanges:** *3 lean meat, 2 vegetable, ½ starch.*

LOADED CHICKEN & GOUDA CALZONES

When I had my daughter, I tried to have a lot of meals in the freezer to make those first few weeks easier. These calzones were one of our favorites! We loved being able to pull them out and have dinner in minutes. Because these freeze in individual portions, they also make for a great lunch. I've dipped these in spaghetti sauce, pesto and ranch dressing, and each was delicious.

—ELISABETH LARSEN PLEASANT GROVE, UT

PREP: 40 MIN. • **BAKE:** 15 MIN.
MAKES: 8 SERVINGS

- 1 tablespoon olive oil
- ½ pound sliced fresh mushrooms
- 1 small onion, finely chopped
- 2 garlic cloves, minced
- 1 package (10 ounces) frozen chopped spinach, thawed and squeezed dry
- 2 cups shredded cooked chicken breast
- 1 cup chopped roasted sweet red peppers, drained
- 6 bacon strips, cooked and crumbled
- ½ teaspoon salt
- ¼ teaspoon pepper
- 2 loaves (1 pound each) frozen whole wheat bread dough, thawed
- 2 cups shredded Gouda cheese
- 1 large egg white, lightly beaten

1. Preheat oven to 400°. In a large skillet, heat oil over medium-high heat. Add mushrooms and onion; cook and stir 3-5 minutes or until tender. Add garlic; cook 1 minute longer. Remove from heat. Stir in spinach, chicken, red peppers, bacon, salt and pepper.

2. On a lightly floured surface, divide each loaf of dough into four portions; press or roll each into an 8-in. circle.

LOADED CHICKEN & GOUDA CALZONES

Place ½ cup filling over half of each circle to within ½ in. of edge. Top each with ¼ cup cheese. Fold dough over filling; pinch edge to seal.

3. Place on greased baking sheets. Brush tops with egg white. Bake 14-17 minutes or until golden brown and heated through. Serve warm.

FREEZE OPTION *Freeze cooled baked calzones in resealable plastic freezer bags. To use, place calzones on greased baking sheets. Cover with foil and reheat in a preheated 350° oven for 25 minutes. Uncover; bake 5-10 minutes longer or until heated through.*

PER SERVING *1 calzone: 528 cal., 17g fat (6g sat. fat), 65mg chol., 1156mg sod., 60g carb. (12g sugars, 8g fiber), 33g pro.*

FAST FIX
SWISS CHICKEN SLIDERS

Friends came over for a spur-of-the-moment bonfire, and I dreamed up these quick chicken sliders so we'd have something to eat. Bake them till the cheese is gooey.

—SARA MARTIN WHITEFISH, MT

START TO FINISH: 25 MIN.
MAKES: 6 SERVINGS

- ½ cup mayonnaise
- 3 tablespoons yellow mustard
- 12 mini buns, split
- 12 slices deli ham
- 3 cups shredded rotisserie chicken
- 6 slices Swiss cheese, cut in half

1. Preheat oven to 350°. In a small bowl, mix mayonnaise and mustard. Spread bun bottoms and tops with mayonnaise mixture. Layer bottoms with deli ham, chicken and cheese; replace tops. Arrange buns in a single layer in a 15x10x1-in. baking pan.

2. Bake, covered, 10-15 minutes or until heated through and cheese is melted.

PER SERVING *2 sliders: 508 cal., 27g fat (6g sat. fat), 100mg chol., 894mg sod., 28g carb. (4g sugars, 1g fiber), 37g pro.*

FAST FIX ▶

CHICKEN VERDE QUESADILLAS

I used the corn, peppers and zucchini in my fridge to create these quick and easy quesadillas. Dollop with sour cream and you're good to go.

—**JULIE MERRIMAN** SEATTLE, WA

START TO FINISH: 30 MIN.
MAKES: 4 SERVINGS

- 2 **tablespoons olive oil, divided**
- 1 **large sweet onion, halved and thinly sliced**
- 1½ **cups frozen corn**
- 1 **small zucchini, chopped**
- 1 **poblano pepper, thinly sliced**
- 2 **cups frozen grilled chicken breast strips, thawed and chopped**
- ¾ **cup green enchilada sauce**
- ¼ **cup minced fresh cilantro**
- ¼ **teaspoon salt**
- ⅛ **teaspoon pepper**
- 8 **flour tortillas (10 inches)**
- 4 **cups shredded Monterey Jack cheese**
  Pico de gallo and sour cream, optional

1. Preheat oven to 400°. In a large skillet, heat 1 tablespoon oil over medium-high heat. Add onion, corn, zucchini and poblano pepper; cook and stir 8-10 minutes or until tender. Add chicken, enchilada sauce, cilantro, salt and pepper; heat through.

2. Brush remaining oil over one side of each tortilla. Place half of the tortillas on two baking sheets, oiled side down. Sprinkle each with ½ cup cheese and top with 1 cup chicken mixture, remaining cheese and tortillas, oiled side up.

3. Bake 7-9 minutes or until golden brown and cheese is melted. If desired, serve with pico de gallo and sour cream.

PER SERVING *1 quesadilla (calculated without pico de gallo and sour cream): 1083 cal., 55g fat (27g sat. fat), 132mg chol., 2449mg sod., 94g carb. (13g sugars, 8g fiber), 56g pro.*

CHICKEN VERDE QUESADILLAS

EAT SMART

THAI CHICKEN LETTUCE WRAPS (PICTURED ON PAGE 197)

Don't be intimidated by the list of ingredients in this recipe. The whole thing truly comes together in no time. You'll love the easy Thai dressing!

—**LAUREEN PITTMAN** RIVERSIDE, CA

PREP: 35 MIN.
MAKES: 6 SERVINGS

- ¼ cup rice vinegar
- 2 tablespoons lime juice
- 2 tablespoons reduced-fat mayonnaise
- 2 tablespoons reduced-fat creamy peanut butter
- 1 tablespoon brown sugar
- 1 tablespoon reduced-sodium soy sauce
- 2 teaspoons minced fresh gingerroot
- 1 teaspoon sesame oil
- 1 teaspoon Thai chili sauce
- 1 garlic clove, chopped
- 3 tablespoons canola oil
- ½ cup minced fresh cilantro

CHICKEN SALAD

- 2 cups cubed cooked chicken breast
- 1 small sweet red pepper, diced
- ½ cup chopped green onions
- ½ cup shredded carrot
- ½ cup unsalted dry roasted peanuts, chopped, divided
- 6 Bibb or Boston lettuce leaves

1. In a blender, combine the first 10 ingredients. While processing, gradually add oil in a steady stream; stir in cilantro. Set aside.

2. In a large bowl, combine the chicken, red pepper, onions, carrot and ¼ cup peanuts. Add dressing and toss to coat. Divide among lettuce leaves; sprinkle with remaining peanuts. Fold lettuce over filling.

PER SERVING *1 ½ cup chicken salad: 284 cal., 19g fat (2g sat. fat), 38mg chol., 222mg sodium, 12g carb. (6g sugars, 2g fiber), 19g pro. **Diabetic Exchanges:** 3 fat, 2 lean meat, 1 starch.*

WEEKNIGHT CHICKEN MOZZARELLA SANDWICHES

⑤INGREDIENTS **FAST FIX**

WEEKNIGHT CHICKEN MOZZARELLA SANDWICHES

My husband is a big garlic fan, so we use garlic bread crumbs and garlic sauce for our baked chicken sandwiches. These are so comforting on a chilly day.

—**BRIDGET SNYDER** SYRACUSE, NY

START TO FINISH: 30 MIN.
MAKES: 4 SERVINGS

- 4 boneless skinless chicken breast halves (6 ounces each)
- 1 cup garlic bread crumbs
- 1 cup garlic and herb pasta sauce
- 1 cup shredded part-skim mozzarella cheese
  Grated Parmesan cheese, optional
- 4 kaiser rolls, split

1. Preheat oven to 400°. Pound chicken with a meat mallet to ½-in. thickness. Place bread crumbs in a large resealable plastic bag. Add chicken, a few pieces at a time; close bag and shake to coat. Transfer to a greased 15x10x1-in. baking pan.

2. Bake, uncovered, 15-20 minutes or until no longer pink. Spoon pasta sauce over chicken. Top with mozzarella and, if desired, Parmesan cheese. Bake 2-3 minutes longer or until cheese is melted. Serve on rolls.

PER SERVING *1 sandwich (calculated without Parmesan cheese): 509 cal., 13g fat (5g sat. fat), 112mg chol., 1125mg sod., 46g carb. (5g sugars, 3g fiber), 50g pro.*

Turn here for change-of-pace meals that come together in a snap. These flame-broiled ribs, weeknight chops and pulled pork sammies are about to become your new favorites!

PORK

PORK [101]

Lean and tender, pork is just as good for everyday cooking as it is for special celebrations.

When it comes serving up succulent meals in a flash, pork is a natural choice. Pork tenderloin can be grilled whole or roasted in the oven in no time. Cut it into medallions or cutlets for quick stovetop entrees, or cube and cook it for hearty additions to kabobs or main-dish salads.

Don't forget about chops, sausages, ham, bacon, ribs and all the other finger-licking favorites that fall in the pork family! These items offer the savory, comforting goodness families crave with only a small amount of prep time.

ZUCCHINI & SAUSAGE STOVETOP CASSEROLE, PAGE 256

THIS LITTLE PIGGY WENT TO MARKET

- Look for pork that is firm and has a pink color and a small amount of fat on the surface.
- Be leery of packages with torn plastic or excessive liquid.
- Pork freezes well. If you're not going to use the meat by the sell-by date, freeze it for future meals.
- For the leanest cuts of pork, look for any cut of loin.

THE WHOLE HOG

- Ounce for ounce, pork tenderloin is as lean as boneless. skinless chicken breast.
- The leanest cuts of pork are boneless loin roasts or chops, boneless sirloin roasts or chops and bone-in pork chops.
- Consider dry-cooking methods such as grilling, roasting and pan-frying when a firm texture is desired from tender cuts.
- Less tender cuts include those in the shoulder and leg areas.

A TOAST TO THE ROAST

- To prepare a pork roast so that it can be stuffed, flatten it by making a lengthwise cut in the center of the roast to within ½ inch of the bottom. Open the roast so it lies flat. Use a mallet to flatten the meat to ¾-inch thickness.
- To carve a roast with rib bones, place the bones to one side of a cutting board. Hold the meat steady with a meat fork, and use a carving knife to slice between the bones.

BRING HOME THE BACON

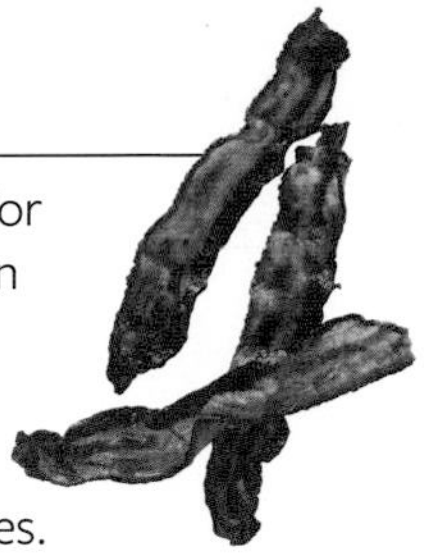

Check the date stamp on packages of bacon for freshness. Once the package is opened, bacon should be used within a week. For long-term storage, freeze bacon for up to one month. Bacon fries well, of course, but it can also be baked on a sheet pan at 350° for 30 minutes.

PORK IS DONE WHEN A THERMOMETER READS

145° (medium-rare) with a 5-minute stand time before carving or eating. For medium doneness, pork should be served at **160°**. Follow suit for large roasts, but increase the stand time to 10-15 minutes. Fully cooked ham should reach a minimum of 140°.

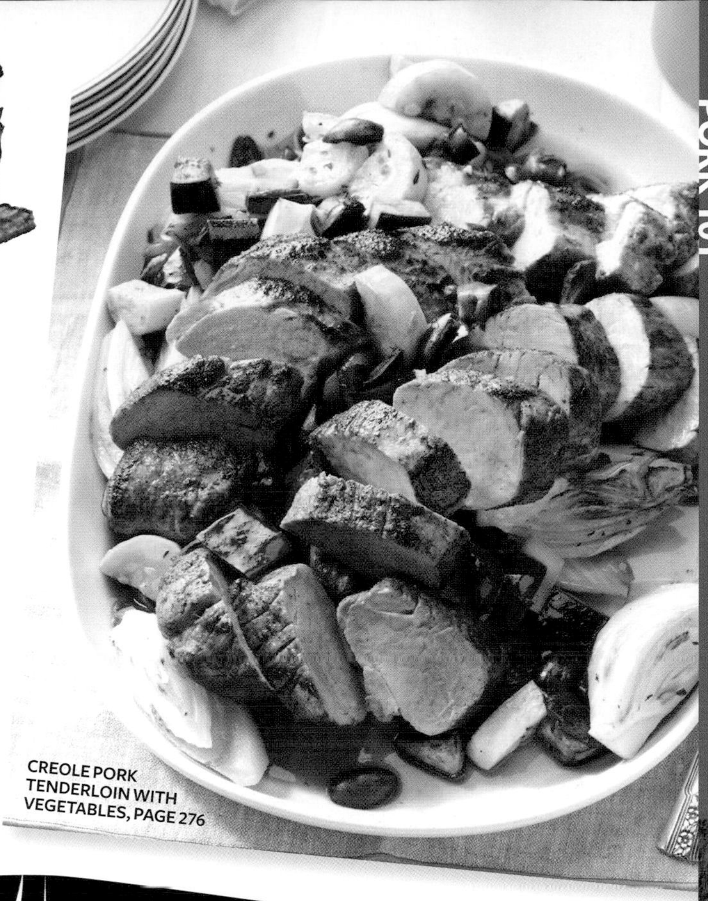

CREOLE PORK TENDERLOIN WITH VEGETABLES, PAGE 276

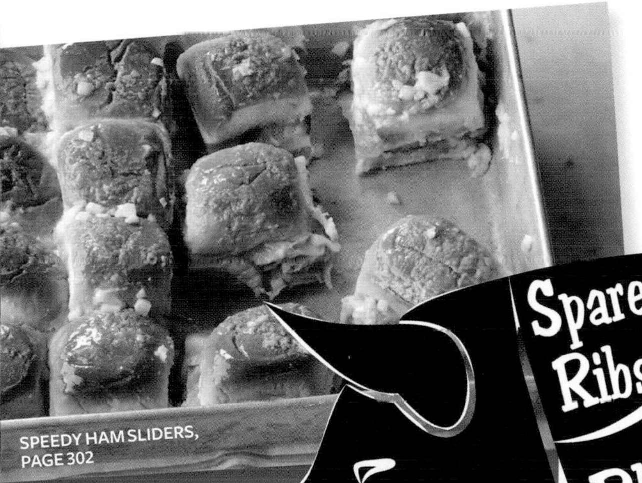

SPEEDY HAM SLIDERS, PAGE 302

Spare Ribs
Head
Blade
Leg
Loin
Belly
Leg/ Ham

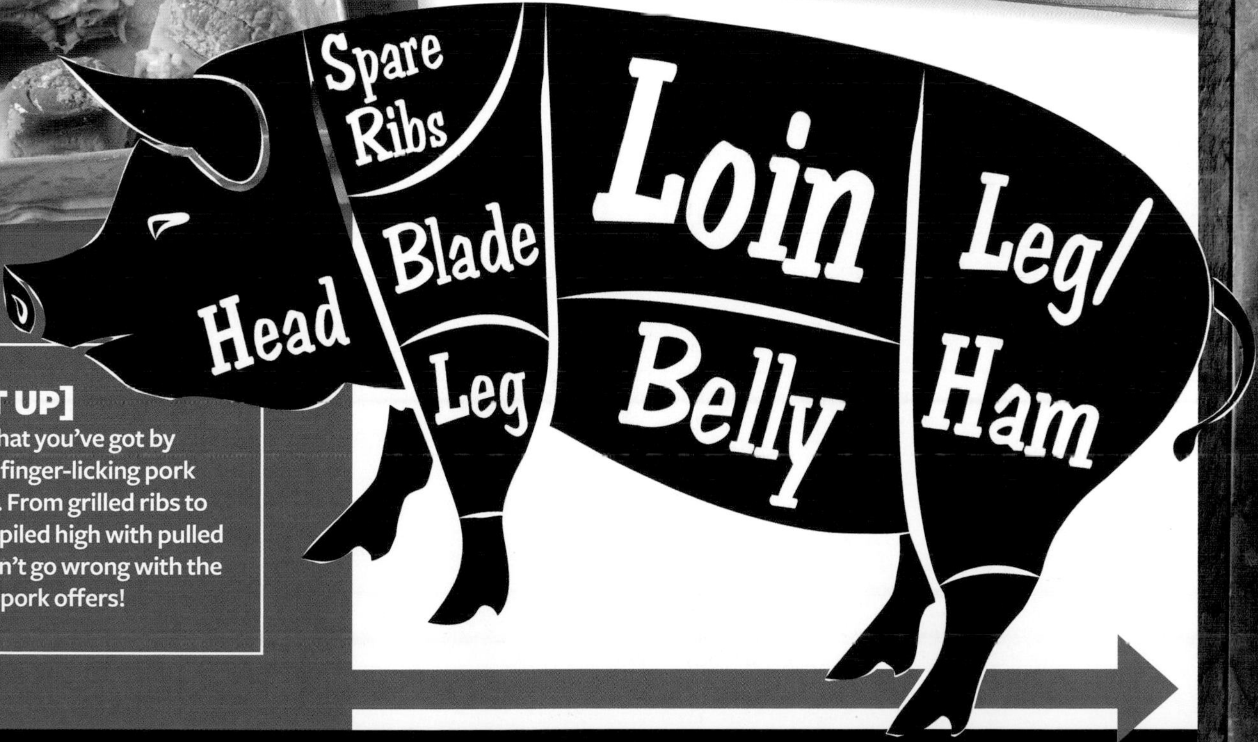

[HAM IT UP]

Show 'em what you've got by serving up a finger-licking pork dish tonight. From grilled ribs to sandwiches piled high with pulled pork, you can't go wrong with the juicy results pork offers!

PIG ILLUSTRATION: CHEMADAN/SHUTTERSTOCK

CARIBBEAN CHIPOTLE
PORK SLIDERS, PAGE 221

BEER AND BRATS
NACHOS, PAGE 224

SPEEDY SNACKS

Looking for hearty appetizers?
Whether you need a buffet of
substantial hors d'oeuvres or
simply a few **comforting bites**
on game day, let this section help!
Pork, sausage, bacon and ham are the
down-home ingredients for stick-
to-your-ribs snacks **people crave.**
Turn the page and give hunger the
cold shoulder today!

SOUTHWESTERN
PULLED PORK
CROSTINI, PAGE 219

BLACK FOREST HAM ROLL-UPS, PAGE 223

MINI MAC &
CHEESE DOGS

MINI MAC & CHEESE DOGS

We wanted to get creative with hot dogs, so we made these cute appetizers. Homemade buns impress your guests, and you can pile on extra cheese, relish and even bacon.
—**JULIE PETERSON** CROFTON, MD

PREP: 25 MIN. + RISING
BAKE: 15 MIN. + COOLING
MAKES: 2 DOZEN

- 1 package (16 ounces) frozen bread dough dinner rolls (12 count), thawed but still cold
- ½ cup panko (Japanese) bread crumbs
- 2 tablespoons chopped onion
- 1 tablespoon canola oil
- ¼ teaspoon salt
- ⅛ teaspoon pepper
- 12 bun-length beef hot dogs
- 1 package (7¼ ounces) macaroni and cheese dinner mix

1. Let dough stand at room temperature 15-20 minutes or until soft enough to shape. Cut each roll in half; shape each half into a 3-in.-long mini hot dog bun. Place 2 in. apart on greased baking sheets.
2. Cover with greased plastic wrap; let rise in a warm place until almost doubled, about 45 minutes. Preheat oven to 350°.
3. Bake buns 12-15 minutes or until golden brown. Remove from pans to wire racks to cool completely.
4. In a 15x10x1-in. baking pan, toss bread crumbs with onion, oil, salt and pepper. Bake at 350° for 5-7 minutes or until golden brown, stirring once.
5. Cook hot dogs and macaroni and cheese according to package directions. To serve, cut hot dogs crosswise in half. Split buns; fill with hot dogs and macaroni and cheese. Sprinkle with toasted crumbs.
PER SERVING *1 mini dog: 198 cal., 12g fat (5g sat. fat), 25mg chol., 446mg sod., 18g carb. (2g sugars, 1g fiber), 6g pro.*

CHEESY PIZZA ROLLS

CHEESY PIZZA ROLLS

The cast-iron skillet browns these delicious pizza rolls to perfection. My family can't get enough. Use whatever pizza toppings your family likes best.
—**DOROTHY SMITH** EL DORADO, AR

PREP: 15 MIN. • **BAKE:** 25 MIN.
MAKES: 8 APPETIZERS

- 1 loaf (1 pound) frozen pizza dough, thawed
- ½ cup pasta sauce
- 1 cup shredded part-skim mozzarella cheese, divided
- 1 cup coarsely chopped pepperoni (about 64 slices)
- ½ pound bulk Italian sausage, cooked and crumbled
- ¼ cup grated Parmesan cheese
  Minced fresh basil, optional
  Crushed red pepper flakes, optional

1. Preheat oven to 400°. On a lightly floured surface, roll dough into a 16x10-in. rectangle. Brush with pasta sauce to within ½ in. of edges.
2. Sprinkle with ½ cup mozzarella cheese, pepperoni, sausage and Parmesan cheese. Roll up jelly-roll style, starting with a long side; pinch seam to seal. Cut into eight slices. Place in a greased 9-in. cast-iron skillet or greased 9-in. round baking pan, cut side down.
3. Bake 20 minutes; sprinkle with the remaining mozzarella cheese. Bake until golden brown, for 5-10 more minutes. If desired, serve with minced fresh basil and crushed red pepper flakes.
PER SERVING *1 pizza roll (calculated without additional pasta sauce): 355 cal., 19g fat (7g sat. fat), 42mg chol., 978mg sod., 29g carb. (3g sugars, 1g fiber), 14g pro.*

ONE-BITE TAMALES

I have always liked Mexican food, and while attending a potluck one night, I fell in love with these tamales. Pork sausage with warm seasonings give a Mexican taste, and there are never any left. They're great in the slow cooker....mix all and forget til ready to serve.

—DOLORES JAYCOX GRETNA, LA

PREP: 40 MIN. • **COOK:** 3 HOURS 20 MIN.
MAKES: ABOUT 5½ DOZEN

- 1¼ cups cornmeal
- ½ cup all-purpose flour
- 5¾ cups V8 juice, divided
- 4 teaspoons chili powder, divided
- 4 teaspoons ground cumin, divided
- 2 teaspoons salt, divided
- 1 teaspoon garlic powder
- ½ to 1 teaspoon cayenne pepper
- 1 pound bulk spicy pork sausage
  Corn chips

1. Preheat oven to 350°. Mix cornmeal, flour, ¾ cup V8 juice, 2 teaspoons chili powder, 2 teaspoons cumin, 1 teaspoon salt, garlic powder and cayenne. Add sausage; mix lightly but thoroughly. Shape into 1-in. balls.

2. Place meatballs on a greased rack in a 15x10-in. pan. Bake until cooked through, 20-25 minutes.

3. Meanwhile, in a 4-qt. slow cooker, mix remaining V8 juice, chili powder, cumin and salt. Gently stir in meatballs. Cook, covered, on low until heated through, for 3-4 hours. Serve with corn chips.

PER SERVING *1 tamale (calculated without corn chips): 37 cal., 2g fat (0g sat. fat), 4mg chol., 172mg sod., 4g carb. (1g sugars, 0 fiber), 1g pro.*

BLUE CHEESE POTATO CHIPS

BLUE CHEESE POTATO CHIPS

Game day calls for something bold, so I top potato chips with tomatoes, bacon and tangy blue cheese. I make two big pans, and they always disappear.

—BONNIE HAWKINS ELKHORN, WI

START TO FINISH: 15 MIN.
MAKES: 10 SERVINGS

- 1 package (8½ ounces) kettle-cooked potato chips
- 2 medium tomatoes, seeded and chopped
- 8 bacon strips, cooked and crumbled
- 6 green onions, chopped
- 1 cup crumbled blue cheese

1. Preheat broiler. In a 15x10x1-in. baking pan, arrange potato chips in an even layer. Top with remaining ingredients.

2. Broil 4-5 in. from heat 2-3 minutes or until cheese begins to melt. Serve immediately.

PER SERVING *215 cal., 14g fat (5g sat. fat), 17mg chol., 359mg sod., 16g carb. (2g sugars, 1g fiber), 6g pro.*

SOUTHWESTERN PULLED PORK CROSTINI

With a meaty take on crostini, these hearty appetizers are great for tailgating and other casual parties. Everyone enjoys the spicy, sweet and salty bites, which makes the recipe even more special to me.

—**RANDY CARTWRIGHT** LINDEN, WI

PREP: 45 MIN. • **COOK:** 6 HOURS
MAKES: 32 APPETIZERS

- 1 boneless pork shoulder butt roast (about 2 pounds)
- ½ cup lime juice
- 2 envelopes mesquite marinade mix
- ¼ cup sugar
- ¼ cup olive oil

SALSA
- 1 cup frozen corn, thawed
- 1 cup canned black beans, rinsed and drained
- 1 small tomato, finely chopped
- 2 tablespoons finely chopped seeded jalapeno pepper
- 2 tablespoons lime juice
- 2 tablespoons olive oil
- 1½ teaspoons ground cumin
- 1 teaspoon chili powder
- ½ teaspoon salt
- ¼ teaspoon crushed red pepper flakes

SAUCE
- 1 can (4 ounces) chopped green chilies
- ⅓ cup apricot preserves
- ⅛ teaspoon salt

CROSTINI
- 32 slices French bread baguette (¼ inch thick)
- ¼ cup olive oil
- ⅔ cup crumbled queso fresco or feta cheese
  Lime wedges, optional

1. Place roast in a 3-qt. slow cooker. In a small bowl, whisk lime juice, marinade mix, sugar and oil until blended; pour over roast. Cook, covered, on low 6-8 hours or until meat is tender.

2. For salsa, in a small bowl, combine corn, beans, tomato and jalapeno. Stir in lime juice, oil and seasonings. In a small saucepan, combine sauce ingredients; cook and stir over low heat until blended.

3. For crostini, preheat broiler. Brush bread slices on both sides with oil; place on ungreased baking sheets. Broil 3-4 in. from heat 1-2 minutes on each side or until golden brown.

4. Remove roast from slow cooker; cool slightly. Shred pork with two forks. To serve, layer toasts with salsa, pork and cheese. Top with sauce. If desired, serve with lime wedges.

PER SERVING *1 crostini: 121 cal., 7g fat (2g sat. fat), 19mg chol., 362mg sod., 9g carb. (3g sugars, 1g fiber), 6g pro.*

SOUTHWESTERN PULLED PORK CROSTINI

TOP TIP

MAKE THEM A MEAL!

These were so delicious, I would make this as a meal on sandwich buns next time!

—EJT325
TASTEOFHOME.COM

LOADED PULLED PORK CUPS

LOADED PULLED PORK CUPS

Potato nests are simple to make and surprisingly handy for pulled pork, cheese, sour cream and other toppings. Make, bake and collect the compliments.

—MELISSA SPERKA GREENSBORO, NC

PREP: 40 MIN. • **BAKE:** 25 MIN.
MAKES: 1½ DOZEN

- 1 **package (20 ounces) refrigerated shredded hash brown potatoes**
- ¾ **cup shredded Parmesan cheese**
- 2 **large egg whites, beaten**
- 1 **teaspoon garlic salt**
- ½ **teaspoon onion powder**
- ¼ **teaspoon pepper**
- 1 **carton (16 ounces) refrigerated fully cooked barbecued shredded pork**
- 1 **cup shredded Colby-Monterey Jack cheese**
- ½ **cup sour cream**
- 5 **bacon strips, cooked and crumbled Minced chives**

1. Preheat oven to 450°. In a large bowl, mix hash browns, Parmesan cheese, egg whites and seasonings until blended. Divide potatoes among 18 well-greased muffin cups; press onto bottoms and up sides to form cups.

2. Bake 22-25 minutes or until edges are dark golden brown. Carefully run a knife around sides of each cup. Cool 5 minutes before removing from pans to a serving platter. Meanwhile, heat pulled pork according to package directions.

3. Sprinkle cheese into cups. Top with pork, sour cream and bacon; sprinkle with chives. Serve warm.

PER SERVING *1 loaded pork cup: 129 cal., 6g fat (3g sat. fat), 19mg chol., 439mg sod., 11g carb. (4g sugars, 0 fiber), 8g pro.*

CARIBBEAN CHIPOTLE PORK SLIDERS

(PICTURED ON PAGE 214)

One of our favorite pulled pork recipes combines the heat of chipotle peppers with cool tropical coleslaw. The robust flavors make these sliders a big hit with guests.

—KADIJA BRIDGEWATER BOCA RATON, FL

PREP: 35 MIN. • **COOK:** 8 HOURS
MAKES: 20 SERVINGS

- 1 **large onion, quartered**
- 1 **boneless pork shoulder butt roast (3 to 4 pounds)**
- 2 **finely chopped chipotle peppers in adobo sauce plus 3 tablespoons sauce**
- ¾ **cup honey barbecue sauce**
- ¼ **cup water**
- 4 **garlic cloves, minced**
- 1 **tablespoon ground cumin**
- 1 **teaspoon salt**
- ¼ **teaspoon pepper**

COLESLAW

- 2 **cups finely chopped red cabbage**
- 1 **medium mango, peeled and chopped**
- 1 **cup pineapple tidbits, drained**
- ¾ **cup chopped fresh cilantro**
- 1 **tablespoon lime juice**
- ¼ **teaspoon salt**
- ⅛ **teaspoon pepper**
- 20 **Hawaiian sweet rolls, split and toasted**

1. Place onion in a 5-qt. slow cooker. Cut roast in half; place over onion. In a small bowl, combine chipotle peppers, adobo sauce, barbecue sauce, water, garlic, cumin, salt and pepper; pour over meat. Cook, covered, on low 8-10 hours or until meat is tender.

2. Remove roast; cool slightly. Skim fat from cooking juices. Shred pork with two forks. Return pork to the slow cooker; heat through.

3. For coleslaw, in a large bowl, combine cabbage, mango, pineapple, cilantro, lime juice, salt and pepper. Place ¼ cup pork mixture on each roll bottom; top with 2 tablespoons coleslaw. Replace tops.

PER SERVING *1 slider: 265 cal., 10g fat (4g sat. fat), 55mg chol., 430mg sod., 27g carb. (15g sugars, 2g fiber), 16g pro.*

BOURBON HAM BALLS

BOURBON HAM BALLS

My Grandma Nette made ham balls, but I re-created them salty-sweet with a bourbon and vinegar kick. Serve them alone, in a sandwich, or over pasta or rice as a change from regular meatballs.

—KIMLA CARSTEN GRAND JUNCTION, CO

PREP: 70 MIN. + FREEZING • **BAKE:** 15 MIN.
MAKES: ABOUT 3½ DOZEN

- 2 **pounds fully cooked boneless ham**
- 1 **thick boneless pork loin chop (8 ounces)**
- ½ **pound bacon strips**
- 1 **cup panko (Japanese) bread crumbs**
- 1 **cup 2% milk**
- 2 **large eggs, lightly beaten**
  Oil for frying

SAUCE

- 1½ **cups packed brown sugar**
- ½ **cup white vinegar**
- ½ **cup bourbon**
- 2 **teaspoons spicy brown mustard**

1. Cut ham, pork chop and bacon into 1-in. pieces; arrange in a single layer in a foil-lined 15x10x1-in. pan. Freeze 30 minutes or until partially frozen.

2. Preheat oven to 350°. Transfer meat to a food processor in batches; pulse until coarsely ground, about 20-24 pulses. In a large bowl, combine bread crumbs, milk and eggs. Add pork mixture; mix lightly but thoroughly. Shape into 1½-in. balls.

3. In a large skillet, heat ¼ in. of oil over medium heat. Add ham balls in batches; cook 3-4 minutes or until cooked through, turning occasionally. Remove from pan; drain on paper towels.

4. In a large bowl, whisk the sauce ingredients; reserve 1 cup for serving. Add ham balls to remaining sauce, a few at a time, allowing the ham balls to soak 1-2 minutes. Transfer ham balls to a foil-lined 15x10x1-in. baking pan. Bake for 15-20 minutes or until heated through, brushing occasionally with remaining sauce from soaking. Serve ham balls with reserved sauce.

PER SERVING *1 ham ball with 1 teaspoon sauce: 138 cal., 8g fat (2g sat. fat), 27mg chol., 276mg sod., 9g carb. (8g sugars, 0 fiber), 6g pro.*

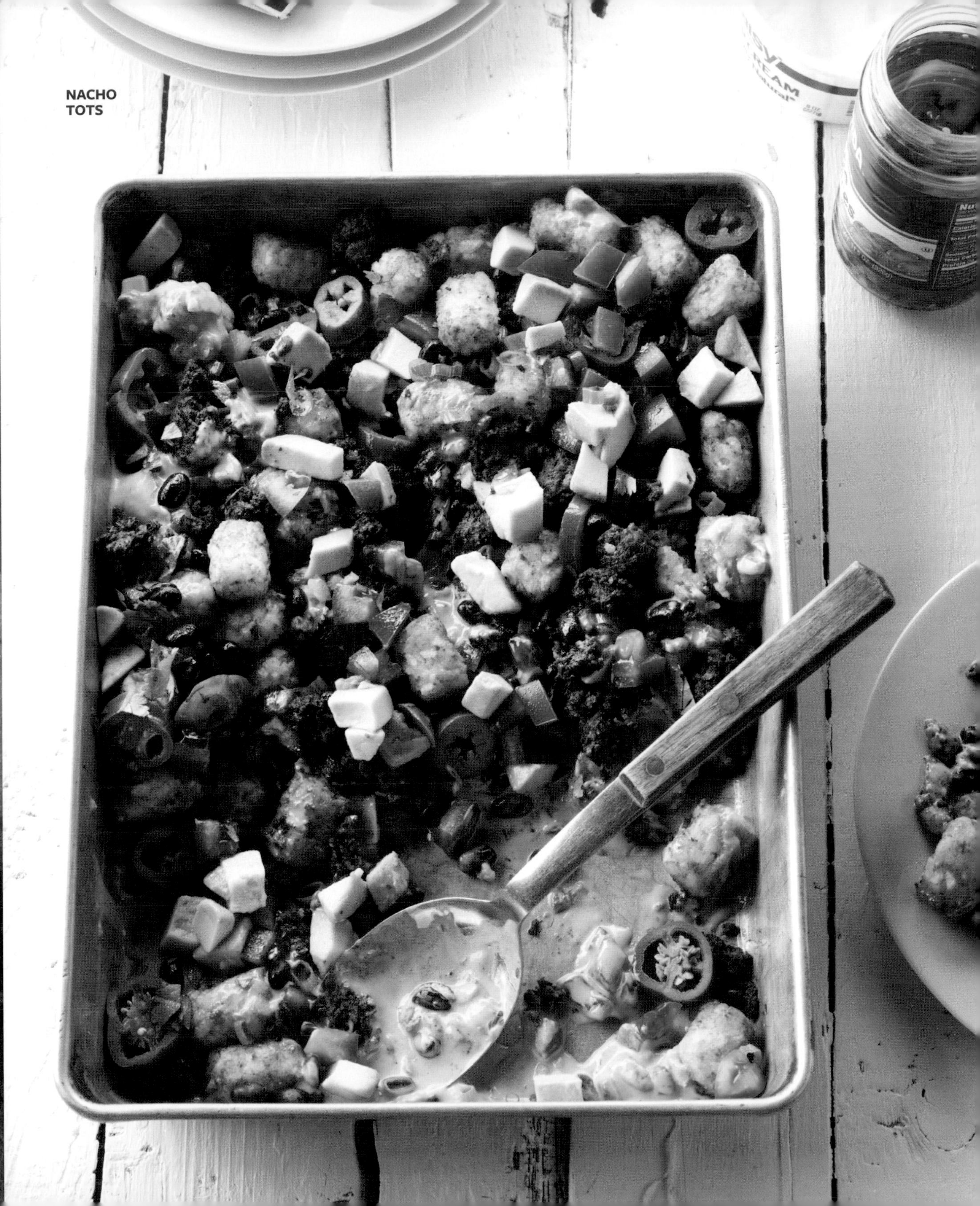

NACHO TOTS

NACHO TOTS

This is an easy, versatile party appetizer that everyone loves. If you can't find chorizo, try ground beef or ground chicken. Top with anything you like!

—**CONNIE KRUPP** RACINE, WI

PREP: 15 MIN. • **BAKE:** 50 MIN.
MAKES: 12 SERVINGS

- 1 package (32 ounces) frozen Tater Tots
- 7 ounces fresh chorizo or bulk spicy pork sausage
- 1 can (14½ ounces) diced tomatoes with mild green chilies, undrained
- 12 ounces process cheese (Velveeta), cubed
- 1 can (15 ounces) black beans, rinsed and drained
- ½ cup pickled jalapeno slices
- ¼ cup minced fresh cilantro
- ⅓ cup thinly sliced green onions
- 1 medium ripe avocado, cubed
- 1 medium tomato, chopped
- ½ cup sour cream

1. Preheat oven to 425°. Place Tater Tots in an ungreased 13x9-in. baking dish. Bake, uncovered, 40 minutes.
2. Meanwhile, in a large skillet, cook chorizo over medium heat until no longer pink, breaking into crumbles; drain. Remove from pan and set aside. In same skillet, add diced tomatoes and cheese. Cook, uncovered, over medium heat until blended and cheese is melted, stirring occasionally. Pour over Tater Tots. Sprinkle with chorizo and black beans.
3. Bake, uncovered, 10 minutes. Sprinkle with jalapenos, cilantro and green onions. Top with avocado and tomato. Serve with sour cream.

PER SERVING *378 cal., 23g fat (9g sat. fat), 45mg chol., 1152mg sod., 29g carb. (5g sugars, 5g fiber), 13g pro.*

BLACK FOREST HAM ROLL-UPS

BLACK FOREST HAM ROLL-UPS

I love to entertain at home and the office. Ham and cheese rolled in tortillas make a quick and appealing appetizer that's super easy to transport.

—**SUSAN ZUGEHOER** HEBRON, KY

PREP: 25 MIN. + CHILLING
MAKES: ABOUT 6½ DOZEN

- 1 package (8 ounces) cream cheese, softened
- 2 teaspoons minced fresh parsley
- 2 teaspoons dried celery flakes
- 2 teaspoons Dijon mustard
- 1 teaspoon lemon juice
- ⅛ teaspoon salt
- ⅛ teaspoon pepper
- ½ cup dried cranberries, chopped
- 2 green onions, chopped
- 5 flour tortillas (10 inches), room temperature
- ½ pound thinly sliced Black Forest deli ham
- ½ pound thinly sliced Swiss cheese

1. In a small bowl, mix the first seven ingredients until blended. Stir in the cranberries and green onions; spread over tortillas. Layer with ham and cheese. Roll up tightly; wrap the tortilla rolls in plastic wrap. Refrigerate at least 1 hour.
2. Just before serving, unwrap and cut each tortilla crosswise into 16 slices.

PER SERVING *1 roll-up: 42 cal., 2g fat (1g sat. fat), 7mg chol., 83mg sod., 3g carb. (1g sugars, 0 fiber), 2g pro.*

ANTIPASTO BAKE

ANTIPASTO BAKE

Stuffed with savory meats, cheeses and even sweet red peppers, this hearty, ooey-gooey appetizer will satisfy an entire offensive line! Wrapped in a crisp and convenient crescent roll crust, it comes together quickly and bakes in under an hour, making it the perfect potluck bring-along.

—BREA BARCLAY, PACKERS WOMEN'S ASSOCIATION GREEN BAY, WI

PREP: 20 MIN. • **BAKE:** 45 MIN. + STANDING
MAKES: 20 SERVINGS

- 2 tubes (8 ounces each) refrigerated crescent rolls
- ¼ pound thinly sliced hard salami
- ¼ pound thinly sliced Swiss cheese
- ¼ pound thinly sliced pepperoni
- ¼ pound thinly sliced Colby-Monterey Jack cheese
- ¼ pound thinly sliced prosciutto
- ¼ pound thinly sliced provolone cheese
- 2 large eggs
- ½ teaspoon garlic powder
- ½ teaspoon pepper
- 1 jar (12 ounces) roasted sweet red peppers, drained
- 1 large egg yolk, beaten

1. Preheat oven to 350°. Unroll one tube of crescent dough into one long rectangle; press perforations to seal. Press onto the bottom and up the sides of an ungreased 11x7-in. baking dish.

2. Layer meats and cheeses on dough in the order listed. Whisk eggs and seasonings until well blended; pour into dish. Top with roasted pepper.

3. Unroll remaining tube of dough into a long rectangle; press perforations to seal. Place over filling; pinch seams tight. Brush with beaten egg yolk; cover with foil. Bake 30 minutes; remove foil. Bake until golden brown, about 15-20 minutes. Let stand 20 minutes.

PER SERVING *1 piece: 229 cal., 15g fat (7g sat. fat), 58mg chol., 662mg sod., 10g carb. (2g sugars, 0 fiber), 11g pro.*

FAST FIX

BEER AND BRATS NACHOS (PICTURED ON PAGE 215)

You just can't beat a platter of these crunchy nacho snacks that are brought to life with a beer-cheese sauce.

—KELLY BOE WHITELAND, IN

START TO FINISH: 30 MIN.
MAKES: 12 SERVINGS

- 1 package (14 ounces) fully cooked smoked bratwurst links, sliced
- 2¼ cups frozen pepper and onion stir-fry blend
- 3 cups (12 ounces) shredded cheddar cheese
- 2½ teaspoons all-purpose flour
- 1 cup chopped onion
- 1 tablespoon olive oil
- 1 garlic clove, minced
- ¾ cup beer or beef broth
- 12 cups tortilla chips

1. In a large skillet, saute the bratwurst for 1 minute. Add stir-fry blend; cook 3-5 minutes longer or until vegetables are tender. Set aside and keep warm.

2. In a large bowl, combine cheese and flour. In a large saucepan, saute onion in oil until tender. Add garlic; cook 1 minute longer. Stir in beer; heat over medium heat until bubbles form around sides of pan.

3. Reduce heat to medium-low; add a handful of the cheese mixture. Stir constantly, using a figure-eight motion, until almost completely melted. Continue adding cheese, one handful at a time, allowing cheese to almost completely melt between additions.

4. Arrange tortilla chips on a large serving platter. Spoon cheese mixture over chips. Top with bratwurst mixture. Serve immediately.

PER SERVING *348 cal., 24g fat (10g sat. fat), 54mg chol., 544mg sod., 20g carb. (1g sugars, 1g fiber), 13g pro.*

MINIATURE CORN DOGS

These little corn dogs add delicious fun to any occasion. Watch out! They always seem to disappear fast.

—DEB PERRY BLUFFTON, IN

PREP: 25 MIN. • **COOK:** 5 MIN./BATCH
MAKES: ABOUT 3½ DOZEN

- 1 cup all-purpose flour
- 2 tablespoons cornmeal
- 1½ teaspoons baking powder
- ¼ teaspoon salt
  Dash onion powder
- 3 tablespoons shortening
- ¾ cup 2% milk
- 1 large egg
- 1 package (16 ounces) miniature smoked sausages
  Oil for deep-fat frying
  Spicy ketchup

1. In a small bowl combine the flour, cornmeal, baking powder, salt and onion powder; cut in shortening until crumbly. Whisk milk and egg; stir into the flour mixture just until moistened. Dip sausages into batter.

2. In an electric skillet or deep fryer, heat oil to 375°. Fry sausages, a few at a time, for 2-3 minutes or until golden brown. Drain on paper towels. Serve corn dogs with ketchup.

PER SERVING *1 corn dog: 68 cal., 6g fat (1g sat. fat), 11mg chol., 136mg sod., 2g carb. (0 sugars, 0 fiber), 2g pro.*

⑤ INGREDIENTS **FAST FIX** ▶

HAM & BRIE PASTRIES

Growing up, I loved pocket pastries. Now with a busy family, I need quick bites, and my spin on the classic ham and cheese delivers at snack or supper time.

—JENN TIDWELL FAIR OAKS, CA

START TO FINISH: 30 MIN.
MAKES: 16 PASTRIES

- 1 **sheet frozen puff pastry, thawed**
- ⅓ **cup apricot preserves**
- 4 **slices deli ham, quartered**
- 8 **ounces Brie cheese, cut into 16 pieces**

1. Preheat oven to 400°. On a lightly floured surface, unfold puff pastry. Roll pastry to a 12-in. square; cut into sixteen 3-in. squares. Place 1 teaspoon preserves in center of each square; top with ham, folding as necessary, and cheese. Overlap two opposite corners of pastry over filling; pinch tightly to seal.

2. Place on a parchment paper-lined baking sheet. Bake 15-20 minutes or until golden brown. Cool on pan 5 minutes before serving.

 FREEZE OPTION *Freeze cooled pastries in a freezer container, separating layers with waxed paper. To use, reheat pastries on a baking sheet in a preheated 400° oven until heated through.*

PER SERVING *1 pastry: 144 cal., 8g fat (3g sat. fat), 17mg chol., 192mg sod., 13g carb. (3g sugars, 1g fiber), 5g pro.*

TOP TIP

GET CREATIVE

Have some fun in the kitchen when you make these pastries. Swap out the apricot preserves with apple jelly, or try sliced turkey in place of the ham. Fig jam is a sweet and tasty addition to Brie cheese, or add a some finely sliced pear or apple. Pieces of rotisserie chicken with cheddar cheese and a thin layer of barbecue sauce also work!

HAM & BRIE PASTRIES

**KANSAS CITY-STYLE
RIBS, PAGE 229**

SPICE-BRINED
PORK ROAST, PAGE 233

FIERY FAVORITES

Juicy roasts, **succulent ribs,** chops glistening with a tangy sauce...these are just a few of the **flame-broiled specialties** you'll find in this chapter. Turn the page and you'll also discover hearty kabobs, tacos and tenderloins **grilled to perfection.** Insatiable staples like these are easy when pork is the main ingredient. Light the coals and **see for yourself!**

GRILLED COUNTRY-STYLE
RIBS, PAGE 242

PINEAPPLE PORK, PAGE 241

LAND AND SEA KABOBS

FAST FIX ▶

LAND AND SEA KABOBS

Basting with lime and curry adds a flavor flourish to my kabobs that you don't want to miss! The combination of pork and shrimp is an unexpected surprise, and the addition of grilled plums and papaya make for a great change-of-pace entree.

—TERESA LAY ELKHART, IN

START TO FINISH: 30 MIN.
MAKES: 2 SERVINGS

- 1   boneless pork loin chop (6 ounces), cut into 1-inch cubes
- 4   cubes fresh pineapple (1-inch)
- 1   medium plum, quartered
- 6   cubes papaya (1-inch)
- 4   uncooked jumbo shrimp, peeled and deveined
- 2   tablespoons canola oil
- 4   teaspoons lime juice
- 1½ teaspoons curry powder
- 1   small garlic clove, minced
- ¼   teaspoon salt
- ¼   teaspoon dried minced onion
- ¼   teaspoon grated lime peel

1. On two metal or soaked wooden skewers, alternately thread the pork, pineapple and plum. On two additional skewers, alternately thread papaya and shrimp. In a small bowl, combine the remaining ingredients; set aside.

2. On a greased grill rack, grill kabobs, covered, over medium heat or broil 4 in. from the heat for 8-12 minutes or until pork juices run clear and shrimp turn pink, turning and basting frequently with lime mixture.

PER SERVING *2 kabobs: 348 cal., 20g fat (3g sat. fat), 103mg chol., 382mg sod., 17g carb. (11g sugars, 3g fiber), 26g pro.*

LOW COUNTRY GRILL

Grilling is one of my family's favorite ways to prepare dinner. This recipe offers a meal-in-one that's perfect for summer nights.
—**ALAINA SHOWALTER** CLOVER, SC

PREP: 20 MIN. • **GRILL:** 50 MIN.
MAKES: 6 SERVINGS

- 2 tablespoons olive oil
- 1 teaspoon salt, divided
- 1 teaspoon garlic powder, divided
- 1 teaspoon seafood seasoning, divided
- 12 small red potatoes, quartered
- ⅓ cup butter, melted
- 1 pound smoked kielbasa or Polish sausage
- 3 medium ears sweet corn, cut in half
- 1½ pounds uncooked medium shrimp, peeled and deveined

1. In a large bowl, combine the oil with ¼ teaspoon each of salt, garlic powder and seafood seasoning. Add potatoes; toss to coat. Spoon onto a greased double thickness of heavy-duty foil (about 18 in. square).
2. Fold foil around potatoes and seal tightly. Grill, covered, over medium heat for 30-35 minutes or until tender, turning once. Set aside and keep warm.
3. In a small bowl, combine the butter with remaining salt, garlic powder and seafood seasoning. Grill kielbasa and corn, covered, over medium heat for 10-12 minutes or until kielbasa is heated through and corn is tender, turning occasionally and basting corn with half of the butter mixture. Keep warm.
4. Thread shrimp onto six metal or soaked wooden skewers; grill, covered, over medium heat for 3-4 minutes on each side or until shrimp turn pink, basting with remaining butter mixture. Slice kielbasa into six pieces before serving. Carefully open foil from the potatoes to allow steam to escape.
PER SERVING *566 cal., 37g fat (15g sat. fat), 215mg chol., 1536mg sod., 26g carb. (2g sugars, 3g fiber), 32g pro.*

KANSAS CITY-STYLE RIBS

KANSAS CITY-STYLE RIBS

Our recipe for ribs has evolved over the years to near perfection. These country-style beauties are legendary in our close circle.
—**LINDA SCHEND** KENOSHA, WI

PREP: 10 MIN. + CHILLING
GRILL: 1 HOUR 25 MIN.
MAKES: 12 SERVINGS

- 1⅓ cups packed brown sugar
- 2 teaspoons each garlic powder, onion powder and smoked paprika
- 1¼ teaspoons each ground cumin, coarsely ground pepper and cayenne pepper
- 12 bone-in country-style pork ribs (about 7 pounds)

SAUCE
- 2 tablespoons canola oil
- 1 medium onion, finely chopped
- 1 cup tomato sauce
- ⅓ cup dark brown sugar
- ¼ cup ketchup
- ¼ cup molasses
- 1 tablespoon apple cider vinegar
- 2 teaspoons Worcestershire sauce
- 1 teaspoon salt
- 1 teaspoon ground mustard
- ¼ teaspoon smoked paprika
- ¼ teaspoon cayenne pepper

1. In a small bowl, mix the brown sugar and seasonings; sprinkle over the ribs. Refrigerate, covered, at least 1 hour.
2. For sauce, in a large saucepan, heat oil over medium heat. Add onion; cook and stir 5-6 minutes or until tender. Stir in remaining ingredients; bring to a boil, stirring occasionally. Remove from heat.
3. Wrap ribs in a large piece of heavy-duty foil; seal edges of foil. Grill, covered, over indirect medium heat 1¼-1¾ hours or until ribs are tender.
4. Carefully remove ribs from foil. Place ribs over direct medium heat; baste with some of the sauce. Grill, covered, 8-10 minutes or until browned, turning and basting occasionally with the remaining sauce.
PER SERVING *1 rib: 453 cal., 18g fat (6g sat. fat) 101mg chol., 452mg sod., 40g carb. (36g sugars, 1g fiber), 31g pro.*

SWEET HORSERADISH GLAZED RIBS

SWEET HORSERADISH GLAZED RIBS

If you like to prep ahead for camping trips, roast these ribs in the oven and wrap them up. Then, finish grilling them at the campsite with the sweet-savory sauce.

—RALPH JONES SAN DIEGO, CA

PREP: 10 MIN. + CHILLING • **COOK:** 2 ¼ HOURS
MAKES: 8 SERVINGS

- 3 racks pork baby back ribs (about 8 pounds)
- 1½ teaspoons salt, divided
- 1½ teaspoons coarsely ground pepper, divided
- 2 bottles (12 ounces each) beer or 3 cups unsweetened apple juice
- 1 jar (12 ounces) apricot preserves
- ¼ cup prepared horseradish, drained
- 2 tablespoons honey or maple syrup
- 1 teaspoon liquid smoke, optional

1. Preheat oven to 325°. If necessary, remove thin membrane from ribs and discard. Sprinkle 1 teaspoon each salt and pepper over ribs. Transfer to a large shallow roasting pan, bone side down; add beer or juice. Bake, covered, until tender, 2-3 hours.

2. Meanwhile, puree preserves, horseradish, honey, remaining salt and pepper and, if desired, liquid smoke in a blender.

3. Drain ribs. Place 1 rib rack on a large piece of aluminum foil. Brush with apricot-horseradish mixture; wrap tightly. Repeat with remaining ribs. Refrigerate up to 2 days.

4. Prepare campfire or grill for medium heat. Remove ribs from foil; grill until browned, 10-15 minutes, turning occasionally.

PER SERVING *1 pound: 690 cal., 42g fat (15g sat. fat), 163mg chol., 674mg sod., 33g carb. (23g sugars, 0 fiber), 45g pro.*

GRILLED PORK TACOS

FAST FIX
GRILLED PORK TACOS

My family raves about this moist pork with smoked paprika and pineapple. I dish it up with brown rice and a salad of avocado and tomatoes. It's ready in just 30 minutes!

—E GELESKY BALA CYNWYD, PA

START TO FINISH: 30 MIN.
MAKES: 4 SERVINGS

- 1 pound boneless pork ribeye chops, cut into ¾-inch cubes
- 2 tablespoons plus 2 teaspoons lime juice, divided
- 1 teaspoon smoked or regular paprika
- ½ teaspoon salt
- ¼ teaspoon pepper
- ¾ cup canned black beans, rinsed and drained
- ½ cup canned unsweetened pineapple tidbits plus 1 tablespoon reserved juice
- 2 tablespoons finely chopped red onion
- 2 tablespoons chopped fresh cilantro
- 4 flour tortillas (6 to 8 inches), warmed Reduced-fat sour cream or plain yogurt, optional

1. In a large bowl, toss cubed pork with 2 tablespoons lime juice and seasonings; let stand 5 minutes. Meanwhile, in a small bowl, mix beans, pineapple with reserved juice, onion, cilantro and the remaining lime juice.

2. Thread pork onto four metal or soaked wooden skewers. On a lightly greased grill rack, grill kabobs, covered, over medium heat 6-8 minutes or until tender, turning occasionally.

3. Remove pork from skewers; serve in tortillas. Top with bean mixture and, if desired, sour cream.

PER SERVING *1 taco with ¼ cup salsa: 383 cal., 16g fat (6g sat. fat), 66mg chol., 636mg sod., 31g carb. (6g sugars, 4g fiber), 27g pro.*

BRAIDED PORK TENDERLOINS

For a summertime family dinner, I served a jerk-spiced marinated pork tenderloin. Braiding the meat, which is easy to do, makes for an attractive presentation.

—**JIM RUDE** JANESVILLE, WI

PREP: 30 MIN. + MARINATING • **GRILL:** 10 MIN.
MAKES: 8 SERVINGS (¾ CUP SAUCE)

- 2 **pork tenderloins (1 pound each)**
- ½ **cup mango nectar**
- ¼ **cup plus 1 tablespoon spiced rum or additional mango nectar, divided**
- 2 **tablespoons olive oil**
- 2 **tablespoons Caribbean jerk seasoning, divided**
- 2 **garlic cloves, minced**
- 1 **tablespoon heavy whipping cream**
- 1 **cup chopped peeled mango**

1. Cut tenderloins in half lengthwise; cut each half into three strips to within 1-in. of one end. In a large resealable plastic bag, combine the mango nectar, ¼ cup rum, oil, 1 tablespoon jerk seasoning and garlic; add pork. Seal bag and turn to coat; refrigerate for up to 4 hours.

2. Drain and discard marinade. Place tenderloin halves on a clean cutting board and braid; secure loose ends with toothpicks. Sprinkle with the remaining jerk seasoning.

3. Grill braids, covered, over medium heat for 4-5 minutes on each side or until a thermometer reads 145°. Discard the toothpicks. Let stand for 5 minutes before slicing.

4. Meanwhile, place the cream, remaining rum and mango in a food processor. Cover and process until smooth. Transfer to a small saucepan; heat through. Serve with pork.

PER SERVING *203 cal., 8g fat (2g sat. fat), 66mg chol., 257mg sod., 6g carb. (5g sugars, 0 fiber), 23g pro.* **Diabetic Exchanges:** *3 lean meat, 1 fat.*

DAD'S BEST PORK CHOPS

DAD'S BEST PORK CHOPS

My son, Kenneth, has loved pork chops since he was little, and he requests them often. He particularly likes this recipe because we pick the mint from the garden.

—**GREG FONTENOT** THE WOODLANDS, TX

START TO FINISH: 25 MIN.
MAKES: 4 SERVINGS

- 2 **medium tomatoes, chopped**
- ¼ **cup chopped onion**
- 3 **tablespoons minced fresh mint**
- 1 **jalapeno pepper, chopped**
- 2 **tablespoons key lime juice**
- 1½ **teaspoons minced fresh rosemary**
- 4 **bone-in pork loin chops (¾ inch thick)**
- ¼ **teaspoon salt**
- ¼ **teaspoon pepper**

1. In a small bowl, combine the first six ingredients. Chill until serving.

2. Sprinkle chops with salt and pepper. Grill chops, covered, over medium heat or broil 4-5 in. from the heat for 4-5 minutes on each side or until a thermometer reads 145°. Let meat stand for 5 minutes before serving. Serve with the salsa.

NOTE *Wear disposable gloves when cutting hot peppers; the oils can burn skin. Avoid touching your face.*

PER SERVING *1 pork chop with ⅓ cup salsa: 342 cal., 19g fat (7g sat. fat), 111mg chol., 229mg sod., 5g carb. (3g sugars, 1g fiber), 37g pro.*

EAT SMART (5) INGREDIENTS FAST FIX

MOLASSES-GLAZED PORK CHOPS

How can you go wrong with these savory chops that call for only a handful of items? Best of all, they're impressive enough to serve to guests.

—ANGELA SPENGLER TAMPA, FL

START TO FINISH: 30 MIN.
MAKES: 4 SERVINGS

- ¼ **cup molasses**
- 1 **tablespoon Worcestershire sauce**
- 1½ **teaspoons brown sugar**
- 4 **boneless pork loin chops (¾ inch thick and 5 ounces each)**

1. In a small bowl, combine molasses, Worcestershire sauce and brown sugar. Reserve 3 tablespoons sauce for serving.
2. Grill pork, covered, over medium heat or broil 4 in. from heat 4-5 minutes on each side or until a thermometer reads 145°, brushing with remaining sauce during the last 3 minutes of cooking. Let stand 5 minutes before serving. Serve with reserved sauce.

PER SERVING *1 pork chop with 2 teaspoons sauce: 256 cal., 8g fat (3g sat. fat), 68mg chol., 89mg sod., 17g carb. (13g sugars, 0 fiber), 27g pro.* **Diabetic Exchanges:** *4 lean meat, 1 starch.*

MOLASSES-GLAZED PORK CHOPS

EAT SMART

SPICE-BRINED PORK ROAST

(PICTURED ON PAGE 227)

This brined and barbecued pork roast is unbelievably tender. Adding seasonings to the coals produces an awesome aroma that draws guests to the grill.

—LORRAINE SCHROEDER ALBANY, OR

PREP: 15 MIN. + CHILLING • **GRILL:** 1½ HOURS
MAKES: 10 SERVINGS

- 2 **quarts water**
- 8 **orange peel strips (1 to 3 inches)**
- ½ **cup sugar**
- ¼ **cup salt**
- 3 **tablespoons fennel seed, crushed**
- 2 **tablespoons dried thyme**
- 2 **tablespoons whole peppercorns**
- 1 **boneless rolled pork loin roast (4 pounds)**

1. In a large saucepan, combine the first seven ingredients. Bring to a boil; cook and stir until salt and sugar are dissolved. Remove from the heat; cool to room temperature.
2. Place a large heavy-duty resealable plastic bag inside a second large resealable plastic bag; add pork. Carefully pour cooled brine into bag. Squeeze out as much air as possible; seal bags and turn to coat. Refrigerate for 12-24 hours, turning several times.
3. Strain brine; discard liquid and set aside seasonings.
4. Lightly grease the grill rack. Prepare grill for indirect heat, using a drip pan. Add reserved seasonings to coals. Place pork over drip pan and grill, covered, over indirect medium heat for 1½-2 hours or until a thermometer reads 160°. Let stand for 5 minutes before slicing.

PER SERVING *6 ounces cooked pork: 225 cal., 8g fat (3g sat. fat), 90mg chol., 75mg sod., 0 carb. (0 sugars, 0 fiber), 35g pro.* **Diabetic Exchanges:** *6 lean meat.*

SWEET GINGER RIBS

People ask what's in the marinade of my glazed ribs with ginger, garlic and peach preserves. Now you know! By the way—it works on steaks and chicken, too.
—**GRACE MCKEONE** SCHENECTADY, NY

PREP: 15 MIN. + MARINATING • **GRILL:** 1½ HOURS
MAKES: 8 SERVINGS

- ½ cup soy sauce
- ½ cup red wine vinegar
- ½ cup ketchup
- ½ cup peach preserves
- ⅓ cup minced fresh gingerroot
- 2 tablespoons stone-ground mustard
- 2 tablespoons brown sugar
- 6 garlic cloves, minced
- ½ teaspoon crushed red pepper flakes
- ½ teaspoon coarsely ground pepper
- 4 pounds pork baby back ribs

1. In a small bowl, whisk the first 10 ingredients until blended. Reserve 1 cup marinade for basting. Divide ribs and remaining marinade between two large resealable plastic bags; seal bags and turn to coat. Refrigerate ribs and reserved marinade in bags overnight.

2. Remove ribs, discarding remaining marinade in bags. Grill ribs, covered, over indirect medium heat 1½-2 hours or until tender, basting occasionally with reserved marinade during the last half hour.

PER SERVING *338 cal., 21g fat (8g sat. fat), 81mg chol., 721mg sod., 13g carb. (10g sugars, 0 fiber), 24g pro.*

SWEET GINGER RIBS

SAUSAGE SHRIMP KABOBS

We love these full-flavored kabobs and fix them often—even in winter. Sweet basting and dipping sauces perfectly round out the colorful combination of sausage, bacon, vegetables and pineapple.

—GLORIA WARCZAK CEDARBURG, WI

PREP: 25 MIN. • **GRILL:** 10 MIN.
MAKES: 4 SERVINGS

- 1 can (8 ounces) pineapple chunks
- 4 bacon strips
- 8 large fresh mushrooms
- 8 uncooked large shrimp, peeled and deveined
- 8 large cherry tomatoes
- 8 ounces smoked sausage, cut into ½-inch slices
- 1 large sweet onion, cut into 8 wedges
- 1 large green pepper, cut into 1-inch pieces
- ½ cup barbecue sauce
- ⅓ cup corn syrup
- ¼ cup ketchup
- 3 tablespoons soy sauce
- 1 tablespoon lime juice
- ½ teaspoon maple flavoring
- ¼ teaspoon garlic powder
- ¼ teaspoon ground ginger
- ⅛ teaspoon dried coriander

1. Drain pineapple, reserving juice. Cut bacon strips in half; wrap each around a mushroom. On metal or soaked wooden skewers, alternately thread the shrimp, pineapple chunks, tomatoes, sausage, bacon-wrapped mushrooms, onion and green pepper.
2. In a large bowl, combine the barbecue sauce, corn syrup, ketchup, soy sauce, lime juice, maple flavoring, seasonings and reserved pineapple juice. Set aside ⅔ cup for serving.
3. Grill kabobs, covered, over medium heat for 10-15 minutes or until vegetables are tender and shrimp turn pink, turning and basting occasionally with remaining sauce. Serve with reserved sauce.
PER SERVING 447 cal., 20g fat (8g sat. fat), 97mg chol., 1967mg sod., 49g carb. (33g sugars, 3g fiber), 21g pro.

PORK TENDERLOIN WITH CRANBERRY-ORANGE RELISH

PORK TENDERLOIN WITH CRANBERRY-ORANGE RELISH

I like how grilled pork and fruit bring out the best in each other. If you have leftover relish, break out the tortilla chips!

—CINDY ESPOSITO BLOOMFIELD, NJ

PREP: 15 MIN. • **COOK:** 15 MIN. + STANDING
MAKES: 4 SERVINGS

- 1½ cups fresh cranberries
- 2 green onions, minced
- 1 seeded jalapeno pepper, minced
- ⅓ cup sugar
- 3 tablespoons minced fresh mint
- 2 tablespoons lime juice
- 1 tablespoon orange juice
- ¼ teaspoon ground ginger
- 2 pork tenderloins (¾ pound each)
- 1 tablespoon olive oil
- ½ teaspoon salt
- ½ teaspoon pepper

1. To make relish, pulse cranberries in food processor until finely chopped. Combine with next seven ingredients. Reserve ½ cup relish for grilling; cover and refrigerate the rest.
2. Brush tenderloins with olive oil; sprinkle with salt and pepper. Grill, covered, over direct heat 12-15 minutes, turning occasionally and spooning with reserved relish, until thermometer reads 145°. Let stand 10-15 minutes. Discard used relish. Slice meat; serve with refrigerated relish.
PER SERVING 319 cal., 9g fat (2g sat. fat), 95mg chol., 366mg sod., 24g carb., 2g fiber, 34g pro.

PLUM-GLAZED PORK KABOBS

CORN-STUFFED PORK CHOPS

With a colorful stuffing of corn, pimiento and green pepper, these pork chops make an eye-catching entree.

—ELIZABETH JUSSAUME LOWELL, MA

PREP: 15 MIN. • **GRILL:** 25 MIN.
MAKES: 6 SERVINGS

6   bone-in center-cut pork loin chops
      (1 inch thick and 10 ounces each)
¾   teaspoon salt, divided
¼   teaspoon pepper, divided
¼   cup chopped onion
¼   cup chopped green pepper
1   tablespoon butter
1½   cups cubed bread, toasted
½   cup frozen corn, thawed
¼   cup egg substitute
2   tablespoons diced pimientos
¼   teaspoon ground cumin

1. Cut a pocket in each pork chop by slicing almost to the bone; sprinkle ¼ teaspoon salt and ⅛ teaspoon pepper in pockets. Set aside.
2. In a small skillet, saute onion and green pepper in butter until tender. Transfer to a bowl. Add the bread cubes, corn, egg substitute, pimientos, cumin and remaining salt and pepper; mix well. Stuff into pork chops; secure with toothpicks.
3. Lightly grease the grill rack. Prepare grill for indirect heat, using a drip pan.
4. Grill chops, covered, over medium indirect heat for 12-15 minutes on each side or until a thermometer reads 145° for meat and 160° for stuffing. Let meat stand for 5 minutes before serving.
PER SERVING *308 cal., 12g fat (5g sat. fat), 102mg chol., 458mg sod., 10g carb. (0 sugars, 1g fiber), 38g pro. **Diabetic Exchanges:** 5 lean meat, ½ starch.*

PLUM-GLAZED PORK KABOBS

Get out there and fire up the grill for pork kabobs, a tasty alternative to chicken and beef. These sweet and gingery beauties make dinnertime happy.

—TONYA BURKHARD PALM COAST, FL

START TO FINISH: 30 MIN.
MAKES: 6 SERVINGS

⅓   cup plum jam
2   tablespoons reduced-sodium soy
      sauce
1   garlic clove, minced
½   teaspoon ground ginger
1   medium sweet red pepper
1   medium green pepper
1   small red onion
2   pork tenderloins (¾ pound each)

1. For glaze, in a small bowl, mix jam, soy sauce, garlic and ginger. Cut vegetables and pork into 1-in. pieces. On six metal or soaked wooden skewers, alternately thread pork and vegetables.
2. On a lightly greased grill rack, grill kabobs, covered, over medium heat for 12-15 minutes or until pork is tender, turning occasionally and brushing with ¼ cup glaze during the last 5 minutes. Brush with the remaining plum glaze before serving.
PER SERVING *196 cal., 4g fat (1g sat. fat), 64mg chol., 239mg sod., 15g carb. (12g sugars, 1g fiber), 24g pro. **Diabetic Exchanges:** 3 lean meat, 1 starch.*

EAT SMART
GRILLED PORK TENDERLOINS

We do a lot of grilling during the summer months, and this recipe is one my family asks for again and again.

—BETSY CARRINGTON LAWRENCEBURG, TN

PREP: 10 MIN. + MARINATING • **GRILL:** 20 MIN.
MAKES: 8 SERVINGS

- ⅓ **cup honey**
- ⅓ **cup reduced-sodium soy sauce**
- ⅓ **cup teriyaki sauce**
- 3 **tablespoons brown sugar**
- 1 **tablespoon minced fresh gingerroot**
- 3 **garlic cloves, minced**
- 4 **teaspoons ketchup**
- ½ **teaspoon onion powder**
- ½ **teaspoon ground cinnamon**
- ¼ **teaspoon cayenne pepper**
- 2 **pork tenderloins (about 1 pound each)**
  Hot cooked rice

1. In a large bowl, combine the first 10 ingredients. Pour half of the marinade into a large resealable plastic bag; add tenderloins. Seal bag and turn to coat; refrigerate 8 hours or overnight, turning occasionally. Cover and refrigerate remaining marinade.

2. Drain and discard marinade from the meat. Grill, covered, over indirect medium-hot heat for 20-35 minutes or until a thermometer reads 145°, turning occasionally and basting with reserved marinade. Let stand 5 minutes before slicing. Serve with rice.

FREEZE OPTION *Freeze uncooked pork in bag with marinade. Transfer reserved marinade to a freezer container; freeze. To use, completely thaw tenderloins and marinade in refrigerator. Grill as directed.*

PER SERVING *3 ounces cooked pork: 196 cal., 4g fat (1g sat. fat), 64mg chol., 671mg sod., 15g carb. (14g sugars, 0 fiber), 24g pro.* **Diabetic Exchanges:** *3 lean meat, 1 starch.*

GRILLED PORK TENDERLOINS

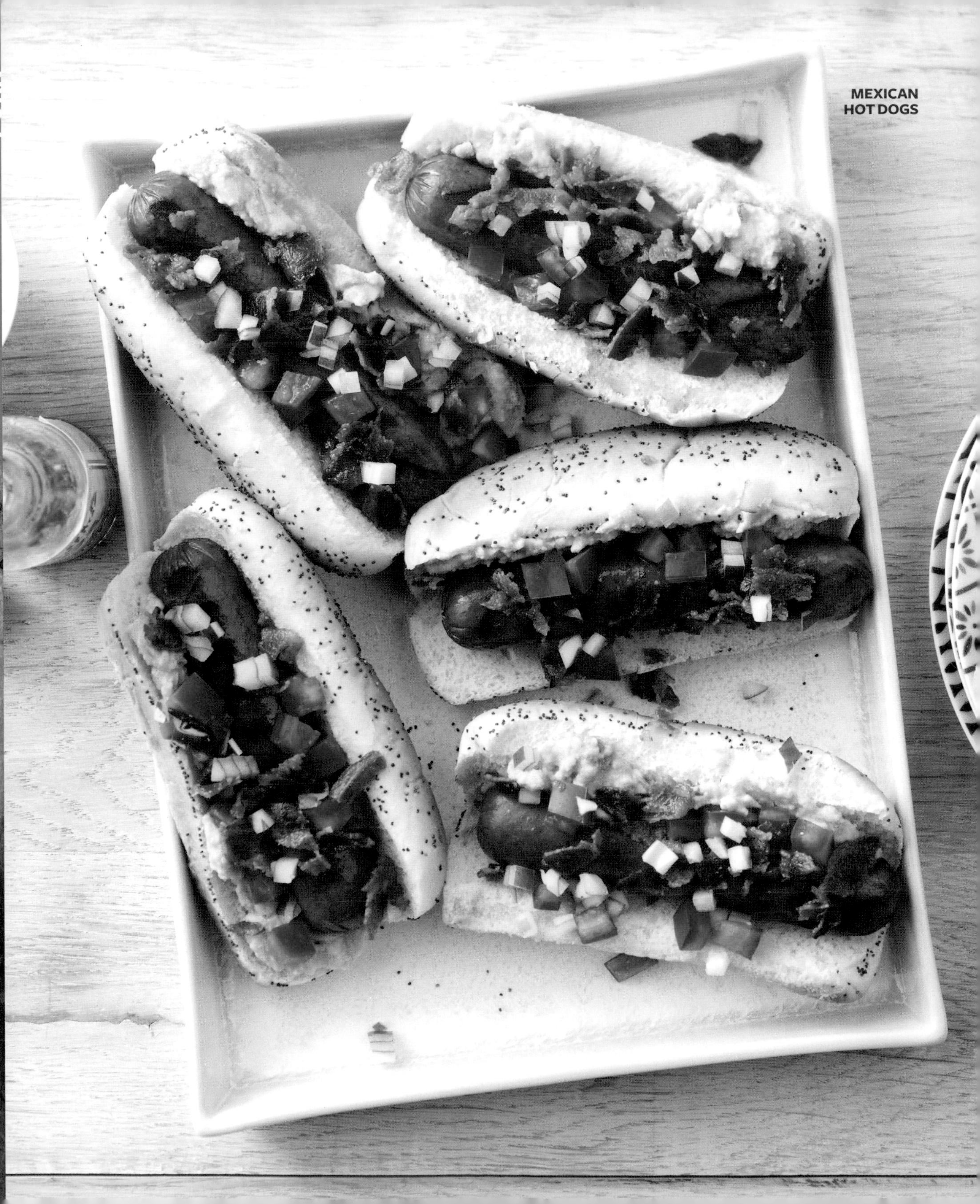

MEXICAN HOT DOGS

MEXICAN HOT DOGS

My stepmom was born in Mexico and introduced us to hot dogs with avocado and bacon. We were instantly hooked. Now our whole family makes them.

—AMANDA BRANDENBURG HAMILTON, OH

START TO FINISH: 20 MIN.
MAKES: 6 SERVINGS

- ½ medium ripe avocado, peeled
- 1 tablespoon lime juice
- ¼ teaspoon salt
- ⅛ teaspoon pepper
- 6 hot dogs
- 6 hot dog buns, split
- 1 small tomato, chopped
- 3 tablespoons finely chopped red onion
- 3 bacon strips, cooked and crumbled

1. In a small bowl, mash avocado with a fork, stirring in lime juice, salt and pepper. Grill hot dogs, covered, over medium heat 7-9 minutes or until heated through, turning occasionally.

2. Serve in buns. Top with avocado mixture, tomato, onion and bacon.

PER SERVING *310 cal., 19g fat (7g sat. fat), 29mg chol., 844mg sod., 25g carb. (4g sugars, 2g fiber), 11g pro.*

 **GRILL SKILL** _____

When direct grilling, place food directly over an even heat source. This method is best for quick-cooking foods such as hot dogs and chops.

With indirect grilling, hot coals are moved to opposite sides of the grill and the food is placed in the center of the grill rack. On a gas grill, a center burner is turned off after the grill preheats, then the food is placed over the unlit burner. Grilling over indirect heat is useful for foods such as roasts that need longer cook times.

GRILLED DIJON PORK ROAST

GRILLED DIJON PORK ROAST

I came up with this recipe one day after not having much in the house to eat. My husband loved it, and it has become the only way we make pork.

—CYNDI LACY-ANDERSEN
WOODINVILLE, WA

PREP: 10 MIN. + MARINATING
GRILL: 1 HOUR + STANDING
MAKES: 12 SERVINGS

- ⅓ cup balsamic vinegar
- 3 tablespoons Dijon mustard
- 1 tablespoon honey
- 1 teaspoon salt
- 1 boneless pork loin roast (3 to 4 pounds)

1. In a large resealable plastic bag, whisk vinegar, mustard, honey and salt. Add pork; seal bag and turn to coat. Refrigerate at least 8 hours or overnight.

2. Prepare grill for indirect heat, using a drip pan.

3. Drain pork, discarding the marinade. Place pork on a greased grill rack over drip pan and cook, covered, over indirect medium heat for 1-1½ hours or until a thermometer reads 145°, turning occasionally. Let stand for 10 minutes before slicing.

PER SERVING *3 ounces cooked pork: 149 cal., 5g fat (2g sat. fat), 56mg chol., 213mg sod., 2g carb. (1g sugars, 0 fiber), 22g pro.* **Diabetic Exchanges:** *3 lean meat.*

PORK

GLAZED PORK CHOPS

GLAZED PORK CHOPS

Rosemary adds a special touch to these beautifully glazed chops that are just right for any meal.

—**LOUISE GILBERT** QUESNEL, BC

PREP: 15 MIN. + MARINATING • **GRILL:** 10 MIN.
MAKES: 8 SERVINGS

- ½ cup ketchup
- ¼ cup packed brown sugar
- ¼ cup white vinegar
- ¼ cup orange juice
- ¼ cup Worcestershire sauce
- 2 garlic cloves, minced
- ½ teaspoon dried rosemary, crushed
- 8 bone-in pork loin chops (¾ inch thick and 7 ounces each)

1. In a small bowl, mix the first seven ingredients. Pour ¾ cup marinade into a large resealable plastic bag. Add the pork chops; seal bag and turn to coat. Refrigerate 8 hours or overnight. Cover and refrigerate remaining marinade.
2. Drain pork, discarding marinade in bag. Lightly grease the grill rack.
3. Grill pork, covered, over medium heat or broil 4 in. from heat 4-6 minutes on each side or until a thermometer reads 145°; brush generously with remaining marinade during the last 3 minutes. Let stand 5 minutes before serving.
PER SERVING *246 cal., 8g fat (3g sat. fat), 86mg chol., 284mg sod., 11g carb. (10g sugars, 0 fiber), 30g pro.* **Diabetic Exchanges:** *4 lean meat, 1 starch.*

GRILLED PORK TENDERLOIN & VEGGIES

PINEAPPLE PORK

(PICTURED ON PAGE 227)

You need just a few ingredients to pull off this special entree of juicy grilled pineapple slices and ginger-flavored pork tenderloin.

—DONNA NOEL GRAY, ME

PREP: 10 MIN. + MARINATING • **GRILL:** 30 MIN.
MAKES: 4 SERVINGS

- 1 **cup unsweetened pineapple juice**
- ¼ **cup minced fresh gingerroot**
- ¼ **cup reduced-sodium soy sauce**
- 4 **garlic cloves, minced**
- 1 **teaspoon ground mustard**
- 2 **pork tenderloins (¾ pound each)**
- 1 **fresh pineapple, cut into 12 slices**

1. In a small bowl, combine the first five ingredients. Pour ⅔ cup marinade into a large resealable plastic bag. Add the pork; seal bag and turn to coat. Refrigerate for 8 hours or overnight. Cover and refrigerate remaining marinade.

2. Drain and discard marinade. Lightly grease the grill rack.

3. Prepare grill for indirect heat, using a drip pan. Place pork over drip pan and grill, covered, over indirect medium heat for 25-30 minutes or until a thermometer reads 160°, basting occasionally with reserved marinade. Let stand 5 minutes before slicing.

4. Meanwhile, grill pineapple slices for 2-3 minutes on each side or until heated through; serve with pork.

PER SERVING *5 ounces cooked pork with 3 pineapple slices: 295 cal., 6g fat (2g sat. fat), 95mg chol., 523mg sod., 23g carb. (16g sugars, 2g fiber), 36g pro.* **Diabetic Exchanges:** *5 lean meat, 1 fruit.*

GRILLED PORK TENDERLOIN & VEGGIES

There's flavor in every bite of this fun supper. Marinate overnight and enjoy easy prep the next day.

—MARIE PARKER MILWAUKEE, WI

PREP: 15 MIN. + MARINATING • **GRILL:** 30 MIN.
MAKES: 4 SERVINGS

- ¾ **cup orange juice**
- ½ **cup olive oil**
- ¼ **cup lime juice**
- 4 **garlic cloves, minced**
- 2 **teaspoons dried oregano**
- 1 **teaspoon grated lime peel**
- 1 **teaspoon ground cumin**
- ½ **teaspoon salt**
- ½ **teaspoon pepper**
- 2 **pork tenderloins (1 pound each)**
- 8 **small carrots, halved lengthwise**
- 2 **medium zucchini, sliced lengthwise**

1. In a small bowl, whisk the first nine ingredients until blended. Pour ½ cup marinade into a large resealable plastic bag. Add tenderloins; seal bag and turn to coat. Refrigerate 8 hours or overnight. Cover and refrigerate the remaining marinade.

2. Drain pork, discarding marinade in bag. Grill tenderloins, covered, over medium heat 18-22 minutes or until a thermometer reads 145°, turning and basting occasionally with ¼ cup of the reserved marinade during the last 10 minutes of grilling. Let stand 5 minutes before slicing.

3. Toss carrots and zucchini with remaining reserved marinade. Grill, covered, over medium heat 4-6 minutes on each side or until crisp-tender. Serve pork with vegetables.

PER SERVING *446 cal., 21g fat (4g sat. fat), 126mg chol., 465mg sod., 17g carb. (9g sugars, 4g fiber), 47g pro.*

GRILLED COUNTRY-STYLE RIBS (PICTURED ON PAGE 227)

Precook these hearty ribs in the microwave, then finish them off on the grill. They turn out moist and tender with a great smoky flavor.

—SUE BENNING MENASHA, WI

PREP: 15 MIN. + MARINATING • **COOK:** 30 MIN.
MAKES: 6 SERVINGS

- 1 **cup water, divided**
- ½ **cup reduced-sodium soy sauce**
- 2 **tablespoons lemon juice**
- 2 **tablespoons canola oil**
- 1 **tablespoon brown sugar**
- 1 **teaspoon garlic powder**
- 1 **teaspoon pepper**
- 6 **bone-in country-style pork ribs (1½ inches thick and 14 ounces each)**

1. In a small bowl, combine ½ cup water, soy sauce, lemon juice, oil, brown sugar, garlic powder and pepper. Cover and refrigerate ½ cup mixture for basting. Pour remaining mixture into a large resealable plastic bag; add the ribs. Seal bag and turn to coat. Refrigerate for 8 hours or overnight.

2. Drain and discard marinade in bag; place ribs and remaining water in a 3-qt. microwave-safe dish. Cover; microwave on high for 20-25 minutes or until meat is tender.

3. Drain ribs. Lightly grease grill rack. Grill ribs, covered, over medium heat or broil 4 in. from the heat for 4-5 minutes on each side or until browned, basting occasionally with reserved marinade.

NOTE *This recipe was tested in an 1,100-watt microwave.*

PER SERVING *462 cal., 27g fat (9g sat. fat), 151mg chol., 995mg sod., 3g carb. (2g sugars, 0 fiber), 48g pro.*

CHEESY HAM & POTATO PACKET

(5) INGREDIENTS **FAST FIX**

CHEESY HAM & POTATO PACKET

I found the technique for grilling ham, potatoes and cheese in foil packets and changed up some ingredients to suit our tastes. I love that this great meal doesn't heat up the kitchen.

—MOLLY BISHOP MCCLURE, PA

START TO FINISH: 30 MIN.
MAKES: 4 SERVINGS

- 1½ **pounds medium red potatoes, halved and thinly sliced**
- 1 **medium green pepper, chopped**
- 1 **medium onion, chopped**
- ¼ **teaspoon pepper**
- 2 **cups cubed deli ham**
- 1 **cup shredded cheddar cheese**

1. In a large bowl, toss potatoes with green pepper, onion and pepper; place in center of a greased 24x18-in. piece of heavy-duty foil. Fold foil around the vegetables and crimp edges to seal.

2. Grill, covered, over medium heat 15-20 minutes or until potatoes are tender. Remove from grill. Open foil carefully to allow steam to escape. Add ham; sprinkle with cheese. Grill opened packet, covered, 2-4 minutes longer or until cheese is melted.

PER SERVING *1½ cups: 341 cal., 13g fat (6g sat. fat), 70mg chol., 1040mg sod., 32g carb. (4g sugars, 4g fiber), 26g pro.*

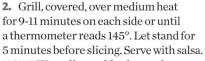
CARIBBEAN-SPICED PORK TENDERLOIN WITH PEACH SALSA

I love this recipe because of the depth of flavor and burst of colors. It's so quick and easy to make. It's best when peaches are in season, but you could try strawberries or pineapple instead.

—HOLLY BAUER WEST BEND, WI

PREP: 15 MIN. • **GRILL:** 20 MIN.
MAKES: 4 SERVINGS (1⅓ CUPS SALSA)

- ¾ **cup chopped peeled fresh peaches**
- 1 **small sweet red pepper, chopped**
- 1 **jalapeno pepper, seeded and chopped**
- 2 **tablespoons finely chopped red onion**
- 2 **tablespoons minced fresh cilantro**
- 1 **tablespoon lime juice**
- 1 **garlic clove, minced**
- ⅛ **teaspoon salt**
- ⅛ **teaspoon pepper**
- 2 **tablespoons olive oil**
- 1 **tablespoon brown sugar**
- 1 **tablespoon Caribbean jerk seasoning**
- 1 **teaspoon dried thyme**
- 1 **teaspoon dried rosemary, crushed**
- ½ **teaspoon seasoned salt**
- 1 **pork tenderloin (1 pound)**

1. In a small bowl, combine the first nine ingredients; set aside. In another small bowl, combine the oil, brown sugar, jerk seasoning, thyme, rosemary and seasoned salt. Rub over pork.

2. Grill, covered, over medium heat for 9-11 minutes on each side or until a thermometer reads 145°. Let stand for 5 minutes before slicing. Serve with salsa.

NOTE *Wear disposable gloves when cutting hot peppers; the oils can burn skin. Avoid touching your face.*

PER SERVING *3 ounces cooked pork with ⅓ cup salsa: 229 cal., 11g fat (2g sat. fat), 63mg chol., 522mg sod., 9g carb. (7g sugars, 1g fiber), 23g pro.* **Diabetic Exchanges:** *3 lean meat, 1½ fat, ½ starch.*

CARIBBEAN-SPICED PORK TENDERLOIN WITH PEACH SALSA

⑤ INGREDIENTS **FAST FIX**

MAPLE HAM STEAK

This main course is very simple to make but has great flavor that everyone will enjoy. With only two ingredients, it's perfect for busy weeknights or any night you don't feel like spending a lot of time preparing dinner.

—JEAN TAYNTOR EATON, NY

START TO FINISH: 15 MIN.
MAKES: 6 SERVINGS

- 1 **bone-in fully cooked ham steak (about 2 pounds and ¾ inch thick)**
- ½ **cup maple syrup, divided**

Grill ham, uncovered, over medium-high heat for 5-7 minutes on each side or until a thermometer reads 140°, basting frequently with ¼ cup syrup. Warm remaining syrup to serve with ham.

PER SERVING *4 ounces: 368 cal., 19g fat (7g sat. fat), 79mg chol., 2035mg sod., 18g carb. (17g sugars, 0 fiber), 30g pro.*

CREAMY SAUSAGE-MUSHROOM
RIGATONI, PAGE 252

HAM STEAKS WITH GRUYERE, BACON & MUSHROOMS, PAGE 257

ON THE STOVETOP

Whether it's **ham, sausage, bacon, chops or medallions,** pork's endless variety means you're never short on choices for **savory home-cooked** meals. Mix it up with potatoes, sauces, cheese or fruit—this versatile meat is never dull and always delicious. Heat up your stovetop and get started—it's **quick, easy** and so very tasty.

ALMOND-CRUSTED CHOPS WITH CIDER SAUCE, PAGE 257

SWEET POTATO AND HAM HASH, PAGE 251

SKILLET PORK CHOPS WITH APPLES & ONION

⟨5⟩INGREDIENTS **FAST FIX**

SKILLET PORK CHOPS WITH APPLES & ONION

Simple recipes that land on the table fast are a lifesaver. I serve skillet pork chops with veggies and, when there's time, corn bread stuffing.

—**TRACEY KARST** PONDERAY, ID

START TO FINISH: 20 MIN.
MAKES: 4 SERVINGS

- 4 **boneless pork loin chops (6 ounces each)**
- 3 **medium apples, cut into wedges**
- 1 **large onion, cut into thin wedges**
- ¼ **cup water**
- ⅓ **cup balsamic vinaigrette**
- ½ **teaspoon salt**
- ¼ **teaspoon pepper**

1. Place a large nonstick skillet over medium heat; brown pork chops on both sides, about 4 minutes. Remove from pan.

2. In the same skillet, combine apples, onion and water. Place the pork chops over the apple mixture; drizzle chops with vinaigrette. Sprinkle with salt and pepper. Reduce heat; simmer, covered, for 3-5 minutes or until a thermometer inserted in chops reads 145°.

PER SERVING *1 pork chop with ¾ cup apple mixture: 360 cal., 15g fat (4g sat. fat), 82mg chol., 545mg sod., 22g carb. (15g sugars, 3g fiber), 33g pro.* **Diabetic Exchanges:** *5 lean meat, 1 fruit, 1 fat.*

TOP TIP

IS IT DONE?

Fresh pork cooks quickly and needs only to reach an internal temperature of 160°-170°. At 160°, the internal color of boneless cuts may be faint pink, while bone-in cuts may be slightly pink near the bone. But if the juices run clear, the meat is properly cooked.

PORK & MANGO
STIR-FRY

ITALIAN-STYLE PORK CHOPS

An Italian version of pork chops was one of the first recipes I tried making in the early days of my marriage. I've changed it over the years to be healthier by reducing the oil and fat and by adding in some vegetables. It works well served over hot rice.

—TRACI HOPPES SPRING VALLEY, CA

START TO FINISH: 30 MIN.
MAKES: 4 SERVINGS

- 2 medium green peppers, cut into ¼-inch strips
- ½ pound sliced fresh mushrooms
- 1 tablespoon plus 1½ teaspoons olive oil, divided
- 4 boneless pork loin chops (6 ounces each)
- ¾ teaspoon salt, divided
- ¾ teaspoon pepper, divided
- 2 cups marinara or spaghetti sauce
- 1 can (3½ ounces) sliced ripe olives, drained

1. In a large skillet, saute peppers and mushrooms in 1 tablespoon oil until tender. Remove and keep warm.
2. Sprinkle chops with ¼ teaspoon salt and ¼ teaspoon pepper. In the same skillet, brown chops in remaining oil. Add marinara sauce, olives, remaining salt and pepper and the reserved pepper mixture. Bring to a boil. Reduce heat; cover and simmer for 10-15 minutes or until a thermometer reads 145°. Let stand for 5 minutes before serving.
PER SERVING *1 pork chop with ¾ cup sauce: 397 cal., 18g fat (5g sat. fat), 82mg chol., 930mg sod., 22g carb. (12g sugars, 5g fiber), 37g pro.*

PORK & MANGO STIR-FRY

You know a recipe is special when everyone in your family raves about it. My finicky eaters give thumbs-up for this hearty, nutty stir-fry.

—KATHY SPECHT CLINTON, MI

START TO FINISH: 25 MIN.
MAKES: 4 SERVINGS

- 1 pork tenderloin (1 pound)
- 1 tablespoon plus 2 teaspoons canola oil, divided
- ¼ teaspoon salt
- ½ teaspoon crushed red pepper flakes, optional
- 6 ounces uncooked multigrain angel hair pasta
- 1 package (8 ounces) fresh sugar snap peas
- 1 medium sweet red pepper, cut into thin strips
- ¼ cup reduced-sugar orange marmalade
- ¼ cup reduced-sodium teriyaki sauce
- 1 tablespoon packed brown sugar
- 2 garlic cloves, minced
- 1 cup chopped peeled mango
- ¼ cup lightly salted cashews, coarsely chopped

1. Cut tenderloin in half lengthwise; cut each half crosswise into thin slices. Toss pork with 1 tablespoon oil, salt and, if desired, pepper flakes. Cook pasta according to package directions.
2. Place a large nonstick skillet over medium-high heat. Add half the pork; stir-fry 2-3 minutes or just until browned. Remove meat from pan; repeat with the remaining pork.
3. Stir-fry snap peas and red pepper in remaining oil for 2-3 minutes or just until crisp-tender. Stir in marmalade, teriyaki sauce, brown sugar and garlic; cook 1-2 minutes longer. Return pork to pan and add mango and cashews; heat through, stirring to combine. Serve with pasta.
PER SERVING *1½ cups pork mixture with ¾ cup pasta: 515 cal., 16g fat (3g sat. fat), 64mg chol., 553mg sod., 58g carb. (23g sugars, 6g fiber), 36g pro.*

HAM PASTA TOSS

This is my favorite meal to make when I'm short on time. You can also use different meats or vegetables depending on what you have on hand.
—SHARON GERST NORTH LIBERTY, IA

START TO FINISH: 25 MIN.
MAKES: 6 SERVINGS

- 12 **ounces uncooked whole wheat spaghetti**
- 3 **tablespoons butter**
- 2 **cups shredded or cubed fully cooked ham**
- 2 **garlic cloves, minced**
- 3 **cups frozen peas (about 12 ounces), thawed**
- 2 **tablespoons minced fresh parsley**
- ¼ **cup grated Parmesan cheese**

1. Cook spaghetti according to package directions; drain. Meanwhile, in a large skillet, heat butter over medium heat. Add ham; cook and stir for 2-4 minutes or until browned. Add garlic; cook for 1 minute longer.
2. Stir in spaghetti, peas and parsley; heat through. Sprinkle with cheese; toss to combine.
PER SERVING *1⅓ cups: 374 cal., 10g fat (5g sat. fat), 46mg chol., 738mg sod., 52g carb. (3g sugars, 10g fiber), 23g pro.*

JUST PEACHY PORK TENDERLOIN

Here's a fresh entree that tastes like summer. I had a pork tenderloin and ripe peaches and decided to put them together. The results couldn't have been more irresistible!
—JULIA GOSLIGA ADDISON, VT

START TO FINISH: 20 MIN.
MAKES: 4 SERVINGS

- 1 **pound pork tenderloin, cut into 12 slices**
- ½ **teaspoon salt**
- ¼ **teaspoon pepper**
- 2 **teaspoons olive oil**
- 4 **medium peaches, peeled and sliced**

JUST PEACHY PORK TENDERLOIN

- 1 **tablespoon lemon juice**
- ¼ **cup peach preserves**

1. Flatten each tenderloin slice to ¼-in. thickness. Sprinkle with salt and pepper. In a large nonstick skillet over medium heat, cook pork in oil until tender. Remove and keep warm.
2. Add peaches and lemon juice, stirring to loosen browned bits from pan. Cook and stir for 3-4 minutes or until the peaches are tender. Stir in the pork and preserves; heat through.
PER SERVING *241 cal., 6g fat (2g sat. fat), 63mg chol., 340mg sod., 23g carb. (20g sugars, 2g fiber), 23g pro.* **Diabetic Exchanges:** *3 lean meat, 1 fruit, ½ starch, ½ fat.*

QUICK TACOS AL PASTOR

My husband and I tried pork and pineapple tacos at a food truck in Hawaii. They were so tasty, I decided to experiment and make my own version at home.
—**LORI MCLAIN** DENTON, TX

START TO FINISH: 25 MIN.
MAKES: 4 SERVINGS (2 TACOS EACH)

- 1 **package (15 ounces) refrigerated pork roast au jus**
- 1 **cup well-drained unsweetened pineapple chunks, divided**
- 1 **tablespoon canola oil**
- ½ **cup enchilada sauce**
- 8 **corn tortillas (6 inches), warmed**
- ½ **cup finely chopped onion**
- ¼ **cup chopped fresh cilantro**
  Optional ingredients: crumbled queso fresco, salsa verde and lime wedges

1. Coarsely shred pork, reserving the juices. In a small bowl, crush half of the pineapple chunks with a fork.

2. In a large nonstick skillet, heat oil over medium-high heat. Add the remaining whole pineapple chunks; cook for 2-3 minutes or until lightly browned, turning occasionally. Remove from pan.

3. Add enchilada sauce and the crushed pineapple to the same skillet; stir in pork and reserved juices. Cook over medium-high heat for 4-6 minutes or until liquid is evaporated, stirring occasionally.

4. Serve in tortillas with whole pineapple chunks, onion and cilantro. If desired, top with cheese and salsa and serve with lime wedges.

PER SERVING *2 tacos: 317 cal., 11g fat (3g sat. fat), 57mg chol., 573mg sod., 36g carb. (12g sugars, 5g fiber), 24g pro.* **Diabetic Exchanges:** *3 lean meat, 2 starch, 1 fat.*

**QUICK TACOS
AL PASTOR**

SWEET POTATO AND HAM HASH
(PICTURED ON PAGE 245)

Tender sweet potatoes match up with ham, eggs and zippy seasonings for an impressive breakfast. Or serve it with salad and have an easy breakfast-for-dinner meal.

—JUDY ARMSTRONG PRAIRIEVILLE, LA

PREP: 20 MIN. • **COOK:** 20 MIN.
MAKES: 4 SERVINGS

- 2 cups cubed peeled sweet potatoes
- 2 tablespoons butter
- 1 tablespoon olive oil
- 1 medium onion, chopped
- 1 small sweet red pepper, chopped
- 3 green onions, chopped
- 1 red chili pepper, seeded and finely chopped
- 3 garlic cloves, minced
- 2 cups cubed fully cooked ham
- ½ teaspoon pepper
- ¼ teaspoon salt
- 4 large eggs
- ¼ cup shredded white cheddar cheese

1. In a large skillet, saute sweet potatoes in butter and oil until crisp-tender. Add onion, red pepper, green onions and chili pepper. Saute 4-5 minutes longer or until tender. Add garlic; cook 1 minute longer. Stir in ham, pepper and salt.
2. With the back of a spoon, make four wells in the potato mixture; add an egg to each well. Sprinkle with cheese. Cover and cook for 4-5 minutes or until the egg whites are completely set.
NOTE *Wear disposable gloves when cutting hot peppers; the oils can burn skin. Avoid touching your face.*
PER SERVING *379 cal., 22g fat (9g sat. fat), 271mg chol., 1237mg sod., 23g carb. (7g sugars, 4g fiber), 23g pro.*

BREADED MUSTARD & SAGE PORK CUTLETS

FAST FIX

BREADED MUSTARD & SAGE PORK CUTLETS

After attending my daughter's back-to-school night and receiving a complementary package of instant potatoes, I had to make something with them. I created these pork cutlets and they were fantastic.

—CARRIE FARIAS OAK RIDGE, NJ

START TO FINISH: 25 MIN.
MAKES: 4 SERVINGS

- 1 large egg
- 2 tablespoons fat-free milk
- 2 tablespoons Dijon mustard
- ¾ cup panko (Japanese) bread crumbs
- ¾ cup mashed potato flakes
- 2 teaspoons ground mustard
- 2 teaspoons minced fresh sage
- ⅓ cup all-purpose flour
- 8 thin boneless pork loin chops (2 ounces each)
- ½ teaspoon salt
- 4 teaspoons canola oil, divided

1. In a shallow bowl, whisk egg, milk and Dijon mustard. In another shallow bowl, mix bread crumbs, potato flakes, ground mustard and sage. Place flour in another shallow bowl. Sprinkle pork with salt.
2. Dip the pork in flour to coat both sides; shake off excess. Dip in the egg mixture, then in the bread crumb mixture, patting to help the coating adhere.
3. In a large skillet, heat 2 teaspoons oil over medium heat. Add pork in batches; cook 2-3 minutes on each side or until a thermometer reads at least 145°. Add more oil as needed.
PER SERVING *2 pork cutlets: 328 cal., 13g fat (3g sat. fat), 101mg chol., 567mg sod., 23g carb. (1g sugars, 1g fiber), 27g pro.* **Diabetic Exchanges:** *3 lean meat, 1½ starch, 1 fat.*

FAST FIX ▶

CREAMY SAUSAGE-MUSHROOM RIGATONI

(PICTURED ON PAGE 244)

While visiting Rome, we enjoyed an amazing dinner at a restaurant near the Pantheon— it lasted three hours! Sadly, the restaurant is now gone, but its memory lives on in this tasty dish.

—BARBARA ROOZROKH BROOKFIELD, WI

START TO FINISH: 30 MIN.
MAKES: 6 SERVINGS

- 1 **package (16 ounces) rigatoni**
- 1 **pound bulk Italian sausage**
- 2 **teaspoons butter**
- 1 **pound sliced fresh mushrooms**
- 2 **garlic cloves, minced**
- ½ **teaspoon salt**
- ¼ **teaspoon pepper**
- 2 **cups heavy whipping cream**
  Minced fresh parsley, optional

1. Cook rigatoni according to package directions.

2. Meanwhile, in a large skillet, cook sausage over medium heat 4-6 minutes or until no longer pink, breaking into crumbles; drain and remove sausage from pan.

3. In same skillet, heat butter over medium heat. Add mushrooms, garlic, salt and pepper; cook, covered, 4 minutes, stirring occasionally. Uncover; cook and stir 2-3 minutes or until the mushrooms are tender and liquid is evaporated.

4. Stir in cream; bring to a boil. Reduce heat; cook, uncovered, 8-10 minutes or until slightly thickened. Return the sausage to the skillet; heat through. Drain pasta; serve with sauce. If desired, sprinkle with parsley.

PER SERVING *½ cup meat mixture with 1 cup pasta: 570 cal., 37g fat (19g sat. fat), 115mg chol., 529mg sod., 46g carb. (5g sugars, 3g fiber), 17g pro.*

HAM AND PEA PASTA ALFREDO

FAST FIX ▶

HAM AND PEA PASTA ALFREDO

When I want a filling meal that even the kids will enjoy, I toss ham and sugar snap peas with Romano cream sauce and pasta.

—CR MONACHINO KENMORE, NY

START TO FINISH: 25 MIN.
MAKES: 8 SERVINGS

- 1 **package (16 ounces) fettuccine**
- 2 **tablespoons butter**
- 1½ **pounds sliced fully cooked ham, cut into strips (about 5 cups)**
- 2 **cups fresh sugar snap peas**
- 2 **cups heavy whipping cream**
- ½ **cup grated Romano cheese**
- ¼ **teaspoon pepper**

1. Cook fettuccine according to package directions. Meanwhile, in a large skillet, heat butter over medium heat. Add ham and peas; cook and stir 5 minutes. Stir in cream, cheese and pepper; bring to a boil. Reduce heat; simmer, uncovered, for 1-2 minutes or until the sauce is slightly thickened and the peas are crisp-tender.

2. Drain fettuccine; add to skillet and toss to coat. Serve immediately.

PER SERVING *1¼ cups: 582 cal., 32g fat (18g sat. fat), 151mg chol., 1032mg sod., 45g carb. (6g sugars, 3g fiber), 33g pro.*

FAST FIX

PORK & RAMEN STIR-FRY

I put a bit of a spin on the stir-fry that you'd normally serve over rice. Ramen noodles are a quick substitute for the rice, and I find that bagged coleslaw mix, along with some fresh broccoli, gives the dish a good crisp-tender bite.

—BARBARA PLETZKE HERNDON, VA

START TO FINISH: 30 MIN.
MAKES: 4 SERVINGS

- ¼ cup reduced-sodium soy sauce
- 2 tablespoons ketchup
- 2 tablespoons Worcestershire sauce
- 2 teaspoons sugar
- ¼ teaspoon crushed red pepper flakes
- 3 teaspoons canola oil, divided
- 1 pound boneless pork loin chops, cut into ½-inch strips
- 1 cup fresh broccoli florets
- 4 cups coleslaw mix
- 1 can (8 ounces) bamboo shoots, drained
- 4 garlic cloves, minced
- 2 packages (3 ounces each) ramen noodles

1. In a small bowl, whisk the first five ingredients until blended. In a large skillet, heat 2 teaspoons oil over medium high heat. Add pork; stir-fry 2-3 minutes or until no longer pink. Remove from pan.

2. In the same pan, stir-fry broccoli in the remaining oil for 3 minutes. Add coleslaw mix, bamboo shoots and garlic; stir-fry 3-4 minutes longer or until the broccoli is crisp-tender. Stir in the soy sauce mixture and pork; heat through.

3. Meanwhile, cook noodles according to package directions; save seasoning packets for another use. Drain noodles; add to pork mixture and toss to combine.

PER SERVING 1¾ cups: 354 cal., 14g fat (5g sat. fat), 44mg chol., 794mg sod., 32g carb. (6g sugars, 3g fiber), 23g pro.

FAST FIX

POLISH SAUSAGE AND VEGGIES

Looking for something different to prepare with Polish sausage one afternoon, I created this entree. My family liked it so much that I've made it time and again since that day.

—RITA KODET CHULA VISTA, CA

START TO FINISH: 30 MIN.
MAKES: 6 SERVINGS

- 4 cups cubed peeled potatoes (about 2½ pounds)
- 1 pound smoked Polish sausage or smoked kielbasa, cut into ¼-inch slices
- ½ cup chopped onion
- ½ cup julienned sweet yellow pepper
- ½ cup julienned sweet red pepper
- 1½ teaspoons Cajun seasoning
- 1 tablespoon canola oil
- 1 tablespoon butter

In a large skillet over medium heat, cook potatoes, sausage, onion, peppers and Cajun seasoning in oil and butter for 15-20 minutes or until the potatoes are tender, stirring occasionally.

PER SERVING 1 cup: 373 cal., 24g fat (9g sat. fat), 59mg chol., 832mg sod., 25g carb. (2g sugars, 2g fiber), 11g pro.

PORK & RAMEN STIR-FRY

SKILLET PORK CHOP DELIGHT

EAT SMART
SKILLET PORK CHOP DELIGHT

Our family loves using apples to brighten savory dishes. We experimented with pork chops and apple recipes to find the perfect pairing, and this recipe is what it came to be.
—**AMANDA JOBE** OLATHE, KS

PREP: 15 MIN. • **COOK:** 20 MIN.
MAKES: 4 SERVINGS

- 4 boneless pork loin chops (4 ounces each and ¾ inch thick)
- 1 teaspoon dried oregano, divided
- ½ teaspoon salt
- ¼ teaspoon coarsely ground pepper
- 1½ teaspoons canola oil
- 2 small apples, cut into ½-inch slices
- 1 cup sliced sweet onion (¼ inch thick)
- ⅓ cup unsweetened applesauce
- ¼ cup cider vinegar

1. Sprinkle pork chops with ½ teaspoon oregano, salt and pepper. Place a large nonstick skillet coated with cooking spray over medium-high heat. Brown the pork chops, about 3 minutes per side; remove from pan.
2. In same pan, heat oil over medium-high heat. Add apples, onion and the remaining oregano; cook and stir for 6-8 minutes or until apples are tender.
3. Reduce heat to medium; stir in applesauce and vinegar. Return the chops to the pan; cook, covered, for 4-6 minutes or until pork is tender. Let stand 5 minutes before serving.
PER SERVING *1 pork chop with ½ cup apple mixture: 215 cal., 8g fat (2g sat. fat), 55mg chol., 329mg sod., 12g carb. (8g sugars, 2g fiber), 22g pro.* **Diabetic Exchanges:** *3 lean meat, ½ fruit, ½ fat.*

FAST FIX
PEAR PORK CHOPS

You'll be tempted to eat this main dish straight out of the pan, but save some for your guests! It's sure to wow them at the dinner table.
—*TASTE OF HOME* **TEST KITCHEN**

START TO FINISH: 30 MIN.
MAKES: 4 SERVINGS

- 1 package (6 ounces) corn bread stuffing mix
- 4 boneless pork loin chops (6 ounces each)
- ½ teaspoon pepper
- ¼ teaspoon salt
- 2 tablespoons butter
- 2 medium pears, chopped
- 1 medium sweet red pepper, chopped
- 2 green onions, thinly sliced

1. Prepare stuffing mix according to package directions. Sprinkle chops with pepper and salt. In a large skillet, brown the pork chops in butter. Sprinkle with pears and red pepper.
2. Top with the stuffing and onions. Cook, uncovered, over medium heat for 8-10 minutes or until a thermometer inserted in chops reads 145°.
PER SERVING *1 pork chop with ¾ cup stuffing mixture: 603 cal., 28g fat (14g sat. fat), 127mg chol., 1094mg sod., 47g carb. (14g sugars, 5g fiber), 38g pro.*

TOP TIP
PEAR POINTERS

To ripen pears, place them in a paper bag at room temperature for several days. When the pears give slightly to pressure, store in the refrigerator. Pears used for cooking should be a little firmer. Before cooking pears, use a vegetable peeler or paring knife to remove the skin. One pound of pears equals about 3 cups sliced.

FAST FIX ▶

SOUTHWEST SKILLET CHOPS

This is one of my go-to meals because I usually have the ingredients for these chops in my kitchen. I can't get enough of the corn relish.

—LINDA CIFUENTES MAHOMET, IL

START TO FINISH: 25 MIN.
MAKES: 4 SERVINGS

- 4 **boneless pork loin chops (6 ounces each)**
- ¾ **teaspoon salt**
- ¼ **teaspoon pepper**
- 2 **tablespoons butter, divided**
- 1 **tablespoon olive oil**
- ½ **small red onion, sliced**
- 1 **jalapeno pepper, seeded and finely chopped**
- ½ **cup frozen corn, thawed**
- 3 **tablespoons lime juice**
- ¼ **cup sliced ripe olives or green olives with pimientos, optional**

1. Sprinkle pork chops with salt and pepper. In a large skillet, heat 1 tablespoon butter and oil over medium-high heat. Brown the pork chops on both sides. Remove from pan.

2. In same skillet, heat the remaining butter. Add onion and jalapeno; cook and stir for 2-3 minutes or until tender. Return the chops to skillet. Add corn, lime juice and, if desired, olives; cook, covered, for 4-6 minutes or until a thermometer inserted in pork reads 145°. Let stand 5 minutes before serving.

NOTE *Wear disposable gloves when cutting hot peppers; the oils can burn skin. Avoid touching your face.*

PER SERVING *1 pork chop with ¼ cup relish: 330 cal., 19g fat (8g sat. fat), 97mg chol., 542mg sod., 6g carb. (1g sugars, 1g fiber), 33g pro.*

SOUTHWEST SKILLET CHOPS

**ZUCCHINI & SAUSAGE
STOVETOP CASSEROLE**

FAST FIX ▶

ZUCCHINI & SAUSAGE STOVETOP CASSEROLE

Gather zucchini from your garden or farm stand and start cooking! My family goes wild for this wholesome casserole. For variety, try coarsely grating the zucchini instead of slicing it.

—**LEANN GRAY** TAYLORSVILLE, UT

START TO FINISH: 30 MIN.
MAKES: 6 SERVINGS

- 1 **pound bulk pork sausage**
- 1 **tablespoon canola oil**
- 3 **medium zucchini, thinly sliced**
- 1 **medium onion, chopped**
- 1 **can (14½ ounces) stewed tomatoes, cut up**
- 1 **package (8.8 ounces) ready-to-serve long-grain rice**
- 1 **teaspoon prepared mustard**
- ½ **teaspoon garlic salt**
- ¼ **teaspoon pepper**
- 1 **cup shredded sharp cheddar cheese**

1. In a large skillet, cook sausage over medium heat 5-7 minutes or until no longer pink, breaking into crumbles. Drain and remove sausage from pan.

2. In same pan, heat oil over medium heat. Add zucchini and onion; cook and stir 5-7 minutes or until tender. Stir in sausage, tomatoes, rice, mustard, garlic salt and pepper. Bring to a boil. Reduce heat; simmer, covered, for 5 minutes to allow the flavors to blend.

3. Remove from heat; sprinkle with cheese. Let stand, covered, 5 minutes or until cheese is melted.

PER SERVING *1⅓ cups: 394 cal., 26g fat (9g sat. fat), 60mg chol., 803mg sod., 24g carb. (6g sugars, 2g fiber), 16g pro.*

FAST FIX ▶

ALMOND-CRUSTED CHOPS WITH CIDER SAUCE

(PICTURED ON PAGE 245)

I use finely ground almonds to give pork chops a crunchy crust. The cider sauce makes them tangy, creamy and sweet.

—**GLORIA BRADLEY** NAPERVILLE, IL

START TO FINISH: 20 MIN.
MAKES: 4 SERVINGS

- ½ cup panko (Japanese) bread crumbs
- ½ cup ground almonds
- ⅓ cup all-purpose flour
- ½ teaspoon salt, divided
- 2 large eggs, beaten
- 4 boneless pork loin chops (¾ inch thick and 4 ounces each)
- 3 tablespoons olive oil
- 1 cup apple cider or juice
- 4 ounces cream cheese, cubed
- 1 tablespoon honey, optional
  Minced chives

1. In a shallow bowl, mix bread crumbs and almonds. In another shallow bowl, mix flour and ¼ teaspoon salt. Place eggs in a separate shallow bowl. Dip pork chops in flour to coat both sides; shake off excess. Dip in egg, then in crumb mixture, patting to help coating adhere.

2. In a large skillet, heat oil over medium heat. Add pork chops; cook 3-4 minutes on each side or until a thermometer reads 145°. Remove chops from pan; keep warm. Wipe skillet clean.

3. In the same skillet over medium heat, combine apple cider, cream cheese, the remaining salt and, if desired, honey. Cook and stir 2 minutes. Serve with pork chops; sprinkle with chives.

PER SERVING *1 pork chop with ¼ cup sauce (calculated without honey): 499 cal., 33g fat (10g sat. fat), 144mg chol., 448mg sod., 21g carb. (8g sugars, 2g fiber), 29g pro.*

HAM STEAKS WITH GRUYERE, BACON & MUSHROOMS

FAST FIX ▶

HAM STEAKS WITH GRUYERE, BACON & MUSHROOMS

This meat lover's breakfast has a big wow factor. It's one of my favorites because the Gruyere, bacon and fresh mushrooms in the topping are a great combination.

—**LISA SPEER** PALM BEACH, FL

START TO FINISH: 25 MIN.
MAKES: 4 SERVINGS

- 2 tablespoons butter
- ½ pound sliced fresh mushrooms
- 1 shallot, finely chopped
- 2 garlic cloves, minced
- ⅛ teaspoon coarsely ground pepper
- 1 fully cooked boneless ham steak (about 1 pound), cut into four pieces
- 1 cup shredded Gruyere cheese
- 4 bacon strips, cooked and crumbled
- 1 tablespoon minced fresh parsley, optional

1. In a large nonstick skillet, heat butter over medium-high heat. Add mushrooms and shallot; cook and stir 4-6 minutes or until tender. Add garlic and pepper; cook 1 minute longer. Remove from pan; keep warm. Wipe skillet clean.

2. In same skillet, cook ham over medium heat 3 minutes. Turn; sprinkle with cheese and bacon. Cook, covered, 2-4 minutes longer or until the cheese is melted and the ham is heated through. Serve with mushroom mixture. If desired, sprinkle with parsley.

PER SERVING *352 cal., 22g fat (11g sat. fat), 113mg chol., 1576mg sod., 5g carb. (2g sugars, 1g fiber), 34g pro.*

SAUSAGE POTATO SUPPER

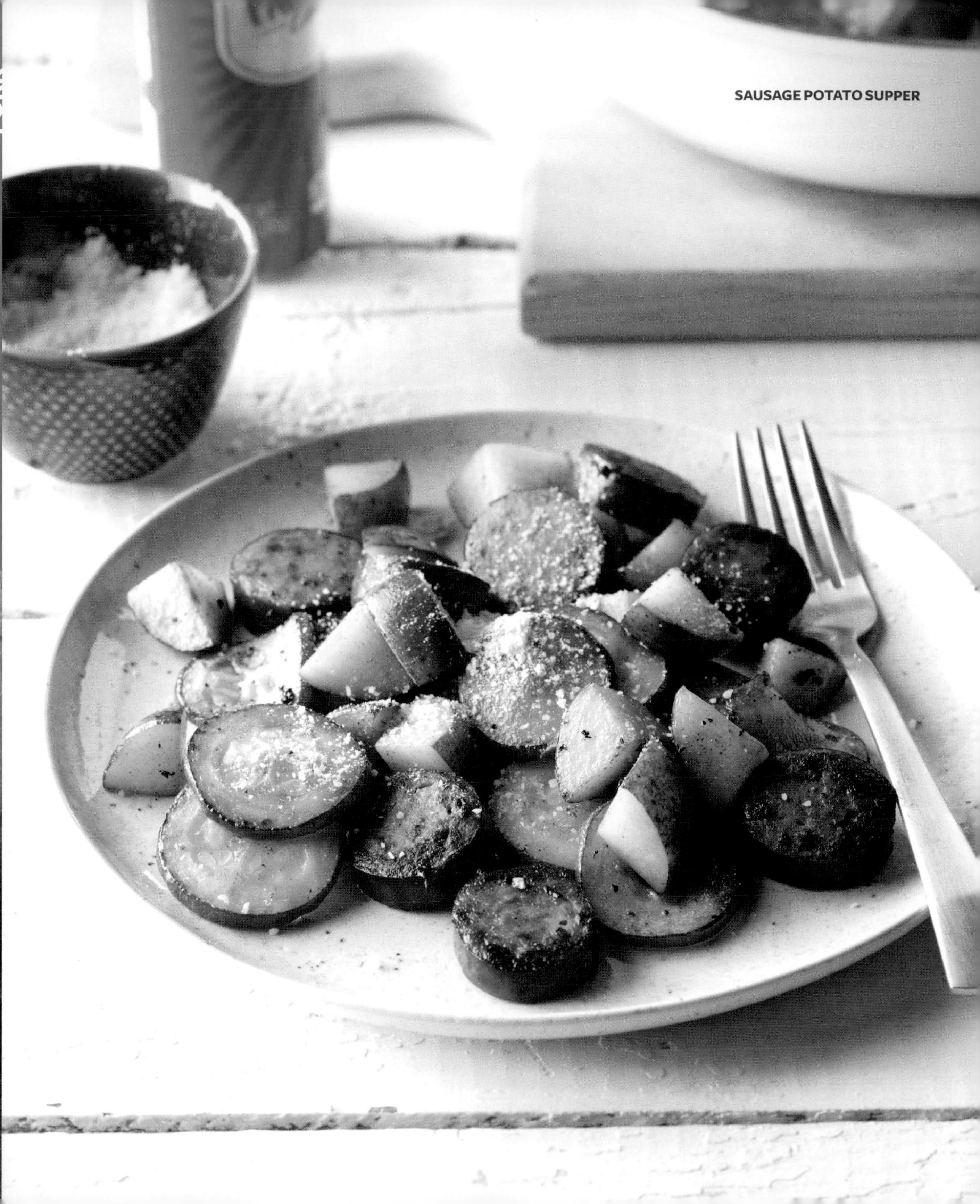

⑤ INGREDIENTS FAST FIX ▶

SAUSAGE POTATO SUPPER

One Saturday night, I cooked sausage with potatoes and zucchini—just the ingredients I had on hand. This spur of the moment supper was a hit with all six of us, and I've made it regularly ever since.
—**NANCY RUSSELL** ENGLEWOOD, CO

START TO FINISH: 25 MIN.
MAKES: 2 SERVINGS

- 2 small red potatoes, cubed
- 1 tablespoon butter
- 1 small zucchini, cut into ¼-inch slices
- ⅛ teaspoon garlic salt
- ½ pound smoked sausage, cut into ½-inch slices
- ⅛ to ¼ teaspoon pepper
  Grated Parmesan cheese, optional

1. In a small saucepan, combine potatoes and enough water to cover; bring to a boil. Reduce heat; cook, uncovered, until tender, 15-20 minutes.
2. In a large skillet, heat butter over medium-high heat; saute zucchini with garlic salt until crisp-tender. Add sausage; cook and stir until browned.
3. Drain potatoes; stir into zucchini mixture. Sprinkle with pepper and, if desired, cheese.
PER SERVING *2 cups: 448 cal., 37g fat (17g sat. fat), 91mg chol., 1396mg sod., 12g carb. (5g sugars, 1g fiber), 18g pro.*

FAST FIX ▶

FETTUCCINE CARBONARA

When a man at church found out how much my family likes fettuccine carbonara, he shared his Italian grandmother's recipe with us. I've made it my own over the last 25 years. Grated Parmesan cheese works just as well as Romano.
—**KRISTINE CHAYES** SMITHTOWN, NY

START TO FINISH: 30 MIN.
MAKES: 6 SERVINGS

- ½ pound bacon strips, chopped
- 1 package (16 ounces) fettuccine
- 1 small onion, finely chopped
- 2 garlic cloves, minced

FETTUCCINE CARBONARA

- 1 cup half-and-half cream
- 4 large eggs, lightly beaten
- ½ cup grated Romano cheese
- ½ teaspoon salt
- ¼ teaspoon pepper
- 1 tablespoon minced fresh parsley
  Additional grated Romano cheese, optional

1. In a large skillet, cook bacon over medium heat until crisp, stirring occasionally. Remove with a slotted spoon; drain on paper towels. Discard drippings, reserving 1 tablespoon in pan.
2. Meanwhile, in a Dutch oven, cook fettuccine according to the package directions. Drain; return to pan.
3. Add onion to the drippings in skillet; cook and stir over medium heat for 2-3 minutes or until tender. Add garlic; cook 1 minute longer. Reduce heat to medium-low. Stir in cream. In a small bowl, whisk a small amount of warm cream into eggs; return all to pan, whisking constantly. Cook for 8-10 minutes or until a thermometer reads 160°, stirring constantly.
4. Stir cheese, salt, pepper and bacon into the sauce. Add to the fettuccine and toss to combine. Sprinkle with parsley and, if desired, additional cheese. Serve immediately.
PER SERVING *1 cup (calculated without additional cheese): 495 cal., 19g fat (9g sat. fat), 162mg chol., 684mg sod., 56g carb. (4g sugars, 3g fiber), 25g pro.*

PORK PANCIT

PORK PANCIT

A dear friend gave me this pork recipe—it's so tempting, we never have leftovers. Try it with other meats like chicken, sausage or even Spam.

—PRISCILLA GILBERT
INDIAN HARBOUR BEACH, FL

START TO FINISH: 30 MIN.
MAKES: 6 SERVINGS

- 8 **ounces uncooked vermicelli or angel hair pasta**
- 1 **pound boneless pork loin chops (½ inch thick), cut into thin strips**
- 3 **tablespoons canola oil, divided**
- 4 **garlic cloves, minced**
- 1½ **teaspoons salt, divided**
- 1 **medium onion, halved and thinly sliced**
- 2½ **cups shredded cabbage**
- 1 **medium carrot, julienned**
- 1 **cup fresh snow peas**
- ¼ **teaspoon pepper**

1. Break vermicelli in half; cook according to package directions. Drain.

2. Meanwhile, in a bowl, toss pork with 2 tablespoons oil, garlic and ½ teaspoon salt. Place a large skillet over medium-high heat. Add half of the pork mixture; stir-fry 2-3 minutes or until browned. Remove from pan. Repeat with remaining pork mixture.

3. In the same skillet, heat the remaining oil over medium-high heat. Add onion; stir-fry 1-2 minutes or until tender. Add remaining vegetables; stir-fry 3-5 minutes or until crisp-tender. Stir in pepper and remaining salt. Return the pork to pan. Add vermicelli; heat through, tossing to combine.

PER SERVING *1⅓ cups: 326 cal., 12g fat (2g sat. fat), 36mg chol., 627mg sod., 34g carb. (3g sugars, 3g fiber), 21g pro.* **Diabetic Exchanges:** *2 starch, 2 lean meat, 1 vegetable, 1 fat.*

SWEET & SOUR PORK

My grandmother made this for me on Valentine's Day when I was a child. Now I make it for my children. I usually make brown rice or rice noodles and add thinly sliced Bok Choy to bump up the vegetable intake. I've never had leftovers.

—BARBARA HINTERBERGER BUFFALO, NY

PREP: 20 MIN. • **COOK:** 15 MIN.
MAKES: 4 SERVINGS

- 1 **can (20 ounces) unsweetened pineapple chunks**
- ⅓ **cup water**
- ⅓ **cup cider vinegar**
- 3 **tablespoons brown sugar**
- 2 **tablespoons cornstarch**
- 1 **tablespoon reduced-sodium soy sauce**
- 1 **teaspoon Worcestershire sauce**
- ½ **teaspoon salt**
- 1 **pound pork tenderloin, cut into ½-inch pieces**
- 1 **teaspoon paprika**
- 1 **tablespoon canola oil**
- 1 **medium green pepper, thinly sliced**
- 1 **small onion, thinly sliced**
- 2 **cups hot cooked brown rice**

1. Drain pineapple, reserving ⅔ cup juice; set pineapple aside. In a small bowl, mix water, vinegar, brown sugar, cornstarch, soy sauce, Worcestershire sauce, salt and the reserved pineapple juice until smooth; set aside.
2. Sprinkle pork with paprika. In a large nonstick skillet coated with cooking spray, brown the pork in oil.
3. Stir the cornstarch mixture and add it to pan. Bring to a boil; cook and stir for 1 minute or until thickened. Add green pepper, onion and pineapple. Reduce heat; simmer, covered, 6-8 minutes or until pork is tender. Serve with rice.
PER SERVING 1¼ cups pork mixture with ½ cup cooked rice: 428 cal., 9g fat (2g sat. fat), 63mg chol., 519mg sod., 61g carb. (30g sugars, 1g fiber), 26g pro.

APPLE-CHERRY PORK MEDALLIONS

EAT SMART **FAST FIX**
APPLE-CHERRY PORK MEDALLIONS

If you're too busy to cook, these pork medallions with tangy apple-cherry sauce, fresh rosemary and thyme deliver the goods in a hurry.

—GLORIA BRADLEY NAPERVILLE, IL

START TO FINISH: 30 MIN.
MAKES: 4 SERVINGS

- 1 **pork tenderloin (1 pound)**
- 1 **teaspoon minced fresh rosemary or ¼ teaspoon dried rosemary, crushed**
- 1 **teaspoon minced fresh thyme or ¼ teaspoon dried thyme**
- ½ **teaspoon celery salt**
- 1 **tablespoon olive oil**
- 1 **large apple, sliced**
- ⅔ **cup unsweetened apple juice**
- 3 **tablespoons dried tart cherries**
- 1 **tablespoon honey**
- 1 **tablespoon cider vinegar**
- 1 **package (8.8 ounces) ready-to-serve brown rice**

1. Cut tenderloin crosswise into 12 slices; sprinkle with rosemary, thyme and celery salt. In a large nonstick skillet, heat oil over medium-high heat. Brown pork on both sides; remove from pan.
2. In the same skillet, combine apple, apple juice, cherries, honey and vinegar. Bring to a boil, stirring to loosen browned bits from pan. Reduce heat; simmer, uncovered, 3-4 minutes or just until the apple is tender.
3. Return the pork to pan, turning to coat with sauce; cook, covered, for 3-4 minutes or until the pork is tender. Meanwhile, prepare rice according to the package directions; serve with the pork mixture.
PER SERVING 3 ounces cooked pork with ⅓ cup rice and ¼ cup apple mixture: 349 cal., 9g fat (2g sat. fat), 64mg chol., 179mg sod., 37g carb. (16g sugars, 4g fiber), 25g pro. **Diabetic Exchanges:** 3 lean meat, 2½ starch.

ORANGE-GLAZED PORK WITH SWEET POTATOES, PAGE 265

DR SPICY BBQ PORK, PAGE 268

HOT FROM THE OVEN

From **tenderloin, chops and roasts** to **casseroles, pizzas and pies,** pork is a versatile choice that plays just as well with rich, elegant glazes as with spicy barbecue sauces. Whether you're planning for a **special celebration** or a **weeknight meal,** get ready for the deliciousness of a **home-cooked** pork dinner!

PORK CHOPS WITH TOMATO-BACON TOPPING, PAGE 272

PIZZA-STYLE MANICOTTI, PAGE 275

TOMATO, SAUSAGE & CHEDDAR BREAD PUDDING

TOMATO, SAUSAGE & CHEDDAR BREAD PUDDING

This savory dish is the perfect excuse to have bread pudding as the entire meal, not just afterward as dessert.

—**HOLLY JONES** KENNESAW, GA

PREP: 30 MIN. • **BAKE:** 45 MIN.
MAKES: 12 SERVINGS

- 3 **cups shredded sharp cheddar cheese**
- 1 **can (28 ounces) diced tomatoes, drained**
- 1 **pound bulk Italian sausage, cooked and crumbled**
- 4 **green onions, thinly sliced**
- ¼ **cup minced fresh basil or 1 tablespoon dried basil**
- ¼ **cup packed brown sugar**
- 1 **teaspoon dried oregano**
- 1 **teaspoon garlic powder**
- 3 **cups cubed French bread**
- 6 **large eggs**
- 1½ **cups heavy whipping cream**
- ½ **teaspoon salt**
- ½ **teaspoon pepper**
- ½ **cup grated Parmesan cheese**

1. Preheat oven to 350°. In a large bowl, combine first eight ingredients. Stir in bread. Transfer to a greased 13x9-in. baking dish.

2. In the same bowl, whisk eggs, cream, salt and pepper; pour over the bread mixture. Sprinkle with Parmesan cheese. Bake for 45-50 minutes or until a knife inserted near the center comes out clean.

PER SERVING *1 piece: 430 cal., 32 g fat (18 g sat. fat), 206 mg chol., 822 mg sod., 16 g carb. (8 g sugars, 2 g fiber), 19 g pro.*

EAT SMART

ORANGE-GLAZED PORK WITH SWEET POTATOES

(PICTURED ON PAGE 262)

When it's chilly outside, I like to roast pork tenderloin with sweet potatoes, apples and an orange. The sweetness and spices make any evening cozy.

—DANIELLE LEE BOYLES WESTON, WI

PREP: 20 MIN. • **BAKE:** 55 MIN. + STANDING
MAKES: 6 SERVINGS

- 1 pound sweet potatoes (about 2 medium)
- 2 medium apples
- 1 medium orange
- 1 teaspoon salt
- ½ teaspoon pepper
- 1 cup orange juice
- 2 tablespoons brown sugar
- 2 teaspoons cornstarch
- 1 teaspoon ground cinnamon
- 1 teaspoon ground ginger
- 2 pork tenderloins (about 1 pound each)

1. Preheat oven to 350°. Peel sweet potatoes; core apples. Cut potatoes, apples and orange crosswise into ¼-in.-thick slices. Arrange on a foil-lined 15x10x1-in. baking pan coated with cooking spray; sprinkle with salt and pepper. Roast 10 minutes.

2. In a microwave-safe bowl, mix orange juice, brown sugar, cornstarch, cinnamon and ginger. Microwave, covered, on high for 1-2 minutes or until thickened, stirring every 30 seconds. Stir until smooth.

3. Place pork over sweet potato mixture; drizzle with orange juice mixture. Roast for 45-55 minutes longer or until a thermometer inserted in the pork reads 145° and the sweet potatoes and apples are tender. Remove from oven; tent with foil. Let stand 10 minutes before slicing.

PER SERVING *4 ounces cooked pork with 1 cup sweet potato mixture: 325 cal., 5g fat (2g sat. fat), 85mg chol., 467mg sod., 36g carb. (21g sugars, 3g fiber), 32g pro.* **Diabetic Exchanges:** *4 lean meat, 2 starch.*

ASPARAGUS, BACON & HERBED CHEESE PIZZA

FAST FIX

ASPARAGUS, BACON & HERBED CHEESE PIZZA

Here's a zesty pizza that's lovely all year round, but especially nice with spring asparagus, mozzarella and bacon.

—DAHLIA ABRAMS DETROIT, MI

START TO FINISH: 30 MIN.
MAKES: 6 SERVINGS

- 1 prebaked 12-inch pizza crust
- 6 teaspoons olive oil, divided
- 1 cup shredded part-skim mozzarella cheese
- 2¼ cups cut fresh asparagus (1-inch pieces)
- 8 bacon strips, cooked and crumbled
- ½ cup garlic-herb spreadable cheese (about 3 ounces)
- ¼ teaspoon crushed red pepper flakes

1. Preheat oven to 450°. Place pizza crust on an ungreased 12-in. pizza pan or baking sheet; brush top with 4 teaspoons of oil. Top with mozzarella, asparagus and crumbled bacon. Drop spreadable cheese by teaspoonfuls over the pizza. Sprinkle with pepper flakes; drizzle with the remaining oil.

2. Bake 12-15 minutes or until cheese is lightly browned.

PER SERVING *1 slice: 407 cal., 24g fat (11g sat. fat), 45mg chol., 748mg sod., 32g carb. (3g sugars, 2g fiber), 18g pro.*

(5) INGREDIENTS

APPLE-PECAN PORK TENDERLOIN

I thought up this recipe when I needed to use up some apple cider—it was so good, it's now a staple for company! I crush the nuts with a rolling pin, but chopping works fine, too.

—ELISABETH LARSEN PLEASANT GROVE, UT

PREP: 10 MIN. + MARINATING
BAKE: 25 MIN. + STANDING
MAKES: 4 SERVINGS

- 1 pork tenderloin (1 pound)
- ½ cup apple cider or juice
- 1 teaspoon salt
- ½ cup finely chopped pecans
- ¼ cup honey
- 2 tablespoons Dijon mustard
   Salt to taste

1. Place pork in a large resealable plastic bag; add apple cider and 1 teaspoon salt. Seal bag and turn to coat. Refrigerate for 4 hours or overnight.

2. Preheat oven to 425°. Spread pecans on a plate. Drain the pork, discarding the marinade. In a small bowl, mix honey and mustard; rub over the pork. Roll the pork in pecans, patting to help nuts adhere.

3. Transfer to a greased 13x9-in. baking dish. Bake for 25-30 minutes or until a thermometer reads 145°. Let stand for 10 minutes before slicing. Season with salt to taste.

PER SERVING *3 ounces cooked pork: 285 cal., 12g fat (2g sat. fat), 63mg chol., 817mg sod., 22g carb. (19g sugars, 1g fiber), 24g pro.*

APPLE-PECAN PORK TENDERLOIN

EAT SMART (5) INGREDIENTS FAST FIX

LEMON-GARLIC PORK CHOPS

These zesty chops spiced with paprika and cayenne are the brainchild of my son James. He'll also mix up a jarful of the dry spices to use as a rub for chops or chicken.
—MOLLY SEIDEL EDGEWOOD, NM

START TO FINISH: 20 MIN.
MAKES: 4 SERVINGS

- 2 **tablespoons lemon juice**
- 2 **garlic cloves, minced**
- 1 **teaspoon salt**
- 1 **teaspoon paprika**
- ½ **teaspoon pepper**
- ¼ **teaspoon cayenne pepper**
- 4 **boneless pork loin chops (6 ounces each)**

1. Preheat broiler. In a small bowl, mix the first six ingredients; brush over pork chops. Place in a 15x10x1-in. baking pan.
2. Broil 4-5 in. from heat 4-5 minutes on each side or until a thermometer reads 145°. Let stand 5 minutes before serving.
PER SERVING *1 pork chop: 233 cal., 10g fat (4g sat. fat), 82mg chol., 638mg sod., 2g carb. (0 sugars, 0 fiber), 33g pro.* **Diabetic Exchange:** *5 lean meat.*

BACON TORTELLINI BAKE

I stirred up this easy pasta and figured that if my family liked it, others might, too. Broccoli and bacon add fabulous texture.
—AMY LENTS GRAND FORKS, ND

PREP: 25 MIN. • **BAKE:** 15 MIN.
MAKES: 6 SERVINGS

- 1 **package (20 ounces) refrigerated cheese tortellini**
- 3 **cups small fresh broccoli florets**
- ½ **pound bacon strips, cut into 1-inch pieces**
- 2 **garlic cloves, minced**
- 1 **tablespoon all-purpose flour**
- 1 **teaspoon dried basil**
- ½ **teaspoon salt**
- ⅛ **teaspoon coarsely ground pepper**
- 2 **cups 2% milk**
- ¾ **cup shredded part-skim mozzarella cheese, divided**
- ¾ **cup grated Parmesan cheese, divided**
- 2 **teaspoons lemon juice**

1. Preheat oven to 350°. Cook tortellini according to package directions, adding broccoli during the last 2 minutes; drain.
2. Meanwhile, in a large skillet, cook bacon over medium heat until crisp, stirring occasionally. Remove with a slotted spoon; drain on paper towels. Discard drippings, reserving 1 tablespoon in the pan.
3. Reduce heat to medium-low. Add garlic to the drippings in pan; cook and stir 1 minute. Stir in flour, basil, salt and pepper until blended; gradually whisk in milk. Bring to a boil, stirring constantly; cook and stir 3-5 minutes or until slightly thickened. Remove from heat.
4. Stir in ½ cup mozzarella cheese, ½ cup Parmesan cheese and lemon juice. Add the tortellini mixture and bacon; toss to combine. Transfer to a greased 13x9-in. baking dish; sprinkle with the remaining cheeses. Bake, uncovered, 15-20 minutes or until heated through and the broccoli is tender.
FREEZE OPTION *Sprinkle remaining cheeses over unbaked casserole. Cover and freeze. To use, partially thaw in refrigerator overnight. Remove from refrigerator 30 minutes before baking. Preheat oven to 350°. Bake casserole as directed, increasing time as necessary to heat through and for a thermometer inserted in center to read 165°.*
PER SERVING *1 cup: 522 cal., 23g fat (11g sat. fat), 80mg chol., 1084mg sod., 52g carb. (6g sugars, 4g fiber), 29g pro.*

BACON TORTELLINI BAKE

DR SPICY BBQ PORK
(PICTURED ON PAGE 263)

I served this at my son's graduation party and kept it warm in a slow cooker after roasting it in the oven. The pork is great piled high on rolls, on top of a BBQ pizza or all by itself.
—**MICHELLE GAUER** SPICER, MN

PREP: 25 MIN. • **BAKE:** 4 HOURS
MAKES: 12 SERVINGS (⅔ CUP EACH)

- 1 **boneless pork shoulder roast (5 to 7 pounds)**
- 1 **teaspoon garlic powder**
- ½ **teaspoon salt**
- ½ **teaspoon freshly ground pepper**
- 6 **chipotle peppers in adobo sauce, finely chopped (about ⅓ cup)**
- 1 **large sweet onion, halved and sliced**
- 2 **tablespoons brown sugar**
- 2 **cans (12 ounces each) Dr Pepper**
- 1 **cup barbecue sauce**
  French-fried onions, biscuits and coleslaw, optional

1. Preheat oven to 325°. Sprinkle roast with garlic powder, salt and pepper; rub with chipotle peppers. Place in a Dutch oven. Top with sweet onion; sprinkle with brown sugar. Pour Dr Pepper around the roast. Bake, covered, 4-4½ hours or until meat is tender.

2. Remove roast; cool slightly. Strain the cooking juices, reserving onion; skim fat from the juices.

3. Shred pork with two forks. Return juices, onion and pork to Dutch oven. Stir in barbecue sauce; heat through over medium heat, stirring occasionally. If desired, sprinkle with french-fried onions and serve with biscuits and coleslaw.

PER SERVING *⅔ cup pork mixture (calculated without optional ingredients): 372 cal., 20g fat (7g sat. fat), 112mg chol., 466mg sod., 15g carb. (14g sugars, 1g fiber), 33g pro.*

BACON-COLBY LASAGNA

BACON-COLBY LASAGNA

My grandmother smattered her cheesy lasagna with bacon, something she borrowed from carbonara-style pasta. Learning by her side taught me so much!
—**CATHY MCCARTNEY** DAVENPORT, IA

PREP: 30 MIN. • **BAKE:** 45 MIN. + STANDING
MAKES: 2 LASAGNAS (12 SERVINGS EACH)

- 24 **uncooked lasagna noodles**
- 2 **pounds lean ground beef (90% lean)**
- 2 **medium onions, chopped**
- 1½ **pounds bacon strips, cooked and crumbled**
- 2 **cans (15 ounces each) tomato sauce**
- 2 **cans (14½ ounces each) diced tomatoes, undrained**
- 2 **tablespoons sugar**
- 1 **teaspoon salt**
- 8 **cups shredded Colby-Monterey Jack cheese**

1. Preheat oven to 350°. Cook noodles according to package directions for al dente; drain.

2. In a 6-qt. stockpot, cook beef and onions over medium-high heat for 10-12 minutes or until beef is no longer pink, breaking up into crumbles; drain. Stir in bacon, tomato sauce, tomatoes, sugar and salt; heat through.

3. Spread 1 cup sauce into each of two greased 13x9-in. baking dishes. Layer each with four noodles, 1⅔ cups sauce and 1⅓ cups cheese. Repeat layers twice.

4. Bake, covered, 40 minutes. Uncover; bake 5-10 minutes longer or until bubbly. Let stand 15 minutes before serving.

FREEZE OPTION *Cool unbaked lasagnas; cover and freeze. To use, partially thaw in refrigerator overnight. Remove from refrigerator 30 minutes before baking. Preheat oven to 350°. Bake the lasagna as directed, increasing time as necessary to heat through and for a thermometer inserted in center to read 165°.*

PER SERVING *1 piece: 357 cal., 18g fat (11g sat. fat), 67mg chol., 744mg sod., 25g carb. (4g sugars, 2g fiber), 23g pro.*

ITALIAN SAUSAGE AND SPINACH PIE

The basic recipe for this pie came from my mother, but I've added a few ingredients. The flavors blend so well, and it even tastes good cold. This makes a hearty supper, especially when served with a side of pasta.

—**TERESA JOHNSON** PERU, IL

PREP: 25 MIN. • **BAKE:** 50 MIN. + STANDING
MAKES: 8 SERVINGS

- 1 pound bulk Italian sausage
- 1 medium onion, chopped
- 6 large eggs
- 2 packages (10 ounces each) frozen chopped spinach, thawed and squeezed dry
- 4 cups shredded mozzarella cheese
- 1 cup ricotta cheese
- ½ teaspoon garlic powder
- ¼ teaspoon pepper
   Pastry for double-crust pie (9 inches)
- 1 tablespoon water

1. In a large skillet, brown sausage and onion over medium heat 6-8 minutes or until the sausage is no longer pink, breaking sausage into crumbles; drain.

2. Separate 1 egg; reserve the yolk. In a large bowl, whisk remaining eggs and the egg white. Stir in sausage mixture, spinach, mozzarella cheese, ricotta cheese, garlic powder and pepper.

3. Preheat oven to 375°. On a lightly floured surface, roll one half of pastry dough to a ⅛-in.-thick circle; transfer to a 9-in. deep-dish pie plate. Trim pastry even with the rim of the pie plate. Add sausage mixture. Roll remaining pastry dough to a ⅛-in.-thick circle. Place over filling. Trim, seal and flute the edge.

4. In a small bowl, whisk water and the reserved egg yolk; brush over pastry. Cut slits in top.

5. Bake 50 minutes or until golden brown. Let stand 10 minutes before serving.

PASTRY FOR DOUBLE-CRUST PIE (9 INCHES) *Combine 2½ cups all-purpose flour and ½ teaspoon salt; cut in 1 cup cold butter until crumbly. Gradually add ⅓ to ⅔ cup ice water, tossing with a fork until dough holds together when pressed. Divide dough in half and shape into disks; wrap each in plastic and refrigerate for 1 hour.*

PER SERVING *1 piece: 608 cal., 40g fat (19g sat. fat), 248mg chol., 787mg sod., 33g carb. (6g sugars, 1g fiber), 28g pro.*

EAT SMART **FAST FIX** ▶

QUICK HAWAIIAN PIZZA

Our family never quite liked the taste of canned pizza sauce, so I tried mixing BBQ sauce into spaghetti sauce to add some sweetness. I've made my pizzas with this special and easy sauce ever since, and my family loves it.

—**TONYA SCHIELER** CARMEL, IN

START TO FINISH: 25 MIN.
MAKES: 6 SLICES

- 1 prebaked 12-inch thin whole wheat pizza crust
- ½ cup marinara sauce
- ¼ cup barbecue sauce
- 1 medium sweet yellow or red pepper, chopped
- 1 cup cubed fresh pineapple
- ½ cup chopped fully cooked ham
- 1 cup shredded part-skim mozzarella cheese
- ½ cup shredded cheddar cheese

1. Preheat oven to 425°. Place crust on a baking sheet. Mix marinara and barbecue sauces; spread over crust.

2. Top with remaining ingredients. Bake until crust is browned and cheeses are melted, 10-15 minutes.

PER SERVING *1 slice: 290 cal., 10g fat (5g sat. fat), 29mg chol., 792mg sod., 36g carb., 5g fiber, 16g pro.* **Diabetic Exchanges:** *2 starch, 2 lean meat, ½ fat.*

ITALIAN SAUSAGE AND SPINACH PIE

HOLIDAY CROWN
PORK ROAST

HOLIDAY CROWN PORK ROAST

Crown roast makes a regal Christmas dinner. Flavored with rosemary, sage and thyme, it's elegant and simple—a real blessing during the hectic holidays.

—LISA SPEER PALM BEACH, FL

PREP: 15 MIN. • **BAKE:** 2 HOURS + STANDING
MAKES: 12 SERVINGS

- 1 **tablespoon paprika**
- 1½ **teaspoons kosher salt**
- 1 **teaspoon dried thyme**
- 1 **teaspoon dried rosemary, crushed**
- 1 **teaspoon pepper**
- ½ **teaspoon rubbed sage**
- 1 **pork crown roast (12 ribs, about 8 pounds)**
  Apples, fresh rosemary sprigs and dried sage leaves, optional

1. Preheat oven to 350°. Mix the first six ingredients; rub over roast. Place on a rack in a large shallow roasting pan. Cover rib ends with foil. Roast 2-2½ hours or until a thermometer reads at least 145°.
2. Remove roast from oven; tent with foil. Let stand 15 minutes. Remove foil; carve between ribs to serve. If desired, serve with apples and fresh herbs.
PER SERVING *1 rib: 301 cal., 15g fat (6g sat. fat), 95mg chol., 298mg sod., 1g carb. (0 sugars, 0 fiber), 39g pro.*

PAN ROASTED PORK CHOPS & POTATOES

A shortcut marinade gives these chops plenty of flavor, and the crumb coating packs on the crunch. For color, I sometimes tuck in a few handfuls of Brussels sprouts.

—CHAR OUELLETTE COLTON, OR

PREP: 20 MIN. + MARINATING • **BAKE:** 40 MIN.
MAKES: 4 SERVINGS

- 4 **boneless pork loin chops (6 ounces each)**
- ½ **cup plus 2 tablespoons reduced-fat Italian salad dressing, divided**
- 4 **small potatoes (about 1½ pounds)**
- ½ **pound fresh Brussels sprouts, trimmed and halved**

PAN ROASTED PORK CHOPS & POTATOES

- ½ **cup soft bread crumbs**
- 1 **tablespoon minced fresh parsley**
- ¼ **teaspoon salt**
- ⅛ **teaspoon pepper**
- 2 **teaspoons butter, melted**

1. Place pork chops and ½ cup salad dressing in a large resealable plastic bag; seal bag and turn to coat. Refrigerate 8 hours or overnight. Refrigerate the remaining salad dressing.
2. Preheat oven to 400°. Cut each potato lengthwise into 12 wedges. Arrange the potatoes and Brussels sprouts in a 15x10x1-in. baking pan coated with cooking spray. Drizzle vegetables with remaining salad dressing; toss to coat. Roast 20 minutes.
3. Drain pork, discarding the marinade. Pat the pork dry with paper towels. Stir vegetables; place pork chops over top. Roast 15-20 minutes longer or until a thermometer inserted in pork reads 145°. Preheat broiler.
4. In a small bowl, combine bread crumbs, parsley, salt and pepper; stir in butter. Top pork with crumb mixture. Broil 4-6 in. from heat 1-2 minutes or until bread crumbs are golden brown. Let stand 5 minutes.
NOTE *To make soft bread crumbs, tear bread into pieces and place in a food processor or blender. Cover and pulse until crumbs form. One slice of bread yields ½ to ¾ cup crumbs.*
PER SERVING *1 pork chop with 1 cup vegetables: 451 cal., 16g fat (5g sat. fat), 87mg chol., 492mg sod., 38g carb. (3g sugars, 5g fiber), 38g pro.* **Diabetic Exchanges:** *5 lean meat, 2½ starch, 2 fat.*

ROAST PORK LOIN WITH ROSEMARY APPLESAUCE

5. Remove roast from oven; tent with foil. Let stand 10 minutes before slicing. Serve with warm applesauce.

PER SERVING *3 ounces cooked pork with 1/3 cup applesauce: 287 cal., 16g fat (6g sat. fat), 72mg chol., 1418mg sod., 15g carb. (11g sugars, 2g fiber), 22g pro.*

(5) INGREDIENTS **FAST FIX**

PORK CHOPS WITH TOMATO-BACON TOPPING

(PICTURED ON PAGE 263)

My husband and I collaborated on these pork chops with sun-dried tomatoes, bacon and rosemary. They're easy enough for any day and fancy enough for special events.

—TRISHA KLEMPEL SIDNEY, MT

START TO FINISH: 30 MIN.
MAKES: 4 SERVINGS

- 4 **thick-sliced bacon strips, chopped**
- 4 **boneless pork loin chops (6 ounces each)**
- ½ **teaspoon salt**
- ¼ **teaspoon pepper**
- ¼ **cup julienned oil-packed sun-dried tomatoes**
- 2 **tablespoons brown sugar**
- 2 **teaspoons minced fresh rosemary or ½ teaspoon dried rosemary, crushed**

1. Preheat broiler. In a large ovenproof skillet, cook bacon over medium heat until crisp, stirring occasionally. Remove with a slotted spoon; drain on paper towels.

2. Sprinkle pork chops with salt and pepper. Add chops to drippings; cook 3-4 minutes on each side or until a thermometer reads 145°. Meanwhile, in a small bowl, mix bacon, tomatoes, brown sugar and rosemary.

3. Spoon tomato mixture over chops. Broil 3-4 in. from heat 1-2 minutes or until brown sugar is melted.

PER SERVING *1 pork chop: 457 cal., 33g fat (12g sat. fat), 108mg chol., 636mg sod., 2g carb. (0 sugars, 0 fiber), 37g pro.*

ROAST PORK LOIN WITH ROSEMARY APPLESAUCE

I made this for a family get-together on my husband's birthday. The homemade rosemary applesauce adds an extra layer of comfort to the tender pork.

—ANGELA LEMOINE HOWELL, NJ

PREP: 15 MIN. + MARINATING
BAKE: 55 MIN.. + STANDING
MAKES: 8 SERVINGS (3 CUPS APPLESAUCE)

- ¼ **cup olive oil**
- 2 **tablespoons salt**
- 4 **teaspoons garlic powder**
- 4 **teaspoons minced fresh rosemary or 1½ teaspoons dried rosemary, crushed**
- 2 **teaspoons pepper**
- 1 **boneless pork loin roast (2 to 3 pounds), halved**

APPLESAUCE
- ¼ **cup butter, cubed**
- 6 **medium Golden Delicious apples, peeled and chopped (about 5 cups)**
- 1 **to 2 teaspoons ground cinnamon**
- 2 **teaspoons brown sugar**
- 1½ **teaspoons minced fresh rosemary or ½ teaspoon dried rosemary, crushed**
- ½ **teaspoon salt**
- 1 **cup water**

1. In a large resealable plastic bag, combine the first five ingredients. Add pork; seal bag and turn to coat. Refrigerate 8 hours or overnight.

2. Preheat oven to 350°. Place pork roast on a rack in a shallow roasting pan, fat side up. Roast 55-65 minutes or until a thermometer reads 145°.

3. Meanwhile, in a large skillet, heat butter over medium heat. Add apples, cinnamon, brown sugar, rosemary and salt; cook 8-10 minutes or until apples are tender, stirring occasionally.

4. Stir in water; bring to a boil. Reduce heat; simmer, uncovered, 10 minutes or until apples are very soft. Remove from heat; mash apples to desired consistency.

PENNE AND SMOKED SAUSAGE

My sausage-pasta dish is a must-try. It just tastes so good when it's hot and bubbly from the oven. The cheddar french-fried onions lend a cheesy, crunchy touch.

—MARGARET WILSON SAN BERNARDINO, CA

PREP: 15 MIN. • **BAKE:** 30 MIN.
MAKES: 6 SERVINGS

- 2 cups uncooked penne pasta
- 1 pound smoked sausage, cut into ¼-inch slices
- 1½ cups 2% milk
- 1 can (10¾ ounces) condensed cream of celery soup, undiluted
- 1½ cups cheddar french-fried onions, divided
- 1 cup shredded part-skim mozzarella cheese, divided
- 1 cup frozen peas

1. Preheat oven to 375°. Cook pasta according to package directions.

2. Meanwhile, in a large skillet, brown sausage over medium heat 5 minutes; drain. In a large bowl, combine milk and soup. Stir in ½ cup onions, ½ cup cheese, peas and sausage. Drain pasta; stir into sausage mixture.

3. Transfer to a greased 13x9-in. baking dish. Cover and bake 25-30 minutes or until bubbly. Sprinkle with remaining onions and cheese. Bake, uncovered, for 3-5 minutes longer or until the cheese is melted.

FREEZE OPTION *Sprinkle remaining onions and cheese over unbaked casserole. Cover and freeze. To use, partially thaw in refrigerator overnight. Remove from refrigerator 30 minutes before baking. Preheat oven to 375°. Bake casserole as directed, increasing time as necessary to heat through and for a thermometer inserted in center to read 165°.*

PER SERVING *1½ cups: 553 cal., 35g fat (14g sat. fat), 70mg chol., 1425mg sod., 36g carb. (7g sugars, 3g fiber), 22g pro.*

PENNE AND SMOKED SAUSAGE

**APRICOT GINGER
MUSTARD-GLAZED HAM**

APRICOT GINGER MUSTARD-GLAZED HAM

Although I usually buy spiral-sliced hams, I decided to do a home-baked ham with a gingery glaze. This is how special-occasion dining is done.

—**ALLY PHILLIPS** MURRELLS INLET, SC

PREP: 15 MIN. • **BAKE:** 2 HOURS
MAKES: 16 SERVINGS

- 1 **fully cooked bone-in ham (7 to 9 pounds)**
- ½ **cup apricot halves, drained**
- ½ **cup stone-ground mustard**
- ⅓ **cup packed brown sugar**
- 2 **tablespoons grated fresh gingerroot**
- 1 **tablespoon whole peppercorns**
- ½ **teaspoon sea salt**
- ½ **teaspoon coarsely ground pepper**

1. Preheat oven to 325°. Place ham on a rack in a shallow roasting pan. Using a sharp knife, score surface of ham with ¼-in.-deep cuts in a diamond pattern. Cover and bake 1¾-2¼ hours or until a thermometer reads 130°.

2. Meanwhile, place the remaining ingredients in a food processor; process until blended. Remove ham from oven. Increase oven setting to 425°. Spread apricot mixture over ham.

3. Bake ham, uncovered, 15-20 minutes longer or until a thermometer reads 140°. If desired, increase oven setting to broil; broil 2-4 minutes or until golden brown.

PER SERVING *4 ounces cooked ham: 201 cal., 6g fat (2g sat. fat), 87mg chol., 1258mg sod., 8g carb. (7g sugars, 0 fiber), 30g pro.*

PIZZA-STYLE MANICOTTI

(PICTURED ON PAGE 263)

Ham, pepperoni and string cheese make little bundles that are stuffed into manicotti shells. It's a fun, hands-on recipe that children can help prepare.

—JUDY ARMSTRONG PRAIRIEVILLE, LA

PREP: 20 MIN. • **BAKE:** 25 MIN.
MAKES: 4 SERVINGS

- 8 uncooked manicotti shells
- 1 jar (24 ounces) spaghetti sauce
- 8 slices deli ham (about 6 ounces)
- 8 fresh basil leaves
- 8 pieces string cheese
- 24 slices pepperoni
- 1 can (2¼ ounces) sliced ripe olives, drained
- 1 cup shredded Parmesan cheese

1. Cook manicotti according to package directions for al dente; drain. Preheat oven to 350°.

2. Pour 1 cup sauce into an 11x7-in. baking dish. On a short side of each ham slice, layer one basil leaf, one piece string cheese and three slices pepperoni; roll up. Insert in manicotti shells; arrange in a single layer in baking dish.

3. Pour remaining sauce over top. Sprinkle with olives and Parmesan cheese. Bake, uncovered, 25-30 minutes or until heated through.

FREEZE OPTION *Cover unbaked casserole and freeze for up to 3 months. Thaw in the refrigerator overnight. Remove from the refrigerator 30 minutes before baking. Cover and bake at 375° for 25-30 minutes or until pasta is tender. Let stand for 10 minutes before serving.*

PER SERVING *2 stuffed manicotti: 618 cal., 32g fat (15g sat. fat), 87mg chol., 2427mg sod., 43g carb. (13g sugars, 4g fiber), 40g pro.*

HAM & SWISS
BAKED PENNE

FAST FIX

HAM & SWISS BAKED PENNE

As a kid I loved to the hot ham and Swiss sandwiches from a local fast-food restaurant. This melty bake makes me think of them.

—ALLY BILLHORN WILTON, IA

START TO FINISH: 30 MIN.
MAKES: 6 SERVINGS

- 2⅔ cups uncooked penne pasta
- 3 tablespoons butter
- 3 tablespoons all-purpose flour
- 2 cups 2% milk
- 1 cup half-and-half cream
- 1½ cups shredded Swiss cheese
- ½ cup shredded Colby cheese
- 2 cups cubed fully cooked ham

TOPPING
- ¼ cup seasoned bread crumbs
- ¼ cup grated Parmesan cheese
- 2 tablespoons butter, melted

1. Preheat oven to 375°. Cook pasta according to package directions for al dente; drain.

2. Meanwhile, in a large saucepan, melt 3 tablespoons butter over medium heat. Stir in flour until smooth; gradually whisk in milk and cream. Bring to a boil, stirring constantly; cook and stir 1-2 minutes or until thickened. Gradually stir in Swiss and Colby cheeses until melted. Add ham and pasta, toss to coat.

3. Transfer to a greased 11x7-in. baking dish. In a small bowl, mix the topping ingredients; sprinkle over pasta. Bake, uncovered, 15-20 minutes or until bubbly.

PER SERVING *1 cup: 559 cal., 30g fat (18g sat. fat), 116mg chol., 905mg sod., 41g carb. (7g sugars, 2g fiber), 31g pro.*

**CREOLE PORK
TENDERLOIN WITH
VEGETABLES**

5 INGREDIENTS

ROSEMARY MARINATED PORK CHOPS

I use fresh rosemary and wine to marinate pork chops. It takes time, so plan ahead. The chops are excellent with noodles tossed in parsley.

—JANE WHITTAKER PENSACOLA, FL

PREP: 10 MIN. + MARINATING • **BAKE:** 20 MIN.
MAKES: 4 SERVINGS

- 1 cup reduced-sodium teriyaki sauce
- ¾ cup sweet white wine
- ¼ cup packed brown sugar
- 2 tablespoons minced fresh rosemary or 2 teaspoons dried rosemary, crushed
- 4 bone-in pork loin chops (1 inch thick and 10 ounces each)

1. In a 13x9-in. baking dish, mix teriyaki sauce, wine, brown sugar and rosemary until blended. Add pork; turn to coat. Refrigerate, covered, at least 4 hours.

2. Remove from refrigerator 30 minutes before baking. Preheat oven to 350°.

3. Bake 20-25 minutes or until a thermometer reads 145°. Let stand 5 minutes before serving.

PER SERVING *1 pork chop with ½ cup sauce: 549 cal., 23g fat (9g sat. fat), 139mg chol., 1382mg sod., 27g carb. (26g sugars, 0 fiber), 49g pro.*

EAT SMART

CREOLE PORK TENDERLOIN WITH VEGETABLES

Fresh summer vegetables are paired with lean pork and tasty Greek olives for a healthy and quick dinner that's great for family or friends.

—JUDY ARMSTRONG PRAIRIEVILLE, LA

PREP: 30 MIN. • **BAKE:** 20 MIN.
MAKES: 8 SERVINGS

- 3½ teaspoons reduced-sodium Creole seasoning, divided
- 2 pork tenderloins (1 pound each)
- 2 tablespoons canola oil
- 2 medium fennel bulbs, trimmed and cut into 1-inch wedges
- 1 medium eggplant, cut into 1-inch cubes
- 2 medium yellow summer squash, halved and cut into ½-inch slices
- 1 large sweet red pepper, cut into 1-inch pieces
- 2 shallots, thinly sliced
- ½ cup pitted Greek olives, coarsely chopped
- 3 garlic cloves, minced
- ½ cup vegetable broth
- 4 teaspoons minced fresh thyme or 1¼ teaspoons dried thyme

1. Preheat oven to 350°. Sprinkle 3 teaspoons Creole seasoning over tenderloins. In a 6-qt. stockpot, heat oil over medium-high heat. Brown tenderloins on all sides. Transfer to a roasting pan.

2. Add fennel, eggplant, squash, pepper and shallots to stockpot; cook and stir over medium heat 3-4 minutes or until lightly browned. Add olives and garlic; cook and stir 1 minute longer. Stir in broth, thyme and remaining Creole seasoning; bring to a boil. Reduce heat; simmer, covered, 6-8 minutes or until fennel is crisp-tender. Spoon vegetables and liquid around pork.

3. Bake, uncovered, 20-25 minutes or until vegetables are tender and a thermometer inserted in pork reads 145°. Let stand 5 minutes before serving. Cut pork into slices; serve with vegetables.

PER SERVING *3 ounces cooked pork with 1 cup vegetables: 247 cal., 10g fat (2g sat. fat), 64mg chol., 575mg sod., 15g carb. (7g sugars, 5g fiber), 25g pro.* **Diabetic Exchanges:** *3 lean meat, 2 vegetable, 1 fat.*

QUESO PORK ENCHILADAS

My husband took these restaurant-style enchiladas to work, and now the guys always ask for them. They're rich and spicy, and you can prepare them with cooked chicken or beef as well.

—ANNA RODRIGUEZ BETHPAGE, NY

PREP: 30 MIN. • **BAKE:** 30 MIN.
MAKES: 6 SERVINGS

- 1 jar (15½ ounces) salsa con queso dip, divided
- 1 can (10 ounces) enchilada sauce, divided
- 1 can (4 ounces) chopped green chilies
- ⅓ cup water
- 2 tablespoons reduced-sodium taco seasoning
- 4 cups cubed cooked boneless country-style pork ribs (from 2 pounds boneless ribs)
- 12 flour tortillas (6 inches), warmed
- 2½ cups shredded Mexican cheese blend, divided
  Shredded lettuce and chopped tomatoes, optional

1. In a large skillet, combine ¾ cup queso dip, ½ cup enchilada sauce, green chilies, water and taco seasoning. Bring to a boil. Reduce heat; simmer, uncovered, for 3 minutes.

2. Spread ⅔ cup sauce mixture into a greased 13x9-in. baking dish. Stir pork into remaining sauce mixture. Place ⅓ cup pork mixture down the center of each tortilla; top with 2 tablespoons cheese. Roll up and place seam side down in prepared dish. Combine remaining queso dip and enchilada sauce; pour over enchiladas.

3. Cover and bake at 350° for 20 minutes. Uncover; sprinkle with remaining cheese. Bake 10-15 minutes longer or until heated through. Serve with lettuce and tomatoes if desired.

FREEZE OPTION *Sprinkle remaining cheese over unbaked casserole. Cover and freeze. To use, partially thaw in refrigerator overnight. Remove from refrigerator 30 minutes before baking. Preheat oven to 350°. Bake casserole as directed, increasing time as necessary to heat through and for a thermometer inserted in center to read 165°.*

PER SERVING *2 enchiladas (calculated without optional ingredients): 705 cal., 41g fat (17g sat. fat), 139mg chol., 1951mg sod., 44g carb. (3g sugars, 3g fiber), 45g pro.*

QUESO PORK ENCHILADAS

TOP TIP

SOFTENING TORTILLAS

If your flour tortillas are too stiff to roll into burritos, enchiladas or veggie wraps, place them between two damp paper towels and warm them in the microwave oven. Check the tortillas every few seconds and remove them when they are soft and pliable.

—KAREN ANN BLAND GOVE, KS

**LIGHT HAM
TETRAZZINI, PAGE 281**

MOM'S SCALLOPED POTATOES AND HAM, PAGE 295

SLOW-COOKED STAPLES

Pork and slow cookers are a perfect match! Pork's mild taste plays well with all the **great flavors** that slow-cooking brings out, from rich and hearty to bright and spicy. Try these **sauces, sandwiches, roasts and more**—all featuring the incredible convenience and fabulous flavors of slow-cooked foods.

PULLED PORK WITH GINGER SAUCE, PAGE 288

PORK ROAST CUBANO, PAGE 285

PORK

SLOW COOKER
TROPICAL
PORK CHOPS

SLOW COOKER TROPICAL PORK CHOPS

Pork and fruit go so nicely together. When you add fresh herbs, you get this fresh, light and bright main dish that everyone loves.

—ROXANNE CHAN ALBANY, CA

PREP: 15 MIN. • **COOK:** 3 HOURS
MAKES: 4 SERVINGS

- 2 jars (23½ ounces each) mixed tropical fruit, drained and chopped
- ¾ cup thawed limeade concentrate
- ¼ cup sweet chili sauce
- 1 garlic clove, minced
- 1 teaspoon minced fresh gingerroot
- 4 bone-in pork loin chops (¾ inch thick and 5 ounces each)
- 1 green onion, finely chopped
- 2 tablespoons minced fresh cilantro
- 2 tablespoons minced fresh mint
- 2 tablespoons slivered almonds, toasted
- 2 tablespoons finely chopped crystallized ginger, optional
- ½ teaspoon grated lime peel

1. In a 3-qt. slow cooker, combine the first five ingredients. Add pork, arranging chops to sit snugly in fruit mixture. Cook, covered, on low 3-4 hours or until meat is tender (a thermometer inserted in pork should read at least 145°).

2. In a small bowl, mix remaining ingredients. To serve, remove pork chops from slow cooker. Using a slotted spoon, serve fruit over pork. Sprinkle with herb mixture.

NOTE *To toast nuts, place in a dry nonstick skillet and heat over low heat until lightly browned, stirring occasionally.*

PER SERVING *(calculated without crystallized ginger)*: *572 cal., 13g fat (4g sat. fat), 69mg chol., 326mg sod., 91g carb. (86g sugars, 3g fiber), 24g pro.*

EAT SMART
LIGHT HAM TETRAZZINI
(PICTURED ON PAGE 278)

This creamy pasta is an easy way to serve a hungry crowd. If you're taking this to a potluck, cook and add the spaghetti to the slow cooker just before heading out.
—**SUSAN BLAIR** STERLING, MI

PREP: 15 MIN. • **COOK:** 4 HOURS
MAKES: 10 SERVINGS

- 2 cans (10¾ ounces each) reduced-fat reduced-sodium condensed cream of mushroom soup, undiluted
- 2 cups cubed fully cooked ham
- 2 cups sliced fresh mushrooms
- 1 cup fat-free evaporated milk
- ¼ cup white wine or water
- 2 teaspoons prepared horseradish
- 1 package (14½ ounces) multigrain spaghetti
- 1 cup shredded Parmesan cheese

1. In a 5-qt. slow cooker, mix the first six ingredients. Cook, covered, on low for 4-5 hours or until heated through.
2. To serve, cook spaghetti according to package directions; drain. Add spaghetti and Parmesan cheese to slow cooker; toss to combine.
PER SERVING *1 cup: 279 cal., 5g fat (2g sat. fat), 26mg chol., 734mg sod., 37g carb. (5g sugars, 4g fiber), 20g pro.* **Diabetic Exchanges:** *2½ starch, 1 lean meat, ½ fat.*

TOP TIP
PASTA TIPS

Many people add oil to the pot when cooking pasta in order to keep the pasta from clumping and sticking; however, the oily residue left on the cooked pasta can make the sauce slide off and make the dish difficult to eat. Instead, just remember to stir the pasta as you add it to the water, and stir several times while it cooks. This will help to separate the strands.

SPICY SAUSAGE FETTUCCINE

SPICY SAUSAGE FETTUCCINE
One time, I accidentally bought hot Italian sausage instead of mild, but wanted to find a way to use it anyway. I tossed it in the slow cooker with mushrooms, tomatoes and wine, which helped to mellow out the heat. Now I buy the hot stuff on purpose!
—**JUDY BATSON** TAMPA, FL

PREP: 25 MIN. • **COOK:** 6 HOURS
MAKES: 8 SERVINGS

- 2 teaspoons canola oil
- 8 hot Italian sausage links
- ½ pound sliced fresh mushrooms
- 1 small sweet onion, chopped
- 2 garlic cloves, minced
- 1 can (14½ ounces) diced tomatoes with mild green chilies, undrained
- ½ cup beef stock
- ½ cup dry white wine or additional stock
- 1 package (12 ounces) fettuccine or tagliatelle
  Grated Parmesan cheese, optional

1. In a large skillet, heat oil over medium heat; brown sausage links on all sides. Transfer to a 3-qt. slow cooker, reserving drippings in pan.
2. In the same skillet, saute mushrooms and onion in the drippings over medium heat until tender, 4-5 minutes. Stir in garlic; cook and stir 1 minute. Stir in the tomatoes, stock and wine; pour over the sausages. Cook, covered, on low 6-8 hours (a thermometer inserted in sausages should read at least 160°).
3. To serve, cook fettuccine according to package directions; drain. Remove the sausages from slow cooker; cut into thick slices.
4. Skim fat from the mushroom mixture. Add the fettuccine and sausage; toss to combine. Serve in bowls. If desired, top with cheese.
PER SERVING *1⅓ cups: 440 cal., 25g fat (7g sat. fat), 57mg chol., 817mg sod., 37g carb., 3g fiber, 19g pro.*

COUNTRY RIBS
DINNER

COUNTRY RIBS DINNER

This is my favorite recipe for a classic rib dinner. It's always a treat for my family when I serve this up!

—**ROSE INGALL** MANISTEE, MI

PREP: 10 MIN. • **COOK:** 6¼ HOURS
MAKES: 4 SERVINGS

- 2 **pounds boneless country-style pork ribs**
- ½ **teaspoon salt**
- ¼ **teaspoon pepper**
- 8 **small red potatoes (about 1 pound), halved**
- 4 **medium carrots, cut into 1-inch pieces**
- 3 **celery ribs, cut into ½-inch pieces**
- 1 **medium onion, coarsely chopped**
- ¾ **cup water**
- 1 **garlic clove, crushed**
- 1 **can (10¾ ounces) condensed cream of mushroom soup, undiluted**

1. Sprinkle ribs with salt and pepper; transfer to a 4-qt. slow cooker. Add the potatoes, carrots, celery, onion, water and garlic. Cook, covered, on low 6-8 hours or until meat and vegetables are tender.
2. Remove the meat and vegetables; skim fat from the cooking juices. Whisk soup into cooking juices; return the meat and vegetables to slow cooker. Cook, covered, for 15-30 minutes longer or until heated through.

PER SERVING *5 ounces cooked meat with 1 cup vegetables and ¼ cup gravy: 528 cal., 25g fat (8g sat. fat), 134mg chol., 1016mg sod., 30g carb. (6g sugars, 6g fiber), 43g pro.*

SLOW-SIMMERING PASTA SAUCE

SLOW-SIMMERING PASTA SAUCE

Spaghetti with sauce is my kids' top pick for dinner. Through trial and error, I came up with my own recipe. This is the winning result.

—**SAMANTHA VICARS** KENOSHA, WI

PREP: 20 MIN. • **COOK:** 6 HOURS
MAKES: 6 SERVINGS

- 1 **pound bulk Italian sausage**
- 1 **medium onion, chopped**
- 3 **garlic cloves, minced**
- 2 **cans (14½ ounces each) diced tomatoes, undrained**
- 1 **can (8 ounces) tomato sauce**
- 1 **can (6 ounces) tomato paste**
- 1 **tablespoon brown sugar**
- 2 **bay leaves**
- 2 **teaspoons dried oregano**
- 2 **teaspoons dried basil**
- 1 **teaspoon salt**
- ½ **teaspoon dried thyme**
- ¼ **cup minced fresh basil, divided**
  Hot cooked pasta

1. In a large skillet, cook sausage and onion over medium heat for 7-8 minutes or until the sausage is no longer pink and the onion is tender. Add garlic; cook 1 minute longer. Drain. Transfer to a 3-qt. slow cooker.
2. Stir in tomatoes, tomato sauce, tomato paste, brown sugar, bay leaves, oregano, dried basil, salt and thyme. Cover and cook on low for 6-8 hours.
3. Discard the bay leaves; stir in half the fresh basil. Serve with pasta. Top with the remaining basil.

PER SERVING *1 cup (calculated without pasta): 327 cal., 20g fat (8g sat. fat), 53mg chol., 1392mg sod., 22g carb. (13g sugars, 4g fiber), 17g pro.*

SPINACH AND SAUSAGE LASAGNA

Dig into rich layers of home-style lasagna featuring plenty of Italian sausage and gooey cheeses. No-cook noodles, frozen spinach and jarred spaghetti sauce simplify the prep, but the result tastes far from ordinary.

—KATHY MORROW HUBBARD, OH

PREP: 25 MIN. • **COOK:** 3 HOURS
MAKES: 8 SERVINGS

- 1 **pound bulk Italian sausage**
- 1 **jar (24 ounces) garden-style spaghetti sauce**
- ½ **cup water**
- 1 **teaspoon Italian seasoning**
- ½ **teaspoon salt**
- 1 **carton (15 ounces) ricotta cheese**
- 1 **package (10 ounces) frozen chopped spinach, thawed and squeezed dry**
- 2 **cups shredded part-skim mozzarella cheese, divided**
- 9 **no-cook lasagna noodles**
   Grated Parmesan cheese

1. Cook sausage in a large skillet over medium heat until no longer pink; drain. Stir in spaghetti sauce, water, Italian seasoning and salt. Combine ricotta, spinach and 1 cup mozzarella cheese in a small bowl.

2. Spread 1 cup of the sauce mixture in a greased oval 5-qt. slow cooker. Layer with three noodles (break noodles if necessary to fit), 1¼ cups sauce mixture and half of the cheese mixture. Repeat layers. Layer with the remaining noodles and sauce mixture; sprinkle with the remaining mozzarella cheese.

3. Cover and cook on low for 3-4 hours or until the noodles are tender. Sprinkle servings with Parmesan cheese.

PER SERVING *1 piece (calculated without Parmesan cheese): 456 cal., 26g fat (11g sat. fat), 70mg chol., 1101mg sod., 33g carb. (11g sugars, 3g fiber), 24g pro.*

SLOW COOKER PEACH BBQ RIBS

SLOW COOKER PEACH BBQ RIBS

For eat-the-whole-rack ribs, start with a rub of chili powder, cumin, paprika and cayenne. Then slather on sweet peachy sauce and keep the napkins coming!

—SUE RYON SHOREWOOD, WI

PREP: 10 MIN. • **COOK:** 5 HOURS
MAKES: 8 SERVINGS (3 CUPS SAUCE)

- 2 **tablespoons chili powder**
- 1 **tablespoon brown sugar**
- 2 **teaspoons ground cumin**
- 2 **teaspoons smoked paprika**
- 2 **teaspoons garlic salt**
- ½ **teaspoon cayenne pepper**
- 4 **pounds pork baby back ribs, cut into serving-size pieces**

SAUCE

- 3 **medium ripe peaches, peeled and chopped**
- 1 **bottle (18 ounces) barbecue sauce**
- ¼ **cup water**
- 1 **jalapeno pepper, thinly sliced**

1. In a small bowl, mix seasonings; rub over meaty side of ribs. Place in a 6-qt. slow cooker. Cook, covered, on low for 5-6 hours or until the meat is tender.

2. Before serving, combine peaches, barbecue sauce and water in a saucepan; bring to a boil. Reduce heat; simmer, covered, 15-20 minutes or until peaches are softened, stirring occasionally. If desired, thin with additional water. Stir in jalapeno. Serve with ribs.

NOTE *These taste amazing even without the sauce, which contributes most of the sodium. Skip the sauce and use 1 teaspoon garlic powder for the 2 teaspoons garlic salt, and sodium falls to 150 milligrams.*

PER SERVING *431 cal., 22g fat (8g sat. fat), 81mg chol., 1048mg sod., 35g carb. (28g sugars, 3g fiber), 24g pro.*

CONGA LIME PORK

Dinner guests won't be too shy to get in line when you set this yummy pork in chipotle and molasses sauce on the buffet table.

—**JANICE ELDER** CHARLOTTE, NC

PREP: 20 MIN. • **COOK:** 4 HOURS
MAKES: 6 SERVINGS

- 1 **teaspoon salt, divided**
- ½ **teaspoon pepper, divided**
- 1 **boneless pork shoulder butt roast (2 to 3 pounds)**
- 1 **tablespoon canola oil**
- 1 **large onion, chopped**
- 3 **garlic cloves, peeled and thinly sliced**
- ½ **cup water**
- 2 **chipotle peppers in adobo sauce, seeded and chopped**
- 2 **tablespoons molasses**
- 2 **cups broccoli coleslaw mix**
- 1 **medium mango, peeled and chopped**
- 2 **tablespoons lime juice**
- 1½ **teaspoons grated lime peel**
- 6 **prepared corn muffins, halved**

1. Sprinkle ¾ teaspoon salt and ¼ teaspoon pepper over roast. In a large skillet, brown pork in oil on all sides. Transfer meat to a 3- or 4-qt. slow cooker.

2. In the same skillet, saute onion until tender. Add garlic; cook 1 minute longer. Add the water, chipotle peppers and molasses, stirring to loosen browned bits from pan. Pour over the pork. Cover and cook on high for 4-5 hours or until the meat is tender.

3. Remove roast; cool slightly. Skim fat from cooking juices. Shred the pork with two forks and return to the slow cooker; heat through. In a large bowl, combine coleslaw mix, mango, lime juice, lime peel and remaining salt and pepper.

4. Place muffin halves cut-side down on an ungreased baking sheet. Broil 4 in. from the heat for 2-3 minutes or until lightly toasted. Serve pork with muffins; top with slaw.

PER SERVING *⅔ cup pork mixture with 1 muffin and ½ cup slaw: 514 cal., 23g fat (7g sat. fat), 135mg chol., 877mg sod., 46g carb. (21g sugars, 3g fiber), 31g pro.*

PORK ROAST CUBANO
(PICTURED ON PAGE 279)

It takes just minutes to prepare this recipe, and the slow cooker does the rest of the work. It's a one-dish meal that's real comfort food for my family.

—**ROXANNE CHAN** ALBANY, CA

PREP: 30 MIN. • **COOK:** 7 HOURS
MAKES: 8 SERVINGS

- 3 **pounds boneless pork shoulder butt roast**
- 2 **tablespoons olive oil**
- 1 **can (15 ounces) black beans, rinsed and drained**
- 1 **medium sweet potato, cut into ½-inch cubes**
- 1 **small sweet red pepper, cubed**
- 1 **can (13.66 ounces) light coconut milk**
- ½ **cup salsa verde**
- 1 **teaspoon minced fresh gingerroot**
- 2 **green onions, thinly sliced**
  Sliced papaya

1. In a large skillet, brown roast in oil on all sides. Transfer to a 5-qt. slow cooker. Add black beans, sweet potato and red pepper. In a small bowl, mix coconut milk, salsa and ginger; pour over top.

2. Cook, covered, on low 7-9 hours or until the pork is tender. Sprinkle with green onions; serve with papaya.

PER SERVING *6 ounces cooked pork with ¾ cup vegetables: 430 cal., 24g fat (9g sat. fat), 101mg chol., 322mg sod., 18g carb. (6g sugars, 5g fiber), 33g pro.*

CONGA LIME PORK

CANTONESE SWEET-AND-SOUR PORK

Step away from the takeout menu. You'll have no reason to dial up delivery once you get a bite of this take on traditional sweet-and-sour pork. The tender vegetables, juicy meat and flavorful sauce are delicious over rice.

—NANCY TEWS ANTIGO, WI

PREP: 20 MIN. • **COOK:** 7½ HOURS
MAKES: 6 SERVINGS

- 1 **can (15 ounces) tomato sauce**
- 1 **medium onion, halved and sliced**
- 1 **medium green pepper, cut into strips**
- 1 **can (4½ ounces) sliced mushrooms, drained**
- 3 **tablespoons brown sugar**
- 4½ **teaspoons white vinegar**
- 2 **teaspoons steak sauce**
- 1 **teaspoon salt**
- 1½ **pounds pork tenderloin, cut into 1-inch cubes**
- 1 **tablespoon olive oil**
- 1 **can (8 ounces) unsweetened pineapple chunks, drained**
  Hot cooked rice

1. In a large bowl, combine the first eight ingredients; set aside.

2. In a large skillet, working in batches, brown pork in oil. Transfer to a 3- or 4-qt. slow cooker. Pour tomato sauce mixture over pork. Cover and cook on low for 7-8 hours or until meat is tender.

3. Add pineapple; cover and cook 30 minutes longer or until heated through. Serve with rice.

PER SERVING *1 cup (calculated without rice): 231 cal., 6g fat (2g sat. fat), 63mg chol., 889mg sod., 19g carb. (14g sugars, 2g fiber), 25g pro.*

CANTONESE
SWEET-AND-SOUR
PORK

HAM WITH CRANBERRY-PINEAPPLE SAUCE

Bookmark this dish for when you crave the mouthwatering combo of cranberry, pineapple and stone-ground mustard served with thick slices of smoky boneless ham.
—**CAROLE RESNICK** CLEVELAND, OH

PREP: 15 MIN. • **COOK:** 5 HOURS
MAKES: 20 SERVINGS (4½ CUPS SAUCE)

- 1 **fully cooked boneless ham (5 to 6 pounds)**
- 12 **whole cloves**
- 1 **can (20 ounces) crushed pineapple, undrained**
- 1 **can (14 ounces) whole-berry cranberry sauce**
- 2 **garlic cloves, minced**
- 2 **tablespoons stone-ground mustard**
- ½ **teaspoon coarsely ground pepper**
- 2 **tablespoons cornstarch**
- 2 **tablespoons cold water**

1. Score the ham, making ½-in.-deep diamond shapes; insert a clove in each diamond. Place ham in a 5-qt. slow cooker. In a large bowl, combine the pineapple, cranberry sauce, garlic, mustard and pepper; pour over ham.
2. Cover and cook on low for 5-6 hours or until a thermometer reads 140°. Remove the meat to a cutting board and keep warm; remove and discard the cloves.
3. Transfer sauce to a small saucepan. Bring to a boil. Combine cornstarch and water until smooth; gradually add to pan, stirring constantly. Bring to a boil; cook and stir for 2 minutes or until thickened. Slice ham and serve with sauce.
PER SERVING *4 ounces ham with 3 tablespoons sauce: 176 cal., 4g fat (1g sat. fat), 58mg chol., 1218mg sod., 14g carb. (10g sugars, 1g fiber), 21g pro.*

PULLED PORK NACHOS

PULLED PORK NACHOS

While home from college, my daughter made these tempting pork nachos—her first recipe ever. My son and I couldn't get enough.
—**CAROL KURPJUWEIT** HUMANSVILLE, MO

PREP: 30 MIN. • **COOK:** 8 HOURS
MAKES: 16 SERVINGS

- 1 **teaspoon garlic powder**
- 1 **teaspoon mesquite seasoning**
- ¼ **teaspoon pepper**
- ⅛ **teaspoon celery salt**
- 3 **pounds boneless pork shoulder butt roast**
- 1 **medium green pepper, chopped**
- 1 **medium sweet red pepper, chopped**
- 1 **medium onion, chopped**
- 1 **can (16 ounces) baked beans**
- 1 **cup barbecue sauce**
- 1 **cup shredded cheddar cheese**
  Corn or tortilla chips
  Optional toppings: chopped tomatoes, shredded lettuce and chopped green onions

1. In a small bowl, mix seasoning ingredients. Place roast in a 5- or 6-qt. slow cooker; rub with seasonings. Add peppers and onion. Cook, covered, on low 8-10 hours.
2. Remove roast; cool slightly. Strain cooking juices, reserving vegetables and ½ cup juices; discard the remaining juices. Skim fat from the reserved juices. Shred pork with two forks.
3. Return the pork, reserved juices and vegetables to slow cooker. Stir in beans, barbecue sauce and cheese; heat through. Serve over chips; top as desired.
 FREEZE OPTION *Freeze cooled pork mixture in freezer containers. To use, partially thaw in refrigerator overnight. Heat through in a saucepan, stirring occasionally and adding a little broth or water if necessary.*
PER SERVING *½ cup pork mixture (calculated without chips and toppings): 233 cal., 11g fat (5g sat. fat), 60mg chol., 416mg sod., 14g carb. (6g sugars, 2g fiber), 18g pro.*

**HAM AND
BEAN STEW**

PORK

PULLED PORK WITH GINGER SAUCE

(PICTURED ON PAGE 279)

It's almost sacrilegious for a South Carolinian from the capitol city to make a pulled pork sauce that isn't mustard-based—but we love this Asian-inspired ginger sauce. Wonderful in a sandwich, it's also great over rice.

—MARY MARLOWE LEVERETTE
COLUMBIA, SC

PREP: 20 MIN. • **COOK:** 7 HOURS
MAKES: 6 SERVINGS

- 2 **medium onions, chopped**
- 1 **boneless pork shoulder butt roast (3 pounds), trimmed**
- 1 **teaspoon salt**
- ½ **teaspoon pepper**
- 1 **cup ketchup**
- 3 **tablespoons lemon juice**
- 2 **tablespoons Worcestershire sauce**
- 2 **tablespoons honey**
- 4 **teaspoons butter, melted**
- 1 **teaspoon ground coriander**
- 1 **teaspoon minced fresh gingerroot**
  Thinly sliced green onions
  Hamburger buns, split

1. Place onions in a 4- or 5-qt. slow cooker. Sprinkle roast with salt and pepper; place over onions. Cook, covered, on low 6-8 hours or until pork is tender.
2. Remove pork and onions; cool slightly. Discard cooking juices or save for another use. Shred pork with two forks. Return pork and onions to slow cooker.
3. In a small bowl, whisk ketchup, lemon juice, Worcestershire sauce, honey, butter, coriander and ginger until blended. Stir into the pork mixture. Cook, covered, on low for 1 hour longer. Sprinkle with sliced green onions; serve on buns.
PER SERVING *1 cup (calculated without buns): 479 cal., 25g fat (10g sat. fat), 141mg chol., 1115mg sod., 23g carb. (20g sugars, 1g fiber), 39g pro.*

⑤INGREDIENTS
HAM AND BEAN STEW
You need only five ingredients to fix this thick and flavorful stew. It's so easy to make and always a favorite with my family. I top the bowls with a sprinkling of shredded cheese.
—TERESA D'AMATO EAST GRANBY, CT

PREP: 5 MIN. • **COOK:** 7 HOURS
MAKES: 6 SERVINGS

- 2 **cans (16 ounces each) baked beans**
- 2 **medium potatoes, peeled and cubed**
- 2 **cups cubed fully cooked ham**
- 1 **celery rib, chopped**
- ½ **cup water**

In a 3-qt. slow cooker, combine all ingredients; mix well. Cover and cook on low for 7 hours or until the potatoes are tender.
PER SERVING *1 cup: 213 cal., 5g fat (2g sat. fat), 30mg chol., 919mg sod., 29g carb. (6g sugars, 5g fiber), 14g pro.*

EAT SMART
CARNE GUISADA

After moving to Michigan, my boyfriend and I grew homesick for the spicy flavors we love. Served with homemade flour tortillas or over rice, this recipe takes us back to Texas.

—KELLY EVANS DENTON, TX

PREP: 25 MIN. • **COOK:** 7 HOURS
MAKES: 12 SERVINGS (ABOUT 2 QUARTS)

- 1 **bottle (12 ounces) beer**
- ¼ **cup all-purpose flour**
- 2 **tablespoons tomato paste**
- 1 **jalapeno pepper, seeded and chopped**
- 4 **teaspoons Worcestershire sauce**
- 1 **bay leaf**
- 2 **to 3 teaspoons crushed red pepper flakes**
- 2 **teaspoons chili powder**
- 1½ **teaspoons ground cumin**
- ½ **teaspoon salt**
- ½ **teaspoon paprika**
- 2 **garlic cloves, minced**
- ½ **teaspoon red wine vinegar**
  Dash liquid smoke, optional
- 1 **boneless pork shoulder butt roast (3 pounds), cut into 2-inch pieces**
- 2 **large unpeeled red potatoes, chopped**
- 1 **medium onion, chopped**
  Lime wedges, chopped fresh cilantro, and whole wheat tortillas or hot cooked brown rice, optional

1. In a 4- or 5-qt. slow cooker, mix first 13 ingredients and, if desired, liquid smoke. Stir in pork, potatoes and onion. Cook, covered, on low until pork is tender, 7-9 hours.

2. Discard the bay leaf; skim fat from the cooking juices. Shred pork slightly with two forks. Serve with remaining ingredients as desired.

NOTE *Wear disposable gloves when cutting hot peppers; the oils can burn skin. Avoid touching your face.*

PER SERVING ⅔ *cup: 261 cal., 12g fat (1g sat. fat), 67mg chol., 200mg sod., 16g carb. (3g sugars, 2g fiber), 21g pro.*
Diabetic Exchanges: *3 medium-fat meat, 1 starch.*

CARNE GUISADA

**EASY AND
ELEGANT HAM**

EASY AND ELEGANT HAM

I love to serve my large family this moist, tender ham. It tastes outstanding, frees up my oven, feeds a crowd and can be readied quickly in the morning. Pineapple, cherries and a delicious orange glaze make it a real showstopper.

—**DENISE DIPACE** MEDFORD, NJ

PREP: 5 MIN. • **COOK:** 6 HOURS
MAKES: 18-20 SERVINGS

- 2 cans (20 ounces each) sliced pineapple
- 1 fully cooked boneless ham (about 6 pounds), cut in half
- 1 jar (6 ounces) maraschino cherries, well drained
- 1 jar (12 ounces) orange marmalade

1. Drain pineapple, reserving juice; set juice aside. Place half of the pineapple in an ungreased 6-qt. slow cooker. Top with ham pieces. Add cherries, the remaining pineapple and reserved pineapple juice. Spoon marmalade over ham. Cover and cook on low for 6-7 hours or until heated through.
2. Remove to a warm platter. Serve pineapple and cherries with sliced ham.
PER SERVING *5 ounces: 212 cal., 5g fat (2g sat. fat), 69mg chol., 1424mg sod., 18g carb. (18g sugars, 0 fiber), 25g pro.*

TOP TIP

RELISH YOUR LEFTOVERS

If you have leftover ham, you can use it to make a tasty spread. Cut the leftover ham into chunks, then grind it in a food processor along with an onion and a few celery ribs. Add yellow mustard, mayonnaise and sweet pepper relish. Serve on bread, crackers or a lettuce leaf— or stuff it into a tomato!

—**DOROTHY L.** ENGLEWOOD, FL

MEAT-LOVER'S PIZZA HOT DISH

I make this hearty casserole for the men who help us out during harvest time. Every year, they say it's the best—hands down. Feel free to throw in any pizza toppings your family likes.

—BROOK BOTHUN CANBY, MN

PREP: 25 MIN. • **COOK:** 3¼ HOURS
MAKES: 10 SERVINGS

- 1 **pound ground beef**
- 1 **pound bulk Italian sausage**
- 1 **medium onion, chopped**
- 1 **cup sliced fresh mushrooms**
- 4 **cans (8 ounces each) no-salt-added tomato sauce**
- 2 **cans (15 ounces each) pizza sauce**
- 1 **package (16 ounces) penne pasta**
- 1 **cup water**
- 1 **can (6 ounces) tomato paste**
- 1 **package (3½ ounces) sliced pepperoni**
- 1 **teaspoon Italian seasoning**
- 2 **cups shredded part-skim mozzarella cheese, divided**
- 2 **cups shredded cheddar cheese, divided**

1. In a large skillet, cook beef, sausage, onion and mushrooms over medium heat 10-12 minutes or until meat is no longer pink and vegetables are tender, breaking up meat into crumbles; drain.

2. Transfer meat mixture to a greased 6-qt. slow cooker. Stir in tomato sauce, pizza sauce, pasta, water, tomato paste, pepperoni and Italian seasoning. Cook, covered, on low 3-4 hours or until pasta is tender.

3. Stir thoroughly; mix in 1 cup mozzarella cheese and 1 cup cheddar cheese. Sprinkle remaining cheese over top. Cook, covered, 15-20 minutes longer or until cheese is melted.

PER SERVING *1⅓ cups: 653 cal., 35g fat (14g sat. fat), 99mg chol., 1482mg sod., 52g carb. (9g sugars, 6g fiber), 36g pro.*

PORK TACOS WITH MANGO SALSA

PORK TACOS WITH MANGO SALSA

I've made quite a few tacos in my day, but you can't beat the tender filling made in a slow cooker. These are by far the best pork tacos we've had—and we've tried plenty. Make the mango salsa from scratch if you have time. Yum!

—AMBER MASSEY ARGYLE, TX

PREP: 25 MIN. • **COOK:** 6 HOURS
MAKES: 12 SERVINGS

- 2 **tablespoons lime juice**
- 2 **tablespoons white vinegar**
- 3 **tablespoons chili powder**
- 2 **teaspoons ground cumin**
- 1½ **teaspoons salt**
- ½ **teaspoon pepper**
- 3 **cups cubed fresh pineapple**
- 1 **small red onion, coarsely chopped**
- 2 **chipotle peppers in adobo sauce**
- 1 **bottle (12 ounces) dark Mexican beer**
- 3 **pounds pork tenderloin, cut into 1-inch cubes**
- ¼ **cup chopped fresh cilantro**
- 1 **jar (16 ounces) mango salsa**
  Corn tortillas (6 inches), warmed

OPTIONAL TOPPINGS
  Cubed fresh pineapple
  Cubed avocado
  Queso fresco

1. Puree first nine ingredients in a blender; stir in beer. In a 5- or 6-qt. slow cooker, combine pork and the pineapple mixture. Cook, covered, on low until pork is very tender, 6-8 hours. Stir to break up the pork.

2. Stir cilantro into salsa. Using a slotted spoon, serve the pork mixture in tortillas; add salsa and top as desired.

FREEZE OPTION *Freeze cooled meat mixture and cooking juices in freezer containers. To use, partially thaw in refrigerator overnight. Heat through in a saucepan, stirring occasionally.*

PER SERVING *⅔ cup pork mixture with 2 tablespoons salsa: 178 cal., 4g fat (1g sat. fat), 64mg chol., 656mg sod., 9g carb., 2g fiber, 23g pro.* **Diabetic Exchanges:** *3 lean meat, ½ starch.*

LOW & SLOW
PORK VERDE

LOW & SLOW PORK VERDE

My family loves this versatile pork dish. We like to serve it over cheesy grits, but it also goes well with rice or potatoes. Leftovers make an excellent starter for white chili.

—**VAL RUBLE** AVA, MO

PREP: 15 MIN. • **COOK:** 5 HOURS
MAKES: 8 SERVINGS

- 1 boneless pork shoulder butt roast (3½ to 4 pounds)
- 1 large onion, chopped
- 1 jar (16 ounces) salsa verde
- 2 cans (4 ounces each) chopped green chilies
- 2 teaspoons ground cumin
- 1 teaspoon dried oregano
- 1 teaspoon salt
- 1 teaspoon pepper
- ¼ teaspoon crushed red pepper flakes
- ⅛ teaspoon ground cinnamon
- ¼ cup minced fresh cilantro
  Hot cooked grits
  Sour cream, optional

1. Place pork and onion in a 4-qt. slow cooker. In a small bowl, combine salsa, chilies, cumin, oregano, salt, pepper, pepper flakes and cinnamon; pour over meat. Cook, covered, on low 5-6 hours or until meat is tender.

2. Remove roast; cool slightly. Skim fat from the cooking juices. Shred pork with two forks. Return meat to slow cooker; heat through. Stir in cilantro. Serve with grits and, if desired, sour cream.

FREEZE OPTION *Freeze cooled meat mixture in freezer containers. To use, partially thaw in refrigerator overnight. Microwave, covered, on high until heated through, gently stirring and adding a little broth if necessary.*

PER SERVING *1 cup (calculated without grits or sour cream): 349 cal., 20g fat (7g sat. fat), 118mg chol., 872mg sod., 8g carb. (3g sugars, 1g fiber), 34g pro.*

CHEESY TATER TOT DINNER

CHEESY TATER TOT DINNER

This slow cooker meal was created to pay homage to my favorite pizza: Hawaiian with bacon and pineapple. The Tater Tots in this recipe make it family-friendly.

—**LISA RENSHAW** KANSAS CITY, MO

PREP: 15 MIN. • **COOK:** 4 HOURS + STANDING
MAKES: 8 SERVINGS

- 1 package (32 ounces) frozen Tater Tots, thawed
- 8 ounces Canadian bacon, chopped
- 1 cup frozen pepper strips, thawed and chopped
- 1 medium onion, finely chopped
- 1 can (8 ounces) pineapple tidbits, drained
- 2 large eggs
- 3 cans (5 ounces each) evaporated milk
- 1 can (15 ounces) pizza sauce
- 1 cup shredded provolone cheese
- ½ cup grated Parmesan cheese, optional

1. Place half of the Tater Tots in a greased 5-qt. slow cooker. Layer with Canadian bacon, peppers, onion and pineapple. Top with the remaining Tater Tots. In a large bowl, whisk eggs, milk and pizza sauce; pour over top. Sprinkle with shredded provolone cheese.

2. Cook, covered, on low for 4-5 hours or until heated through. If desired, sprinkle with Parmesan cheese; let stand, covered, 20 minutes.

PER SERVING *1½ cups (calculated without Parmesan cheese): 439 cal., 21g fat (8g sat. fat), 85mg chol., 1216mg sod., 43g carb. (14g sugars, 4g fiber), 17g pro.*

**APPLE-CINNAMON
PORK LOIN**

⑤ INGREDIENTS

CHERRY BALSAMIC
PORK LOIN

After having a wonderful cherry topping on Brie cheese at a local market, I just knew I had to create one for pork. If you're crazy about cherries, add even more to the dish.

—SUSAN STETZEL GAINESVILLE, NY

PREP: 20 MIN. • **COOK:** 3 HOURS + STANDING
MAKES: 8 SERVINGS (1⅓ CUPS SAUCE)

- 1 boneless pork loin roast
  (3 to 4 pounds)
- 1 teaspoon salt
- ½ teaspoon pepper
- 1 tablespoon canola oil
- ¾ cup cherry preserves
- ½ cup dried cherries
- ⅓ cup balsamic vinegar
- ¼ cup packed brown sugar

1. Sprinkle roast with salt and pepper. In a large skillet, heat oil over medium-high heat. Brown roast on all sides.

2. Transfer to a 6-qt. slow cooker. In a small bowl, mix preserves, cherries, vinegar and brown sugar until blended; pour over roast. Cook, covered, on low for 3-4 hours or until tender (a thermometer inserted in pork should read at least 145°).

3. Remove roast from slow cooker; tent with foil. Let stand 15 minutes before slicing. Skim fat from cooking juices. Serve pork with sauce.

PER SERVING *5 ounces cooked pork with 2 tablespoons sauce: 359 cal., 10g fat (3g sat. fat), 85mg chol., 128mg sod., 34g carb. (31g sugars, 0 fiber), 33g pro.*

EAT SMART ⑤ INGREDIENTS

APPLE-CINNAMON
PORK LOIN

I love making this slow-cooked dinner for my family on chilly fall days—the comforting apple-cinnamon aroma fills our whole house. The pork roast tastes even better served with homemade mashed potatoes.

—RACHEL SCHULTZ LANSING, MI

PREP: 20 MIN. • **COOK:** 6 HOURS
MAKES: 6 SERVINGS

- 1 boneless pork loin roast (2 to
  3 pounds)
- ½ teaspoon salt
- ¼ teaspoon pepper
- 1 tablespoon canola oil
- 3 medium apples, peeled and sliced,
  divided
- ¼ cup honey
- 1 small red onion, halved and sliced
- 1 tablespoon ground cinnamon
  Minced fresh parsley, optional

1. Sprinkle roast with salt and pepper. In a large skillet, brown roast in oil on all sides; cool slightly. With a paring knife, cut about sixteen 3-in.-deep slits in the sides of the roast; insert one apple slice into each slit.

2. Place half the remaining apples in a 4-qt. slow cooker. Set the roast over the apples. Drizzle with honey; top with onion and the remaining apples. Sprinkle with cinnamon.

3. Cover and cook on low for 6-8 hours or until the meat is tender. Remove pork and apple mixture; keep warm.

4. Transfer the cooking juices to a small saucepan. Bring to a boil; cook until the liquid is reduced by half. Serve with pork and apple mixture. Sprinkle with parsley if desired.

PER SERVING *290 cal., 10g fat (3g sat. fat), 75mg chol., 241mg sod., 22g carb. (19g sugars, 2g fiber), 29g pro.* **Diabetic Exchanges:** *4 lean meat, 1 starch, ½ fruit, ½ fat.*

TWO-MEAT MANICOTTI

I wanted to create my ideal version of a stuffed manicotti, which requires a fantastic filling and a meat sauce to die for. This recipe is the final result, and I don't mind saying it's a huge success!

—SHALIMAR WIECH GLASSPORT, PA

PREP: 45 MIN. • **COOK:** 4 HOURS
MAKES: 7 SERVINGS

- ½ **pound medium fresh mushrooms, chopped**
- 2 **small green peppers, chopped**
- 1 **medium onion, chopped**
- 1½ **teaspoons canola oil**
- 4 **garlic cloves, minced**
- ¾ **pound ground sirloin**
- ¾ **pound bulk Italian sausage**
- 2 **jars (23½ ounces each) Italian sausage and garlic spaghetti sauce**
- 1 **carton (15 ounces) ricotta cheese**
- 1 **cup minced fresh parsley**
- ½ **cup shredded part-skim mozzarella cheese, divided**
- ½ **cup grated Parmesan cheese, divided**
- 2 **large eggs, lightly beaten**
- ½ **teaspoon salt**
- ¼ **teaspoon pepper**
- ⅛ **teaspoon ground nutmeg**
- 1 **package (8 ounces) manicotti shells**

1. In a large skillet over medium-high heat, saute the mushrooms, peppers and onion in oil until tender. Add garlic; cook 1 minute longer. Remove from pan.

2. In the same skillet, cook beef and sausage over medium heat until no longer pink; drain. Stir in the mushroom mixture and spaghetti sauce; set aside.

3. In a small bowl, combine ricotta cheese, parsley, ¼ cup mozzarella cheese, ¼ cup Parmesan cheese, eggs and seasonings. Stuff into uncooked manicotti shells.

4. Spread 2¼ cups of the sauce onto the bottom of a 6-qt. slow cooker. Arrange five stuffed manicotti shells over the sauce; repeat two times, using four shells on the top layer. Top with remaining sauce; sprinkle with remaining cheeses. Cover and cook on low for 4-5 hours or until the pasta is tender.

BAKE OPTION *Spread half of the sauce mixture into a greased 13x9-in. baking dish. Arrange stuffed manicotti shells in a single layer over sauce. Top with remaining sauce. Cover and bake at 375° for 45-55 minutes or until pasta is tender. Uncover; sprinkle with remaining cheeses. Bake 10-15 minutes longer or until cheese is melted. Let stand 5 minutes before serving.*

PER SERVING *2 manicotti: 657 cal., 33g fat (14g sat. fat), 155mg chol., 1609mg sod., 55g carb. (22g sugars, 7g fiber), 39g pro.*

TWO-MEAT MANICOTTI

MOM'S SCALLOPED POTATOES AND HAM

(PICTURED ON PAGE 279)

My mom's friend gave her this recipe years ago, and Mom shared it with me. It's the most requested recipe at my house when we have leftover ham to use up.

—KELLY GRAHAM ST. THOMAS, ON

PREP: 20 MIN. • **COOK:** 8 HOURS
MAKES: 9 SERVINGS

- 10 **medium potatoes (about 3 pounds), peeled and thinly sliced**
- 3 **cups cubed fully cooked ham**
- 2 **large onions, thinly sliced**
- 2 **cups shredded cheddar cheese**
- 1 **can (10¾ ounces) condensed cream of mushroom soup, undiluted**
- ½ **teaspoon paprika**
- ¼ **teaspoon pepper**

1. In a greased 6-qt. slow cooker, layer half of the potatoes, ham, onions and cheese. Repeat layers. Pour soup over top. Sprinkle with paprika and pepper.

2. Cover and cook on low for 8-10 hours or until the potatoes are tender.

PER SERVING *1½ cups: 344 cal., 13g fat (7g sat. fat), 53mg chol., 995mg sod., 40g carb. (4g sugars, 3g fiber), 17g pro.*

**COBB SALAD SUB,
PAGE 309**

PINEAPPLE-DIJON
HAM SANDWICHES,
PAGE 301

SAMMIES, SUBS & MORE

You can't go wrong with deli subs **piled high with taste,** shredded pork sandwiches **loaded with juicy appeal** and grilled sausages **guaranteed to please.** Turn here for meatball sliders, BLT classics, party-size hoagies and more. **Guy-food greats** are always at your fingertips in this chapter!

BLT WITH PEPPERED
BALSAMIC MAYO, PAGE 305

CRISPY PORK TENDERLOIN SANDWICHES, PAGE 302

MEATBALL
SLIDERS

PEAR, HAM & CHEESE
PASTRY POCKETS

⑤ INGREDIENTS

MEATBALL SLIDERS

Meatballs stuffed with cheese? There's no hesitation when it comes to enjoying these incredible bites!

—HILARY BREINHOLT GLENWOOD, UT

PREP: 15 MIN. • **BAKE:** 25 MIN.
MAKES: 16 SERVINGS

- 1½ **pounds bulk Italian sausage**
- 16 **cubes part-skim mozzarella cheese (1-inch; about 8 ounces total)**
- 1 **jar (24 ounces) spaghetti sauce**
- 1 **jar (8.1 ounces) prepared pesto**
- 16 **dinner rolls, split and toasted**

1. Divide sausage into 16 portions. Shape each portion around a cube of cheese. Place on a greased rack in a shallow baking pan. Bake at 350° for 25-30 minutes or until meat is no longer pink. Remove to paper towels to drain.

2. In a large saucepan, combine spaghetti sauce and pesto; bring just to a boil over medium heat, stirring occasionally. Add meatballs; heat through, stirring gently. Serve on rolls.

PER SERVING *1 slider: 334 cal., 20g fat (6g sat. fat), 50mg chol., 889mg sodium, 25g carb. (6g sugars, 3g fiber), 13g pro.*

TOP TIP

MAKE-AHEAD STRATEGY

If Meatball Sliders are on your menu for an upcoming party, you can save yourself from last minute rush. Cook the meatballs and the sauce a day or two ahead and store in the fridge. When it's party time, simply reheat, assemble and serve.

FAST FIX ▶

PEAR, HAM & CHEESE PASTRY POCKETS

I came up with this recipe on the fly one night. Add a cup of soup and supper's ready. The sweet-savory flavor combo makes it a good brunch choice, too.

—TERRI CRANDALL GARDNERVILLE, NV

START TO FINISH: 30 MIN.
MAKES: 8 SERVINGS

- 1 **package (17.3 ounces) frozen puff pastry, thawed**
- ¼ **cup honey Dijon mustard**
- 1 **large egg, lightly beaten**
- 8 **slices deli ham**
- 4 **slices Muenster cheese, halved diagonally**
- 1 **medium red pear, very thinly sliced**
- 1 **small red onion, thinly sliced**

1. Preheat oven to 400°. Unfold each sheet of puff pastry. Cut each into four squares. Spread 1½ teaspoons mustard over each square to within ½ in. of edges. Brush egg over edges of pastry.

2. On one corner of each square, layer ham, cheese, pear and onion. Fold opposite corner over filling, forming a triangle; press edges with a fork to seal. Transfer to ungreased baking sheets. Brush tops with remaining egg.

3. Bake 10-14 minutes or until golden brown. Serve warm.

FREEZE OPTION *Freeze cooled pockets in a freezer container, separating with waxed paper. To use, reheat pockets on a baking sheet in a preheated 400° oven until crisp and heated through.*

PER SERVING *1 pocket: 403 cal., 21g fat (6g sat. fat), 43mg chol., 540mg sod., 43g carb. (6g sugars, 6g fiber), 12g pro.*

BBQ SANDWICHES

BBQ SANDWICHES

Friends love these warm ham sandwiches and often ask me to make them. Since I know they are a crowd-pleaser, I double the recipe and serve them at potlucks.

—**DANA KNOX** BUTLER, PA

PREP: 20 MIN. • **COOK:** 2 HOURS
MAKES: 16 SERVINGS

- 3 cups ketchup
- ¾ cup chopped onion
- ¾ cup chopped green pepper
- ¾ cup packed brown sugar
- ½ cup lemon juice
- ⅓ cup Worcestershire sauce
- 1 tablespoon prepared mustard
- 1¼ teaspoons ground allspice
- 1½ teaspoons liquid smoke, optional
- 3 pounds thinly sliced deli ham
- 16 kaiser or ciabatta rolls, split

1. In a large saucepan, combine the first eight ingredients; if desired, stir in liquid smoke. Bring to a boil over medium-high heat. Reduce heat; simmer, uncovered, 5 minutes, stirring occasionally.

2. Place ham in a 5- or 6-qt. slow cooker. Add sauce; stir gently to combine. Cook, covered, on low 2-3 hours or until heated through. Serve on rolls.

PER SERVING *1 sandwich: 348 cal., 4g fat (0 sat. fat), 38mg chol., 1744mg sod., 57g carb. (26g sugars, 2g fiber), 21g pro.*

TOP TIP

COOK HAS A TERRIFIC TOPPING IDEA

I really enjoyed these sandwiches. My kitchen smelled amazing, and my husband loved them. I topped my sandwich with some coleslaw. Delicious!

—**HAVINGFUNWITHMYFAMILY**
TASTEOFHOME.COM

PINEAPPLE-DIJON HAM SANDWICHES

(PICTURED ON PAGE 297)

My kids like ham, but it's a challenge to come up with different ways to prepare it. I like the combo of ham and pineapple, so I decided to throw them in the slow cooker, and the result was amazing. Even my two youngest ones ate their sandwiches right up.

—CAMILLE BECKSTRAND LAYTON, UT

PREP: 20 MIN. • **COOK:** 3 HOURS
MAKES: 10 SERVINGS

- 2 pounds fully cooked ham, cut into ½-inch cubes
- 1 can (20 ounces) crushed pineapple, undrained
- 1 medium green pepper, finely chopped
- ¾ cup packed brown sugar
- ¼ cup finely chopped onion
- ¼ cup Dijon mustard
- 1 tablespoon dried minced onion
- 10 hamburger buns, split
- 10 slices Swiss cheese
  Additional Dijon mustard, optional

1. In a greased 4-qt. slow cooker, combine the first seven ingredients. Cook, covered, on low 3-4 hours or until mixture is heated through.
2. Preheat broiler. Place bun bottoms and tops on baking sheets, cut side up. Using a slotted spoon, place ham mixture on bottoms; top with cheese. Broil 3-4 in. from heat 1-2 minutes or until cheese is melted and tops are toasted. Replace tops. If desired, serve with additional mustard.
PER SERVING *1 sandwich (calculated without additional mustard): 396 cal., 8g fat (3g sat. fat), 67mg chol., 1283mg sod., 52g carb. (30g sugars, 2g fiber), 28g pro.*

GRILLED BEER BRATS WITH KRAUT

GRILLED BEER BRATS WITH KRAUT

I made this for my son's 21st birthday bonfire, attended by both friends and family. The kraut flavors are a fabulous topping for these tasty brats, precooked in dark beer.

—KEELEY WEBER STERLING HEIGHTS, MI

PREP: 45 MIN. • **GRILL:** 35 MIN.
MAKES: 12 SERVINGS

- 6 bacon strips, chopped
- 1 large onion, chopped
- 1 medium apple, peeled and thinly sliced
- 2 garlic cloves, minced
- 1 can (14 ounces) sauerkraut, rinsed and well drained
- 3 tablespoons spicy brown mustard
- 1 tablespoon brown sugar
- 12 uncooked bratwurst links
- 1 bottle (12 ounces) dark beer
- 12 hoagie buns, split

1. In a large skillet, cook bacon over medium heat until crisp, stirring occasionally. Remove with a slotted spoon; drain on paper towels.
2. Cook and stir onion in bacon drippings until softened. Reduce heat to medium-low; cook 15-20 minutes or until deep golden brown, stirring occasionally. Add apple and garlic; cook 2 minutes longer. Stir in sauerkraut, mustard, brown sugar and cooked bacon.
3. Transfer to a 13x9-in. disposable foil pan. Arrange bratwurst over top. Pour beer over bratwurst. Place pan on grill rack over medium heat; cook, covered, 30-35 minutes or until sausages are no longer pink. Remove pan from heat.
4. Remove bratwurst and return to grill. Grill, covered, 2-3 minutes on each side or until browned. Serve on buns with the sauerkraut mixture.
PER SERVING *1 brat: 582 cal., 34g fat (11g sat. fat), 71mg chol., 1473mg sod., 44g carb. (9g sugars, 2g fiber), 22g pro.*

EAT SMART **FAST FIX**

CRISPY PORK TENDERLOIN SANDWICHES

(PICTURED ON PAGE 297)

This breaded tenderloin rekindles memories of a sandwich shop in my Ohio hometown. Even though I've moved away, I'm happy to say my family can still enjoy them, thanks to this quick, easy recipe.

—ERIN FITCH SHERRILLS FORD, NC

START TO FINISH: 25 MIN.
MAKES: 4 SERVINGS

- 2 tablespoons all-purpose flour
- ½ teaspoon salt
- ¼ teaspoon pepper
- 1 large egg, lightly beaten
- ½ cup seasoned bread crumbs
- 3 tablespoons panko (Japanese) bread crumbs
- ½ pound pork tenderloin
- 2 tablespoons canola oil
- 4 hamburger buns or kaiser rolls, split
  Optional toppings: lettuce leaves, tomato and pickle slices and mayonnaise

1. In a shallow bowl, mix flour, salt and pepper. Place egg and the combined bread crumbs in two separate shallow bowls.

2. Cut tenderloin crosswise into four slices; pound each with a meat mallet to ¼-in. thickness. Dip in flour mixture to coat both sides; shake off excess. Dip in egg, then in crumb mixture, patting to help adhere.

3. In a large skillet, heat oil over medium heat. Cook pork 2-3 minutes on each side or until golden brown. Remove from pan; drain on paper towels. Serve in buns with toppings as desired.

PER SERVING *1 sandwich: 289 cal., 11g fat (2g sat. fat), 43mg chol., 506mg sod., 29g carb. (3g sugars, 1g fiber), 17g pro.* **Diabetic Exchanges:** *2 starch, 2 lean meat, 1½ fat.*

SPEEDY HAM SLIDERS

FAST FIX

SPEEDY HAM SLIDERS

It's easy to make these delicious Cuban-style sliders by the panful, which is great because they go fast! Bake the pan until the rolls are lightly toasted and the cheese melts, then set them out and watch them disappear.

—SERENE HERRERA DALLAS, TX

START TO FINISH: 30 MIN.
MAKES: 2 DOZEN

- 2 packages (12 ounces each) Hawaiian sweet rolls
- 1¼ pounds thinly sliced deli ham
- 9 slices Swiss cheese (about 6 ounces)
- 24 dill pickle slices

TOPPING

- ½ cup butter, cubed
- 2 tablespoons finely chopped onion
- 2 tablespoons Dijon mustard

1. Preheat oven to 350°. Without separating rolls, cut each package of rolls in half horizontally; arrange the bottom halves in a greased 13x9-in. baking pan. Layer with ham, cheese and pickles; replace top halves of rolls.

2. In a microwave, melt butter; stir in onion and mustard. Drizzle over rolls. Bake, covered, 10 minutes. Uncover; bake until golden brown and heated through, 5-10 minutes longer. Remove from pan; cut into sliders.

PER SERVING *2 sliders: 382 cal., 19g fat (11g sat. fat), 84mg chol., 1065mg sod., 34g carb. (12g sugars, 2g fiber), 19g pro.*

APPLE CIDER PULLED PORK

For potlucks and tailgates, we slow-cook pork with cider, onions and spices. Served with sweet potato fries, these tangy sliders make a winning barbecue plate.
—**RACHEL LEWIS** DANVILLE, VA

PREP: 15 MIN. • **COOK:** 8¾ HOURS
MAKES: 12 SERVINGS

- 2 **teaspoons seasoned salt**
- ½ **teaspoon ground mustard**
- ½ **teaspoon paprika**
- ¼ **teaspoon ground coriander**
- ¼ **teaspoon pepper**
- 2 **medium Granny Smith apples, peeled and coarsely chopped**
- 1 **medium onion, chopped**
- 1 **celery rib, chopped**
- 1½ **cups apple cider or juice**
- 1 **boneless pork shoulder butt roast (3 pounds)**
- 2 **tablespoons cornstarch**
- 2 **tablespoons water**
- 24 **mini buns, warmed**
  Additional apple slices, optional

1. Mix first five ingredients. Place apples, onion, celery and cider in a 5-qt. slow cooker; top with roast. Sprinkle roast with seasoning mixture. Cook, covered, on low until tender, 8-10 hours.
2. Remove roast; shred with two forks. Skim fat from the cooking juices. Mix cornstarch and water; stir into cooking juices. Cook, covered, on high until thickened, 10-15 minutes. Stir in pork; serve on buns. If desired, top with additional apple slices.

FREEZE OPTION *Freeze cooled meat mixture in freezer containers. To use, partially thaw in refrigerator overnight. Heat through in a saucepan, stirring occasionally and adding a little broth or water if necessary.*
PER SERVING *2 sliders: 375 cal., 15g fat (5g sat. fat), 69mg chol., 563mg sod., 35g carb. (9g sugars, 2g fiber), 25g pro.*

FAST FIX
CUBAN PORK WRAPS

Hot and juicy pork with Swiss, ham and pickles—those are the makings of a classic Cuban sandwich. These wraps pile on all the best-loved flavor, but they're quicker to prepare because they're simply wrapped in flour tortillas and baked in the oven.
—**AIMEE BACHMANN** NORTH BEND, WA

START TO FINISH: 20 MIN.
MAKES: 4 SERVINGS

- ¾ **pound thin boneless pork loin chops, cut into strips**
- 1 **tablespoon canola oil**
- ⅛ **teaspoon pepper**
- 1 **tablespoon Dijon mustard**
- 4 **multigrain tortillas (10 inches)**
- 8 **ounces sliced deli ham**
- 8 **slices Swiss cheese**
- 4 **thin sandwich pickle slices**
- ¼ **cup thinly sliced red onion**

1. Preheat oven to 350°. In a bowl, toss pork with oil and pepper. Place a large skillet over medium-high heat. Add pork; cook and stir for 2-3 minutes or until browned. Remove from heat.
2. To assemble, spread mustard onto center of tortillas; layer with ham, cheese, pickle, onion and pork. Fold bottom and sides of tortillas over filling and roll up. Place on an ungreased baking sheet; bake 4-6 minutes or until heated through.
PER SERVING *1 wrap: 501 cal., 22g fat (8g sat. fat), 86mg chol., 1230mg sod., 37g carb. (5g sugars, 7g fiber), 39g pro.*

APPLE CIDER PULLED PORK

(5) INGREDIENTS FAST FIX ▶

HAM & SWISS STROMBOLI

This is a comforting meal on hectic weeknights. It's also easy to change up the recipe with your favorite meats or cheeses.
—**TRICIA BIBB** HARTSELLE, AL

START TO FINISH: 30 MIN.
MAKES: 6 SERVINGS

- **1 tube (11 ounces) refrigerated crusty French loaf**
- **6 ounces sliced deli ham**
- **¼ cup finely chopped onion**
- **8 bacon strips, cooked and crumbled**
- **6 ounces sliced Swiss cheese**
  Honey mustard, optional

1. Preheat oven to 375°. Unroll dough on a baking sheet. Place ham down center third of dough to within 1 in. of ends; top with onion, bacon and cheese. Fold long sides of dough over filling, pinching seam and ends to seal; tuck ends under. Cut several slits in top.

2. Bake 20-25 minutes or until golden brown. Cut into slices. If desired, serve with honey mustard.

FREEZE OPTION *Securely wrap and freeze the cooled unsliced stromboli in heavy-duty foil. To use, reheat stromboli on an ungreased baking sheet in a preheated 375° oven until heated through and a thermometer inserted in center reads 165°.*

PER SERVING *1 slice: 272 cal., 11g fat (5g sat. fat), 40mg chol., 795mg sod., 26g carb. (3g sugars, 1g fiber), 18g pro.*

HAM & SWISS STROMBOLI

FAST FIX ▶

BLT WITH PEPPERED BALSAMIC MAYO

(PICTURED ON PAGE 297)

Here's my twist on a classic. Creamy avocado plus some balsamic mayo make it a keeper. For a lighter take, I often use turkey bacon.
—AMI BOYER SAN FRANCISCO, CA

START TO FINISH: 25 MIN.
MAKES: 4 SERVINGS

- 8 bacon strips, halved
- ½ cup mayonnaise
- 1 tablespoon balsamic vinegar
- ½ teaspoon pepper
- ⅛ teaspoon salt
- 8 slices bread, toasted
- 2 cups spring mix salad greens
- 8 cherry tomatoes, sliced
- 1 medium ripe avocado, peeled and sliced

1. In a large skillet, cook the bacon over medium heat until crisp. Remove to paper towels to drain.
2. In a small bowl, mix mayonnaise, vinegar, pepper and salt. Spread half of the mixture over four toast slices. Layer with bacon, salad greens, tomatoes and avocado. Spread remaining mayonnaise over remaining toast; place over top.
PER SERVING *1 sandwich: 501 cal., 37g fat (6g sat. fat), 27mg chol., 870mg sod., 32g carb. (4g sugars, 5g fiber), 11g pro.*

TOP TIP

MUST-TRY MAYO

This peppered balsamic mayo is so good, and I'm already thinking of other ways to use it. It was a very nice complement to a regular BLT, along with the avocados which added a nice creaminess. With a bowl of gazpacho, they made a great light summer meal!
—VALANDDANSMITH
TASTEOFHOME.COM

COLORFUL PORK PITAS

EAT SMART ⑤INGREDIENTS FAST FIX ▶

COLORFUL PORK PITAS

Cracked black pepper and garlic give the pork some pop. Then fill the pitas up with sweet red peppers, leaf lettuce and caramelized onions. Top (or not) with mayo for an awesome weeknight meal.
—KATHY WHITE HENDERSON, NV

START TO FINISH: 20 MIN.
MAKES: 4 SERVINGS

- 1 pound boneless pork loin chops, cut into thin strips
- 1 tablespoon olive oil
- 2 teaspoons coarsely ground pepper
- 2 garlic cloves, minced
- 1 jar (12 ounces) roasted sweet red peppers, drained and julienned
- 4 whole pita breads, warmed
  Garlic mayonnaise and torn leaf lettuce, optional

In a small bowl, combine pork, oil, pepper and garlic; toss to coat. Place a large skillet over medium-high heat. Add the pork mixture; cook and stir until no longer pink. Stir in red peppers; heat through. Serve on pita breads. Top with mayonnaise and lettuce if desired.
PER SERVING *1 pita (calculated without mayonnaise): 380 cal., 11g fat (3g sat. fat), 55mg chol., 665mg sod., 37g carb. (4g sugars, 2g fiber), 27g pro.* **Diabetic Exchanges:** *3 lean meat, 2 starch, 1 fat.*

HAM & POTATO
SALAD SANDWICHES

PORK PICADILLO LETTUCE WRAPS

I think that warm pork tenderloin and cool, crisp lettuce are a combination born in culinary heaven. My spin on a lettuce wrap is loaded with scrumptious flavor and spice.

—**JANICE ELDER** CHARLOTTE, NC

PREP: 30 MIN. • **COOK:** 2½ HOURS.
MAKES: 2 DOZEN

- 3 **garlic cloves, minced**
- 1 **tablespoon chili powder**
- 1 **teaspoon salt**
- ½ **teaspoon pumpkin pie spice**
- ½ **teaspoon ground cumin**
- ½ **teaspoon pepper**
- 2 **pork tenderloins (1 pound each)**
- 1 **large onion, chopped**
- 1 **small Granny Smith apple, peeled and chopped**
- 1 **small sweet red pepper, chopped**
- 1 **can (10 ounces) diced tomatoes and green chilies, undrained**
- ½ **cup golden raisins**
- ½ **cup chopped pimiento-stuffed olives**
- 24 **Bibb or Boston lettuce leaves**
- ¼ **cup slivered almonds, toasted**

1. Mix garlic and seasonings; rub over pork. Transfer to a 5-qt. slow cooker. Add onion, apple, sweet pepper and tomatoes. Cook, covered, on low 2½ to 3 hours or until meat is tender.

2. Remove pork; cool slightly. Shred meat into bite-size pieces; return to slow cooker. Stir in raisins and olives; heat through. Serve in lettuce leaves; sprinkle with almonds.

PER SERVING *1 lettuce wrap: 75 cal., 3g fat (1g sat. fat), 21mg chol., 235mg sod., 5g carb. (3g sugars, 1g fiber), 8g pro.*

FAST FIX ▶
HAM & POTATO SALAD SANDWICHES

These open-faced sandwiches with zingy toppings are super easy to put together. The bites originated in a deli in Prague, where they're a really popular winter party food.

—**CARA MCDONALD** WINTER PARK, CO

START TO FINISH: 15 MIN.
MAKES: 6 SERVINGS

- 1½ **cups deli potato salad**
- 6 **diagonally cut French bread baguette slices (½ inch thick)**
- 6 **ounces fully cooked ham, thinly sliced**
- 6 **slices tomato**
- 12 **dill pickle slices**
- 2 **hard-cooked eggs, sliced**
- 2 **slices red onion, separated into rings**

Spread ¼ cup of potato salad on each baguette slice. Layer with ham, tomato, pickle, egg and onion.

PER SERVING *1 open-faced sandwich: 229 cal., 10g fat (2g sat. fat), 96mg chol., 821mg sod., 25g carb. (3g sugars, 2g fiber), 12g pro.*

SLOW COOKER SAUSAGE SANDWICHES

My Italian sandwiches actually started out as pork chops and sausage over angel hair pasta. Now we have a handy new slow-cooked version of a beloved family recipe.

—**DEBRA GOFORTH** NEWPORT, TN

PREP: 20 MIN. • **COOK:** 6 HOURS
MAKES: 8 SERVINGS

- 3 **bone-in pork loin chops (7 ounces each)**
- 4 **Italian sausage links (4 ounces each)**
- 1 **can (28 ounces) whole plum tomatoes, undrained**
- 1 **can (6 ounces) tomato paste**
- 1 **teaspoon Italian seasoning**
- 3 **garlic cloves, minced**
- ¼ **teaspoon crushed red pepper flakes**
- 1 **large onion, halved and sliced**
- 1 **large sweet red pepper, cut into strips**
- 1 **large green pepper, cut into strips**
- 1 **jar (16 ounces) mild pickled pepper rings, drained**
- 8 **submarine buns, split**
- 1 **cup (4 ounces) shredded Italian cheese blend**

1. Place pork chops and sausage in a 5- or 6-qt. slow cooker. Place tomatoes, tomato paste, Italian seasoning, garlic and pepper flakes in a food processor; pulse until chunky. Pour over meats. Cook, covered, on low 4 hours.

2. Add onion and peppers to slow cooker. Cook, covered, on low 2-3 hours longer or until pork is tender, a thermometer inserted in sausages reads 160°, and vegetables are crisp-tender. Remove pork chops and sausages from slow cooker. Remove pork from bones; discard bones. Shred meat with two forks and cut sausages into 2-in. pieces; return to slow cooker. Serve on buns with cheese.

PER SERVING *1 sandwich: 554 cal., 26g fat (10g sat. fat), 77mg chol., 1218mg sod., 48g carb. (10g sugars, 6g fiber), 31g pro.*

SLOW COOKER SAUSAGE SANDWICHES

COBB SALAD SUB

FAST FIX ▸

COBB SALAD SUB

When we need a quick meal to share, we turn Cobb salad into a sandwich masterpiece. Sometimes I swap out the bread for tortillas and make wraps instead.

—KIMBERLY GRUSENDORF MEDINA, OH

START TO FINISH: 15 MIN.
MAKES: 12 SERVINGS

- 1 **loaf (1 pound) unsliced Italian bread**
- ½ **cup balsamic vinaigrette or dressing of your choice**
- 5 **ounces fresh baby spinach (about 6 cups)**
- 1½ **pounds sliced deli ham**
- 4 **hard-cooked large eggs, finely chopped**
- 8 **bacon strips, cooked and crumbled**
- ½ **cup crumbled Gorgonzola cheese**
- 1 **cup cherry tomatoes, chopped**

Cut loaf of bread in half; hollow out top and bottom, leaving a ¾-in. shell (discard removed bread or save for another use). Brush vinaigrette over bread halves. Layer spinach, ham, eggs, bacon, cheese and tomatoes on bread bottom. Replace top. Cut in half lengthwise; cut crosswise five times to make 12 total pieces.

PER SERVING *1 piece: 233 cal., 10g fat (3g sat. fat), 97mg chol., 982mg sod., 17g carb. (3g sugars, 1g fiber), 18g pro.*

ASIAN SHREDDED PORK SANDWICHES

No one guesses the secret ingredient behind my slow-cooked sandwiches—canned plums! They add a little sweetness to the juicy pork and help tenderize the meat. The pork freezes well, and it's easy to keep on hand.

—HOLLY BATTISTE BARRINGTON, NJ

PREP: 30 MIN. **• COOK:** 6 HOURS
MAKES: 10 SERVINGS

- 1 **can (15 ounces) plums, drained and pitted**
- 1 **tablespoon Sriracha Asian hot chili sauce**
- 1 **tablespoon hoisin sauce**

- 1 **tablespoon reduced-sodium soy sauce**
- 1 **tablespoon rice vinegar**
- 1 **tablespoon honey**
- 2 **garlic cloves, minced**
- 1 **teaspoon pepper**
- 1 **teaspoon sesame oil**
- ½ **teaspoon ground ginger**
- ¼ **teaspoon salt**
- 2 **tablespoons canola oil**
- 1 **boneless pork shoulder butt roast (3 pounds)**
- 4 **medium carrots, finely chopped**
- 10 **ciabatta rolls, split**
  Shredded napa or other cabbage

1. Mix first 11 ingredients. In a large skillet, heat oil over medium-high heat. Brown roast on all sides.

2. Place carrots in a 4- or 5-qt. slow cooker. Add roast; pour plum mixture over top. Cook, covered, on low until pork is tender, 6-8 hours.

3. Remove pork; shred with two forks. Skim fat from carrot mixture; stir in pork and heat through. Serve the pork on rolls with cabbage.

FREEZE OPTION *Freeze cooled pork mixture in freezer containers. To use, partially thaw in refrigerator overnight. Heat through in a covered saucepan, stirring gently and adding a little broth if necessary.*

PER SERVING *1 sandwich: 637 cal., 21g fat (6g sat. fat), 81mg chol., 864mg sod., 85g carb., 5g fiber, 34g pro.*

GENERAL RECIPE INDEX

This index lists every recipe by food category, major ingredient and/or cooking method, so you can quickly find recipes that best suit your needs.

ALPHABETICAL RECIPE INDEX